Nicko

THE POCKET HISTORY

OF

FREEMASONRY

THE POCKET HISTORY OF FREEMASONRY

By

FRED L. PICK and G. NORMAN KNIGHT

Revised by

FREDERICK SMYTH

FREDERICK MULLER LIMITED
LONDON

First published in Great Britain in 1953 by
Frederick Muller Limited, London, SW19 7JZ
Second Impression, 1953
Second (Revised) Edition, 1954
Third Edition, 1956
Fourth Edition, 1963
Fifth Edition 1969, Reprinted 1971
Sixth Edition, 1977
Seventh Edition, 1983

Copyright © 1953 Fred L. Pick and G. Norman Knight

All rights reserved. No part of this publication may be reproduced, stored in a retrieval system, or transmitted, in any form or by any means, electronic, mechanical, photocopying, recording or otherwise, without the prior permission of Frederick Muller Limited.

British Library Cataloguing in Publication Data

Pick, Fred Lomax
  The pocket history of Freemasonry. — 7th edition
  1. Freemasons — History
  I. Title II. Knight, Gilfred Norman III. Smyth, Frederick

ISBN 0-584-11039-1

Typeset by Texet, Leighton Buzzard, Bedfordshire
Printed in Great Britain by
Redwood Burn Ltd., Trowbridge, Wiltshire

CONTENTS

	Foreword by Harry Carr	7
	Preface	9
	The Authors	10
I	The Origin of Freemasonry	13
II	Medieval Operative Masonry	19
III	The Old Charges	30
IV	Pre-Grand Lodge Freemasonry	43
V	The Grand Lodge Period, 1717-50	68
VI	English Grand Lodges, 1751-1813	88
VII	United Grand Lodge Freemasonry, 1813-1975	108
VIII	Irish Freemasonry	145
IX	Scottish Freemasonry	177
X	The Holy Royal Arch	200
XI	The Order of Mark Masonry and the Royal Ark Mariner's Degree	211
XII	Other Degrees and Orders	222
XIII	Freemasonry in the Forces	242
XIV	Freemasonry in Europe	255
XV	Freemasonry in America	268
XVI	Freemasonry in Africa	298
XVII	Freemasonry in Australasia	301
XVIII	Freemasonry in Asia	308
XIX	Unrecognized Orders	314
	'A Daily Advancement' and Short List of Recommended Books	320
	Some Notable Masonic Dates	323
	Some Famous Freemasons	326
	Index	333

FOREWORD
by
BROTHER HARRY CARR, P.J.G.D.
Secretary and Editor, 1961-73, of the
QUATUOR CORONATI LODGE No. 2076
THE PREMIER LODGE OF MASONIC RESEARCH

It is a great pleasure for a masonic historian to have been granted the opportunity of writing a foreword to this new edition of a work which has already earned a high place for itself among the 20th century publications in this field.

Masonic books in general are plentiful; but the works that can be honestly recommended to the general masonic reader are all too scarce. So much has been written and published by worthy brethren whose feet were planted firmly in the clouds. Of course they meant well, but they were unable to resist the strong temptation to fill the numerous gaps in our history, and especially in our pre-history, with statements and theories which had no foundation in fact, and which could not withstand even the most elementary test.

The joint authors of the first four editions of this book were both men of the 'Authentic School'. Bro. Fred L. Pick was a full member and Past Master of the Quatuor Coronati Lodge, whose masonic studies, published in *A.Q.C.*, and in the Transactions of many other English Research Lodges, had long demonstrated his abilities. His collaborator, a retired Civil Servant, Bro. G. Norman Knight, M.A., a Barrister-at-Law and a freelance indexer, was in 1967 awarded a Gold Medal by the Library Association for his work on the Winston S. Churchill biography. During my twelve years as Editor of the annual volumes of the Quatuor Coronati Lodge *Transactions (A.Q.C.),* eight of those volumes were proof-read and indexed by Bro. Norman Knight and I am very glad to pay tribute to the meticulous accuracy and the wide masonic knowledge he always displayed.

Bro. Frederick Smyth who was called in as joint author (following the death of Bro. Pick in 1966) had already done useful work on the Additional Degrees and on Freemasonry under various Grand Lodges overseas. He contributed much valuable material under those heads to the 5th edition and this has been brought up to date in the present volume, which will more particularly enhance its interest because those aspects of modern Masonry are almost unknown to the general masonic public.

The Pocket History of Freemasonry has long had its place among the first three books on the Quatuor Coronati list of works recommended especially for beginners; the present much-enlarged edition will help to maintain that position, and there is much in it that will interest the more advanced student as well.

December 1975   Harry Carr

It is sad to have to record that Norman Knight died on 17th August 1978.

In this 7th edition the opportunity has been taken to correct minor errors in the text and to update statistics and other changeable information.

PREFACE

The *Pocket History of Freemasonry* was first published in 1953, the work of Fred Pick (whose death in 1966 was an irreparable loss to masonic research) and Norman Knight (1891–1978), distinguished for all time in the world of books for having raised the art of indexing to its present highly professional level, and well-versed in the story of the English Craft and its ancestry.

Norman Knight invited Frederick Smyth to work with him on the extensive revisions and to contribute additional material demanded by the 5th edition because, as Fred Pick had been, he was a member of many Orders and Degrees beyond the Craft and, additionally, he had strong links with Freemasonry overseas.

Twenty-three years have passed since the first copies of this book came off the press and a 7th edition is now called for. This has not been so radically revised as was the last edition but the masonic world has seen many events in the intervening years and these have been faithfully recorded. Not a few readers have sent comments and criticisms to the authors, for all of which they are truly grateful. The majority of them have influenced amendments which have now been incorporated in the text.

The authors, present and past, have sought the aid of many experts as each edition was being prepared and due acknowledgement has been given in the relevant prefaces. It is impossible, and indeed unnecessary, here to give mention to all but especial thanks are due to J. D. E. Barnard, Deputy Grand Secretary of the United Grand Lodge of England, T. O. Haunch, Grand Lodge's Librarian, the Secretaries of the four Masonic Charities, R. E. Parkinson (Ireland), George S. Draffen of Newington (Scotland), Harold V. B. Voorhis (America) and — most particularly — to Harry Carr, Secretary Emeritus of the Quatuor Coronati Lodge No. 2076 of London and for many years the editor of its splendid transactions (*Ars Quatuor Coronatorum*), for advice always generously given and for bringing up to date the Foreword which he wrote for the 5th edition.

F.S.

THE AUTHORS

FRED PICK

Fred Lomax Pick (1898-1966) was born in Blackpool, educated at Preston, worked for much of his life in the public service at Oldham and, after retirement therefrom, gave eleven busy years as Provincial Grand Secretary for East Lancashire (holding comparable offices in the Royal Arch and Mark Provinces). He was initiated into Freemasonry in 1926 and, within three years, had joined the Manchester Association for Masonic Research. In 1934 he was a founder of the lodge which sprang from that Association and became its Master in 1939 before having taken that chair in any other lodge. He edited the Manchester *Transactions* from 1956 until his death. Of his masonic activities outside his home county we need elaborate only on a few. He was elected to full membership of the Quatuor Coronati Lodge in 1937, *while still a Master Mason*, and was elected to the chair in 1943. In 1948 he was appointed Prestonian Lecturer and, two years later, was invested as Past Assistant Grand Director of Ceremonies, being promoted to Past Grand Deacon in 1958. Comparable honours came to him in the Royal Arch, Mark Masonry, the Allied Masonic Degrees and the Societas Rosicruciana. He was also a Royal Ark Mariner, a Knight Templar and a member of the Ancient and Accepted Rite.

He was the author of many valuable papers on Freemasonry and is perhaps best known for his work on the Gilds, a subject in which he had specialized since his Preston school days.

NORMAN KNIGHT

Gilfred Norman Knight, M.A. (Oxon) (1891—1978), was educated at Bradfield and Balliol. A Tancred Scholar, he was called to the Bar at Lincoln's Inn in 1918. His civil career was mainly in the service of the Crown, a notable period being spent as first assistant secretary to the West India Committee.

His mother lodge was the Old Bradfield, of which he was a Past Master, and he was a founder member of the Caribbean and Rudyard Kipling Lodges. He held London Grand Rank and was long a member of the Correspondence Circle of the Quatuor Coronati Lodge.

Norman Knight was internationally acclaimed for his work in the field of professional indexing. He founded the Society of Indexers in 1957 and was instrumental in raising the art and science of creating an index to its present high level. He was also a chess-player of considerable repute.

His published works include some highly entertaining and widely-praised anthologies on chess, together with books on indexing and he contributed much to periodicals and transactions on those subjects as well as on the West Indies and — of course — Freemasonry.

FREDERICK SMYTH

Frederick Smyth (b.1919) is a West Countryman and studied at Exeter School. He began a civil service career in 1937 and, with war service in the British and Indian Armies, has spent quite a few years 'on tour' to the detriment of his masonic life.

He was initiated in the Punjab in 1943 and at once became interested in research which he facilitated by early membership of the Royal Arch, Mark, Rose Croix and other degrees and Orders, affiliating also to the Scottish and Irish Constitutions. In 1948 he gave his first talk on the Craft and his first published paper appeared in *The Northern Freemason*. During service in Germany he joined the Association of British Freemasons there, acting for a while as Secretary to its Central Committee before returning to England in 1953. When at last able to put down domestic and masonic roots, he joined Hazara, an ex-Indian lodge, becoming its Master in 1966. He is also a Past Master of the Connaught Army and Navy Lodge and has presided in many other degrees and Orders. He has been advanced to the 32° of the Ancient and Accepted Rite, is a Past Grand Junior Overseer of the Grand Lodge of Mark Master Masons, and has been similarly honoured in other masonic Orders.

In masonic research, he became Master of the Quatuor Coronati Lodge in 1979. He is a Fellow of the American Lodge of Research, New York, and holds associate memberships in other United States lodges and societies, as well as in France and New Zealand.

He is especially interested in overseas Masonry, the degrees and Orders beyond the Craft (in all countries), and masonic music and musicians. On these and other subjects he has written many papers, published in many countries (including translation into French and Finnish), and is frequently called upon to give talks to lodges and other masonic bodies.

CHAPTER I

THE ORIGIN OF FREEMASONRY

An immense amount of ingenuity has been expended on the exploration of possible origins of Freemasonry, a good deal of which is now fairly generally admitted to have been wasted.

In a system, fundamentally ethical, which makes a wide use of symbolism in its manner of imparting instruction, it would be surprising if there were not many points of contact with a variety of religions, old and new, in addition to the classical 'Mysteries', and even ancient Chinese philosophy, in which, for example, the square is known to have been employed as an illustration or emblem of morality.

Many of the doctrines or tenets inculcated in Freemasonry belong to the vast traditions of humanity of all ages and all parts of the world. Nevertheless, not only has no convincing evidence yet been brought forward to prove the lineal descent of our Craft from any ancient organization which is known to have, or even suspected of having, taught any similar system of morality, but also, from what we know of the Craft in the few centuries prior to the formation of the first Grand Lodge in 1717, it is excessively unlikely that there was any such parentage. Indeed, it can be very plausibly argued that a great deal of the symbolism which we find in the Craft today is actually a comparatively modern feature and that some was not introduced until after the beginning of the eighteenth century.

Without attempting to give an exhaustive list of ancient bodies or organizations which have at various times been claimed as the ancestors of Freemasonry, it may be said that, roughly, they fall into five groups, which will be shortly reviewed in what appears to be the order of increasing plausibility.

THE ORIGIN OF FREEMASONRY

Druids, Culdees and Rosicrucians

First come certain bodies such as the Druids and the Culdees, of whom we know nothing, or next to nothing, as to what rites or ceremonies they may have practised; and who thus provide admirable opportunities for guess-work as to any possible or probable ancestorship. Of both these it need only be said that they certainly existed and functioned in the British Isles, but that our knowledge of neither justifies any attempt at establishing a relationship to Freemasonry.

Again the Rosicrucians, no less mysterious, have been claimed as among our ancestors. But, whether there ever was such a body at all and, if so, whether it possessed any peculiar ritual or secrets, are extremely doubtful; and in any case there can have scarcely have been such a fraternity until after the beginning of the seventeenth century, and by that date Freemasonry was widely distributed over Scotland, and probably over England.

The Essenes and the Ancient Mysteries

Next must come the 'esoteric' moral systems of the past, such as that of the Essenes (who flourished from an early date in Hebrew history until well into our era), the ancient Mysteries of Egypt and Greece, and the Mithraic cult. These, undoubtedly, taught morality through symbolism, used elaborate rituals and inculcated such doctrines as that of the immortality of the soul.

Here we do in some cases know rather more regarding their tenets and practices; but the differences are more pronounced than the resemblances, and the latter are in such details as might have developed quite independently in widely separated places or ages.

The Collegia, Travelling Architects and Comacine Masters

Thirdly, there are several known or fancied bodies of operative builders or architects, who have been suspected of having handed down and propagated moral teachings and symbolism which finally came into the possession of the medieval operative masons, to blossom at last into the Craft as we have it today. There are three main 'theories' (if such a term is permissible); and, as the technique of operative masonry has undoubtedly been handed down from generation to generation

COLLEGIA, COMACINE MASTERS, ETC.

for perhaps several thousand years, we cannot ignore entirely the possibility that some esoteric teaching has come to us through the same channels. The three main theories will be dealt with separately.

The *Collegia* were part-religious, part-social and part-craft 'clubs' which flourished, encouraged by the Roman authorities, at the height of the Empire. It is quite likely (but there is no evidence) that such bodies, primarily devoted to the craft of building, accompanied or followed the Roman armies to Britain in mid-first century; and that when the Romans withdrew from this country towards the end of the fourth century, some of the personnel remained behind, so that their teaching survived and was handed down until it found utterance again among the stone-builders of the Anglo-Saxon period. It is not impossible that this may have been the case; but as there is no evidence that the *Collegia* possessed any esoteric teaching; as there was an almost complete break of several centuries in stone-building after the departure of the Romans; and as there is no evidence even of craft-organization among the masons until the tenth century (and then only very slender evidence), the chances of an inheritance from the *Collegia* would appear highly remote.

Again, there is a remark of Dugdale, the seventeenth-century antiquary and herald, recorded somewhat casually by John Aubrey, to the effect that 'about Henry the Third's time the Pope gave a Bull or diploma to a Company of Italian Architects to travell up and downe over all Europe to build Churches. From these are derived the *Fraternity of Free-Masons*'. This, again, is not impossible; but, in spite of intensive search in Papal archives and elsewhere, no evidence is yet available in support of the statement. We can safely, therefore, dismiss it as a guess, at the same time emphasizing that, though much research has been carried out in recent years on operative documents, there is still no reason for supposing that any special body of masons was ever employed exclusively on church- or abbey-building in this country. On the contrary, a mason took any job which came his way, whether church or castle.

Lastly, much has been said and written of recent years of a supposed body of masons who called themselves the *Comacine Masters*, so-called, it is said, because their original headquarters

THE ORIGIN OF FREEMASONRY

were situated on an island in Lake Como. Now it is certainly true that the early development of Romanesque architecture was much influenced by Lombard builders, who were in wide demand over western Europe, and whose work in some of its characteristic features is distinctive. But it is extremely doubtful if they ever formed an organized body; while, even if they did so, there is no reason whatever for supposing that they possessed any of the features, such as symbolic teaching or secret signs or words, which are among the peculiarities of the freemasons. Consequently, though the rather attractive idea that we had found here our lineal ancestors gained considerable hold forty or fifty years ago, it has long since been abandoned as a working hypothesis.

The Steinmetzen

The theory that our fraternity derived from the *Steinmetzen*, or stonecutters, of Germany became very popular over a century ago following the publication in 1848 of the writings of Fallou who failed, however, to submit any evidence in support of his claim. His lead was followed uncritically by later writers, including several of much greater eminence. The Abbot Wilhelm, of Hirschau, is said to have introduced an institution of lay brothers but examination of the records shows that these were not connected with the building trades. Another claim, like that of the *Comacines*, is that the *Steinmetzen* were established by Papal Bulls but these have never been traced. As in other countries, lodges (*Bauhütten*) were set up in connection with the building of the great cathedrals and their rules and customs tend to follow a common pattern. It must be remembered that for several reasons there was a constant interchange of staff and there would be a tendency for the best ideas evolved in one place quickly to spread to others. The earliest known text of their rules was drawn up at Regensburg in 1459 and the Torgau Statutes of 1462 record the acceptance by masters from several places of the ordinances previously drawn up. These regulations were confirmed by imperial authority in 1498 and again in 1563. Translations may be found in Gould's *History of Freemasonry* but we may here mention briefly that though some of their provisions are found in the Old Charges of England the latter do not in the main follow those documents. The Apprentice, when declared free, was required to enter into an obligation among other things not unlawfully to communicate the mason's greeting and grip and not to alter without permission the mark conferred on him. The Torgau Ordinances contain detailed instructions on the conferment and use of the mark and even on its *loan* to an apprentice when his master has no work for him. The nature of the 'greeting' is unknown today but was probably a formula rather than a Word such as was given in Scotland.

There was in the organization a chain of authority not established in England, a much more compact country. The lodge was subordinate to its provincial lodge and the chief lodge of Strasbourg was predominant over all. There is no evidence of any direct connection between the *Steinmetzen* and Freemasonry.

The Compagnonnage

Turning to France we find an association much more closely akin to Freemasonry than the *Steinmetzen*, one curiously overlooked by many French authorities. The French gild system has a much greater antiquity than anything in Britain, in fact, of all parts of Europe the shadow of the dark ages passed over none so lightly as the South of France. There were many trade fraternities and we hear of an organization of stonemasons as early as 1365, while a code of the masons of 1407 is preserved in the archives of Amiens. A still earlier code, of 1260, of an organization of masons, stonemasons, plasterers and mortarers is especially interesting as it refers to a privilege granted by Charles Martel, who also figures in the English Old Charges.

But there was another organization in France, among the journeymen masons and members of allied trades and, curiously, its very existence was only known by the fact that encounters between members of rival sections were generally the prelude to the outbreak of bloody fighting, hardly kept in check by the threat of the galleys. In 1841, one Agricol Perdiguier published the *Livre du Compagnonnage*, the first really detailed account to appear. The *Compagnonnage* contained three great divisions, the Sons of Solomon, the Sons of Maître Jacques and the Sons of Soubise. Maître Jacques, according to his legend, was one of the first masters of Solomon and a colleague of Hiram. He was the son of Jacquin, a

THE ORIGIN OF FREEMASONRY

celebrated architect, and his life was attempted and, after one rescue, a further attempt was successful.

The newly-admitted journeyman was expected to make the *tour de France* in search of employment and wider experience and measures were taken for the reception of travelling craftsmen who were provided with work or helped on their way. The similarities between their initiation and English masonic catechisms are suggestive but it is unfortunate that so little is known of them before Perdiguier, by which time much may have been adopted from Freemasonry which had been popular and widespread for a century. (In this country we know remarkably little about Friendly Society ritual which was so generally borrowed from the masonic that the Foresters took an especial pride in their alleged independence.)

In Britain, operative masonry lost its ritual which passed over into the keeping of and was elaborated by the speculatives, whereas the *Compagnonnage* retained theirs and remained aloof from French speculative Freemasonry. Though this *Compagnonnage* cannot be claimed to be in any way one of the origins of Freemasonry, yet it is more than likely that it did exercise considerable, if indirect, influence upon speculative Freemasonry in the sixteenth century, just as other institutions in England and Scotland were similarly influenced from across the Channel in this period.

Freemasonry a British product

Up to the present time, no even plausible theory of the 'origin' of the freemasons has been put forward. The reason for this is probably that the Craft, as we know it, originated among the operative masons of Britain. No doubt it incorporated from the earliest times shreds of ritual, folk-lore and even occult elements, of time-immemorial antiquity. But it is almost certainly a British product and of British origin.

CHAPTER II

MEDIEVAL OPERATIVE MASONRY

The history of Freemasonry is not so much the story of the development of a Craft Gild, culminating in such organizations as the Masons' Company of London, as the development of a body of 'moral instruction' communicated by means of meetings held under the seal of secrecy. For this reason that history is not to be found written in the stone buildings which successive generations of masons have left behind them.

Nevertheless, in order to understand the possibility of such a development, the forms which it took and the terms which it employed, it is necessary to know something of the organization under which they were developed. Though, therefore, we need not consider the various styles of architecture that prevailed successively in the medieval period, we shall have to look into the status of the different classes of masons, the conditions under which they worked, the trade customs and legal enactments by which they were bound, and (so far as we can) the Craft system which grew up as a consequence of those conditions and customs.

Inter-communication among Masons

Until the fourteenth century we have no evidence at all of organization. Yet, from the rapidity with which each new 'style' seems to have spread far and wide soon after its appearance, it is evident that there must have been at least a high degree of inter-communication among the masons. To take a single instance — it seems likely that scarcely fewer than 5,000 churches were built in England during the twenty years immediately following the Norman Conquest (1066-86). Among those which remain not only is there a remarkable similarity in size, proportion and general lay-out, but they differ appreciably from the surviving churches which are known to date from the half century or so before that period. It looks almost as if some central authority had prescribed (roughly) what sort of building was to be erected. Yet we know of no such central authority; it may be, quite simply, that the movement of the masons from one site to another was sufficient to spread the 'specification' (if we may so call it) of a church of that date.

There is visual evidence of such movement when some of the work at Selby Abbey in Yorkshire and Waltham Abbey in Essex is compared with that at Durham Cathedral.

The Secret Signs

To indicate the direction in which our study of the period must tend let it be said now that two features of the Craft, even in those early days, probably played a part in rendering it susceptible to the development of an 'esoteric' element.

In the first place, the mason's occupation must have required him to accept a degree of mobility. With very few exceptions, all the stone buildings erected in Britain in the Middle Ages were cathedrals, abbeys, churches or castles; on completion of one job he had to travel, possibly far, in search for the next. Thus a mason must have been joining parties or lodges of hitherto complete strangers and the possession of some secret sign or word to prove his *bona fides* would at least be appropriate — not so much, perhaps, to guarantee his ability (which could easily be tested practically) as to satisfy his employer that he was familiar with, and had pledged his fidelity to, the established customs and usages of the Craft.

In the second place, for several (perhaps many) years at a time the body of masons employed on a building enterprise would form a more or less isolated community, lodging close to their work and having comparatively little intercourse with the inhabitants of the nearest town or village.

The Gilds

Before passing on to consider the 'background' of the medieval mason we must consider the Gild system. Many crafts had their trade secrets; many, perhaps most, from the tenth century onwards tended to form Gilds for the better governing of their members and for securing a high standard of technical skill. The masons, too, had their trade secrets of a

THE GILDS

technical character but they were in a different position from other crafts, the members of which generally followed their trade throughout life in the same locality.

The Craft Gilds were essentially products of the larger communities, their members well-known to each other, contributing regularly to a common purse for sick benefits, burial and other purposes, and maintaining an altar at which they met on the Festival of their Patron Saint. The mason, on the other hand, went where the work was available; sometimes he went under compulsion when royal castles were under construction.

In Tudor and Stuart times we find the masons formed into actual Gilds in conjunction with other building trades, but their medieval organization was of a regional or national character. Exactly how this functioned we do not know but there are references to a periodical assembly of masons in the Old Charges, which will be considered later. Another occupation which was not confined to the towns was that of the minstrels and they have left definite traces of regional assemblies.

Though the organization of masons was distinct from that of the Gilds generally, much of the gild machinery was known to and adopted by the Craft, as will be seen in the Old Charges. It has also been suggested that our ritual may have been inspired by the annual productions of miracle plays, sections or interludes of which were taken over by various Gilds.

Here we run into difficulty. Four complete cycles of miracle plays are still in existence and many other individual plays, but in none with which the masons were concerned is there a thread of connexion with our masonic ceremonial, nor is there any play based on the building of King Solomon's Temple. On the other hand no part of the Old Testament story was more fully dramatized than the building of the Ark and there was in very early times a ritual based on this structure. As the Craft in general adopted much from the Gilds, so there are parallels between the dramas enacted in public by the Craft Gilds and the essentially private productions of masons.

The Lodge

We may now refer to some 'operative' usages. Several *were* common in other trades or crafts, but in Freemasonry there are many interesting survivals.

A lodge was originally the mason's working place, as

MEDIEVAL OPERATIVE MASONRY

distinguished from the place where he slept and ate. The earliest known reference occurs in 1277 in the building accounts of Vale Royal Abbey, where *logias* and *mansiones* were erected for the workers as no doubt the building was being carried out far from town or village. Later operative documents have many allusions to 'lodges', which in some cases (for example at York in 1399) served also as repositories for tools and implements.

It is an interesting theory that these lodges were usually placed on the southern side of buildings under construction so that the only available light had to come from the south.

The body of masons working there may well have been referred to also as a 'lodge' quite early, but we have no clear indication of such a practice before the (Scottish) Aitchison's Haven minutes of 1598, and the Schaw Statutes of 1598 and 1599; in the latter, three organized bodies of masons are spoken of as the Lodges of Edinburgh, Kilwinning and Stirling.*

Apprentices

The system of apprenticeship was, of course, known and used in many trades and crafts from early days. It seems to date from the first part of the thirteenth century, the earliest known London regulation being dated about 1230 although that was nearly a century before it began to be insisted upon and to come into general use.

Early references to mason apprentices are rare but this may well be because our knowledge of Craft organization is largely based on building accounts; these usually relate to important buildings such as abbeys or castles, at the erection of which apprentices would scarcely be encouraged.

The *Entered Apprentice* was a feature of Scottish operative masonry at least as early as 1598 though the term is not heard of in English masonry before the first *Book of Constitutions*, written in 1723 by a Scotsman!

According to the Scottish practice an apprentice, after completing his (nominally) seven years under indenture, was 'entered' in the lodge and became an Entered Apprentice. He was then allowed to do a certain amount of work on his own account but was not yet free to undertake a building enterprise involving the employment of subordinate labour.

See Chapter IX.

APPRENTICES, FELLOWS, ETC.

Fellows and Fellow Crafts

The Entered Apprentice's full freedom came some seven years later (but the length of time varied considerably) when he became a Fellow (of) Craft, which term is again unknown in England until 1723. He was then fully qualified as regards membership of his lodge, and could also undertake contracts as an employer. Incidentally, it is fully established that as early as 1598 the admission to the grades of both Entered Apprentice and Fellow Craft was of an esoteric nature.

In English documents the term 'Fellow' is first found near the end of the fourteenth century when it is used in the sense of one of a body or member of a fraternity, with no grade significance. After the middle of the fifteenth century it is used in Craft regulations with that implication, but the Fellow was by then of a status superior to that of the 'mere' mason and qualified, if called on, to take charge or to employ masons under him — a status roughly equivalent to that of the Fellow Craft of Scottish documents.

The Warden

This office was a normal feature of the Gilds, whence the masonic office was derived. In our Craft the Warden begins to appear about 1400. At York in 1408 the Warden and other senior masons took the oath of obedience to the regulations as well as to the Master. In several cases, as for instance in London in 1481, the Warden was in charge of the lodge's cash.

The Master, or Master Mason

Until the end of the seventeenth century, this was a term applied solely to the mason in charge of a building operation. The earliest recorded example in this country is John of Gloucester who was Master Mason at the erection of Westminster Hall from 1254 to 1262.

In Scottish lodges, although the presiding officer was usually known as the Deacon, Warden or Preses, we find near the end of the seventeenth century the title Master Mason applied to him; it is not quite clear, however, whether this was an operative practice.

Masons and 'Free' Masons

The earliest known use of the word freemason occurs in

MEDIEVAL OPERATIVE MASONRY

1376 when it implies an *operative* mason of a somewhat superior class, though not very clearly defined; indeed it is by no means certain that there was actually any technical distinction between a mason and a freemason. During the seventeenth century a number of examples of the use of the latter word suggest that it was beginning to be applied especially to the non-operative mason.

Curiously enough the very meaning of the term is not certain. By many it is taken to imply a 'freedom' in varying senses: free from restrictive laws and regulations; free from tolls and taxes; or free as emancipated skilled artisans. Unlike practically every other craft or trade, in which the 'freedom' of a city or borough was required to qualify the craftsman to exercise his occupation, the Masons' Craft could be and was called on to build anywhere, regardless of town regulations, and it may be that this is what is implied in the term 'free' mason.

On the other hand, the accepted opinion of many notable authorities is that the term was originally an abbreviated form of 'freestone mason' — one whose work would involve the cutting and shaping of the finer kinds of stone, called freestone, found in a region stretching from Dorset to Yorkshire and also imported from Normandy. This would require more skill than was possessed by one who was occupied with the roughstone, or stone of inferior quality, which was more or less incapable of being properly squared.

Although there is perhaps a majority opinion that 'freemason' originally meant a worker in freestone, yet the insistence on physical freedom that is freedom from serfdom, in the Old Charges (*see* next Chapter) and in the modern ritual, must be noted. The probable explanation is that the term 'free' in freemason had different implications in successive periods of Freemasonry.

The Layer (or Setter)

This name, which figures largely in the early building accounts, was given to a separate class of workman whose job it was to build up the prepared stones. The craft of the layer (or setter) was less skilled than that of the mason (or hewer) and there may have been a certain amount of jealousy between them. Nevertheless, there is some evidence as to the interchangeability of the two trades and that the authorities in

THE LAYER AND THE COWAN

London in the middle of the fourteenth century tried to avoid demarcation disputes; but the distinction between the two classes persisted.

The layer's chief tool was the trowel which even today occupies a comparatively minor place in the English ritual.

The Cowan

We first hear of the cowan in the Schaw Statutes of 1598 (*see* Chapter IX), and he had no exact counterpart in England or Ireland. He was a working mason who had not properly joined the Fraternity — who had not, in fact, been admitted into a lodge after serving his term under indentures. No doubt there were many such, capable of doing good work. But the official attitude to them is clearly indicated by the following regulation from the Schaw Statutes:

> Item, that no master or fellow of craft receive a cowan to work in his society or company, nor send any of his servants to work with cowans, under pain of twenty pounds [Scots] so oft as any person offends in this respect.

According to a minute of the Mother Kilwinning Lodge in 1707 'No Meason shall employ no cowan which is to say without the word to work', which (by leaving out the last two important words) has given rise to the definition of a cowan as 'a mason without the word'. Mention of him does not enter English Freemasonry until Anderson's second *Book of Constitutions*, 1738.

The Assembly

So far we have documentary evidence for all that has been said. We are on less safe ground when we come to consider the Assembly of Masons. According to the earliest two of the Old Charges such a governing body existed, meeting every year or every third year and possessing certain legislative powers; every Master was bound to attend. Its origin is there attributed (with no historical probability) to the time of King Athelstan. The much later Roberts 'family' of Old Charges speak of *annual* assemblies.

It is just possible that such General Assemblies of Masons were actually held, either annually or triennially, in medieval times. But it is at least curious that, beyond those two Old

MEDIEVAL OPERATIVE MASONRY

Charges, there is no contemporary evidence to confirm their existence since it is now believed that the Statutes of 1360 and 1425 (*see* next Section), which banned confederations of masons, were more likely to have been aimed at illegal organizations formed to increase wages.

In the second edition (1738) of his *Constitutions* Dr. Anderson gives a detailed account of an attempt to break up a General Assembly at York in 1561. No authority has been found for this account, although the Doctor assures us that 'this tradition was firmly believ'd by all the old English Masons'. According to his narrative Queen Elizabeth, 'hearing the Masons had certain *Secrets* that could not be reveal'd to her (for that she could not be *Grand Master*) and being jealous of all secret Assemblies, she sent an armed Force to break up their annual *Grand Lodge* at *York* on St. *John's* Day, Dec. 27, 1561. . . . But Sir Thomas Sackville, Grand Master, took care to make some of the chief Men sent *Fre-masons*, who then joining in the *Communication*, made a very honourable Report to the Queen; and she never more attempted to dislodge or disturb them, but esteem'd them as a peculiar sort of Men that cultivated Peace and Friendship, Arts and Sciences without meddling in the Affairs of Church or State.'

For the tradition of a General Assembly in 1663, *see* page 65.

The advent of Grand Lodge in 1717 was, according to Anderson, a revival not so much of Freemasonry as of the General Assembly.

The Statutes Affecting the Masons

The Statutes of the realm provide the only evidence, apart from the Old Charges and such records as the building accounts already mentioned, of the existence of Freemasonry in England before the initiation of Elias Ashmole in 1646 (*see* p. 45).

In Edward III's reign the Black Death swept away more than half of the four million population of England; the demand for the labour of the survivors became so great that wages rose to heights unknown before. In consequence there was enacted the restrictive Statute of Labourers of 1350, the following clause of which applies to the masons:

> Item, that carpenters, masons and tilers and other work-

THE STATUTES AFFECTING THE MASONS

men of houses shall not take for their work, but in such manner as they were wont; that is to say, a master carpenter iiid., and another iid.; a master freestone mason iiiid., and other masons iiid., and their servants id.

This was confirmed by a Statute of ten years later which also declared that

> All alliances and covines of masons and carpenters, and congregations, chapters, ordinances and oaths betwixt them ... shall be from henceforth void and wholly annulled; so that every mason ... shall be compelled by his master whom he serveth to do every work that to him pertaining to do, or of free stone, or of rough stone.

In 1425, the third year of King Henry VI's reign, it was enacted that

> Whereas by the yearly Congregations and Confederacies made by the Masons in their general Chapters assembled, the good Course and Effect of the Statutes of Labourers be openly violated and broken ... Our said Lord the King ... hath ordained and established ... that such Chapiters and Congregations shall not be hereafter holden ... and that all ... Masons that come to such Chapiters and Congregations be punished by Imprisonment of their Bodies, and make Fine and Ransom at the King's Will.

Piquancy is added to this Statute by the once commonly held belief, endorsed by Dr. Anderson, that Henry VI himself later became a freemason. There is nothing in the Statutes of 1360 and 1425 to connect the 'covines', congregations, confederacies and 'chapters' therein mentioned with the General Assembly of the first two Old Charges; it is far more likely that they arose in revolt against the low wages fixed by the Statute of 1350.

The various Statutes of Labourers were codified, and in part repealed, by an Act of 1563 in Queen Elizabeth's reign; one clause is of especial interest. Among many tradesmen allowed to have their sons apprenticed to them is specified the 'roughe mason', whereas in previous legislation the term 'freemason' had been used. The explanation may be that the latter expression had by this time already lost its purely operative significance.

MEDIEVAL OPERATIVE MASONRY

Later laws affecting the (speculative) freemasons, such as the Unlawful Societies Act of 1799 and the Unlawful Oaths in Ireland Act of 1823, will be referred to in their proper places.

The Four Crowned Martyrs

This seems a fitting place for telling the story of the Christian stonemason martyrs, who suffered under Diocletian. They were to become the Patron Saints of the building trades, though their commemorative day, 8th November, was less popularly observed by English masons than among the German *Steinmetzen* and on the Continent generally.

Actually there were *five* masons: Claudius, Castorius, Nicostratus, Simphorianus and Simplicius, and (including four soldiers) *nine* martyrs in all, who are commemorated under the name of Quatuor Coronati.

The five masons, who were highly skilled sculptors, refused to fashion a statue of the heathen god Aesculapius for the Emperor who thereupon ordered that they be buried alive in leaden coffins and cast in the River Tiber. Forty-two days later the chests were recovered by Nicodemus, a fellow Christian. When the image had been made by other hands Diocletian ordered the city militia to offer incense and four Christian soldiers who declined to do so were scourged to death. Their bodies, which were thrown to the dogs, were rescued and buried with the other Saints. The dates assigned to the two sets of martyrdoms were A.D. 298 and 300 respectively.

In 1313 Pope Melchiades built for the relics a Basilica on the Caelian Hill, dedicated to the Four Crowned Ones and the Five Sculptor Martyrs. But, as it was always called by the first part of the title, the memory of the Five became blended in the Four.

The Basilica was rebuilt by Pope Honorius I in 622, but three years earlier a Church of the Four Crowned Martyrs had been erected in Canterbury, probably where St. Alphege's Church now stands. Of the Old Charges, the earliest — the Regius Poem — alone mentions the Quatuor Coronati; this it does as follows:

> Pray we now to God Almyght,
> And to hys swete Moder Mary Bryght,
> That we nowe keepe these Artyculus here,

THE FOUR CROWNED MARTYRS

And these poynts wel al-y-fere
As dede these holy Martyres fowre,
That yn thys Craft were of grete Honoure;
They were as gode Masonus as on earthe schul go
Gravers and ymage-makers they were also.

In speculative Freemasonry the name of Quatuor Coronati survives in that of the oldest and best-known lodge of masonic research, No. 2076, London, warranted in 1884. (The same name has been adopted by other research lodges, including one at Bayreuth in Germany and one in Rome under the Grand Orient of Italy.)

CHAPTER III

THE OLD CHARGES

This is a subject about which the average brother hears more than he learns. At each Installation meeting a 'Summary of the Ancient Charges and Regulations' is read out to the Master-elect and most freemasons will have read this for themselves in the *Book of Constitutions*. But few read the fuller version which follows in the same book; this is, however, all that survives in present-day form of a mass of manuscripts of varying age which played a very vital part in the lives of our operative ancestors. Although parallels will be found here and there, no other medieval body — craft, religious or otherwise — is known to have possessed such documents.

No fewer than 125 copies are now known and classified (as compared with the ten only that were known in 1882) and most are available in reliable reproductions, while the original documents can be seen in the British Museum, or in the Grand Lodge or other masonic libraries, although a few remain in private hands.

The Regius and Cooke MSS

The two oldest are in the British Museum: the *Regius MS* is believed to have been written about 1390 and the *Cooke MS* about 1410. The *Grand Lodge No. 1 MS*, in the possession of the Grand Lodge of England, is dated 1583; several others are ascribed to the seventeenth century and still more were written in the eighteenth century *after* the formation of Grand Lodge. Great attention has been paid to them by students during the past ninety years or so and, by examining in great detail the various copies, it has been possible to work out lines of descent for, as in many manuscripts, 'differences' occur between copy and copy. They are essentially English or of English origin and, as Professor Douglas Knoop was of the opinion that there was

THE OLD MANUSCRIPTS

little trace of any masonic organization in England before about 1375, it will be realized that they bring us very close to the earliest operative Craft system.

Their use will be discussed later; let us first describe them. The two old copies are in book form as are a few of the more recent ones, but many are written on skins stitched end to end in the form of a roll.

The text falls into three parts — a prayer, a historical section and the Charges.

The Prayer

First, a prayer of invocation. The following example is taken from *Grand Lodge No. 1 MS* of 1583:

> THE MIGHTE OF THE FFATHER OF HEAVEN and the wysedome of the glorious Soonne through the grace & the goodnes of the holly ghoste yt been three p'sons & one god be wth us at or beginning, and giue us grace so to gou'ne us here in or lyuing that wee maye come to his blisse that neur shall haue ending. AMEN.

The History

The following is an abstract of the version given in the *Beswicke-Royds MS* which was discovered in 1915 and is now in the possession of the Province of East Lancashire.

This version was probably written in the early part of the sixteenth century and consists of four pieces of parchment about six inches wide stitched together to form a continuous strip six feet ten inches in length.

The Liberal Arts and Sciences

The historical statement opens with an account of the Seven Liberal Arts and Sciences. These are still referred to in connection with the second degree but in medieval times they formed the normal curriculum of the universities. The place of Geometry will be realized by the following passage:

> ... The wch seaven liberall scienc's bee as it were all one science that is to say Geometry for thus may a man proue that all the scienc's in the world bee found by Geometry for it teacheth meat & measure ponderacon & weight of all maner of kynd & earth and there is no man that worketh

by any craft but hee worketh by some measure and no man buyes or sells but by measure & weight and all is Geometry. And Craftsmen & merchants fynd no other of the VII scienc's espetially plowe-men & tillers of graine both corne seeds vynes plants & sellers of all other fruits, for *Gram^r* neither Astronomy nor any of these can fynd a man one measure or meat without Geometry wherefore I thinke that science most worthy that fyndeth all others,

The Two Pillars

The story proper begins with Lamech and his two sons by one wife and one son and one daughter by another. These children were the founders of all crafts in the world: Jabal of geometry, Jubal of music, Tubal Cain of the smith's craft and the sister who discovered weaving. These children knew that God would take vengeance for sin either by fire or water.

. . . wherefore they writt these scienc's wch were found in twoe pillars of Stone that they might bee found at after the flood. The one ftone was called marble that cannot burne with fire. The othr was called Lateras that cannot drowne wth watr. Our Intent is now to tell you truly howe & in what manner these stones were found whereon these Crafts were written. The Greek Hermenes that was sonne vnto Cus and Cus was Sonne vnto Sem who was sonne vnto Noah This same Hermenes was afterwards called Hermes the father of wise men and hee found out the twoe pillars of stone wherein the scienc's were written and taught them forth. And at the makinge of the Tower Babilon there was the Craft of Masonry then first found & made much of and the kinge of Babilon who was called Hembroth or Nembroth was a mason and loved well the Craft as it is said wth the mr of the stories.

Here we have the original legend of the Pillars, not those with which we are familiar today but two others erected by the inhabitants of the ancient world to carry over the knowledge of mankind over an impending destruction which proved to be Noah's flood. Of all our traditions this has the longest pedigree for it was taken by the compiler of the early version from *Polychronicon*, a world history written by Ranulf Higden, a monk of Chester, who died about 1364. Higden copied from

THE HISTORY

Josephus who in turn took it from the Greek historian, Berosus, who wrote about 300 B.C. and is believed to have copied from the Sumerian account of about 1500 B.C.

The first Charge was given by the King of Babylon to a party of sixty masons sent to assist in the building of the city of Nineveh. We then pass to the removal of Abraham and Sarah into Egypt where the patriarchs taught the seven sciences to the Egyptians, a worthy scholar being Euclid.

> ... And it befell in his dayes That the lords and states of this Realme had so many sonnes that they had begotten some by their wyues and some by ladies of the realme, for that land is an hott land & plenteous generacon and they had no Competent living for their children wherefore they made much sorrowe And the kinge of that land called a great Counsell & a pliamt to knowe how they might fynd *there children* meanes and they could fynd no good wayes. Then hee caused a Cry to bee made throughout the Realme That if there were any man that could informe him that hee should come vnto him and hee should bee well rewarded and hould himselfe well paid. And after this Crye was made, this worthy Clarke Euclid came and said to the kinge and all his great Lords If you will haue yor children gouerned & taught honestly as gentlemen should bee vnder Condision that you will grant them & mee a Comifsion that I may haue power to rule them honestly as those sciencs ought to bee ruled And the kinge wth his Counsell granted them & sealed that Comifsion And then the worthy docter tooke the Lords sonnes and taught them the science of Geometry in practice to worke masonry and all manner of worthy workes that belonged to building of Castles & all maner of Courts Temples Churchs with all other building & hee gaue them a charge in this manner first that they should bee true vnto the kinge and vnto the lord they serued and that they should loue well togethr and bee true one to anothr and that they should call one & other fellowes & not servant or knaue nor othr foule names and that they should truly serue for their paym^t the lord they serued.

Building of the Temple

The next major episode is the building of the Temple.

THE OLD CHARGES

... Longe after the Children of Israel came into the land of Behest wch nowe is called amongst vs is called Jerusalem kinge Dauid began the temple of Jerusalem called wth them Templu' Domini And the same kinge Dauid loued Masons well & cherished them and gaue them paymt And hee gaue them chargs as you shall here afterwards. And after the decease of Kinge Dauid Solomon that was sonne vnto Dauid pformed out the Temple his father had begun and hee sent after Masons into dyvers lands and gathered them togeather so that hee had foure score thoufand workers of stone and they were named Masons and hee had three thoufand of them wch were ordeyned maisters & governors of that worke And there was a kinge of another Region that men called Hyram and hee loved well kinge Solomon & gaue him timber for his worke and hee had a Sonne that was named Aynon and hee was mr of Geometry and hee was chiefe mr of all his masons and mr of all his Graveinge works & of all othr masons that belonged to the Temple and this witnefseth the Byble in libro Regn IIII^{to} capite VII. And this sonne Solomon confirmed both charges & manners wch his father had given to masons and thus was the worthy craft of masons confirmed in the Cuntry of Jerusalem and in many othr kingdomes glorious craftsmen walkinge abrode into dyuers Cuntryes some because of learninge more craft & other some to teach their craft.

Naymus Graecus

The reference above to the son of King Hiram 'named Aynon' is interesting. This person is introduced in various guises in the different versions of the Old Charges. Another curious name follows in the next section, Naymus Graecus. the man with the Greek name, possibly a reference to Pythagoras, but there are many alternative theories. Charles Martel, who is also referred to, is Charlemagne (througout this history anachronisms must be overlooked).

... And so it befell yt a curious mason named Naymus Graecus who had beene at the makinge of Solomons Temple came into france & there taught the Craft of masonry to the men of France. And then there was one of the royall blood of france called Charles Martell & hee loued

NAYMUS GRAECUS & ST. ALBAN

well this Craft and hee drewe to him this Naymus Graecus & learned of him the Craft & tooke upon him the Charges & manners & afterwards by the grace of God hee was elected kinge of france & when hee was in his state hee tooke to him many masons and made mafons there that were none before and sett them on worke & gaue them charges & manners & good paymt wch hee had learned of other masons & hee confirmed them a Charter from year to year to hould an afsembly & thus came the Craft of masonry into ffrance.

St. Alban

There immediately follows the story of the introduction of Masonry into England with an account of the fixing of the rate of pay. This is regarded by many authorities as confirmative of the theory that the original traditional history was devised shortly after the Black Death with its economic upheaval.

... England all this season stood void both of any Charge & Masonry vntill the tyme of St. Albon and in his tyme the kinge of England yt was a pagan and hee walled the Towne wch is nowe called St Albons and so in Albons tyme a worthy knight was chiefe steward to the kinge & had goumt of the Realme & alfo of makinge the towne walls & hee loued masons well & cherished them & made their paymt right good standinge wages as the Realme did require for hee gaue them euery three weeks III^s VI^d their double wages whereas before that tyme through all the whole land a mason tooke but a peny a day till the tyme that St Albon mended it and gott them a charter of the kinge and his Counsell and gaue it the name of an Afsembly & was thereat himselfe & made masons & gaue them charges as you shall here hereaftr.

The Assembly at York

There followed a period of inactivity until the time of King Athelstan and here we find an account of the alleged Assembly at York around which a masonic legend persisted for many centuries.

... and he had a sonne that was named Hedwine and hee loued masons much more than his father for hee was full of

THE OLD CHARGES

the practice of Geometry wherefore hee drewe himselfe to commune wth masons & to learne of them the Craft & afterwards for loue hee had to masons & the craft hee was made mason himselfe & hee gott of his father the kinge a Charter & a Comifsion to hould euer yeare an Afsembly where they would within the realme & to correct wthin themselues by statute Trespafses if they were done wthin the Craft. And hee held himselfe an afsembly at work & there hee made masons & gaue them charges and taught them the manners of masons and comannded that Rule to bee houlden euer after and to him he betooke the Charter & Comifsion to keepe & ordeyned That it should bee ruled from kinge to kinge. when the Afsembly was gathered togethr hee caufsed a Cry to bee made that all masons both ould & yonge That had any writings or vnderstanding of the Charges that were made before either in this land or any othr that they should shewe them forth and there was some in french some in Greeke & some in Englishe and some in othr langages and the Intent thereof was found, and thereof hee commannded a booke to bee made, how the Craft was first found & made and Comannded that it should bee read & tould when any mafon should bee made & to giue them the charge and from tyme till this masonry hath beene kept in that forme and order as well as men might Gouerne the same, And furthermore at dyvers afsemblies hath beene putt to and added certaine charges more by the best aduice of maisters & fellowes.

The Obligation

This ends the historical statement and, at this point in several versions, we find an instruction to take an obligation on the Volume of the Sacred Law. In the *Haddon MS* of 1723, this instruction is interposed in Latin:

> Tunc unus ex Senioribus teneat Librum, ut illi vel ponat, vel ponat manus super Librum et tunc praecipta deberunt legi.*

---

*Then one of the senior brethren holds the Book in such a manner that he either places it before the candidate or else places his (the candidate's) hand upon it and thus the charges ought to be read.

36

THE CHARGES

The Charges

The Charges differ widely from the general character of Gild ordinances and, while some set out regulations for the conduct of the work, others may be described as general rules of behaviour. Internal evidence shows that the Charges in the *Cooke MS* of about 1410 were taken from an earlier original version than the *Regius MS* of about 1390 and again the evidence points to the middle of the fourteenth century.

Here are the Charges as set forth in the *Beswicke-Royds MS*:

here followeth the worthy & godly oath of masons (vizt)

EUERY man that is a mason take heed right well of this charge if you fynd yor selfe guilty of any of these that you may amend you againe espetially yo^u that are to bee charged take good heed that you may keepe this Charge for it is a great prill for a man to forsweare himselfe vpon a Booke.

1. The first charge is that you shall bee true man to God and holy church, and that you vse no heresie or error by your vnderstandinge or by teachinge of indiscreet men.
2. Alfo you shall bee true liegemen to the kinge wthout treason or fallshood and that you knowe no treason but that you amend it if you may or ells warne the kinge or his Counfell thereof.
3. Alfo you shall be true one to another, that is to say to euery mr & fellowe of the Craft of masonry that bee mafons allowed & that you doe to them as you would they should doe to you.
4. And alfo that euer mason keepe Counsell of lodge and chamber truly & all othr Counsell that ought to bee kept by the way of masonry.
5. Alfo that no mason bee thiefe in Company so farr forth as you shall knowe.
6. And alfo that you shall bee true vnto the lord & mr that you ferue & truly to see for his profitt & advantage.
7. Alfo that you doe no villany in that house whereby the Craft may be slandered.

These bee the Charges in Gen'all wch euery mason should hould both maisters & fellowes

Now followe other Charges in pticuler for maisters & fellowes.

1. first that no mr take vpon him any lords worke nor other

THE OLD CHARGES

worke butt that he knowe himselfe able of Cuninge to pforme the same so that the Craft haue no disworship but that the lord may bee ferued truly.

2 Alfo that no mr take any worke but that hee take it reasonably so that the lord may be truly ferved wth his owne goods & the mr liue honestly & truly pay his fellowes their pay as the manner of the Craft doth require.

3 Alfo that no mr nor fellowe supplant other of their worke (that is to say) if they haue taken a worke or stand mr of a lorde's worke you shall not putt him out vnles hee bee unable of Cunning to end the worke.

4 Alfo that no mr or fellowe take any prentice to bee allowed his aprentice but for seaven years and that the apprentice bee able of birth & limms as hee ought to bee.

5 Alfo that no mr nor fellowe take allowance to bee made mafon wthout the afsent of his fellowes at the leaft fyve or six.

6 And alfo that hee that is to bee made masons bee free borne of good kinred & no bondman & that hee haue his right lims as a man ought to haue.

7 Alfo that no mr putt a lords worke to taske that was vsed to goe to journey.

8 Alfo that euery mason giue pay to his fellowes *but* as hee may deserue so that hee bee not deseaued by false workmen.

9 Alfo that no fellowe slandr anothr falsly behind his backe to make him loose his good name or his worldly goods.

10 Alfo that no fellowe wthin the lodg or wthout answer another vngodly wthout reasonable cause.

11 Alfo that euery mason preferr his elder & putt him to worship.

12 Alfo that no mason shall play at cards hazards or any othr vnlaw^{ll} game wherby they may bee slandered.

13 Alfo that no mason comitt Ribaldry or leachery to make the Craft slandered & that no fellowe goe into the towne where there is a lodge of masons wthout a fellowe to bear him witnes that hee was in honest Company.

14 Alfo that euer mr & fellowe come to the Afsembly if hee bee wthin fifty myles & hee haue warning & to ftand to the award of maisters and fellowes.

15 Alfo that euery mr & fellowe if hee haue trespafsed shall

THE CHARGES

stend to the award of mrs & fellowes to make them accord & if they cannot to goe to the Common lawe.

16 Alfo that no mason make moulds sware or rule to any rough layers.

17 Alfo that no mason sett layers wthin a lodge or wthout to haue mould ftones wth moulde of his owne makinge.

18 Alfo that euery mason shall receave and cherish strange masons when they come ouer the Cuntry & sett them on worke as the manner is (that is to say) if they haue mould ftones in place hee shall sett him a fortnight on worke at the least & giue him his hyre & if there bee no stones for him then to refresh him wth some money to bringe him to the next lodge, and also euery mason shall serue truly the workes and truly make an end of the worke bee it taske or Journey if hee haue his pay as he ought to haue.

> These charges that are here rehearsed and all other that belonge to masonry you shall truly keepe to the vttermost of yor knowledge
>
> So helpe you God and by
> the Contents of this Book.

The English character of the Charges is indicated by the fact that in the Scottish versions we find the craftsmen pledging obedience to the King of England, a very curious provision before the union of the two countries.

Use of the Old Charges

We have now described very briefly the general form of the Old Charges. What were their uses?

We gather from the historical portion that Prince Edwin, son of Athelstan, collected the writings and understandings of the Craft at his Assembly at York. It is doubtful whether this history was ever read or recited in full but the possession of a copy seems to have served very much the same purpose as a lodge Warrant today. This is borne out in the *Sloane 3848 MS* to the effect that it was finished by Edward Sankey on the 16th day of October, 1646. This was the day on which Elias Ashmole was initiated at Warrington,* the earliest recorded initiation of a speculative mason in an *English* lodge. Richard Sankey was one of the members and it is almost certain that the document was prepared for use on that occasion. There is

*See p. 45.

THE OLD CHARGES

a note on the *Scarborough MS* of a meeting at Scarborough in 1705 when six gentlemen were admitted.

The last section — the Charges, general and particular — poses some interesting questions. They are of different classes. How came they to be included?

They reveal a mixture of what we may call the operative and the speculative sides. About a score contain an Apprentice Charge of a definitely operative character; of these, some — mainly, though not exclusively, associated with the latter part of the pre-Grand Lodge era — contain new articles of a *speculative* character, and other copies refer to masonic secrets.

It is a curious fact that these documents contain no mention of the use of the Mason's Mark, a very essential feature of operative life which comes into full prominence in Scottish records.

There was a ritual side. Two distinguished brethren, the late E. L. Hawkins and the late R. H. Baxter, devoted much time to analysing and identifying passages which have now passed into the ritual or may have inspired it. One small group of these old manuscripts goes so far as to describe the ceremonial at the conferment of secrets. These were written in the latter part of the sixteenth and early part of the seventeenth century and link up with another type of document which is more closely associated with speculative Freemasonry and will be described later.

Here are a few further examples from versions of the Old Charges. They were selected by R. H. Baxter.

Buchanan MS (Second half seventeenth century)
These Charges that you have Received you shall well and truly keepe, not discloseing the Secrecy of our Lodge to man, woman, nor child: stick nor stone, thing moueable nor immoueable: so God you helpe and his holy Doome. Amen.

Harris MS, No. 1 (Second half seventeenth century)
These Charges wch wee now rehearse to you and all other the Charges, Secrets and Mysteries belonging to Free-Masonry, you shall faithfully and truely keep together with

OBLIGATIONS

the Council of this Lodge or Chamber. You shall not for any Gift, Bribe or Reward, favour or affections, directly or Indirectly, for any Cause whatsoever divulge or disclose to either Father or Mother, Sister or Brother, Wife, Child, friend, Relation or Stranger, or any other prson whatsoever. So help you God your Holydoom and the Contents of this Book.

Harleian MS No. 1942 (Second half seventeenth century)
I A: B: Doe in the presence of Almighty god & my fellowes and Brethren here present, promise and declare that I will not at any time, hereafter, by any Act, or Circumstance whatsoever, Directly or Indirectly, Publish, discover, reveale or make knowne any of the secrets privilidges, or Councells of the ffraternity or fellowship of free masonry, which at this time, or any time hereafter shalbee made knowne vnto mee, soe helpe me god & the holy contents of this booke.

Dumfries No. 4 MS (First half eighteenth century)
The charges we now w Rehearse to you wt. all other charges and secrets otherways belonging to free masons or any that enter their interest for curiocitie together wt. the counsels of this holy ludge chamber or hall you shall not for any gift bribe or Reward favour of affection directly or indirectly nor for any case qt. soever devulge disclose ye same to ether father or mother sister or brother or children or stranger or any person qt.soever. So help you God.

You yt. are under vouees take hee yt. you keep ye ath and promise you made in presence of allmighty God think not yt. a mental reservation or equivocation will serve for to be sure every word you speak the whole time of your Admission is ane oath.

The Working Tools are suggested by the *Melrose No. 2 MS* (1674) '... and he ought not to let you know the priviledge of ye compass, Square, levell and ye plum-rule'.

There is an interesting endorsement on the *Grand Lodge No. 1 MS* which, as we have already mentioned, is dated 1583. The addition was probably made about a couple of centuries

THE OLD CHARGES

later but is very suggestive of early Royal Arch Freemasonry.

> In the beginning was the Word,
> And the Word was with God,
> And the Word was God.
> Whose Sacred and universal Law
> I shall endeavour to observe
> so Help me God.

The original Grand Lodge of England underlined the importance of the Old Charges when in 1719 they requested the Craft to bring in old records. This and its sequel will be considered later (p. 72).

The first *Book of Constitutions* published in 1723 is claimed by its author, Dr. James Anderson, to contain a digest of the old Records. We may here mention that two copies of the *Cooke MS* (the *Woodford MS* and the *Supreme Council MS*) were made in 1728. The former bears the endorsement,

> This is a very Ancient Record of Masonry wch was copyed for me by Wm. Reid Secretary to the Grand Lodge 1728.

It is a curious fact that, despite this display of official interest, the study of the Old Charges did not seriously begin for more than a century and was then inspired by a non-mason who drew public attention to the long-overlooked document now known as the *Regius MS*. The first analysis into what we know today as 'families', enabling lines of descent of groups of these documents to be ascertained and studied, was undertaken by a German, Dr. Begemann, and was continued and developed in this country by those two giants of masonic research, W. J. Hughan and R. F. Gould. The two great experts of this century, so far, have been the late Douglas Knoop and the late Reverend Herbert Poole. As has already been mentioned, the majority of these Old Charges are available for study in facsimile or reliable transcript.

CHAPTER IV

PRE-GRAND LODGE FREEMASONRY

We have discussed briefly various suggested sources of Freemasonry and given some account of medieval operative Masonry and the Old Charges. We now reach the important task of describing the evolution of our speculative system. In addition to several copies of the Old Charges we have in England certain seventeenth-century records but nothing of the nature of lodge minutes, whereas in Scotland there are not only minute books — one running back as far as 1598 — but also the tradition of the Mason Word.

Economic Changes

The economic changes of the fifteenth and sixteenth centuries had far-reaching effects on the mason craft. The building of churches and the older ashlar-faced castles had declined and the classical style of architecture was being introduced. At the same time there was a drastic fall in the value of money; this stimulated building but diminished the reward of labour. It is not always realized today that 'direction of labour' is no new thing; it was commonly resorted to in connection with the building of royal castles and residences and was still occurring in the seventeenth century.

Later Gilds and the Masons' Company of London

There were in several places Gilds or Companies of Masons, often in conjunction with other building trades. The records of the London Masons' Company are extant from 1620 onwards and it is at about this time that we begin to find traces of lodges or other bodies as well as records of individuals connected with the craft of Masonry but not themselves practising it. For the sake of convenience we call them speculative freemasons but, though the word 'speculative' is found in the

PRE-GRAND LODGE FREEMASONRY

Cooke MS of about 1410,* it is not found in general use before the middle of the eighteenth century. Thus we have the picture of an entirely operative craft in 1600 which has given place to the speculative side by the middle of the eighteenth century.

The London Masons' Company was probably not in existence before 1356, though there is a record that in 1306 the journeymen combined and threatened to beat newcomers if they accepted lower wages than was customary. In 1376 four masons were elected to the Common Council and there was a grant of arms in 1472 while in 1481 ordinances were adopted and approved. Other incorporations including masons were found at Canterbury, Durham, Exeter, Gateshead, and elsewhere.

There was, within the London body, an inner fraternity known as the Acception, membership of which did not necessarily follow membership of the Company. Those admitted paid a fee of 20s. if of the Company, 40s. if strangers. Seven members of the Company enrolled in the Acception in 1620-21; Nicholas Stone, the King's Master Mason, who was Master of the Company in 1633, did not join the Acception until 1639.

Initiation of Sir Robert Moray

Shortly afterwards occurred the earliest recorded initiation *on English soil*. Some members of the Lodge of Edinburgh (Mary's Chapel) No. 1, to give it its present-day title, had entered England with the Scottish Army and on 20th May 1641 they initiated 'Mr. the Right Honerabell Mr. Robert Moray, General Quarter Mr. to the armie off Scotlan.' This was at Newcastle-on-Tyne which was evacuated by the Scottish Army the following July, after which those responsible reported the fact to the lodge and the matter was rectified and recorded in the minutes. Sir Robert Moray also attended a meeting of the lodge in 1647, when he signed the minutes.

Elias Ashmole

The next event is particularly interesting. Elias Ashmole, the antiquary, left a diary in which are mentioned many

*'For of speculatyf he was a master.' Here it refers to theory as opposed to practice.

ELIAS ASHMOLE

matters of astrological or other occult significance and there are two references to Freemasonry:

1646. Oct. 16. 4 H 30' p.m. I was made a Freemason at Warrington in Lancashire with Coll: Henry Mainwaring of Karincham in Cheshire. The names of those who were then of the Lodge, Mr. Rich Penket, Warden, Mr. James Collier, Mr. Rich Sankey, Henry Littler, John Ellam, Rich: Ellam and Hugh Brewer.

Most of these have been identified as men of good social position and there was not a single operative member. We have already mentioned that the *Sloane 3848 MS* was transcribed by Edward Sankey, possibly the son of Richard Sankey, one of the members of the lodge.

Nearly thirty-six years later, Ashmole sat in lodge again, this time in London.

March, 1682.
10 — About 5 P.M. I rec^d: a Sumons to app^r at a Lodge to be held the next day, at Masons Hall London.
11 — Accordingly I went, & about Noone were admitted into the Fellowship of Free Masons,
Sr William Wilson Knight, Capt. Rich: Borthwick, Mr Will: Woodman, Mr Wm Grey, Mr Samuell Taylour & Mr William Wise.
I was the Senior Fellow among them (it being 35 yeares since I was admitted) There were p^{r}sent beside my selfe the Fellows after named.
Mr Tho: Wise M^r of the Masons Company this p^{r}sent yeare. Mr Thomas Shorthose, Mr Thomas Shadbolt, Waindsford Esqr Mr Nich: Young Mr John Shorthose, Mr William Hamon, Mr John Thompson, & Mr Will: Stanton.
Wee all dyned at the halfe Moone Taverne in Cheapeside, at a Noble dinner prepaired at the charge of the New-accepted Masons.

This is truly valuable. All but three of those present were members of the Masons' Company; several were Masters of it in various years. Also it was evidently possible for gentlemen to become members of the lodge without the formality of joining the Company and taking up the Freedom of the City.

PRE-GRAND LODGE FREEMASONRY

There is in a number of pamphlets, some of which are now exceedingly rare, ample confirmation of the fact that Freemasonry was familiar to more Londoners than the members of the Company or the Acception. A skit on the 'Company of Accepted Masons' was published in *Poor Robin's Intelligencer* in 1676; an anti-masonic leaflet of 1698, now in the Library of Grand Lodge, is addressed 'To all Goodly People of the Citie of London.' There are two well-known references to 'Pretty Fellows' who have their 'Signs and Tokens like Freemasons' in *The Tatler* of 1709 and 1710.

Dr. Robert Plot

In the Midlands Dr. Robert Plot, Keeper of the Ashmolean Museum, Oxford, published his *Natural History of Staffordshire* in 1686. This contains not only an abstract and criticism of part of the Old Charges but a contemporary account of our fraternity:

> To these add the *Customs* relating to the *County*, whereof they have one, of admitting Men into the *Society* of *Free-Masons*, that in the *moorelands* of the *County* seems to be of greater request, than any where else, though I find the *Custom* spread more or less all over the *Nation*, for here I found persons of the most eminent quality, that did not disdain to be of this *Fellowship*. Nor indeed need they, were it of that *Antiquity* and *honor*, that is pretended in a large *parchment volum* they have amongst them, containing the *History* and *Rules* of the craft of *masonry*. Which is there deduced not only from *sacred writ*, but *profane story*, particularly that it was brought into *England* by St *Amphibal*, and first communicated to S. *Alban*, who set down the *Charges* of *masonry*, and was made paymaster and Governor of the *Kings* works, and gave them *charges* and *manners* as St *Amphibal* had taught him. Which were after confirmed by King *Athelstan*, whose youngest son *Edwyn* loved well masonry, took upon him the *charges*, and learned the *manners*, and obtained for them of his Father, a *free-Charter*. Whereupon he caused them to assemble at *York*, and to bring all the old *Books* of their *craft*, and out of them ordained such *charges* and *manners*, as they then thought fit: which *charges* in the said *Schrole* or *Parchment volum*, are in part declared; and thus was the *craft* of

masonry grounded and confirmed in *England*. It is also there declared that these *charges* and *manners* were after perused and approved by King *Hen.* 6. and his *council*, both as to *Masters* and *Fellows* of this right Worshipfull *craft*.

Into which *Society* when any are admitted, they call a *meeting* (or *Lodg* as they term it in some places), which must consist at lest of 5 or 6 of the *Ancients* of the *Order*, whom the *candidats* present with *gloves*,* and so likewise to their *wives*, and entertain with a *collation* according to the Custom of the place: This ended, they proceed to the *admission* of them, which chiefly consists in the communication of certain *secret signes*, whereby they are known to one another all over the *Nation*, by which means they have maintenance whither ever they travel: for if any man appear though altogether unknown that can shew any of these *signes* to a *Fellow* of the *Society*, whom they otherwise call an *accepted mason*, he is obliged presently to come to him, from what company or place soever he be in, nay, tho' from the top of a *Steeple* (what hazard or inconvenience soever he run), to know his pleasure, and assist him; *viz.*, if he want *work* he is bound to find him some; or if he cannot doe that, to give him *mony*, or otherwise support him till *work* can be had; which is one of their *Articles*; and it is another, that they advise the *Masters* they work for, according to the best of their *skill*, acquainting them with the goodness or badness of their *materials*; and if they be any way out in the *contrivance* of their *buildings*, modestly to rectify them in it; that *masonry* be not dishonoured: and many such like that are commonly known: but some others they have (to which they are *sworn* after their fashion), that none know but themselves, which I have reason to suspect are much worse than these, perhaps as bad as this *History* of the *craft* it self; than which there is nothing I ever met with, more false or incoherent.

Randle Holme

Five heraldic painters and genealogists of Chester bore the name of Randle Holme. The third of the line, who was born in 1627 and died in 1699, was, like his father and grandfather

---

*The presentation of gloves remains a practice in many continental lodges.

before him, a deputy to Garter King of Arms. He was the author of the *Academie of Armory* in which were several references to Freemasonry of the greatest importance as indicating the relationship of a non-operative to the fraternity in the seventeenth century, for instance

> A Fraternity, or Society, or Brotherhood, or Company; are such in a corporation, that are of one and the same trade, or occupation, who being joyned together by oath and covenant, do follow such orders and rules, as are made, or to be made for the good order, rule, and support of such and every of their occupations. These several Fraternities are generally governed by one or two Masters, and two Wardens, but most Companies with us by two Aldermen, and two Stewards, the later, being to pay and receive what concerns them.

Again, he refers to various tools without, apparently, moralizing upon them (this came much later in the development of Freemasonry) and in a later passage said

> I cannot but Honor the Fellowship of the Masons because of its Antiquity; and the more, as being a Member of that Society, called Free-Masons. In being conversant amongst them I have observed the use of these several Tools following some whereof I have seen being born in Coats of Armour.

He attached some importance to Pillars and they were depicted in an illustration of the Arms of the Masons (the familiar three castles).

Among the loose papers in the *Harleian MS 2054* is a version of the Old Charges transcribed by this Randle Holme and immediately following this there is written on a small scrap of paper 'There is seu^{r}all words & signes of a free Mason to be revailed to y^u wch as y^u will answ: before God at the Great & terrible day of Iudgm^t y^u keep Secrete & not to revaile the same to any in the heares of any pson w but to the M^{rs} & fellows of the said Society of free Masons so helpe me God, xc.

The significance of this cannot be doubted. The next leaf contains further notes by the same writer obviously relating to an existing lodge and including a list of members and certain figures apparently connected with entrance fees and subscriptions. Much study has been devoted to this record and the majority of the persons concerned have now been almost positively identified. They were members of various trades, including some masons or followers of other building trades, but obviously persons of culture with whom Randle Holme would feel at home.

Much of his work can still be seen in Chester and he was enrolled as a foreign burgess at the celebration of Preston Gild in 1662, his son, Randle Holme IV, being similarly enrolled in 1682.

It is convenient at this point to refer to an interesting fact often overlooked by masonic students. Attempts have been made to enlist the support of the Craft in various political controversies and this has been sternly discouraged from the very beginning in English Freemasonry. Of the three individuals most prominently considered in this chapter, Sir Robert Moray was serving with the Army of Scotland, then allied to the Parliamentary side, Ashmole was a staunch Cavalier and Randle Holme III was also a Royalist.

John Aubrey

John Aubrey (1626-97) published *The Natural History of Wiltshire* in 1686. He repeats therein the fable of the Papal Bull from which so many legendary accounts of Freemasonry have derived.

> Sr William Dugdale told me many years since, that about Henry the third's time, the Pope gave a Bull or diploma (Patents) to a Company of Italian Architects (Freemasons) to travell up and downe over all Europe to build Churches. From those are derived the *Fraternity of Free-Masons*. (Adopted-Masons) They are known to any other by certayn Signes & Markes ['Markes' is erased] and Watch-words: it continues to this day. They have Severall Lodges in severall Counties for their reception: and when any of them fall into decay, the brotherhood is to relieve him, &c. The manner of their Adoption is very formall, and with an Oath of Secrecy.

This was taken from the original in the Bodleian and the additions in parentheses indicate alternative wordings written above the original. Aubrey therefore felt the subject was of sufficient importance to polish considerably.

PRE-GRAND LODGE FREEMASONRY

On the reverse of folio 72 we have the famous reference to Sir Christopher Wren:

1691. Mdm, this day (May the 18th, being Monday) [another interpolation — after Rogation Sunday] is a great convention at St. Paul's Church of the Fraternity of the Free Masons: [again Aubrey strikes out the word Free and inserts 'Accepted'] where Sr Christopher Wren is to be adopted a Brother: and Sr Henry Goodric ... of ye Tower & divers others — There have been kings, that have been of this Sodalitie.

Sir Christopher Wren

This great and controversial figure was born in 1632. He became a professor of Astronomy in 1657 and of Mathematics in 1661, being also appointed Assistant Surveyor General of the Royal Buildings. After the Fire of London he was entrusted with the great work of reconstruction and, though many of his plans were not followed, we owe to him the magnificent St. Paul's Cathedral and many churches and other buildings. The first *Book of Constitutions*, edited for Grand Lodge by Dr. Anderson and published in 1723, refers but briefly to him as 'the ingenious Architect' and as the architect of the Sheldonian Theatre, Oxford. At that time, however, Wren was not in favour with George I but, when the second edition of the *Book of Constitutions* appeared in 1738, Anderson felt himself at liberty to give much greater prominence to the famous architect. Unfortunately, as we shall see later, Anderson was no reliable authority and his story of Wren's masonic offices, including that of Grand Master, are simply without foundation though it is almost certain that he was a member of the Craft (*see* page 70*n*.)

Anderson's account, for what it is worth, may thus be summarized:

1669. Completed the Sheldonian Theatre and the 'pretty Museum'.
1673.*Grand Master Rivers levelled the Footstone of St. Paul's, designed by D. G. Master Wren.

*The foundation stone was in fact laid on 21st June 1675. E. T. Floyd Ewin, Registrar and Receiver of St. Paul's, has said that this was done 'probably with some masonic ceremony'.

SIR CHRISTOPHER WREN

1685. Upon the death of Grand Master Arlington, the Lodges met and elected Sir Christopher Wren Grand Master, who appointed Mr. Gabriel Cibber and Mr. Edward Strong, Grand Wardens.
1707. Lodges in the South neglected by Wren.
1708. St. Paul's completed.

Some few Years after this Sir *Christopher Wren* neglected the Office of *Grand Master*; yet the *Old Lodge* near St. *Paul's* and a few more continued their stated meetings.

An account, written by Sir Christopher's son, of the building of St. Paul's Cathedral was published by his grandson, Stephen Wren, who mentions that 'The highest or last Stone on the Top of the Lantern, was laid by the Hands of the *Surveyor's* son, *Christopher Wren* deputed by his Father, in the Presence of that excellent Artificer Mr Strong, his Son, and other *Free and Accepted Masons*, chiefly employed in the Execution of the Work.'

The Swalwell and Alnwick Lodges

At Swalwell, County Durham, there was a lodge of operative masons with archives dating from 1725 and the tradition of earlier beginnings. In 1735 it accepted a Warrant from the Grand Lodge of England but its Minutes show that it was still transacting 'operative' business nearly twenty years later. It is still very much alive as the Lodge of Industry No. 48 at Gateshead, whither it transferred itself in 1845, and is the only instance of an English operative lodge surviving in speculative form.

Another famous operative lodge met at Alnwick in Northumberland. Although this never changed its character — it seems to have died out in or after 1763 — its Minutes[*] run from 1703 and are the only records known today of an English operative lodge of the pre-1717 period. It is important to add that a copy of the Old Charges was included among its papers, together with a code of rules devised by the lodge in 1701.

A particularly interesting Alnwick minute of 1708 describes the essential masonic dress of the day as the 'apron and common square fixed in the belt thereof'. A Swalwell minute of

[*]They were published in 1895 in book form.

1734 specifies 'gloves and aprons', this being a year before it came under Grand Lodge rule. Also in the early Swalwell records is evidence that a ceremony involving, at least, the *recital* of the legendary history took place in lodge, but there is no hint of degrees, as we now understand them, in 'operative' practice.

York

No name appeals more strongly to the masonic imagination than York but, alas, imagination has too often been too freely used. Prince Edwin's Assembly of 926 and Queen Elizabeth's 'raid' of 1561 are the best-known examples. But York has a masonic antiquity, operative and speculative, of its own. On the operative side we have the *Fabric Rolls* of York Minster and the original of the *Levander-York MS* of the Old Charges, said to have been written in 1560.

Another version of those Charges, the *York MS* copied in 1693, bears below the signature of the copyist the names of five members of 'the Lodg'. Unfortunately, neither copyist nor members can be traced among the Freemen of York. There is an endorsement on the back of the *Scarborough MS* recording the admission of six persons at a private lodge at Scarborough on 10th July 1705. The original Minute Book of the York Lodge, later to assume Grand Lodge status, has been lost for some years but extracts were taken in 1778 from which we know that Sir George Tempest presided in 1705 and that in 1713 '18 gentlemen of the first families in the Neighbourhood were made Masons' at Bradford.

A Central Organization

Though there is a family resemblance between many of the bodies we have described in this chapter there is no evidence of the existence during the early eighteenth century of any central authority, but the Catechisms, which will be considered later, suggest a remarkable uniformity of procedure. There is, too, a hint in some of the later versions of the Old Charges that the establishment of such a body was at least under consideration.

Early Freemasonry in Scotland and Ireland

The contemporary situation in Scotland is discussed in

EARLY FREEMASONRY IN SCOTLAND & IRELAND

Chapter IX but a word or two at this point may be useful. We have already mentioned that the Old Charges were essentially English. Scotland has, however, an abundance of other old records including lodge Minutes far older than anything south of the Border. She has the registration and use of the Mason's Mark, the Edinburgh Minutes of 1599 being attested by the Mark of the Warden and the Lodge of Aberdeen being in possession of a beautiful Mark Book which began in 1670. Above all, Scotland has the Mason Word, no trace of which has been found in English medieval records.

The old Scottish lodge Minutes are those of essentially operative bodies yet non-operatives were admitted to membership from a very early date. By the late sixteenth century there was a measure of co-operation and uniformity which suggests the possible existence of some central influence. Was this the function of a test word? The skilled mason could give practical proof of his ability; possession of the means of recognition proved him to be a member of the organization.

We have a description written in 1691 by the Rev. Robert Kirk, Minister of Aberfoyle, 'like a Rabbinical Tradition, in way of comment on Jachin and Boaz, the two Pillars erected in Solomon s Temple (I Kings vii. 21) with ane Addition of some secret Signe delyvered from Hand to Hand, by which they know and become familiar with one another.'

A letter of 1697 tells that the Lairds of Roslyn 'are obliged to receive the masons' word which is a secret signall masons have thr'out the world to know one another by. They alledge 'tis as old as Babel, when they could not understand one another and they conversed by signs. Others would have it no older than Solomon.'

A remarkable document which is preserved in the Library of Trinity College, Dublin, and is quoted on p. 147 of Chapter VIII, clearly suggests that in 1688 a masonic society was well established in the 'fair city'.

'The Bridge'

A suggestion was made recently, and gave rise to much controversy, that the bridge between operative and speculative Masonry would rest mainly on Scotland at the operative end and on England at the speculative. What can we gather from the information available?

PRE-GRAND LODGE FREEMASONRY

The Position of the Old Charges

The Old Charges were still held in veneration and we find many instances of their use in an assembly wholly or partially non-operative: Ashmole's, Randle Holme's, Scarborough and York have been quoted here.

The Social Board

Ashmole tells how the brethren at London dined together at the expense of the newly-admitted masons. Something of the nature of an initiation fee or paying one's footing is indicated here. In Plot we find the candidates presenting the brethren and their wives with gloves as well as entertaining them with a collation. Randle Holme left what appears to be a subscription list.

Working Tools

These are referred to at Chester by Randle Holme. The moralizing with which we are familiar was introduced much later.

Dress

The only account of masonic dress in the lodge is found at Alnwick in 1708 (*see* pp. 51-2).

Relief

There is an elaborate gibe at the duty to relieve a distressed brother in the *Trinity College, Dublin MS*. Plot also waxes satirical on this point and his remark probably inspired a later parody of the Entered Apprentice Song:

> If on House ne'er so high,
> A Brother they spy,
> As his Trowel he dextrously lays on,
> He must leave off his Work,
> And come down with a Jerk,
> At the Sign of an Accepted Mason.

Ritual

It will surprise many to learn that the English ritual of today was consolidated only after the Union of 1813. For earlier information we rely on a mass of documents and printed exposures from which we gather that the three degrees in *something* like their present form were fully established by 1730. But, when we take our researches back to before that date, we find that several schools of thought have existed — even for the period immediately after the formation of Grand Lodge in 1717. The leading masonic historians at the beginning of the present century could not agree on whether the lodges of that period recognized and practised one, two or three degrees. Much has been discovered in more recent years and the students of today generally accept that at least two separate ceremonies were then worked and that within their framework was to be found a good deal of the esoteric teaching now divided between the three Craft degrees. Some would add that the Royal Arch ritual also contains material from those early ceremonies.

We have mentioned the Mason Word in Scotland; we have seen Randle Holme's cryptical reference to the secrecy to be observed in regard to several words and signs. Aubrey leaves a similar hint but, at the beginning of this twentieth century, *pre*-Grand Lodge ritual was virtually unknown.

The Haughfoot Minute

The Haughfoot Lodge (Scottish and Speculative), now extinct, left its Minute Book for posterity, but some scrupulous brother removed the first pages so that the record begins on 22nd December 1702 with:

... of entrie as the apprentice did Leaving out (The Common Judge). Then they whisper the word as before — and the Master Mason grips his hand after the ordinary way.

The same day Sr James Scott of Gala Thomas Scott his Brother, David Murray in Philliphaugh James Pringle in Haughfoot Robert Lowrie in Stowtonherd and John Pringle Wright gave in ther petition each for themselves earnest desiring to be admitted into the s^d Society of Masons and ffellow Craft

Which ther desir being maturely considered was accordingly agreed to and granted and they each of them by them selves were dueiy and orderly admitted apprentices and ffellow Craft. And ther was imposed on them the soumes following to be payed in to the box quh they accordingly each of them for himself promised to pay, viz.:

PRE-GRAND LODGE FREEMASONRY

    Sir James Scott   half a guinie or 7^{lb} 2^{sh}
    Thomas Scott   Three punds
    David Murray   One pund
    James Pringle   One pund
    Robert Lowrie   One pund
    John Pringle   One pund

    Thereafter the meeting resolved with one voice y^t y^r shall be ane yearly meeting of those concerned in this Lodge att Haughfoot in all tyme comeing upon St John's Day.

    They also committed to Andrew Thompson one of y^r number to provide a Register book against their next meeting.

    And they committed to John Hoppringle of y^t Ilk to appoint the next meeting and give timely advertisement thereof to all concerned.

We have here a most important minute indicating in a few lines the progress from one degree to another, the acceptance of candidates and their admission fees (in Scots currency). The lodge was also putting its affairs in order by purchasing a register and arranging an Annual Meeting — on St. John's Day.

For the student of masonic ritual the 29 words at the head of this Minute, usually described as the 'Haughfoot fragment', are of the utmost importance because they represent the earliest item of ritual procedure that can be associated with actual lodge practice.

The three oldest surviving ritual texts (discussed below) are the *Edinburgh Register House MS* of 1696, the *Chetwode Crawley MS* of c. 1700 and the *Kevan MS* of c. 1714. All three purport to describe the two-degree system that was practised in those days. By themselves, without any kind of authentication, they must necessarily have remained of doubtful value but the 'Haughfoot fragment', which corresponds almost exactly with the relevant portion of the second degree in all three texts, provides the important piece of evidence which proves that these rituals were in actual use.

The Catechisms

The next evidence is provided by a group of sixteen manuscripts and prints ranging in date from 1696 to 1730. Each is

CATECHISMS

cast in catechetical form, hence the name given to the group. Though certain relationships are apparent it is not possible to divide them into 'families', as has been done with the Old Charges.

The Chetwode Crawley and the Edinburgh Register House MSS

About 1900, several years after the publication of the first edition of Gould's great *History of Freemasonry* and much of Hughan's early work, some volumes were purchased from a second-hand dealer and among them was discovered a masonic catechism. Thanks to the efforts of W. J. Hughan, it was secured for the Grand Lodge of Ireland and named after the great Irish masonic student, W. J. Chetwode Crawley. The paper, watermark and writing indicate the origin about the end of the seventeenth century or the beginning of the eighteenth. The drawback, from the point of view of the student, was that it *might* have been written after the formation of the Grand Lodge of England and the great spread of interest in Freemasonry; hence it was not completely accepted in evidence before 1930 when the *Edinburgh Register House MS* was discovered in the Scottish Archives after which it is named. This is definitely dated, the endorsement being 'Some Questiones Anent the mason Word 1696' and the document is headed 'Some Questiones that Masons use to put to Those who have ye Word before they will acknowledge them.'

Although the two documents have obviously not been copied one from another they are as obviously closely related. Many of the questions are identical and most of the others approximately so; the 'form of giving the Mason Word' is very similar and this appears in different parts of the two documents.

The following transcript of the *Edinburgh Register House MS* is taken by permission, from the *Transactions of the Manchester Association for Masonic Research*.

> SOME QUESTIONES THAT MASONS USE TO PUT TO THOSE WHO HAVE THE WORD BEFORE THEY WILL ACKNOWLEDGE THEM.

Quest. 1   *Are you* a mason. Answer Yes.
    Q. 2   How shall I know it? Ans. you shall know it in time and place convenient. Remark the fors[ai]d answer is only to be made when there is company present

PRE-GRAND LODGE FREEMASONRY

who are not masons. But if there be no such company by, you should answer by signes tokens and other points of my entrie.

Q. 3 What is the first point? Ans. Tell me the first point ile tell you the second. The first is to heill and conceall, second, under no less pain, which is then cutting of your throat. For you most make that sign when you say that.

Q. 4 Where was you entered? An. At the honourable Lodge.

Q. 5 What makes a true and perfect Lodge? An. Seven masters, five entered apprentices, A dayes journey from a burroughs town without bark of dog or crow of cock.

Q. 6 Does no less make a true and perfect lodge? An. Yes five masons and three entered apprentices &c.

Q. 7 Does no less. An. The more the merrier the fewer the better chear.

Q. 8 What is the name of your lodge An. Kilwinning.

Q. 9 How stands your lodge. An. east and west as the temple of Jérusalem.

Q. 10 Where was the first lodge. An. in the porch of Solomons Temple.

Q. 11 Are there any lights in your lodge An. Yes three the north east, S W, and eastern passage. The one denotes the master mason, the other the warden. The third the setter croft.

Q. 12 Are there jewells in your lodge. An. Yes three, Perpend esler a square pavement and a broad ovall.

Q. 13 Where shall I find the key of your lodge. Yes [*sic lege* An.] Three foot and a half from the lodge door under a perpend esler, and a green divot. But under the lap of my liver where all my secrets of my heart lie.

Q. 14 Which is the key of your lodge. An. a wool hung tongue.

Q. 15 Where lies the key. Ans. In the bone box.

After the masons have examined you by all or some of these Questions and that you have answered them exactly and made the signes, they will acknowledge you, but not a master mason or fellow croft but only as [*sic lege* An.] apprentice,

58

THE EDINBURGH REGISTER HOUSE MS.

soe they will say I see you have been in the kitchine but I know not if you have been in the hall. Ans. I have been in the hall as weel as in the kitchine.

Quest. 1 Are you a fellow craft Ans. Yes.
Quest. 2 How many points of the fellowship are there Ans. Fyve viz. foot to foot, knee to knee, Heart to Heart, hand to hand and ear to ear. Then make the sign of fellowship and shake hand and you will be acknowledged a true mason. The words are in . . . . and in . . . .

THE FORME OF GIVEING THE MASON WORD

Imprimis you are to take the person to take the word upon his knees and after a great many ceremonies to frighten him to make him take up the bible and laying his right hand on it you are to conjure him to secrecie by threatning that if [he] shall break his oath the sun in the firmament will be a witness ag[ain]st him and all the company then present, which will be an occasion of his damnation and that likewise the masons will be sure to murder him. Then after he hes promised secrecie. They give him the oath a[s] follows By god himself and you shall answer to god when you shall stand naked before him, at the great day, you shall not reveal any pairt of what you shall hear or see at this time whether by word not write not put it in wryte at any time nor draw it with the point of a sword, or any other instrument upon the snow or sand, nor shall you speak of it but with an entered mason, so help you god.

After he hes taken the oath he is removed out of the company with the youngest mason, where after he is sufficiently frighted with 1000 ridicolous postures and grimaces, He is to learn from the s[ai]d mason the manner of makeing his due guard which is the signe and the postures and words of his entrie which are as follows First when he enters again into the company he must make a ridicolous bow, then the signe and say God bless the honourable company. Then putting off his hat after a very foolish manner only to be demonstrated then (as the rest of the signes are likewise) he sayes the words of his entrie which are as follows

PRE-GRAND LODGE FREEMASONRY

Here come I the youngest and last entered apprentice As am, sworn by God and St John by the square and compass and common judge to attend my masters service at th honourable lodge from munday in the morning till saturda at night and to keep the keyes therof under no less pai then haveing my tongue cut out under my chin and o being buried, within the flood mark where no man sha' know, then he makes the sign again withdrawing his han under his chin alongst his throat which denotes that it b cut out in case he break his word.

Then all the mason[s] present whisper amongst themselve the word beginning at the youngest till it come to th master mason who gives the word to the entered apprentic Now it is to be remarked that all the signes and words a yet spoken of are only what belong to the entered appren tice, But to be a master mason or fellow craft there is mor to be done which after follows. First all the prentices are t be removed out of the company and none suffered to sta but masters.

Then he who is to be admitted a member of fellowship i putt again to his knees, and gets the oat[h] administrate to him of new afterwards he must go out of the compan with the youngest mason to learn the postures and signes o fellowship, then comeing in again He makes the master sign, and sayes the same words of entrie as the apprentic did only leaving out the common judge then the mason whisper the word among them selves beginning at th youngest as formerly afterwards the youngest mason mus advance and put himself into the posture he is to receive th word and sayes to the eldest mason in whispering

> The worthy masters and honourable company greet yo weel, greet you weel, greet you weel.

Then the master gives him the word and gripes his han after the masons way, which is all that is to be done t make a a perfect mason.

A third MS, now named the *Kevan MS*, was discovered i 1954. It is similar to the *Chetwode Crawley* and *Edinburg Register House MSS* but was probably written shortly befor the formation of the Grand Lodge of England.

THE DUMFRIES AND GRAHAM MSS.

The Dumfries No. 4 MS

The experts date this document from about 1710 and it has always been in the possession of the Dumfries Kilwinning Lodge No. 53, Scotland, which originated in 1687.

It consists of a masonic catechism combined with an unusually corrupt version of the Old Charges and some notes on King Solomon's Temple. It was obviously at one time of practical use as it shows signs of considerable handling.

The MS begins with the Charges, the last in this instance being to the Apprentice; there follows a set of questions and answers in some respects similar to other catechisms but also introducing scriptural matter. A reference to the Master's dress echoes test questions found in early Irish Freemasonry and elsewhere.

Q. would you know your master if you saw him. A. yes Q. what way would ye know him A. by his habit Q. what couller is his habit A. yellow & blew meaning the compass w^c is bras & Iron.

Then follows 'The Strangers Salutation' which is succeeded by 'Questions concerning the Temple', some of which are found in other catechisms. The writer describes quite fully the Pillars of King Solomon's Temple but a question immediately preceding this apparently refers to the earlier antediluvian pillars.

Q. where [was] the noble art or science found when it was lost A. it was found in two pillers of stone the one would not sink and the other would not burn

The whole concludes with eight lines of doggerel verse:

> A caput mortuu here you see
> To mind you of mortality . . .

The Graham MS

One of the most valuable discoveries of this century occurred in Yorkshire, in 1936, after the Initiation of the Rev. H. I. Robinson, in whose family the MS had been for a considerable time. The date is rather vague and could be read as 1672 or 1726 and the latter is generally accepted as authentic. The examination follows closely conventional masonic lines, containing parallels to other catechisms, notably that in a broad-

PRE-GRAND LODGE FREEMASONRY

sheet entitled *The Whole Institution of Free-Masons Opened* printed in 1725. There are also similarities to the *Dumfrie No. 4 MS* described in the previous section.

The candidate is tested after his entering *and* after hi raising and the latter differs from anything else known in Free masonry for the traditional history is devoted to an attempt to extract from the body of Noah the secrets he had carried with him from the antediluvian world. Here is the counterpart of our traditional history.

> we have it by tradition and still some refferance to scrip ture cause shem ham and Japheth ffor to go to their fathe noahs grave for to try if they could find anything abou him ffor to Lead them to the vertuable secret which thi famieous preacher had for I hop all will allow that al things needfull for the new world was in the ark with noah Now these 3 men had allready agreed that if they did no ffind the very thing it self that the first thing that they found was to be to them as a secret they not Douting bu did most ffirmly be Leive that God was able and woule allso prove willing through their faith prayer and obediance for to cause what they did find for to prove as vertuable to them as if they had received the secret at ffirst from God himself at its head spring so came to the Grave finding nothing save the dead body all most consumed away take ing a greip at a ffinger it came away so from Joynt to Joyn so to the wrest so to the Elbow so they R Reared up the dead body and suported it setting ffoot to ffoot knee to knee Breast to breast Cheeck to cheeck and hand to back and cryed out help o ffather as if they had said o father of heaven help us now for our Earthly ffather cannot so Laid down the dead body again and not knowing what to do — so one said here is yet marow in this bone and the second said but a dry bone and the third said it stinketh so they agreed for to give it a name as is known to free masonry to this day so went to their undertakings and afterwards works stood: yet it is to be beleived and allso understood that the vertue did not proceed from what they ffound or how it was called but ffrom ffaith and prayer so thus it Contenued the will pass for the deed

The narrative passes on to the building of King Solomon's

THE GRAHAM MS.

Temple with an ingenious method of differential payments of interest to present-day Mark Master Masons.

> now it is holden fforth by tradition that there was a tumult at this Errection which should hapened betwext the Labourours and masons about wages and ffor to call me all and to make all things easie the wise king should have had said be all of you contented ffor you shall be payed all alike yet give a signe to the Masons not known to the Laborours and who could make that signe at the paying place was to be payed as masons the Laborours not knowing thereof was payed as fforesaid

The description of the secrets indicates some primitive symbolism including the five points of fellowship.

> So all Being ffinised then was the secrets off ffree Masonry ordered aright as is now and will be to the E End of the world for such as do rightly understand it — in 3 parts in refferance to the blesed trinity who made all things yet in 13 brenches in refferances to Christ and his 12 apostles which is as follows a word ffor a deveine Six ffor the clargey and 6 ffor the ffellow craft and at the ffull and totall agreement thereoff to ffollow with five points off ffree Masons fellowshipe which is ffoot to ffoot knee to knee breast to breast cheeck to cheeck and hand to Back which ffive points hath refferance to the ffive cheife signes which is head ffoot body hand and heart and allso to the ffive points off artitectur and allso to the ffive orders of Masonry yet takes thire strength ffrom five primitive one devine and ffour temporall which is as ffollows ffirst christ the chiefe and Cornnerston secondly Peter called Cephas thirdly moses who cutte the commands ffourthly Bazalliell the best of Masons ffifftly hiram who was ffilled with wisdom and understanding.

The signature of this interesting document is 'Tho Graham Chanceing Master of Lodges outher Enquam Ebo.' A palaeographer suggested that the third word was misread and was possibly part of the name. If this be so (and the point is not generally admitted), 'outher' might refer to the instructor of candidates sometimes found (especially in Scotland) and the last two pseudo-Latin words appear to be an anagram (give or

63

PRE-GRAND LODGE FREEMASONRY

take a letter or two) of a word familiar to Master Masons!

Slade's 'Free Mason Examin'd'

It is convenient at this point to mention a work which appeared over half a century later. *The Free Mason Examin'd* by Alexander Slade was published in 1754 and ran to half a dozen editions in the course of the next five years. There was at the time quite a craze for alleged revelations of the secrets of Freemasonry. This one differed from all others in that the ceremonies are based on the building of the Tower of Babel. The three degrees are called the Minor's Part, the Major's Part and the Officer's Part, and the Officers are the six sons of Cush, the eldest son of Ham and the grandson of Noah.

The pamphlet has been largely discounted by students and the following reasons put forth as possible causes of its publication:

Firstly — It was a picture of a branch of masonic work in 1754. Although Nimrod (a son of Cush) does not appear in our ritual, he figured in some of the Old Charges. Slade explains that his grandfather was made a free-mason about 1708 when Sir Christopher Wren was Grand Master and it is just possible that it represents a working of that time.

Secondly — It was published as a counterblast to the newly formed rival Grand Lodge, the Antients, of which more will be heard in Chapter VI.

Thirdly — that it was an ingenious parody designed to confuse the minds of those who were too eagerly buying the exposures then widely printed and sold.

Fourthly — It was a purely financial speculation.

Our earliest ritual

What was the form of our earliest ritual? From the evidence we have discussed, it is clear that before the formation of the first Grand Lodge more than one version was to be found. How the change was made from Pillars of the Old Charges, constructed to preserve the knowledge of mankind from an impending destruction, to the Pillars in which so much of today's interest centres is a mystery that may never be solved. But it is probable that, before the Craft finally settled on the

MOVING TOWARDS ORGANISATION

building of King Solomon's Temple and the loss and subsequent recovery of certain knowledge, other prototypes were tried out perhaps by small groups of masons in isolated parts of the country. The evidence in favour of the Temple rite as a general basis is overwhelming but the *Graham MS* of undeniable authenticity and the Slade pamphlet of dubious parentage at least hint of rites based on Noah's Ark and the Tower of Babel.

Moving towards organization

Mention has already been made of a small group of the Old Charges containing new orders. These are set out in full in the Roberts version published in 1722, five years *after* the formation of the first Grand Lodge and shortly before the issue of the first official *Book of Constitutions.*

We do not know what truth there is in the heading of the new articles but they suggest an attempt at metropolitan organization:

ADDITIONAL ORDERS AND CONSTITUTIONS MADE AND AGREED UPON AT A GENERAL ASSEMBLY HELD AT...... ON THE EIGHTH DAY OF DECEMBER, 1663.

I. That no Person, of what Degree soever, be accepted a *Free-Mason*, unless he shall have a Lodge of five *Free-Masons* at the least, where-of one to be a Master or Warden of that Limit or Division where such Lodge shall be kept, and another to be a Workman of the Trade of *Free-Masonry*.

II. That no Person hereafter shall be accepted a *Free-Mason*, but such as are of able Body, honest Parentage, good Reputation, and Observers of the Laws of the Land.

III. That no Person hereafter, which shall be accepted a *Free-Mason*, shall be admitted into any Lodge, or Assembly, until he hath brought a Certificate of the Time and Place of his Acception, from the Lodge that accepted him, unto the Master of that Limit and Division, where such Lodge was kept, which said Master shall enroll the same on Parchment in a Roll to be kept for that Purpose, and give an Account of all such Acceptions, at every General Assembly.

IV. That every Person, who is now a *Free-Mason*, shall bring to the Master a Note of the Time of his Acception, to the end the same may be enrolled in such Priority of Place, as the Person deserves, and to the end the whole Company

PRE-GRAND LODGE FREEMASONRY

and Fellows may the better know each other.

V. That for the future the said Society, Company and Fraternity of *Free-Masons*, shall be regulated and governed by one Master, and as many Wardens as the said Company shall think fit to chuse at every Yearly General Assembly

VI. That no Person shall be accepted a *Free-Mason*, unless he be One and Twenty Years Old, or more.

VII. That no person hereafter be accepted a *Free Mason*, or know the Secrets of the said Society, until he shall have first taken the Oath of Secrecy here following, *viz.:*

I, A.B. DO HERE IN THE PRESENCE OF GOD ALMIGHTY, AND OF MY FELLOWS AND BRETHREN HERE PRESENT, PROMISE AND DECLARE, THAT I WILL NOT AT ANY TIME HERE AFTER BY ANY ACT OR CIRCUMSTANCE WHATSOEVER DIRECTLY OR INDIRECTLY, PUBLISH DISCOVER, REVEAL OR MAKE KNOWN ANY OF THERE SECRETS, PRIVITIES OR COUNCILS OF THE FRATERNITY OR FELLOWSHIP OF FREE MASONS, WHICH AT THIS TIME, OR AT ANY TIME HEREAFTER SHALL BE MADE KNOWN UNTO ME. SO HELP ME GOD AND THE TRUE AND HOLY CONTENTS OF THIS BOOK.

FINIS

Immediately after this date, London was visited by a double calamity. One-fifth of the population was killed by the Great Plague of 1665, and, a year later, two-thirds of London's houses and almost one hundred of its churches, including St. Paul's Cathedral, perished in the Great Fire.

A major building problem arose and it is fortunate that there was available a genius such as Sir Christopher Wren to deal with it. An Act of Parliament was passed encouraging all manner of building trade workers to settle in the City of London and promising their freedom on the completion of seven years' residence and work there. At the same time, King Charles II exercised his influence with the corporations of other towns for the rehabilitation of those who had lost their homes and businesses in the fire.

This move brought hundreds of masons flocking into the city. We have no records of their organization but operative masonry must have been given an enormous impetus and, following the tendency of the time, 'accepted' masons were no doubt admitted into the lodges.

By the early part of the eighteenth century, the stage was

MOVING TOWARDS ORGANIZATION

set for the first assembly of Free and Accepted Masons which we can confidently record and for the establishment of the Grand Lodge of England.

CHAPTER V

THE GRAND LODGE PERIOD, 1717-50

The Formation of Grand Lodge

1717 is the most important date in the history of Freemasonry. For it was in the third year of the reign of King George I and two years after the first of the two attempts to restore the Stuart line to the throne of the United Kingdom that, conceived the year before, the Grand Lodge of England had its birth. Now it has been truly observed that 'all Freemasonry in existence today can be traced, through one channel or another, to the Grand Lodge of England.'*

Since no Minutes were then kept, Dr. James Anderson's second (1738) edition of his *Book of Constitutions* is practically our sole authority for the proceedings of Grand Lodge during the first six years of its existence, and his account, in which is mentioned a preliminary meeting the preceding year, runs as follows:

> A.D. 1716, the few *Lodges* at *London* . . . thought fit to cement under a *Grand Master* as the Center of Union and Harmony, *viz.* the *Lodges* that met,
>
> 1. At the *Goose and Gridiron* Ale-house in *St. Paul's Church Yard*.
> 2. At the *Crown* Ale-house in *Parker's Lane* near *Drury-Lane*.
> 3. At the *Apple-Tree* Tavern in *Charles-street, Covent-Garden*.
> 4. At the *Rummer and Grapes* Tavern in *Channel-Row, Westminster*.
>
> They and some old Brothers met at the said *Apple-Tree*, and having put into the Chair the *oldest Master* Mason (now the Master of a *Lodge*) they constituted themselves a

*Dr. W. J. Chetwode Crawley.

THE FORMATION OF GRAND LODGE

GRAND LODGE pro Tempore in *Due Form*, and forthwith revived the Quarterly *Communication* of the *Officers* of Lodges (call'd the **Grand Lodge**) resolv'd to hold the *Annual* ASSEMBLY *and Feast*, and then to chuse a GRAND MASTER from among themselves, till they should have the Honour of a *Noble Brother* at their Head.

Accordingly

On St. *John Baptist's* Day, [24th June], A.D. 1717, the ASSEMBLY and *Feast* of the *Free and accepted Masons* was held at the foresaid *Goose and Gridiron* Ale-house.

Before Dinner, the *oldest Master* Mason (now the *Master* of a *Lodge*) in the Chair, proposed a List of proper Candidates; and the Brethren by a Majority of Hands elected

Mr. ANTHONY SAYER, Gentleman, *Grand Master* of Masons, who being forthwith invested with the Badges of Office and Power by the said *Oldest Master*, and install'd, was duly congratulated by the Assembly who pay'd him the *Homage*.

{ Capt. *Joseph Elliot*
  Mr. *Jacob Lamball*, Carpenter }   *Grand Wardens*

SAYER *Grand Master* commanded the *Masters* and *Wardens* of Lodges to meet the *Grand* Officers every *Quarter* in *Communication*, at the Place that he should appoint in his Summons sent by the *Tyler*.

Of the above two Grand Wardens we meet the Junior again as Acting Junior Grand Warden in 1735, but Captain Elliot fades entirely from sight.

The above Assembly represents the so-called 'revival of Freemasonry', wrongly so named since in its earliest years the Grand Lodge claimed jurisdiction over lodges in London and Westminster alone.

The above account is supplemented by a reference to the formation of Grand Lodge in *The Complete Free-mason; or, Multa Paucis for Lovers of Secrets*, which, published as late as 1763, substantially confirms Anderson's statement, but gives as the number of sponsoring lodges, six. The additional two, which may have been represented by 'some old brothers' as above, are not named.

THE GRAND LODGE PERIOD, 1717-50

The Four Old Lodges

Original No. 1. According to the *Engraved List of Lodges* of 1729 this lodge was constituted in 1691, but it probably had a far earlier origin and had almost certainly been the operative lodge most connected with the rebuilding of St. Paul's Cathedral (1675-1708, *see* p. 51). In 1723 it had twenty-two members, including Thomas Morrice and Josiah Villeneau, who both at different times served as Grand Wardens. But in those early days its members seem not to have had the same social significance as for example those of Original No. 4. When lodges began to cease to be known by their meeting-places it became in 1760 the West India and American Lodge and ten years later adopted the title of the Lodge of Antiquity, which it still bears. It is now No. 2 on the Grand Lodge roll, having drawn lots in 1813 with the Grand Master's Lodge (No. 1 of the Antients) for the honour of heading the list — and having lost the hazard.

One of its most famous Masters was William Preston (*see* p. 97), the author of *Illustrations of Masonry*, who asserted that Sir Christopher Wren had regularly attended the lodge and had presented it with three mahogany candlesticks and the maul* with which Charles II levelled the foundation-stone of St. Paul's. There is confirmation of only the three candlesticks.** It was largely through Preston that for ten years, from 1777 to 1787, the lodge was rent in twain; the majority of members seceded from Grand Lodge and actually became one on their own, the Grand Lodge of England South of the River Trent, being so constituted by the York Grand Lodge. Other distinguished members included the Duke of Sussex, son of George III and Grand Master for thirty years (1813-43), the Duke of Albany, youngest son of Queen Victoria, and Thomas Harper, Deputy Grand Master of the Antients.

Original No. 2 had 1712 as the official date of its constitu-

---

*'This historic Wren Maul', as the Pro Grand Master described it, was brought into Grand Lodge and 'presented' to him by R. W. Bro. Sir Eric Studd, W. M. of the Lodge of Antiquity, on the occasion of the Installation of the Duke af Kent as Grand Master on 27 June 1967.

**A Minute of the lodge dated 3 June 1723 (only a month or two after Wren's death) refers to these candlesticks as having been 'presented to this lodge by *its worthy old Master*, Sir Christopher Wren'. The words in italics (ours) are surely conclusive of Wren's having been a freemason.

ion. It had only a short life under Grand Lodge as it came to an end between 1736 and 1738.

Original No. 3 was somehow induced to accept, 'though they wanted it not', in 1723 a Grand Lodge Warrant which, as one of the 'Time Immemorial' lodges, it scarcely required, and in consequence found itself in 1729 ousted from its proud seniority and, despite its protests, relegated by the Committee of Precedence to the eleventh place. In 1768 it became the Lodge of Fortitude and, having amalgamated with the Old Cumberland Lodge in 1818, is now the Fortitude and Old Cumberland Lodge No. 12. In 1967 its petition to be allowed to surrender its Warrant and regain its Immemorial constitution was granted, but it still retains its precedence after No. 11. It has the honour of having supplied from its members the first Grand Master.

Original No. 4 was the aristocrat of the Old Lodges. Of its seventy-one members in 1724 ten were noblemen, three were honourable, four baronets or knights and two general officers, while the three senior lodges possessed not a single 'Esquire'. The second and third Grand Masters were both members of this lodge, as well as Dr. James Anderson. The Duke of Richmond was its Master in 1724 until being elected Grand Master the same year.

The lodge took Original No. 3's place in 1729 and eleven years later advanced to No. 2, which number it retained until the Union of Moderns and Antients in 1813 (*see* p. 108). In 1747 it was erased from the list for non-attendance at Quarterly Communications, but was restored in 1751 on the intercession of the second Grand Master.

The lodge moved in 1723-4 from the Rummer and Grapes Tavern to the Horn Tavern, Palace Yard, and was called by the name of the latter tavern for many years. Unfortunately there was formed a new Lodge at the Horn, which became the more fashionable, and in 1774, 'finding themselves in a declining state,' the members agreed to amalgamate with the Somerset House Lodge. It is now known as the Royal Somerset House and Inverness Lodge, and is once again No. 4.

The First Grand Master

Little enough is known of Anthony Sayer, gentleman. Two years after his Grand Mastership he was appointed Senior

THE GRAND LODGE PERIOD, 1717-50

Grand Warden in the reign of Dr. Desaguliers. He was a member of No. 3 of the four old lodges, of which he was Warden in 1723 and remained a member until at any rate 1730.

His financial circumstances seem to have been poor and a petition from him is recorded in Grand Lodge Minutes in 1724 — with what result is not known. A second petition for relief was made in 1730, when 'the Question having been put it was agreed that he should have £15 on Acct. of his having been Grand Master,' and a final sum of two guineas was paid to him from the General Charity in 1741.

More pleasant is it to picture Anthony Sayer as walking last in a procession of ten Grand Masters, arranged in order of juniority, at the installation of the Duke of Norfolk in 1730. Unfortunately the same year saw him arraigned before Grand Lodge on a complaint of his having committed irregularities, their nature not being specified. 'The Deputy Grand Master told Bro. Sayer that he was acquitted of the charge against him and recommended it to him to do nothing so irregular for the future' — the equivalent of a verdict of 'Not Guilty, but don't do it again'.

At the time of his death in January, 1742, he was Tyler of what is now the Old King's Arms Lodge No. 28.

The Second and Fourth Grand Master

George Payne was on 24th June, 1718, 'duly invested, install'd, congratulated and homaged' as Grand Master of Masons, after which he 'desired any brethren to bring to the Grand Lodge any old *Writings* and *Records* concerning *Masons* and *Masonry* in order to shew the Usages of antient Times'. Anderson further states that during that year several copies of the Gothic (i.e. MS) Constitutions were produced and collated.

During his second term of office as (the last commoner) Grand Master (1720-1) he produced the *Cooke MS* in Grand Lodge and also compiled the General Regulations which were enshrined in Anderson's *Constitutions*, 1723. What was from our point of view a tragedy of this year was that in some private lodges several valuable MSS (probably Old Charges) 'were too hastily burnt by some scrupulous Brothers, that those Papers might not fall into strange Hands'.

He was Master of No. 4 Lodge in 1723, and it was out of respect to him that Grand Lodge restored that lodge to its

EARLY GRAND MASTERS

place in 1751. He was appointed Junior Grand Warden in 1725 and acted as Grand Master on a special occasion in 1735, continuing as an active member of Grand Lodge until 1754, in which year he was appointed a member of the committee set up to revise the *Constitutions*; the new edition was published in 1756. George Payne was of considerably more substance than the first Grand Master, and when he died in 1757 he held the post of Secretary of the Tax Office.

The Third Grand Master

Dr. John Theophilus Desaguliers, D.C.L., F.R.S., succeeded George Payne in 1719. Of French descent and attractive personality if forbidding aspect, he had been educated at Christ Church, Oxford, where he took orders in 1710. In the same year he became a lecturer on experimental philosophy and in one of his books on this subject, published in 1734, he showed himself (as Bernard Jones points out) a prophet, over two hundred years before the event, of the splitting of the atom!

While Grand Master, it is recorded that he 'reviv'd the old regular and peculiar Toasts or Healths of the *Free Masons*'. It was also during his rule that it was agreed that the Grand Master should have the power of appointing his Grand Wardens, who had hitherto been annually elected, and a Deputy Grand Master. The first Deputy Grand Master was Dr. John Beale, appointed by the Duke of Montagu in 1721. Dr. Desaguliers himself was Deputy Grand Master to the Duke of Wharton in 1722, and held the same office again in 1723 and 1726. Like his predecessor he was a staunch supporter of the General Charity when it came to be established in 1724.

The high-light of his masonic career may be said to have been his famous visit to Edinburgh in 1721, which he undertook for professional reasons, but while there he sought an interview at the Lodge of Edinburgh, the Master Masons of which, 'finding him duly qualified in all points of Masonry, received him as a Brother into their Societie'. This visit is believed to have accelerated to some degree the transition from operative to speculative membership of Scottish lodges.

It was Dr. Desaguliers who was responsible for the initiation of the first Royal freemasons. These were the Duke of Lorraine (later the Emperor Francis I), who was admitted into the Craft by the Doctor at The Hague in 1731, and Frederick, Prince of

THE GRAND LODGE PERIOD, 1717-50

Wales (whose Chaplain he was), at an 'Occasional Lodge' at Kew Palace in 1737.

On his death in 1744 he was buried in the Chapel Royal in the Savoy. His son, Lieut.-Gen. Thomas Desaguliers, who served for fifty-seven years in the Royal Artillery, was a well-known freemason, and the remarkable number of lodges in that Corps during the second half of the eighteenth century may well have been due to his influence.

A lineal descendant, Lord Shuttleworth, was Junior Grand Warden in 1951-52.

Noblemen as Grand Masters

In 1721 John, Duke of Montagu, was chosen as Grand Master, which office has since been invariably held by one of noble or Royal blood. In that year, Dr. William Stukeley, the antiquarian, had been, according to his *Diary*

> made a Freemason at the Salutation Tavern, Tavistock Street ... I was the first person made a Freemason in London for many years. We had great difficulty to find members enough to perform the ceremony. Immediately upon that it took a run and ran itself out of breath thro' the folly of the members.

What led him to become a freemason is explained in his *Autobiography:*

> His curiosity led him to be initiated into the mysterys of Masonry, suspecting it to be the remains of the mysterys of the antients; when, with difficulty, a number sufficient was to be found in all London. After this it became a public fashion, not only spred over Brittain and Ireland, but all of Europe.

Stukeley was present at the installation of the Duke of Montagu.

An important discovery relating to the latter's term of office was made in 1930, when the new Bank of England was being built. This was a 'Foundation Stone' bearing the following names:

ANDERSON

Mr. Thomas Dunn } Masons.
Mr. John Townsend
  Anno Masonry 5722
Ld. Montacute, G. Master

Now Brothers Dunn and Townsend have been identified as having been apprenticed masons in 1694 and as belonging in 1723 to the lodge held at the 'Ship behind the Royal Exchange.' Here is further proof of the continuity of descent from operative to speculative masonry.

The next Grand Master (1722-3) was Philip, Duke of Wharton, who was most probably the original of Lovelace in Richardson's *Clarissa* and in any case proved an unsatisfactory Freemason.* He appointed Dr. Desaguliers as his Deputy and the Rev. James Anderson as one of his Wardens.

Dr. James Anderson (1684-1739)

This important masonic pioneer was the second son of James Anderson, 'Glassier and Measson', whose name is recorded as a member of the Aberdeen Lodge in 1670. Educated at Marischal College, Aberdeen, he was licensed as a minister of the Church of Scotland about 1702, but moved to London in 1709, receiving the degree of Doctor of Divinity in 1731 from Aberdeen University.

There is no trace of his having been present at the formation of Grand Lodge or of ever having attended until 1721. It is not known in what lodge he was initiated or whether it was a Scottish or English one, but we do know that he was a member of the Horn Lodge (Original No. 4, *see* p. 71). He achieved some fame at the time by the publication of his *Royal Genealogies*, but it is his masonic activities that have saved his name from oblivion.

According to his own account, at a meeting of Grand Lodge in 1721, when sixteen lodges were represented,

> His Grace's *Worship* and the *Lodge* finding fault with all the Copies of the *old Gothic Constitutions*, order'd Brother *James Anderson*, A.M., to digest the same in a new and better method.

---
*He is thus summed up in Pope's *Moral Essays:*
> Wharton, the scorn and wonder of our days,
> Whose ruling passion was the lust of praise.

but it is more likely that the suggestion came from Anderson himself, who was commercially as well as masonically motivated and not only sought and obtained the approval of Grand Lodge for the preparation of the second edition of his *Constitutions* (which appeared in 1738), but also throughout retained the property in both editions, and actually secured from Grand Lodge a motion discouraging members from buying Smith's *Pocket Companion*, which 'pyrated' his work in 1735.

At any rate Anderson produced his manuscript which, after being examined by a committee of '14 learned Brothers', who reported that they had perused Brother Anderson's *History, Charges, Regulations and Master's Song* and had approved of it with certain amendments, was ordered to be printed. This was done, with the addition of *The Antient Manner of Constituting a Lodge*. After the publication of his work in 1723 he stayed away from Grand Lodge for seven years.

Anderson's Constitutions, 1723

This small quarto volume of ninety-one pages contains a remarkable frontispiece representing a classical arcade with two noble Grand Masters in the foreground, and behind them attendants, one of whom carries aprons and gloves; in the centre is a diagram of Euclid's 47th (Pythagoras's) proposition with underneath it the Greek word 'eureka', which exclamation however, is commonly ascribed to Archimedes rather than to Pythagoras. There is a Preface from the pen of Dr. Desaguliers, followed by the History, in which Anderson excels himself. Whereas the Old Charges had traced Masonry, or geometry, from Lamech, Anderson must needs go back to Adam. Many English monarchs are claimed as having belonged to the Order, but it is noteworthy that although 'the ingenious architect, Sir Christopher Wren', (*see* p. 50) is mentioned, he is not referred to in this edition as Grand Master.

More important is the introduction of several phrases derived from Scottish operative masonry, including 'Entered Apprentice' and 'Fellow-craft' (the old operative expressions in England having been 'Apprentice' and 'Fellow'), although Anderson leaves the word 'cowan' until his second edition in 1738.

Of 'The Charges of a Free-Mason' the most striking, and one that, as we shall see, was to have far-reaching consequences, is the first, which states that "'tis now thought more expedient only to oblige them [freemasons] to that Religion to which all men agree, leaving their particular opinions to themselves'. Now, in spite of Anderson's explanation that in ancient times masons were charged in every country to be of the religion of that country, this article was definitely an innovation, since the Old Charges have almost without exception a positively Christian character.

This First Charge ('Concerning God and Religion') has long been the subject of considerable controversy and two leading members of the Quatuor Coronati Lodge are at variance as to its meaning and effects, Bro. J. R. Clarke holding that it definitely implied a change from Christianity to Deism, while Bro. Lt.-Col. Eric Ward believes that it was meant to ease the Masonic path for the Dissenters (of whom Anderson as a Presbyterian was one) and that the English Craft did not move solidly towards monotheism much before the end of the eighteenth century. But a fact of which neither brother seems to have been aware is that the Craft already contained at least two practising Jews,* who were members of the Lodge of Antiquity as early as 1721, *two years before the First Charge.* Is it not therefore far more probable that, in wording his Charge as he did ("'tis now thought more expedient ..."), Anderson deliberately intended to give retrospective coverage for these Jewish admissions?

The thirty-nine General Regulations, which formed the chief feature of the work, were based on a code compiled by George Payne during his second Grand Mastership in 1720. No. XIII has always been a headache to masonic historians. It lays down quite simply that 'Apprentices must be admitted Masters and Fellow Crafts only here [in the Grand Lodge] except by dispensation'. This at once raises the question whether Masters and Fellow Crafts are intended here as separate degrees.

How Many Degrees?

It is quite certain that in the great majority of lodges at this time there were only two degrees, that of Initiate or (Entered) Apprentice and that of Fellow, the latter being quite eligible to become Master of his lodge or even a Grand Officer. The working of these two degrees was in no sense identical with

*see footnote to pp. 88-9.

that of our own first two degrees, but most probably covered between them most of those degrees together with part of our third. The two degrees were commonly bestowed on the candidate on the same evening.

On the other hand there is evidence that fairly early in the eighteenth century a few speculative lodges were admitting masons, passing them to the degree of Fellow Craft and making Master Masons in three separate steps. This was an innovation since the 'Master' of the Old Charges referred to the mason who organized the building operations or else the contractor, and not the Master Mason in our present meaning.

Whatever may have been the reason for imposing regulation No. XIII, its observance (if it ever was observed) must have been extremely inconvenient to London lodges and have been resented even more by the growing number of provincial lodges under Grand Lodge jurisdiction. That it was impracticable is shown by its repeal two years later.

The wording 'Masters and Fellow Crafts' in the regulation we can only conclude to have been one of Anderson's importations from Scotland, where the two expressions meant much the same thing. That they were intended to convey the same grade is shown by the omission of 'Fellow Crafts' from the repealing resolution.

At any rate we may rest assured that by 1730 quite a number of lodges were working the third degree, complete with the Hiramic legend — it is not known exactly when this made its appearance in Freemasonry — and that three degrees were officially recognized in the 1738 *Constitutions*, although for long afterwards some lodges persisted in confining themselves to the old two degrees. The wording 'sublime degree' does not make its appearance until after 1750.

Grand Lodge Minutes

Hitherto for our account of the proceedings of Grand Lodge we have had to rely mainly on the History in Dr. Anderson's second (1738) *Book of Constitutions*. But in 1723 William Cowper, the House of Lords' Clerk, was appointed its first Secretary,* and thenceforth we have contemporary and reliable Minutes to which to refer. It was not, however, until 1741 that the Secretary was to be declared automatically a

*The title of *Grand* Secretary is first referred to in the Minutes of 1737.

member of Grand Lodge. Cowper presumably served as secretary until 1727 but he is recorded as Chairman of the Committee of Charity in 1725 and was Deputy Grand Master in 1727. He was an uncle of the poet.

His first Minutes, dated 24th June 1723, record that, on the election of the Earl of Dalkeith to succeed the Duke of Wharton, the latter appealed against the new Grand Master's appointment of Dr. Desaguliers as his Deputy, whereupon the Duke's action was held to be 'unprecedented, unwarrantable, and irregular' and His Grace seems to have left the hall in a huff.

At the meeting of Grand Lodge in February, 1724, it was agreed that a brother must not belong to more than one lodge at one time 'within the Bills of Mortality'. The last is a curious phrase, often met with at this period, and is explained by Bernard Jones as having had its origin about five hundred years before, when London began to issue weekly lists of deaths. Curiously enough, the provision of 1724 has never been repealed, the reason being that, to the relief of many ardent London brethren, it was never enforced.

The Gormogons

During 1724 there first came to public notice a rival and definitely anti-masonic body, regarding whom the following appeared in the *Daily Post* of the 3rd September:

> Whereas the truly ANTIENT NOBLE ORDER of the Gormogons, instituted by Chin-Quaw Ky-Po, the first Emperor of China ... many thousand years before Adam and of which the great philosopher Confucius was Œcumenical Volgee, has lately been brought into England by a Mandarin and he, having admitted several Gentlemen of Honour into the Mystery of that most illustrious order, they have determined to hold a Chapter at the Castle Tavern in Fleet Street, at the particular request of several persons of Quality. This is to inform the public, that there will be no drawn Sword at the Door, nor Ladder in a dark Room, nor will any Mason be receiv'd as a Member till he has renounced his Novel Order and been properly degraded ... The Mandarin will shortly set out for Rome, having a particular Commission to make a Present of this Antient Order

to His Holiness and it is believed the whole Sacred College of Cardinals will commence Gormogons.

The last sentence rather points to the Roman Catholics (and perhaps the Jacobites) as having been behind the movement. A later news-sheet asserted that 'many eminent freemasons have degraded themselves' and seceded to the Gormogons. while, according to the *British Journal* of the 12th December:

> A Peer of the first Rank, a noted Member of the Society of Free Masons, hath suffered himself to be degraded as a member of that Society and his Leather Apron and Gloves to be burnt and thereupon enter'd himself as a Member of the Society of Gormogons, at the Castle Tavern.

This last cutting established the connexion with the movement of the first and last Duke of Wharton, 6th Grand Master, whose flighty and unstable character well fits in with such a derogatory gesture.

When exactly the Gormogons died out is not known, but two considerations seem to render untenable Gould's theory that 'the Order is said to have become extinct in 1738'. In the first place the existence of a Lancashire Gormogon in the person of John Collier, better known as Tim Bobbin (1708-86), was revealed by the chance stumbling upon a poem of his, *The Goose*, by the late Bro. Fred Pick, one of the authors of the present work. The first known appearance of the poem is in Tim Bobbin's *Collected Poems* of 1757 and in any case very little of his verse is ascribed to a period before the last forty years of his life. *The Goose* has a dedication:

> As I have the honor to be a member of the ancient and venerable order of the Gormogons, I am obliged by the laws of the great *Chin-Quaw-Ki-Po*, emperor of *China*, to read, yearly, some part of the ancient records of that country ...

The poem describes, in part, the spinning of a coin to settle a dispute about the payment for a goose:

> No sooner said than done -- both parties willing
> The Justice twirls aloft a splendid shilling;
> While she (ah nature, nature) calls for tail,
> And pity 'tis, poor soul, that she should fail!
> But chance decrees -- up turns great *Chin-Quaw-Ki-Po*,
> Whose very name my belly sore doth gripe-oh!

THE GORMOGONS

Secondly, Gould's theory is further stultified by the existence of some very rare but undoubtedly Gormogon medals which bear every evidence of having been minted as late as 1799.

The Musical Society

A curious minute of Grand Lodge in 1725, ordering William Gulston and six other brethren to attend the next Quarterly Communication (but with no further elucidation from that source), is explained by the minutes of the *Philo-Musicae et Architecturae Societas*, which had been instituted the same year by those seven brethren from the Lodge at the Queen's Head in Holles Street. It was a condition of membership that the applicant must be a mason; failing this the society would make him one; it went so far as to pass Fellow Crafts and even make Master Masons, despite Regulation XIII (*see* p. 77), then in force.

George Payne as Junior Grand Warden visited the society to see for himself and there followed a letter from the Duke of Richmond, the Grand Master, calling attention to the irregular makings. The society paid no attention, but went on with its practices without any action being taken by Grand Lodge; indeed a week later Francis Sorrell, Senior Grand Warden, is shown to have been a guest of the society. The Musical Society died out early in 1727.

The Grand Lodge of York

Although the once firmly believed account of Edwin's Assembly of Masons at York (*see* p. 35), is purely apocryphal, there was undoubtedly an old (operative) lodge at York of considerable antiquity. Its extant records start from 1712, when it was in process of becoming speculative. In these the Master of the lodge is usually referred to as 'President' and initiates are invariably 'admitted and sworne' or 'sworne and admitted' — a gild term.

On the Festival of St. John, 1725, called now the 'Grand Feast', the lodge met in slightly strange circumstances since the President of previous years had now become 'the Grand Master', while a Deputy Grand Master and Grand Wardens were also elected.

The reason for this translation (in the sense of Bottom in *The*

THE GRAND LODGE PERIOD, 1717-50

Midsummer Night's Dream) is clearly a Grand Lodge's having been set up in London eight years previously, and the explanation of the sudden burst of pride is furnished in the famous Oration next year of Francis Drake, Junior Grand Warden, wherein he asserts that

> Edwin, the first Christian King of the *Northumbers*, about the six hundredth year after *Christ*, and who laid the Foundation of our Cathedral, sat as Grand Master. This is sufficient to make us dispute the superiority with the Lodges at *London*. But as nought of that kind ought to be amongst so amicable a fraternity, we are content they enjoy the Title of Grand Master of *England*; but the *Totius Angliae* (of All England) we claim as an undoubted right.

Incidentally, in this speech Dr. Drake addresses the 'Working Masons; persons of other Trades and Occupations; and Gentlemen,' showing that the lodge still contained operative members, and also alludes to 'E.P. [Entered 'Prentice], F.C. and M.M.', thus making it clear that three degrees were already worked in this lodge.

The new Grand Lodge drew up nineteen 'Articles agreed to be kept and observ'd by the Antient Society of Free Masons in the City of York', which read more like the rules for a single lodge than the regulations of a Grand Lodge. Although its independence is acknowledged in Anderson's *Constitutions* of 1738, York Grand Lodge did not attempt to warrant lodges or indulge in other similar Grand Lodge activities until after its revival in 1761 (*see* p. 94).

The Duke of Norfolk

When this nobleman was proclaimed and installed in January 1730, nine former Grand Masters, as already recorded, 'walk'd one by one according to Juniority — viz.: Lord Coleraine, *Earl* of Inchiquin, *Lord* Paisley*, *Duke* of Richmond, *Earl* of Dalkeith†, *Duke* of Montagu, Dr. Desaguliers, George Payne, Esq., and Mr. Anthony Sayer.' The only one absent was the Duke of Wharton, who died the following year.

Thomas Howard, 8th Duke of Norfolk, was a Roman Catholic (and consequently suffered from inability to secure

---
*later James, 7th Earl of Abercorn.

†later Francis, 2nd Duke of Buccleuch.

state office). It was he who presented to Grand Lodge its Sword of State (still in use), which Anderson claimed (1738 *Book of Constitutions*) to have belonged to King Gustav II Adolph of Sweden and carries that great warrior's name on its blade. It is only fair to add that its one-time possession by the King has been queried by the National Grand Lodge of Sweden.

The General Charity

Up to the establishment of Grand Lodge the disbursement of relief had been the affair of individual lodges. It was not until 1724 that a centralized charity scheme was seriously mooted and a Committee of Charity (today's Board of Benevolence) appointed. Five years later the first contributions from lodges were received, each newly constituted lodge being assessed at two guineas.

In 1730, and even more in 1733, the functions of that Committee were considerably extended, and duties which today would fall to the Board of General Purposes were entrusted to it.

We have already spoken of the case of Anthony Sayer. Other early applicants for relief were Joshua Timson, who had been Grand Warden in 1722, and Edward Hall, whose petition in 1732 was personally recommended by the Duke of Richmond, he at the Lodge at the Swan in Chichester having been 'made a Mason by the late Duke of Richmond Six and thirty Years agoe'. Brother Hall got six guineas.

It was suggested in Grand Lodge in 1735 that the General Charity might be the cause of masons' being made irregularly, for the purpose of participating in the benefits therefrom.

Extension of Grand Lodge Jurisdiction

It has already been observed that the Grand Lodge that was founded by the four (or possibly six) old lodges in 1717 did not claim any jurisdiction over lodges outside London and Westminster, that is a total of three square miles. The first three years were quiet ones but after that came a spate of activity.

In 1723 we find Grand Lodge legislating for lodges 'in or near London', 'within the Bills of Mortality' and 'within ten miles of London', and in the same year the further 'regular constituted lodges' are recorded as having been situated in Edgeworth (Edgware?), Acton and Richmond. In the *Engraved List of Lodges* of 1725 are to be found sixty-four lodges in all and the sphere of jurisdiction extended to such places as Bath — this spa may well have had the honour of having in its Queen's Head Lodge the first at any distance from London to come under Grand Lodge — Bristol, Carmarthen, Chester, Chichester, Gosport, Norwich, Reading, Salford and Warwick. In 1726 it became necessary to appoint the first Provincial Grand Masters,* and in the next two years came the constitution of the first overseas lodges, at Fort William in Bengal, Gibraltar and Madrid. The last had been originally constituted, personally but irregularly, by the erratic Duke of Wharton in 1728. By 1732 there were 102 lodges in all on the *Engraved List*.

Next the vexed question of precedence began to trouble the lodges but this was in 1729 settled for the time being, but naturally not without a certain want of harmony, by Grand Lodge's arranging the order according to the dates of their constitution as lodges, or what they themselves considered to be those dates.

Prichard's Exposure

Masonry Dissected by Samuel Prichard, 'late member of a constituted lodge', first published in 1730, was so successful that it ran though three editions in eleven days and was reprinted in numerous editions in many countries for the remainder of the century. It had two effects: in the first place, unlike its contemporary fellow-exposure, *The Mystery of Free-Masonry*, this thirty-two page catechism definitely establishes the working of three degrees, and the great stimulus given to the use of the third degree in lodges at this time may well have been the result of its enormous sales. Secondly, although the ritual it displays was not wholly accurate, yet its disclosures were enough to cause alarm and despondency in Grand Lodge, one result being a tightening up of the regulations regarding a lodge's admission of a visitor, who had thenceforth to be personally vouched for by a member.

*These were for North and South Wales, having their headquarters at Chester and Carmarthen respectively. Chester already had an *elected* Provincial Grand Master, as well as his Deputy and Wardens, all also elected. *See* 'Provincial Grand Lodges' on p. 109.

PRICHARD'S EXPOSURE

A further and more important consequence was that, in the words of John Noorthouck's *Book of Constitutions* of 1784, 'some variations were made in the established forms' at this time, the better to detect impostors. What exactly these 'variations' were is not now clear* but it is certain that they gave a decided impetus to the dispute between Antients and Moderns, leading to the setting up of a rival Grand Lodge, as dealt with in the next chapter.

It remains to add that an anonymous and allegedly impartial counterblast to *Masonry Dissected* was duly forthcoming under the title of *A Defence of Masonry*. Its authorship is commonly attributed to Martin Clare, who was to be Deputy Grand Master in 1741. The *Defence* was reprinted in the *Book of Constitutions*, 1738, but no copy of the original pamphlet has been preserved.

The Grand Stewards

In 1728, on the proposition of Dr. Desaguliers, twelve Stewards were nominated to look after the Great Feast, and this number remained until the Union of 1813, when it was increased to eighteen, being raised to the present nineteen in 1904. Starting in 1735 a custom arose of appointing Grand Officers only from the body of past Stewards of Grand Lodge and this was given legislative effect by a Grand Lodge motion in 1779 which required all such appointments to be confined to subscribing members of the Stewards' Lodge. This had been founded as No. 117 in 1735 but in 1792 became the Grand Stewards' Lodge and was placed at the head of the list without a number.

Their red aprons and collars were granted to the Grand Stewards in 1731 and in 1735 they were allowed to wear, after their year of office, a special jewel designed by the great William Hogarth, who had himself been one of their number the year before.

In 1736 Grand Lodge was declared to consist of the four present and all former Grand Officers, the Master and Wardens of all regular lodges and, in the case of the Stewards' Lodge, of nine other representatives as well, the nomination of whom was left to that lodge.

To this day it is still the custom that the nineteen Grand

But see p. 89(3).

THE GRAND LODGE PERIOD, 1717-50

Stewards for the year share the cost of the Grand Festival.

The Second Book of Constitutions, 1738

A good deal has already been said about the new and revised edition, which was again the work of Dr. Anderson and appeared the year before his death. One of the chief additions to his previous volume is an imposing list of pre-Grand Lodge Grand Masters, including Grand Masters Moses, Nebuchadnezzar, Alfred the Great, Cardinal Wolsey and Sir Christopher Wren. (For the last, *see* p. 50.) It is easy to laugh at such absurdities of spurious erudition, but it must be remembered that Anderson's *Constitutions* exercised an enormous influence all over the world and that his reputation as *the* historian of the Craft survived his death by nearly two hundred years. Nowadays the Doctor's historical statements, except those within his own masonic experience or fully corroborated, are usually disregarded.

Masonic Processions

Up to 1747 it had been the custom for brethren, dressed in full masonic clothing, to move in procession through the streets to the Great Feast. But owing to the number of mock processions, often of an elaborate and expensive character, which had been taking place with the object of deriding the Order, the practice was discontinued for the future.

Further, a regulation of 1754 forbade a brother's joining any public procession clothed as a mason, except by dispensation.

A Period of Neglect, 1747-1750

Lord Byron, a great-uncle of the Poet, was elected Grand Master in 1747 at the age of 25 — there had already been one (Lord Raymond in 1739) 22 years of age — and during his five years' reign he attended Grand Lodge but thrice, while the same Grand Officers and Stewards remained in office throughout. Everything points to this having been a period of slackness and neglectful conduct of the Society's affairs. There were increasing complaints of 'irregular makings', and one London tavern is recorded as having displayed a notice: 'Masons made here for 2s.6d.' Horace Walpole had remarked in 1743:

THE 18TH-CENTURY LODGE

> The Freemasons are in ... low repute now in England ... I believe nothing but a persecution could bring them into vogue again.

If there was to be no persecution, there was to ensue a fierce dissension in their ranks, as the next chapter will reveal.

The Eighteenth-century Lodge

In almost every case the brethren met in a tavern or coffeehouse. The lodge room would be graced with an 'oblong-square' table down the centre. Shortly before the opening of lodge two brethren enter and unlock the lodge box, with two, sometimes three, keys. They take out the properties and place them on the table round which the working is to be done; these include a tinder box for striking a flame to light the candles. They also see that the punch bowl and firing glasses are properly arranged, together with the long clay churchwarden pipes, for throughout this century lodge work was accompanied by smoking and drinking.

The brethren do not enter in procession but just stroll in, habited in their white aprons. When the Master enters, the members take their seats after he is seated. The Master takes off his hat on declaring the lodge open and the other brethren follow suit but do not replace their hats as the Master does his.

The Master and Wardens then chalk the 'lodge' on the floor according to which ceremony is to be performed, filling in the outline with a few simple figures, such as the two pillars, square, level, plumb rule and the letter 'G' (the last being introduced after 1730; it then signified 'geometry'). Later in the century the Tyler was paid to 'draw the lodge' — the precursor of the Tracing Board. When a candidate has been initiated he has to take mop and pail and wash out the drawing before taking his seat.

A lecture (in the form of a catechism) is then worked, the Master asking the questions of the members in turn. When it is concluded, there is a very simple closing — the Master giving his command and the Senior Warden saying, 'It is our Master's will and pleasure that this lodge stand closed.'

In some instances the (inner) lodge was in triangular form, the Master sitting at the apex in the east, and both Wardens in the west.

CHAPTER VI

ENGLISH GRAND LODGES, 1751-1813

The Great Dissension — Antients and Moderns

Throughout the latter half of the eighteenth century Freemasonry in England (and likewise in much of the English-speaking world) was rent into two bitterly opposed camps, that of the 'Antients', who in 1751 formed a rival Grand Lodge 'under the Old Institutions', and that of the 'Moderns' (so dubbed), who loyally adhered to the original Grand Lodge.

Until comparatively recently it was customary to describe the Antients as 'seceders' and 'schismatics', but both terms are quite unjustified seeing that not one of the first dissidents belonged to any lodge under the jurisdiction of the premier Grand Lodge, and also that their ritual and customs differed scarcely at all from those of their Irish and Scottish brethren, whose Grand Lodges, as we shall see, were later to recognize the new as *the* Grand Lodge of England.

Later secessions of masons and lodges from the Moderns to the Antients *did* occur, just as there are recorded instances of secession from the Antients to the Moderns (e.g. William Preston, *see* p. 97).

The Causes of the Dissension

These can be found partly in the slackness and weak administration of the original governing body at this time, as alluded to in the preceding chapter, and partly in certain changes in custom and ritual which had been made, some deliberately (*see* p. 85). These changes can be stated with some certainty to have included the following:

(1) The opening of the Craft to men of non-Christian faith (often *wrongly* described as 'the de-Christianization of Freemasonry') which had started at least as early as 1721.* (see p.89).

(2) Neglect of the days of St. John as special masonic

festivals.† Between 1730 and 1753 not one ('Modern') Grand Master was installed on either of those Saints' days. Now among eighteenth-century freemasons this was regarded as a serious matter.

(3) A transposition of the modes of recognition in the first and second degrees. Probably one of the 'variations in the established forms' deliberately made about 1739, as earlier recorded, it certainly destroyed any claim of Freemasonry to be 'universal' and it is likely that this removal of a land-mark incensed the Antients most of all.

(4) Abandonment of the esoteric part, slight though it then was, in the ceremony of installing a lodge's Master.

(5) Neglect of the catechisms attached to each degree.

Other variations in working, as practised by Antients and strict Moderns included:

(a) Differences in the passwords for the second and third degrees; (b) Different words for one of the substituted secrets of a Master Mason, resulting in the alternative forms in use today; (c) The method of placing the Three Great Lights and the Wardens; (d) The employment of Deacons in lodges. These officers are known to have functioned in Ireland as early as 1727, but in strict Modern lodges their duties were performed by Stewards until the Articles of Union in 1813; (e) The refusal of the premier Grand Lodge officially to recognize the Royal Arch degree.

The Traditioners

We have used the expression 'strict Moderns' because it must not be imagined that by all means all of the lodges under the jurisdiction of the 'Modern' Grand Lodge allowed themselves to be influenced by its edicts to the extent of changing their customs. For those — and additional instances are coming

*In that year two practising Jews, Nathan Blanch and John Hart, were (according to W. Bro. John Shaftesley) initiated in the Lodge of Antiquity, then No. 1. The first Jew to reach Grand Rank was David Lyon, who in the Antients' Grand Lodge in 1763 was elected Grand Tyler and two years later was appointed Grand Pursuivant. The first Moderns' instance was not till 1785, when W. Bro. Moses Isaac Levi was appointed both Junior and Senior Grand Warden in the same year.

†The traditional birthday of St. John the Baptist is celebrated on June 24, while St. John the Evangelist's Day is December 27.

to light very frequently — who remained faithful at once to their own Constitution and their old ritual, Brother Heron Lepper, late Librarian of Grand Lodge, coined (in this sense) the excellent term 'Traditioners'.

For the most part the 'strict Modern' lodges are found to have been those in or near London, while the Traditioner lodges flourished further afield.

The Antients' Grand Lodge

When exactly the Grand Committee, which preceded the Grand Lodge of the Antients, was formed is not known; some have put it even as early as 1739. What we do discover from the first records is the meeting of a Committee of 'a General Assembly' in July, 1751, when the 'Rules and Orders to be Observ'd by the Most ANTIENT and HONble Society of FREE and ACCEPTED MASONS' were agreed by five members, including a 'Grand Secretary'.

Next year we find the Grand Committee a *fait accompli*, and its first Minutes record the presence of representatives of nine duly numbered lodges, 'all the Antient Masons in and adjacent to London.' There was undoubtedly a large Irish element in these lodges, whose members were mainly mechanics or shopkeepers.

It was not until December, 1753, that a Grand Master was chosen in the person of Robert Turner, 'Master of No. 15' (whose Warrant is now held by the Newcastle-upon-Tyne Lodge No. 24), who then appointed a Deputy. With the election of Grand Wardens the transformation into a Grand Lodge was complete.

Laurence Dermott

The Minutes of 1752 already quoted record the appointment as the second Grand Secretary of one who has been characterized as 'the most remarkable mason that ever existed.' This was Laurence Dermott, who was born in Ireland in 1720. Initiated there at the age of 20, he was made Master of a Dublin lodge in 1746 and in the same year was exalted in the Royal Arch, the allusion to this in the records of the Antients being one of the earliest known references to the degree.

Coming to England about 1748 as a journeyman painter, at which trade he often worked a twelve-hour day, he at first

LAURENCE DERMOTT

...ned a lodge under the premier Grand Lodge but later trans-...rred his allegiance to Nos. 9 and 10 of the Antients (now the ...nt Lodge, No. 15 and the Royal Athelstan Lodge, No. 19 ...spectively). He afterwards became a wine merchant and pros-...red. Of no mean education, he had at least a smattering of ...atin and Hebrew, his polemic style was a match for that of ...y of his 'Modern' antagonists, and such was the force of his ...aracter that he was the life and soul of the Antient move-...ent almost until his death in 1791.

Laurence Dermott fulfilled the duties of Grand Secretary ...th triumphant success until 1771, when he resigned after ...sputes with his Deputy and successor, William Dickey; from ...at year until 1787 he was often chosen as Deputy Grand ...aster. One of his first acts as Grand Secretary was to produce ... model set of by-laws for private lodges, and in 1756 he com-...led, like Anderson before him, a book of Constitutions. To ...is he gave the curious title of

...himan Rezon

or, A Help to a Brother (the Hebrew words can barely ...retch to this interpretation). This edition, which, it is worthy ...f note, contains not a single word derogatory to the ...loderns', was in fact copied very largely from Anderson and ...om Spratt's *Constitutions for the Use of Lodges in Ireland*, ...751. Three more editions, with a greater use of original matter ...nd increasingly strong strictures on the premier Grand Lodge, ...ere to be published in the lifetime of the compiler and pro-...rietor, and a further four before the Union of 1813.

Of the 224 pages of the 1764 edition no fewer than 118 ...ere devoted to poetry and songs. In the 1778 edition there is ... note to the third Charge (forbidding the initiation of women ...r eunuchs) which runs: 'This is still the law of Antient ...lasons, though disregarded by our Brethren (I mean our ...isters) the Modern Masons.' (*see* p. 104).

That the title of the book was often misunderstood by ...lasons is shown by the reference to it in a Lodge Inventory ... 1838) as '*A. H. Iman's Reasons*'!

R. H. Baxter, in the Transactions of the Manchester Asso-...iation for Masonic Research, Vol. XVIII, put forward ...roposition that 'Ahiman Rezon' could — by an ingenious use ...f the familiar masonic cipher -- be found (with a few minor errors of transcription) to have been derived from the wor[d] 'Freemasonry'.

Progress of the Antients

The first country lodge, at Bristol, was constituted in 175[4]. By next year there were thirty-six lodges on the register, whic[h] seventeen years later accounted for seventy-four lodges [in] London, eighty-three country lodges and forty-three in ove[r]seas countries. In that same year, 1771, the 'Modern' Gran[d] Lodge had under it 157 London, 164 country and 100 ove[r]seas lodges.

In 1754 a Committee of Charity, known as the Steward[s] Lodge, was set up with powers very much the same as those o[f] the similar Committee of the Moderns, (*see* p. 83). A curiou[s] Minute of Grand Lodge the same year runs as follows:

> Bro. Cowen, Master of Lodge No. 37, proposed payin[g] one guinea into the Grand Fund for No. 6, now vacan[t]. This proposal was accepted and the Brethren of No. 37 ar[e] to rank as No. 6 [since 1819 the Enoch Lodge No. 11] fo[r] ye future.

The efforts of Laurence Dermott and others to find a nobl[e] Grand Master were successful in 1756 when the Earl o[f] Blesington, who as Viscount Mountjoy had already ruled th[e] Grand Lodge of Ireland in 1738 and 1739, was installed a[s] Grand Master of the Antients *in proxy*, as indeed the four year[s] of his term of office were to be continued. His absence can[,] however, be accounted for by the fact that the Seven Year[s] War (1756-63) made it necessary for him to be in Ireland. I[t] was no doubt to promote the Earl's acceptance of the Gran[d] Mastership that Dermott had discreetly dedicated his *Ahima[n] Rezon* to him.

In 1758 a 'strict union' was established with the Gran[d] Lodge of Ireland, and Scotland followed suit in 1773, the thir[d] Duke of Atholl, then head of the Grand Lodge of the Antients[,] being at the same time Grand Master-elect of Scotland.

Four years later it was decided that no one should be mad[e] a mason for less than two guineas, of which five shillings wa[s] to be paid to the Fund of Charity, and one shilling to th[e] Grand Secretary. Curiously enough we read that later the sam[e] year 'David Fisher, late Grand Warden Elect' had 'attempted t[o]

PROGRESS OF THE ANTIENTS

rm a Grand Lodge of his own and offered to Register Masons erein for 6d. each' — which is a little reminiscent of the vern notice mentioned on p. 86. Brother Fisher was quite derstandably 'deem'd unworthy of any office or seat in the and Lodge'.

In 1767 Thomas Mathew, who according to Dermott had a rtune of £16,000 a year (worth more than ten times that nount today), was privately installed as Grand Master. He as a Roman Catholic, but despite the Papal Bulls of 1738 and 751 was

> so fond of the Craft that wherever he resided, whether in Great Britain, Ireland, or France, he also held a Regular Lodge among his own Domesticks.

e Atholl Masons

When the third Duke of Atholl was installed Grand Master 1771, he chose Laurence Dermott as his Deputy, and William ckey was elected to succeed the latter as Grand Secretary. e two seem to have worked in complete harmony from this ne.

Next year it was agreed that the Masters and Wardens of lodges within five miles of London must attend every meeting of Grand Lodge, or in default pay a fine of five shillings d threepence 'to be levy'd on the Warrant.'

After expressing satisfaction that the 'Antient Craft is gaining its ground from the Moderns' the third Duke died in 774 — he drowned himself in a 'fit of delirium'. He was succeded both as Duke and Grand Master by his son, who, *at the e of 19*, was initiated, passed, raised, installed Master of the rand Master's Lodge and elected Grand Master of the ntients, all in four days. His installation in the last office me after a further four months, and the above must conitute something of a record in rapid advancement in the raft. There was no counterpart in the premier constitution to e Grand Master's Lodge, which (under the Antients) was en No. 1, and is so listed today.

Thus breathlessly installed, the fourth Duke was to reign, ith one ten-year interval, until 1813. It is little wonder that e Antients came to be known as 'Atholl Masons' and their odges as 'Atholl Lodges'. John Murray, fourth Duke of

Atholl, came of a family which had been connected wi[th]
Masonry since 1641; the initiation of his blood relation, [Sir]
Robert Moray in that year is related on page 44.

In 1783 Robert Leslie was appointed Grand Secretary a[nd]
despite a serious conflict with Dermott retained that positi[on]
with one brief interval, until the Union with the Moderns [in]
1813. The Grand Secretary at this time does not appear [to]
have been overpaid. His salary was five guineas a year, [in]creased in 1790 to fifteen, paid 'quarterly or half-yearly, as [he]
pleased to take it'.

There was a glimmer of the dawning of reconciliation wi[th]
the Moderns in 1798, when it was moved to appoint a co[m]mittee to effect with one from the rival Grand Lodge a uni[on]
between the two controlling bodies. But the time was not y[et.]

Remakings

At the height of the feud both Grand Lodges fulminat[ed]
against a member of the rival body's being admitted to one [of]
their own lodges, even as a visitor, and it was consequently t[he]
custom for both Modern and Antient lodges to 're-make' [a]
brother of the other persuasion who sought admission. Som[e]times this was carried to ridiculous lengths, as in the case [of]
Milbourne West, who as an Irish and Antient freemason h[ad]
been elected Provincial Grand Master of Canada under t[he]
Modern Grand Lodge. When, however, he applied for membe[r]ship of what is now the Royal Cumberland Lodge, No. 41, [at]
Bath, that experience was of no avail, and he had to [be]
'remade', but without fee.

In the sixties the situation seems to have softened som[e]what, at any rate in London, and we find William Dicke[y]
when Grand Secretary of the Antients, being made a Mode[rn]
mason without in any way diminishing his allegiance to t[he]
Antients' Grand Lodge, of which he subsequently becam[e]
Deputy Grand Master from 1777-81 and from 1794 till h[is]
death in 1800.

The York Grand Lodge

Before relating the further history of the Moderns it will [be]
necessary to say something of two other Grand Lodges. The[se]
were the Grand Lodge of All England, situated at York, [to]
which allusion has already been made on p. 82, and the Gra[nd]

THE YORK GRAND LODGE

Lodge of England South of the River Trent, deriving from it.

The original Grand Lodge of York was dormant from 1740-60. The occasion of its revival in 1761 by 'Six of the surviving Members of the Fraternity' was the warranting of a lodge which met at the Punch Bowl, York, by the Grand Lodge of the Moderns, which had already chartered lodges in Scarborough, Halifax and Leeds and appointed a Provincial Grand Master for Yorkshire.

The Lodge at the Punch Bowl did not last long and the York Grand Secretary wrote to the Moderns' Grand Lodge in 1767 that it 'had been for some years discontinued, and that the most Antient Grand Lodge of All England held for time immemorial in this City is the only Lodge held therein.' He went on to say:

> That this Lodge acknowledges no Superior, that it pays Homage to none, that it exists in its own Right, that it grants Constitutions, and Certificates in the same Manner, as is done by the Grand Lodge in London, and as it has from Time immemorial had a Right and use to do . . .

The collapse of the Lodge at the Punch Bowl did not deter the Moderns' Grand Lodge from constituting other lodges in York at this time, one of which is the famous York Lodge, No. 236, constituted as the Union Lodge in 1777.

Noorthouck's *Constitutions* of 1784 stated that 'the ancient York Masons were confined to one Lodge, which is still extant, but consists of very few members, and will probably be soon altogether annihilated'. This last wish or prophecy was to be fulfilled although not immediately. The Grand Lodge was never dissolved, but lingered on until about 1792, when it gradually faded out.

During its heyday the jurisdiction of the 'Grand Lodge of All England' never extended beyond Yorkshire, Lancashire and Cheshire, but it is to be observed that the 'York Rite' and 'York Masonry' have always been regarded and notably in the United States as denoting the oldest and purest form of Freemasonry. During the sixty-seven years of its existence the Grand Lodge constituted, so far as is known, not more than fourteen lodges and one Grand Lodge, namely

ENGLISH GRAND LODGES, 1751-1813

The Grand Lodge of England South of the River Trent (1779-89)

Under this high-sounding title masquerades our old friend the Lodge of Antiquity, first of the four Old Lodges. How did it come about that this mainstay of the original Grand Lodge should desert its allegiance and set itself up as a rival organization? The cause was the antipathy existing between the famous William Preston, then Master of the lodge, and John Noorthouck, its Treasurer. Preston had been appointed Assistant Grand Secretary and employed by the Grand Secretary, James Heseltine, in preparing a new edition of the *Book of Constitutions*. When this was nearly completed, the job was taken away from him and given to Noorthouck, whereupon Preston threw up his Assistant Grand Secretaryship in disgust.

Next came a complaint from Noorthouck to Grand Lodge that on St. John the Evangelist's Day, 1777, Preston had instigated a procession in masonic dress from St. Dunstan's Church (actually a distance of a few yards) in contravention of the Grand Lodge regulation already mentioned (p. 86). When Preston was arraigned for this offence he pleaded that by virtue of its immemorial constitution the Lodge of Antiquity had certain privileges that more modern lodges did not possess. Although he was induced to withdraw this plea and just when reconciliation seemed in sight, fresh fuel was added to the flames by the action of the lodge in expelling Noorthouck and two of his faction.

Grand Lodge demanded their reinstatement without effect and meanwhile the lodge Secretary had been in touch with the York Grand Lodge and obtained its consent to constituting the majority members of the Lodge of Antiquity as the Grand Lodge of England South of the River Trent. This was followed by a severance of relations with the original Grand Lodge and the publication of a manifesto acknowledging the authority of the Grand Lodge of York as the senior body.

The expelled minority, backed by Grand Lodge, continued to style themselves the Lodge of Antiquity, but Preston and his associates had secured the lodge furniture, which they moved by night to fresh rooms. Of the new Grand Lodge John Wilson was the first Grand Master and John Sealy the Grand Secretary, while Preston himself was appointed Deputy Grand

GRAND LODGE SOUTH OF THE TRENT

Master and Grand Orator. The leading seceders were formally expelled from the original Grand Lodge. There were thus two Lodges of Antiquity operating at the same time and under different Constitutions, one of them having a dual capacity, that of a private lodge and that of a Grand Lodge.

Two new lodges were constituted by it during the ten years of its existence, but little else was accomplished to bring glory either to itself or to the Yorkist cause which had sponsored it. In 1789 Preston and those expelled with him submitted to Grand Lodge and were restored to their privileges, while the warring members of the lodge of Antiquity were reunited in that harmony which the lodge has preserved ever since. The Grand Lodge of England South of the River Trent thus came painlessly to its end, but it should be noted that during its brief lifetime it formed one of *four* Grand Lodges in simultaneous existence in England.

William Preston (1742-1818)

The author of *Illustrations of Masonry*, which was first published in 1772 and ran to eleven further editions in his lifetime, came in 1760 from Edinburgh to London, where he became a journeyman printer. At the age of twenty he was the second initiate of an Antients' lodge of Edinburgh brethren in London, whom he persuaded to be reconstituted by the Moderns' Grand Lodge in 1772. That lodge is today the Caledonian Lodge No. 134.

Two years later he joined the Lodge of Antiquity and within three months was elected its Master. The story of this 'time immemorial' lodge fascinated him and he devoted much of his time to increasing its membership and winning recognition for its prestige.

Always adept in composing and delivering masonic lectures, William Preston, 'little Solomon' as his opponents dubbed him, may be regarded as the father of the modern Preceptor. When he died in 1818 he left £500 to the Fund of Benevolence and another £300 in Consols as the endowment which has allowed the celebrated Prestonian Lectures to be given to this day — annually except for breaks from 1862 to 1925 and during the second World War.* (see p. 98).

William Preston lies buried in St. Paul's Cathedral.

ENGLISH GRAND LODGES, 1751-1813

The Moderns' Grand Lodge after 1750

After several ineffective Grand Masters, the 9th Baron Blayney was installed in that high office in 1764. This Irish nobleman was a solider and may have been initiated in a military lodge; at any rate he was undoubtedly a Traditioner in his outlook on ritual and he took his duties as Grand Master very seriously. During his three years of office he constituted seventy-four lodges, sixty-two of them in England and Wales, nineteen of which are still in existence, while in the same period only twenty-four lodges were warranted by the Grand Lodge of the Antients.

Sale of Lodge Constitutions

There was at this time more than one case of the illegal sale of lodge constitutions, and a notable instance occurred in 1767 when the members of the George Lodge, then No. 3, which met at the Sun and Punch Bowl, High Holborn, agreed to sell their Warrant and regalia for thirty guineas to 'some Honourable Gentlemen Newly Made'. These newly made gentlemen included Thomas Dunckerley, of whom we shall be hearing more, and Thomas French, who was next year to be appointed Grand Secretary. The new lodge was the present famous Lodge of Friendship No. 6†. At its first meeting the Duke of Beaufort was initiated and elected to the chair; a few months later he was elected Grand Master.

Meanwhile, the Committee of Charity, to whom the irregular sale of the constitution had been reported, decided that 'as a mark of high respect to his Grace the Duke of Beaufort and the other Noblemen and Honourable Gentlemen who meet under the name of the Lodge of Friendship and in consideration of their being very young masons', the constitution of No. 3 should remain with them, this decision not to be looked upon as a precedent.

Thomas Dunckerley (1742-95)

This outstanding freemason was a natural son of King George II, although his royal descent was not acknowledged

The Collected Prestonian Lectures, 1925-1960, edited by Harry Carr and containing all but three (whose esoteric contents made them unsuitable for printing), was published by the Quatuor Coronati Lodge in 1965.

†In 1856 it was found that out of twenty Grand Wardens recently appointed, no fewer than thirteen had come from the ranks of the Lodge of Friendship.

by George III until 1767. He joined the Navy, from which he retired about 1764 with the rank of gunner. Having been initiated in Portsmouth in 1754, he formed masonic lodges in several of the ships in which he served, and one of these, that meeting in H.M.S. *Prince*, has long met in London as the Royal Somerset House and Inverness No. 4.

Like Lord Blayney he was a Traditioner. In 1767 that Grand Master appointed him the first Provincial Grand Master of Hampshire, and at a time when, as his biographer, Henry Sadler, points out, that office was virtually dormant in England (as were also most of those who held it!) he carried out his duties with the utmost enthusiasm and energy. Eventually he held no fewer than eight out of the thirty-four Provincial Grand Masterships, and was honoured in 1786 by being appointed Past Grand Warden.

His connexions with the Royal Arch and Mark degrees will be related in their proper places.

Proposed Charter of Incorporation, 1769

The Duke of Beaufort was anxious to obtain a Royal Charter of Incorporation for the Society and in 1769 the project was approved by Grand Lodge after the lodges had voted in its favour by 168 to 43. But determined opposition now arose, the Caledonian Lodge even entering with the Attorney General a caveat against the move (for which they narrowly escaped erasure). The Antients' Grand Lodge were also alarmed, holding that the scheme was directed against themselves.

In any case, the Moderns' Deputy Grand Master, the Hon. Charles Dillon, when due to move the appropriate Bill in the House of Commons, moved instead that its consideration should be deferred *sine die*. The scheme had failed but, in the picturesque wording of Heron Lepper, 'in vanishing from human ken, like the fiend of folklore, it left behind a nauseous stench to remind men that something unholy had passed that way'. The Antients, of course, jeered jubilantly.

But, apart from the prestige conferred, a Royal Charter of Incorporation has distinct advantages, such as the right to sue in the courts, and it may be pertinent to inquire if in the altered circumstances of today the time has not come for the Society to seek to be so incorporated.

ENGLISH GRAND LODGES, 1751-1813

Freemasons' Hall, 1776

Another venture of the Duke of Beaufort's was far more successful. In 1769 he proposed the raising of a fund for defraying the expenses of building a new hall, and four years later a Hall Committee (of which William Preston was originally a member) was set up to superintend the scheme. Hitherto Grand Lodge had usually held its ordinary meetings at various taverns.

The Committee bought 'two large commodious dwelling houses and a large garden situated in Great Queen Street' for £3,180 and, with the customary optimism of building estimates, it was reckoned that the complete structure could be erected for a further £3,180. Actually the building cost no less a sum than £20,000. This naturally required paying for and there was much groaning among the brethren of the time at the increased charges payable to Grand Lodge.

The first Freemasons' Hall took little more than a year to build and in 1776 it was ceremoniously opened and dedicated to Masonry, Virtue, Universal Charity and Benevolence.

Three new Grand Officers were appointed in connexion with the new hall. These were a Grand Chaplain (Dr. William Dodd who, however, was expelled from the Society in 1777 on being convicted of having forged a bond from his patron, the Earl of Chesterfield, for which he was executed despite eloquent pleas by Dr. Johnson and others), a Grand Architect (Thomas Sandby) and a Grand Portrait Painter (Rev. William Peters). The last two appointments were intended to be purely personal and not to be perpetual offices.

Lord Petre

Freemasons' Hall was completed during the Grand Mastership of Lord Petre, who had succeeded the Duke of Beaufort in 1772 and ruled for five years. Robert Edward, 9th Lord Petre, was looked upon as the head of the Roman Catholic community in England. Although he was not the first Catholic to hold the English office of Grand Master (*see* p. 82), he was the only one to do so in the original Grand Lodge after the Papal denunciations of 1738 and 1751, since we can except the Marquess of Ripon, who in 1874 resigned the supreme office in Freemasonry on adopting the Catholic religion. William Preston praised Lord Petre's masonic enthusiasm.

LORD PETRE, WILKES & SMITH

John Wilkes (1727-97)

A mystery attaches to the initiation of the famous (or notorious) 'Friend of Liberty'. The Minutes of the then Jerusalem Lodge No. 44* of 1769 record that John Wilkes was made a mason 'by virtue of a dispensation under the hand and seal of Charles Dillon, Deputy Grand Master'. This is supplemented by a notice in the contemporary press that the ceremony took place in King's Bench Prison in the presence of Grand Officers, who are named in the minutes as having been Bro. Dobson, the Worshipful Master, who was also Past Assistant Grand Master, Bro. Maschall, a Provincial Grand Master and Bro. French, Grand Secretary.

Although the dispensation and the presence of Grand Officers were both officially denied a few days later (also in the press), we may take it for granted that the facts recorded above are correct and that what Grand Lodge was nervous about was the revelation that Wilkes had been initiated in prison; this is confirmed by the subsequent fate of

Captain George Smith

This officer was Junior Grand Warden and Provincial Grand Master for Kent. His book *The Use and Abuse of Freemasonry* the Grand Lodge declined to sponsor. In 1783 he was arraigned for 'making Masons in a clandestine manner in the King's Bench Prison'. His defence was that he had done so as Master of the itinerant Royal Military Lodge, the Master of which having the constitution (warrant) had the right to hold a lodge and make masons. But Grand Lodge set its face against this plea, declaring it to be inconsistent with the principles of Masonry to hold a freemasons' lodge for making, passing or raising masons in any place of confinement.

Captain Smith was subsequently in more serious trouble, being charged with 'uttering an Instrument purporting to be a certificate of the Grand Lodge, recommending two distressed Brethren', for which he was expelled from the Society.

Royal Freemasons

The Duke of Cumberland, a brother of King George III, was

---

*Warranted 1731, erased 1780; not to be confused with the present Jerusalem Lodge, 197, which — constituted in 1771 — is one of the nineteen 'Red Apron' lodges.

ENGLISH GRAND LODGES, 1751-1813

elected Grand Master in 1782, and the Earl of Effingham, whom he nominated as Acting Grand Master, was installed as his proxy. Five years later, the Prince of Wales and his brother, Prince William (afterward William IV), were initiated. Four of the other sons of George III, that is all (except the Duke of Cambridge) who reached manhood, became members of the Craft, and we shall hear more of the Duke of Kent and the Duke of Sussex.

Fifth Book of Constitutions, 1784

The third editor of the *Book of Constitutions* was John Noorthouck, the antagonist of William Preston. The new edition, which as we have seen had been started by William Preston, was an improvement on any that had gone before, and what is more carried for the first time a full index 'without which no publication beyond the size of a pamphlet can be deemed compleat'. With this sentiment, expressed in its preface, the present authors heartily concur.

The Masonic Charities

This period saw the start of the great charities of the Craft. The Royal Cumberland Free Masons' School (now the Royal Masonic Institution for Girls), the first of them, was founded in 1788, largely through the exertions of the Chevalier Bartholomew Ruspini, Grand Sword Bearer (1791-1813) and a founder of the Nine Muses Lodge (now No. 235); he was the Prince of Wales's dentist. Two of his grandchildren were subsequently admitted as pupils at the school. In his charitable endeavour he was ably seconded by Thomas Dunckerley and James Heseltine, the Grand Secretary.

The school was first sited at Somers Place East, near the present St. Pancras Station, and was able to accommodate fifteen girls, but it had already proved inadequate by 1795, when a new building was erected in St. George's Fields at a cost of £3,000. The number of pupils was now increased to thirty, which was again doubled by 1802.

The second of the great charities, the Royal Masonic Institution for Boys was, unlike its predecessor, established by the Antients. In 1798 William Burwood, P.M., of the United

THE MASONIC CHARITIES

Mariners' Lodge (now No. 30), with other members, set up the Institution for Clothing and Educating the Sons of Indigent Freemasons, of whom the number first to be cared for was six. In 1801 the fourth Duke of Atholl became its Patron, while towards the end of its separate existence the Antients' Grand Lodge contributed a proportion of the fees it had received for the initiation of candidates. In 1810, to commemorate the fiftieth year of George III's reign, the number of pupils was increased to fifty.

The subsequent history of the first two of the great charities, as well as the founding of the third, will be briefly related in the following chapter.

The Chevalier d'Eon (1728-1810)

In the person of this French gentleman and freemason English Freemasonry became indirectly involved in one of the major scandals of the eighteenth century. It is an extraordinary story.

An expert swordsman and dragoon officer, the Chevalier was the trusted servant of both Louis XV and Louis XVI and at the end of the Seven Years War was appointed Ambassador at the Court of St. James. When in 1764 he was superseded in his post by a personal enemy, he carried away the state papers relating to his mission; they included details of a scheme for invading this country.

In 1777 he accepted an offer by Louis XVI to increase his pension in return for the papers, accompanied by the amazing stipulation that he should 'lay aside the uniform of a Dragoon ... and resume the garments of *her* sex.' Now rumours that he was in reality Mlle la Chevalière had been growing ever since they were started by his enemy the French Ambassador, and to such an extent that several hundreds of thousands of pounds were freely wagered on his sex. One of these 'insurance policies' had been brought to the Law Courts in 1777; a French surgeon gave evidence from his surgical knowledge and another Frenchman swore from his carnal knowledge that d'Eon was a woman. Lord Mansfield, the judge, rejected the argument that he must be a man since he had been admitted a freemason and the jury legally decreed him a woman.

The Chevalier had in fact been initiated in 1767 by 'L'Immortalité de L'Ordre', one of several ('Modern') French

ENGLISH GRAND LODGES, 1751-1813

lodges constituted in London at this time, and rose to be its Junior Warden; his writings show how keen he was on the Craft. When the rumours recounted above were at their height he took refuge with Earl Ferrers, who had been Grand Master in 1762-3.

The amazing sequel is that, although hitherto he had stoutly protested his manhood without, however, agreeing to put it to the proof, after accepting King Louis's offer he proclaimed himself a female and for the remaining thirty-three years of his life so attired himself; he never re-entered a lodge. The actual truth about his sex did not come to light until his death, when he was divested of his (female) clothes for burial.

The judgment of the High Court was the origin of Laurence Dermott's jibe in *Ahiman Rezon* (1778), already quoted, concerning 'our brethren (I mean sisters) the modern-masons . . . And upon a late tryal at Westminster, it appeared that they had admitted a woman named Madame D'E—.'

The Earl of Moira

It was a fortunate day when, in 1790, the Earl of Moira was appointed Acting Grand Master of the Moderns by the Grand Master, the Duke of Cumberland, and he was continued in that office by the latter's successor, the Prince of Wales, afterwards King George IV. This outstanding military commander and fine freemason was styled 'Acting Grand Master of India'* in 1813, when he went as Governor-General of Bengal and Commander-in-Chief of India.

As a member of the Committee set up to effect a reconciliation with the Antients, his efforts towards that desirable end were tremendous. Equally useful was his help in securing the immunity of freemasons from the provisions of the Unlawful Societies Act of 1799, which is dealt with in the succeeding section.

His only not wholly successful action was the founding, in 1799, of the Masonic Benefit Society, which flourished for a while but perished about 1830.

He was Acting Grand Master of Scotland from 1806-1808 (*see* p. 192). In 1816 he was created the 1st Marquess of Hastings. He died in 1826.

*His patent was dated 17th January 1818.

THE EARL OF MOIRA

The Unlawful Societies Act, 1799

At the height of the Wars of the French Revolution Parliament passed an Act for the suppression of seditious societies. It enacted that all societies, the members of which are required to take an oath not authorized by law, shall be deemed unlawful combinations. Owing to the efforts of the Duke of Atholl and the Earl of Moira a clause was inserted exempting all lodges of 'freemasons from its operation, except that lodge Secretaries were required to make an annual return of their members' names and addresses to the local Clerk of the Peace.' (It was assumed at first that the Act precluded the consituting of new lodges, thus doubling the perils of erasure, but this proved not to be the case.)

In 1967 the Unlawful Societies Act, 1799, was repealed by Section 13(2) of the Criminal Law Act. It is curious to find the noble Order of Freemasonry associated in any way with either unlawful societies or criminal law.

Steps towards Reconciliation

After nearly half a century of severance a new generation of freemasons of both societies had arisen, many of whom were heartily sick of the internecine warfare between the two bodies.

The first move came from the Antients' Grand Lodge, as already recorded on page 94. Five years later the next attempt to heal the breach, which was made by the Moderns, was also unsuccessful and matters were not improved by their expulsion in 1803 of Brother Thomas Harper who, curiously enough, held important positions in both bodies, sitting as a Past Grand Steward on the Committee of Charity of the elder, while at the same time serving as Deputy Grand Master of the Antients.

In 1809 the Moderns' Grand Lodge, which had meanwhile entered into fraternal alliances with the Grand Lodges of Scotland (of which the Earl of Moira was Acting Grand Master) and of Ireland, took an important step, resolving that

> It is not necessary any longer to continue in force those Measures which were resorted to in or about 1739 respecting irregular Masons and do therefore enjoin the several Lodges to revert to the Antient Land Marks of the Society,

and next year Thomas Harper was reinstated. It is generally believed that this brother, while professing to be keen on the

Union, was in reality opposed to it, since he believed that his trade as a jeweller, supplying masonic regalia, would be affected.

In 1810, however, the Atholl Grand Lodge resolved that

> a Masonic Union on principles equal and honourable to both Grand Lodges, and preserving the Land Marks of the Ancient Craft, would be ... expedient and advantageous to both.

Meetings followed between the Earl of Moira and the Duke of Atholl and between special committees of the rival Grand Lodges.

The Lodge of Promulgation

The Moderns' negotiating committee had been formed in 1809 as the Lodge of Promulgation, which lasted until 1811. Its original object was to report on the differences of ritual as practised by Antients and Moderns. Ceremonies were rehearsed in front of the Duke of Sussex, Master of the Lodge of Antiquity (who was to succeed the Prince of Wales as Grand Master in 1813 and was easily the most cultured of the sons of King George III), and the Masters of eight other London lodges.

In the result the working adopted was mainly that of the Antients, notably in the use of Deacons, which had hitherto been confined to Antient lodges, and in the Installation ceremony for Masters of lodges; it is considered that the expression 'Board of Installed Masters' dates from this time.

Among other recommendations of the lodge to the Earl of Moira was one for appointing a 'Professor of the Art and Mystery of Speculative Freemasonry,' to settle all doubtful points. Such an officer never materialized.

The Articles of Union

In 1813 the Duke of Atholl, who had ruled the Antient Masons (with one ten-year interval) since 1774, was succeeded by the Duke of Kent, the father of Queen Victoria. This Prince who was far from being generally popular, certainly showed his best side in his masonic contacts. Royal brothers were thus in command of the two branches of the English Craft and the Duke of Kent had also, as a mark of reconciliation, been appointed his Deputy by the Duke of Sussex, the new Grand Master of the Moderns.

THE UNION OF 1813

In the same year twenty-one Articles of Union between the two Grand Lodges were signed and sealed by both Grand Masters and other important officers, including Thomas Harper.

The second Article lays down that 'pure Ancient Masonry consists of three degrees and no more, viz. those of the Entered Apprentice, the Fellow Craft and the Master Mason, including the Supreme Order of the Royal Arch'.

The fifth Article set up a Lodge of Reconciliation, consisting of representatives of both fraternities, to visit lodges for the purpose of obligating and instructing members.

The Articles of Union were very soon ratified by both Grand Lodges and thus was born the present United Grand Lodge of England, with the Duke of Sussex (proposed by the Duke of Kent) as its first Grand Master. Thus also was happily ended the feud of sixty years. Probably the feud itself, but certainly the terms of settlement, have been of inestimable benefit to the present Craft.

CHAPTER VII

UNITED GRAND LODGE FREEMASONRY 1813-1975

However wonderful the Union must have seemed to English freemasons, it was not unattended by difficulties; one was that it was not equally welcomed in other parts of the world, and notably in America; another was the question of the

New Numbering of Lodges

This was solved by the respective No. 1 lodges of the two Constitutions drawing lots for the first place; the (Antients') Grand Master's Lodge won, so that the Lodge of Antiquity, as already recorded on page 70, has from thenceforth become No. 2. The remaining lodges on the two lists were given alternate numbers, the Antients taking the odd numbers and the Moderns the even, so far as the old Ancient lodge numbers lasted. Where, however, there were gaps in the numbers of one system but not of the other, the latter was allotted one or more successive numbers.*

At this time there were altogether 647 numbered lodges carried forward, plus the (Moderns') Grand Stewards' Lodge which kept its place at the head of the roll without a number.

There were further closings-up of numbers in 1832 and in 1863; the order and numbers stabilized in the latter year are likely to remain permanent and final, whether or not further lodges drop out.

The Lodge of Reconciliation (1813-16)

This lodge, appointed by the Articles of Union, included

---

*The last constituted Antients' lodge is Mount Sinai, now No. 121 at Penzance whose Warrant is dated but six days before the Grand Assembly of 27 December 1813 at which the Act of Union was ratified. The last lodge chartered by the premier Grand Lodge, in October 1813, survives as Unanimity No. 339 at Penrith.

THE LODGE OF RECONCILIATION

among its eighteen members some of the ablest ritualists of the day, and the present Craft working is vastly indebted to the labours of these brethren. The Rev. Dr. S. Hemming, a Modern mason, was the Worshipful Master.

In 1814 there was a certain amount of dissension about the obligations of the three degrees. This was fomented by Bro. J. H. Goldsworthy, Past Master of the Lodge of Fidelity No. 3 (who at its start was a member of the Lodge of Reconciliation and was later to become a member of the Board of General Purposes and a noted Preceptor), and by members of the Phoenix Lodge No. 289 and other Antient lodges.

But the trouble, which at one time threatened to develop into a schism, was patched up with the result that in Grand Lodge in 1816

> The Ceremonies and Practices, recommended by the Lodge of Reconciliation, were exhibited and explained; and alterations on two points in the Third Degree [one of which was that the Master's Light was never to be extinguished while the Lodge was open] having been resolved upon, the several Ceremonies . . . were approved and confirmed.

And so, its labours being ended, the lodge was thanked for its 'unremitting Zeal and Exertion' and ceased to be.

Another important result of the Act of Union was the setting up of the Board of General Purposes, which soon became a most important instrument of Grand Lodge.

Provincial Grand Lodges

A further result of the Union was the regularization of the Provincial Grand Lodges in something of their present shape. They had grown up, as the late R. W. Bro. W. R. S. Bathurst has pointed out,* as a result of a series of historical accidents. The first Provincial Grand Master was Col. Francis Columbine who, with Deputy and Wardens, was *elected* Grand Master Provincial for Cheshire by the Sun Lodge, Chester, in 1725. He presided over several local lodges when they dined together after a Church Service. His unofficial sort of Provincial Grand Lodge was tacitly recognized by Desaguliers, who as Deputy Grand Master visited Chester in 1727.

Grand Lodge, 1717-1967, Appendix B.

109

UNITED GRAND LODGE FREEMASONRY

In 1726 Grand Lodge had appointed two Provincial Grand Masters and by 1730 eleven had been appointed, five in England and Wales and six overseas. But neither Anderson in his 1738 *Book of Constitutions* nor the Rev. John Entick in that of 1756 makes any mention of Provincial Grand Lodges. In the latter's 1767 edition, however, Article III empowers Provincial Grand Masters to 'appoint a Deputy, Wardens, Treasurer, Secretary and Sword Bearer'. These Provincial Grand Officers were 'entitled to wear the Cloathing of Grand Officers while they officiate as such within that particular district'. They normally formed part of what R. W. Bro. Bathurst in his Prestonian Lecture (1966) termed a 'Pocket Provincial Grand Lodge', i.e. existing within a privileged lodge in the Province, usually the oldest, as the Sun Lodge had been in Chester in 1725. The Provincial Grand Master's chief function was to constitute new lodges in his Province. We have already mentioned Thomas Dunckerley's eight Provincial Grand Masterships between 1776 and 1790.

After the Union of 1813, Provincial Grand Lodges were recognized as such for the first time in the *Book of Constitutions* written by William Williams in 1815. Their members are to be the present and Past Provincial Grand Officers and the Masters, Past Masters and Wardens of every lodge in the Province. They must keep Minutes of their meetings, which must not be fewer than one a year. They may have a local charity fund. The officers' clothing is differentiated. Not until 1887 were any appreciable number of Provincial Grand Officers admitted to Past rank in Grand Lodge.

On rare occasions, when accusations against a Provincial Grand Master have had to be investigated (Bristol, 1814, and Somerset, 1819) or when the office has been in abeyance, as in the case of Lancashire just before its division into the Eastern and Western Divisions (1822-6), the Province has been placed under the jurisdiction of the Grand Registrar. Only one Provincial Grand Master has been deposed by the Grand Master. This was in 1853, when an example was made of William Tucker, the Provincial Grand Master for Dorset, for wearing the 'robe of the 33rd Degree'* over his Craft regalia.

In 1866, the title of 'Provinces' overseas was changed to

*There is no *robe* worn in England today for any of the regularly worked degrees of the Ancient and Accepted Rite.

PROVINCIAL GRAND LODGES

'Districts' but the Provincial and District Grand Masters rank together according to seniority.

The International Compact, 1814

With the establishment of the United Grand Lodge of England it became necessary for the sister Grand Lodges of Ireland and Scotland to be asssured that the working sanctioned by the new authority was in conformity with their own. Accordingly at the end of 1814 there took place at Freemasons' Hall an historic meeting between the Duke of Sussex, the Duke of Leinster, Grand Master of Ireland, and Lord Kinnaird, the Scots' Grand Master Mason, together with other brethren from the three Grand Lodges, and at this the eight resolutions that form the International Compact were unanimously agreed to.

By these the definition of pure Ancient Masonry was declared in the same wording as in the second Article of Union (*see* p. 107) and provision was made for a 'constant fraternal intercourse, correspondence and communion' to be maintained for ever between the three Grand Lodges, each agreeing not to issue Warrants for lodges within the others' jurisdiction.

Although the last of the resolutions ordered the circularization of the Compact to all lodges under the rule of the three Grand Lodges, the only known official record of it in full is contained in the Minutes of the Irish Grand Lodge.

The Book of Constitutions, 1815

New Constitutions were clearly necessary and these were published in 1815, the editor being Bro. W. Williams.* For the first time the fabled history of Freemasonry was omitted.

The Ancient Charges were scarcely altered, with the exception of the first, 'Concerning God and Religion' (*see* p. 77), which is now made to run:

> Let a man's religion or mode of worship be what it may, he is not excluded from the order, provided he believe in the glorious architect of heaven and earth, and practise the sacred duties of morality (*see* p. 132).

By the Regulations of 1815 Provincial Grand Masters

---

* Provincial Grand Master for Dorset, 1812-1839.

ranked after Past Deputy Grand Masters and before the Grand Wardens, while past rank was not to be given to the holder of any Grand office below that of Deacon. The least sum payable by an applicant for initiation was fixed at three guineas, which was raised in 1883 to five guineas in the case of lodges at home. The same Master was precluded from remaining in the chair for more than two years, and at least a month must elapse between different degrees for any one freemason. Official sanction, moreover, was for the first time given to the ceremony of consecrating a lodge.

The General Regulations were revised in 1818, the chief amendments being to restore to Grand Lodge the election of the Grand Treasurer and to add all Past Masters to the Masters and Wardens as admissible to Grand Lodge.

Lodges of Instruction and Preceptors

With the Union's newly agreed ritual, lodges of instruction began to flourish, fifteen existing in 1814. The most famous were the Stability Lodge (No. 217) of Instruction, founded in 1817, and the Emulation Lodge of Improvement which was founded six years later. While the systems taught by the two lodges now differ widely in detail, there is evidence that at one time they more nearly coincided. It must be remembered that the working of the Lodge of Reconciliation was not committed to writing and may have been variously recollected by those present; in 1836 the *Freemasons' Quarterly Review* (*see* p. 115) rebuked Emulation for lapses from the standard of accuracy demanded by Peter Gilkes, while in 1856 Bro. Muggeridge, leader of Stability, said that the differences between the two lodges' teaching were of form only and not of substance. The printed *aides-mémoire** came only gradually into general use.

In an age rich in Preceptors the following outstanding ones, all of whom were elected to the Board of General Purposes, must be briefly mentioned — Peter Gilkes, whose name was one to conjure with in the Emulation Lodge of Improvement;

---

*The first 'respectable' printed ritual — *i.e.* one that was not published as an exposure — was published in 1838. It was George Claret's *The Ceremonies of Initiation, Passing and Raising ... Opening and Closing in the Three Degrees ... with the Ceremony of Installing the W. Master and his Officers*. No printed ritual has ever been officially recognized.

LODGES OF INSTRUCTION

Lawrence Thompson, who by the Grand Master's command delivered for many years the Prestonian Lecture (*see* p. 97) in the Lodge of Antiquity No. 2; Peter Thomson, who became a Life Governor of all the Craft charities; Philip Broadfoot, a founder of the Stability Lodge of Instruction; and John Goldsworthy, already referred to in connexion with the Lodge of Reconciliation.†

Although all had colourful personalities and lived to a great age, they were not entirely free from jealousy, as witness Peter Gilkes's attempt in 1819 to induce Grand Lodge to suppress some unauthorized lectures by Philip Broadfoot. This came to nothing but is noteworthy as an early instance of the rivalry between Stability and Emulation workings.

Erasure of Lodge 31, 1821

The erasure of this Liverpool lodge arose out of the presentation of a Memorial to Grand Lodge through the Provincial Grand Lodge of Lancashire. When later the latter asked for its withdrawal the Duke of Sussex merely pigeonholed the document without informing either Grand Lodge or the Board of General Purposes of its receipt. Lodge No. 31 was far from satisfied, accused the Board of General Purposes of having detained the Memorial and protested rather contumaciously.

Other Lancashire lodges joined in and, after Grand Lodge's efforts at patient explanation and appeasement had proved of no avail, it became necessary to suspend sixty-eight masons belonging to eleven lodges. Subsequently forty-two duly submitted and were restored. The twenty-six recalcitrants were expelled and Lodge No. 31 was erased.

Thus was stamped out what might have led to a dangerous mutiny but the affair left behind much bitter feeling.

The Grand Lodge of Wigan, 1823

Four more erased and disgruntled Lancashire lodges formed a new Grand Lodge in 1823; it constituted six lodges of which only one, the Lodge Sincerity of Wigan (since 1913 chartered as No. 3677, E.C.), survives today. With occasional periods of dormancy the new Grand Lodge struggled on till about 1866

† For an excellent record of the activities of these, and many more, Preceptors the reader is recommended to refer to *Emulation – A Ritual to Remember* by Colin Dyer (1973).

UNITED GRAND LODGE FREEMASONRY

but Lodge Sincerity continued on its independent way for upwards of another forty years.

It was the privilege of one of the original authors of this work* to dine with one of the last surviving members of the 'Grand Lodge of Free and Accepted Masons of England according to the Old Institutions' of Wigan.

A Grand Lodge Library Started, 1837

This invaluable adjunct was added to Grand Lodge when on the suggestion of the Grand Registrar, Bro. John Henderson, £100 was voted for the purpose. In 1847 Bro. J. R. Scarborough proposed an annual grant of £20 to the library and museum, emphasizing

> the desirability of possessing the means of cultivating intellectuality more than gastronomy; that the other bottle did not do half so much good as the other volume, that it was laughable to tell a poor but inquiring brother to make a daily advance in masonic study — if we withheld from him the means of doing so, and did not even give him a hint where masonic knowledge could be gathered.

Although this was equally impressively seconded by Dr. Crucefix, of whom we shall be hearing more in next section, nothing much was done until 1880, when Grand Lodge voted an annual grant of £25 and added a Library Committee to the Board of General Purposes.

A Grand Lodge Librarian and (Museum) Curator was appointed in 1887,† and assistants in 1920; these offices have been occupied by masons of high scholastic attainment, who have proved their worth in the field of masonic research and in their unfailing helpfulness to inquiring students. Grand Lodge library now comprises nearly 30,000 volumes, as well as numerous valuable pamphlets and MSS.

The Royal Masonic Benevolent Institution, 1838-1976

We have already dealt with the start of two earlier charities (*see* p. 102). The third, although his was not the inception of the idea, will always be associated with the name of Dr. Robert

---

*the late Fred Pick.
†The brother appointed was Henry Sadler, the famous author of *Masonic Facts and Fictions* (1887) who was at the time also Grand Tyler.

THE BENEVOLENT INSTITUTION

Crucefix who, despite determined opposition from the highest quarters, nevertheless stoutly persevered in his laudable project for the erection of an Asylum for Worthy and Decayed Freemasons, as the charity was at first called. He even started the *Freemasons' Quarterly Review*, which he edited for several years, to provide propaganda for the cause.

At the first meeting of subscribers, held in June, 1835, Bro. Crucefix, who presided, was able to announce that the Earl of Durham (Deputy Grand Master) and the Grand Treasurer had agreed to act as trustees. A few weeks later, however, the Earl withdrew, stating that he had been under the impression that the consent of the Duke of Sussex had been obtained.

When that Prince was tackled it was found that he had numerous objections to the scheme, at first on the grounds that a third charity could only harm the existing ones, and that the proposed Asylum would 'tend to hold out an inducement for an improper class of individuals to enter the Fraternity', and later because he preferred a system of annuities to the erection of a building. Meanwhile Bro. Crucefix, who was Junior Grand Deacon, had in 1837 obtained from Grand Lodge a unanimous resolution recommending the contemplated Asylum to the favourable consideration of the Craft.

Then in 1840, owing to the Grand Master's continued opposition, came a clash between Grand Lodge and Dr. Crucefix, caused by the latter's having printed certain proceedings of Grand Lodge in his *Review* — he had already been suspended in connexion with remarks made at an Asylum Committee meeting. It was proposed to expel him from the Society, but this fate was averted by his making a very humble apology.

In 1842 Grand Lodge launched the Duke of Sussex's rival scheme in the shape of the 'Royal Masonic Benevolent Annuity Fund' and in 1849 the scheme was extended to cover a Widows' Fund.

In spite of the theft by an absconding trustee of its funds, amounting to £620, the Asylum Committee did not lose sight of its object and, a site having been found near Croydon, the foundation stone of a building to house fifty annuitants was laid in May, 1849.

Next year came the eagerly awaited amalgamation of the Asylum and the Annuity Fund, the two charities being united

UNITED GRAND LODGE FREEMASONRY

under the style of the Royal Masonic Benevolent Institution for Aged Freemasons and their Widows. Unfortunately Bro. Crucefix did not live to see this final fruition for which he had striven so valorously.

In 1876 the annuities were increased to £40 for each brother and £32 for each widow. The full rates today are £210 for a married brother and £140 for a bachelor, widower, widow, spinster daughter or spinster sister of a deceased freemason. In 1974 the Institution was paying annuities to over 2,200 beneficiaries. The cost of annuities, funeral grants and Christmas gifts in that year amounted to nearly £225,000.

The story of the Institution is one of increasing progress and its record of care of the elderly is outstanding. In 1955 the Croydon Home was replaced by a newly erected block of 104 very modern flats named Harewood Court at Hove, Sussex. (This now has 100 flats, but also a 4-bedded sick bay and a supervisory wing with 25 bed-sitting rooms.) The Institution in 1962 extended its objectives by deciding to build additional homes in which residential accommodation and nursing care would be provided not only for annuitants but also for those freemasons and their dependants who were of limited financial resources but were able to make a contribution towards their stay in the homes. These new homes are erected in different parts of the country and 1966 saw the completion of the first of the original 'trinity' when Devonshire Court was opened at Oadby, Leicestershire, by Queen Elizabeth, the Queen Mother. Scarbrough Court at Cramlington in Northumberland was opened by Princess Alexandra in 1967, and the third – Prince George Duke of Kent Court at Chislehurst in Kent – which was to have been opened by his widow, Princess Marina, was in fact opened by her son, the Most Worshipful Grand Master in 1968 as she lay stricken by her last illness.

The next home, Connaught Court, Fulford, York, was opened in 1971 by H.R.H. the Duchess of Kent. The building of Lord Harris Court, Sindlesham, Berkshire (named after the then Grand Master of Mark Masonry) was made possible by the magnificent gift of £500,000 from Mark Grand Lodge to celebrate the centenary of the Mark Benevolent Fund. This home received its first residents in October 1972 and was officially opened in May of the following year by the Grand Master of the Craft.

THE BENEVOLENT INSTITUTION

The newest home of the Royal Masonic Benevolent Institution, Albert Edward Prince of Wales Court, Porthcawl, South Wales, was opened in 1973 by M. W. Bro. The Earl Cadogan, Pro Grand Master, who had laid its foundation stone in 1970. In 1975 over 650 residents were accommodated in the seven homes of the Institution. There are plans to build three more by 1980 and work was begun on the first of these at Llandudno in 1975, to be ready for occupation by 1977.

The Bagnall Report, published in 1974 (*see* p. 141), stated quite clearly that the work of the Royal Masonic Benevolent Institution must continue and that the standard of the homes maintained by the Institution should not be reduced. The Committee of Management of the Institution considered at a special meeting the main recommendations of the Bagnall Report as they related to the work of the Institution and decided as a matter of policy to continue the nursing of residents who are ill within the homes and, additionally, to provide facilities for the care of the chronic sick and to admit such residents to special care units. The Committee at that meeting was entirely in favour of amalgamating with the Board of Benevolence but was opposed to any amalgamation with the Royal Masonic Hospital.

There were other aspects of the Bagnall Report which did not meet with the Committee's approval but the members were unanimous in their intention that the work of the Royal Masonic Benevolent Institution should not only be continued but should be expanded to meet the growing need of the aged.

It is wonderfully encouraging to be able to report that the 1976 Festival of the Institution, under the presidency of Lord Swansea, Provincial Grand Master for South Wales (Eastern Division) raised the record amount of £1,508,825 to enable those intentions to be advanced. That sum was, in fact, a record for any Masonic Festival.

The Girls' School, 1813-1975

At the Union both the Royal Masonic Institution for Girls and that for boys became available equally to the children of both Atholl Masons and Moderns. In 1814 it was resolved by Grand Lodge that the charge of registering new-made masons initiated in London should be one guinea, of which five shillings would be applied towards the maintenance of the schools,

UNITED GRAND LODGE FREEMASONRY

and in the case of initiations in distant, foreign and military lodges the charge should be half-a-guinea, of which two and sixpence would be similarly applied.

In 1851 a new girls' school (*see* p. 102) was built facing Wandsworth Common and was dedicated by the Earl of Zetland (Grand Master) at a Grand Lodge meeting specially held at the school. Up to about 1858 the general conception of an orphanage or 'charity school' still prevailed and the training fitted the pupils to be little more than domestic servants. Since then, however, the curriculum has been completely modernized and the education now provided can rank with that of any girls' school anywhere.

In 1918 a Junior School, which accommodated a hundred little girls between the ages of seven and ten, was opened at Weybridge and this school continued successfully and celebrated its jubilee in 1968. With the passing of the years, however, it was found that there was less demand for boarding school places for girls taking their junior education and in 1973, owing to the falling-off in the number of pupils, the cost per girl became uneconomic. So, with the greatest regret, the Committee decided that the school should be closed.

In 1934 the then Senior School was moved from Wandsworth to magnificent new buildings, situated in 315 acres of parkland at Rickmansworth, Hertfordshire. The opening was performed by H.M. Queen Mary. Here some 400 girls are being educated and a further 350 are receiving 'out-education' at training colleges, universities and other schools. making a total of nearly 800 who are provided for by the Institution.

A Royal Charter was granted to the Royal Masonic Institution for Girls in 1952. Two years later the Duchess of Kent laid the foundation stone of the new domestic science wing. The fine Halsey Memorial Pavilion was presented by the Province of Hertfordshire in 1957 and during the next year the Mark Centenary Hall, the gift of Grand Lodge of Mark Master Masons, was opened. The senior school was visited by H.M. Queen Elizabeth II in 1955 and by H.R.H. Princess Alexandra in 1961.

An extensive building programme (1967-9) provided a new science block with the most up-to-date equipment; a new library, to encourage research; two residential blocks for the staff; also alterations to the existing school houses to allow for

ats for the house mistresses and matrons and eighty study/
bedrooms for sixth form girls. A second film of the School has
also been produced and is available to lodges.

The Institution's annual expenditure now runs at £8-900,000.
The highest amount raised at one of its Festivals was at its
84th (held in 1972), sponsored by the Province of East
Lancashire. This totalled £1,129,544.

The Boys' School, 1813-1975

This Charity which, as already stated on page 102, had been
started by the Antients, was amalgamated in 1817 with a
similar one which had been originated by Bro. F. Columbine
Daniel and other members of the (Moderns') Royal Naval
Lodge No. 59 in 1808. The combined masonic institution
became 'Royal' on King William IV's agreeing to act as its
Patron in 1832. In 1838 Grand Lodge's annual contribution
was fixed at £150. It has today risen to £2,000.

In 1856 the first school building was bought at Wood
Green, London, where the erection of a larger school was
begun in 1862, the premises being opened three years later by
the Earl de Grey and Ripon, then Deputy Grand Master. They
were extended in 1873 and again in 1883 through the
generosity of the Craft.

The Prince of Wales presided at the Centenary celebrations
in 1898 when the collection of the then record sum of
£141,000 made possible the erection of the Institution's
school buildings at Bushey, Hertfordshire. These were completed in 1902 and in 1929 a junior school was added; as an
economic measure this was merged with the senior school in
1970.

The Royal Masonic Institution for Boys, which received a
Charter of Incorporation from King George V in 1926, subsequently amended by Supplemental Charters in 1958 and
1966, provided in 1975 educational benefits for over 600
boys, nearly 400 of whom were then still in the Bushey school.
The remainder were being assisted at schools elsewhere or were
obtaining higher education.

In 1975, however, it was decided by the Court of the Institution with the very greatest reluctance and regret that the
school must be closed not later than 31 August 1977. This was
to avoid further and even greater differences between income

and expenditure, the greater part of the discrepancy being due to the cost of running the school.

This decision had been arrived at quite independently of the recommendation of the *Bagnall Report* (*see* p. 141), which had suggested that either the school would have to amalgamate with the Royal Masonic Girls' School to form one coeducational establishment or else it would have to close down.

All the alternatives to closure had received full deliberation and discussion:

(1) Merger with the girls' school was ruled out as involving an operation of great complexity which would necessitate a capital outlay of millions of pounds, so that by the time that the scheme would have been put into full operation the Institution's finances would have been completely exhausted.

(2) A special appeal to the Craft, if allowed, would do no more than defer for a few years the insolvency of the Institution at the then rate of expenditure.

(3) The admission of some day pupils paying full economic fees, as is the practice in the girls' school, would have no significant effect on the Institution's financial future, while also it would not be in accordance with the provision of the Royal Charter which states that 'the primary object of the Institution shall be to benefit those sons of Freemasons who are in need'. It is from this clause that its whole charitable status is derived.

Those boys still at the school when it would be closed would be found suitable places at either day- or boarding-schools in accordance with the parents' choice.

The sale of the school buildings and their valuable site would provide a useful contribution to the Institution's ailing funds. But it was stressed that the closure would not mean any lessening of the real need for the Craft's support.

The 159th Anniversary Festival in June 1970 brought a record total of £687,647, of which the Province of Kent alone contributed no less a sum than £566,262.

An interesting development has been the formation of Old Masonians' Lodges, of which five now exist: No. 2700 (London, 1898); No. 6762 (Midland, at Handsworth, 1948); No. 7322 (Northern, at Salford, 1953); No. 7658 (Middlesex, at Kenton, 1957); No. 7702 (West Lancashire, at Liverpool, 1960). After the closure of the Boys' School in 1976, however, it is difficult to see how those excellent lodges will be able to survive for more than a limited period so long as their recruitment of new members is confined to Old Masonians.

The Duke of Sussex, Grand Master, 1813-43

We must now return from the present time to the second decade of the nineteenth century. Something has already been said of the Duke's share in the achievement of a United Grand Lodge of England. In 1838, to commemorate his twenty-five years' Grand Mastership, the Craft presented him with a testimonial valued at one thousand guineas, and when he died in 1843 he had ruled over English freemasons for the then record period* of thirty years. The Earl of Zetland succeeded him as Grand Master until 1870.

Although the Duke of Sussex exercised his powers in a somewhat arbitrary and dictatorial manner, as seen in his dealings with Lodge 31 and Dr. Crucefix, there was no other Modern (with the exception of the Earl of Moira) who could have retained the loyal fidelity of such (Antient) Past Deputy Grand Masters as Agar and Harper for the rest of their lives and enjoyed the complete trust of the whole English Craft.

Of his brother, King William IV, it is related that once when a deputation of influential freemasons waited on him, expecting a ceremonious audience, they were somewhat astonished when 'gentlemen,' exclaimed the bluff Sailor King, who was Grand Patron of the Craft, 'if my love for you equalled my ignorance of everything concerning you, it would be boundless!'

An Impostor, 1847

It is not often that Grand Lodge allows itself to be hoodwinked but it so happened in 1847, when a visiting American, who styled himself Major-General George Cooke, LL.D., and gave out that he was Chancellor of the University of Ripley, joined the Prince of Wales's Lodge No. 259. A generous supporter of the masonic charities, he became Vice-President of the Girls' School and a Life Governor of the Boys' School and of the Benevolent Institution.

---

*The actual record was the thirty-eight year reign of the Duke of Connaught (1901-39) (*see* p. 124). This was exceeded in Ireland by the Duke of Leinster, who was Grand Master for sixty-one years. (*See* pp. 162-3.)

UNITED GRAND LODGE FREEMASONRY

Before he left England the Grand Master conferred on him the rank of Past Grand Warden and appointed him his representative at the Grand Lodge of New York. A fund was even raised for the purpose of putting his bust in Freemasons' Hall. It was not until Cooke was safely back in the States that it came to light that so far from being a Major-General or a Doctor of Laws he was in reality a mere medical quack who advertised his wares.

He was accordingly stripped of his masonic rank, expelled from Grand Lodge and reimbursed the sums he had subscribed to the charities.

John Havers

John Havers, a pupil of Peter Thomson whom he called the greatest mason he had ever known, was in 1855 'the most disliked brother in the Craft' and even described himself as 'an incendiary and red republican', but lived to be entertained by his old opponents and to have his bust placed in Freemasons' Hall.

In that year the Craft was at the dictation of Bro. W. H. White, who had served as Grand Secretary for no less than forty-six years and of three other influential Grand Officers, and was seething with unrest, largely because Grand rank seemed to be the perquisite of three or four London lodges. The Earl of Zetland, the Grand Master, then placed John Havers, P.S.G.D., in charge of affairs and, within three years, he had largely succeeded in restoring harmony.

John Havers became Junior Grand Warden in 1862 and was for many years on the Board of General Purposes and on the Committee of Management of the Masonic Benevolent Annuity Fund (*see* p. 115).

A New Freemasons' Hall, 1866

The building of the second Hall was started in 1864. An improvement on the old Hall but of course nothing like as commodious or impressive as the present Masonic Peace Memorial (*see* p. 127), it took just under two years to complete. For the first time Freemasons' Tavern (now the Connaught Rooms) was separated from the Hall.

During the reconstruction, the Building Committee, under the chairmanship of John Havers, found the great chairs which had — with the great throne (*see* p. 135) — been made for the Grand Master and his two Wardens in the days when the Prince of Wales (later George IV) had been at the head of the Craft. Repaired and re-gilded, the chairs have since been reserved for their original purpose.

After a disastrous fire in 1883, by which the Grand Temple was almost completely destroyed as well as most of the portraits of previous Grand Masters, the building was reconstructed and the Temple enlarged.

Some Masonic Miscreants

Although they have been fortunately few and far between, there have been occasional black sheep and backsliders in the Craft. The case of Bro. Dr. William Dodd, the forger who rose to be Grand Chaplain, has already been mentioned on page 100. Then there have been two brethren who were notorious poisoners. One of these was Dr. Edward William Pritchard, who had been initiated in Winchester and was a Past Master of lodges in Scarborough and district as well as one in Glasgow; he was hanged in 1865 for administering antimony to his wife and mother-in-law in the last named city; he may also have been guilty of murdering a maidservant.

The other was Frederick Henry Seddon, a miserly murderer who in 1911 poisoned a woman lodger with arsenic, obtained (it was said) from fly-papers. Having defrauded her of all her savings during her lifetime, he caused his victim to be buried in a pauper's grave, charging the undertaker 7s. 6d. commission for recommending him.

It is related that during his trial at the Old Bailey, under relentless pressure in cross-examination, he made signs of distress to Mr. Justice Bucknill whom Seddon knew to be a prominent mason. But the judge promptly rebuked him, saying that if the prisoner did not desist he would order a retrial before another judge.

When asked if he had anything to say before sentence, 'I declare,' said Seddon, 'before the Great Architect of the Universe, I am not guilty, my Lord.'

The judge was deeply moved as the black cap was placed on his head. When he was able to speak, he said:

You and I know that we both belong to the same brother-

hood and it is all the more painful for me to have to s…
what I am saying. But our brotherhood does not encoura…
crime; on the contrary, it condemns it. I pray you again…
make your peace with the Great Architect of the Univers…

The prisoner was then sentenced to death.

Grand Masters, 1870-1939

When the Earl of Zetland gave up his Grand Mastership…
1870, he was presented with a testimonial in the form…
£2,730, which he transferred to the Zetland Fund for t…
relief of distinguished brethren who might become distresse…
He was succeeded by the Marquess of Ripon (then Earl…
Grey and Ripon) who resigned four years later on becoming…
Roman Catholic.

His successor in 1874 was the Prince of Wales whose Insta…
lation ceremony at the Royal Albert Hall was attended by t…
largest assembly of freemasons that had ever met. Two yea…
later his brother, the Duke of Connaught, became Senic…
Grand Warden, and in 1886 the Duke was made Provinci…
Grand Master for Sussex — the first time such an office ha…
been held by a Prince of the Blood Royal. During his visit t…
India in 1875, the Prince of Wales was presented by th…
masons of Bengal with a magnificent casket of gold and silve…
elaborately embellished with emblems of Craft and Roy…
Arch Masonry. This was graciously presented to United Gran…
Lodge Museum by H.M. Queen Elizabeth II in 1967.

When the Prince of Wales ascended the Throne in 1901 a…
King Edward VII, he resigned his Grand Mastership an…
became Protector of the Craft. He was intensely devoted t…
Freemasonry and wore a special masonic ring, to be seen i…
his portrait by Fildes in Freemasons' Hall. His Majesty was sti…
wearing it when he died in 1910.

He was succeeded as Grand Master by the Duke o…
Connaught whose thirty-eight years' reign was marked by th…
greatest success and prosperity of the Craft. These, in som…
difficult years, were largely due to the active interest taken b…
the Pro Grand Master (1908-35), Lord Ampthill, the Deput…
Grand Master (1903-26), Sir Frederick Halsey, and the Presi…
dent of the Board of General Purposes (1913-31), Sir Alfre…
Robbins, who was also the first Chairman of the Peac…
Memorial Committee.

LONDON (GRAND) RANK

London (Grand) Rank, 1908

The members of London lodges (i.e. those held within ten miles of Freemasons' Hall) had long felt it somewhat unfair that, unlike their brethren in the Provinces and Districts, they were ineligible for honours intermediate between those conferred in private lodges and office in Grand Lodge itself. Accordingly Grand Lodge decided in 1907 that there should be instituted a new rank to be called London Rank, with distinctive regalia. The Grand Master was empowered to confer this award upon a certain number of Past Masters of London lodges who had rendered long and meritorious service. There were 598 brethren originally appointed to London Rank in 1908, but the number of annual recipients thereafter was at first limited to 150, being increased to 263 three years later. In 1930 annual awards were fixed at one for every three London lodges, recently revised to one for every two. Since 1933 the rank has been conferred by official investiture in the Grand Stewards' Lodge by the Assistant Grand Master. London *Grand* Rank became the official designation in 1939. In 1961 it was enacted that for 'members' and 'recipients' of London Grand Rank there should be substituted the title 'holders'. Although it is not an office, it is roughly the equivalent of Provincial or District Grand office and the holders can enjoy a corporate character by joining the London Grand Rank Association, which has now over 8,000 members. In the words of a Secretary of that Association, London Grand Rank is, 'the most democratic honour that is conferred in Freemasonry, after election to the chair of a lodge. It is, as it were, a peerage conferred by one's peers.'

(A comparable honour, Overseas Grand Rank, exists for conferment upon Past Masters of lodges overseas which are not governed by a District Grand Master but are under Grand Inspectors or administered directly by Grand Lodge.)

A similar award for London Royal Arch masons is known as London Grand Chapter Rank.

There are now senior levels of London Grand and London Grand Chapter Ranks to which promotions can be made after long and worthy service in the basic ranks.

Bicentenary of Grand Lodge, 1917

This was duly celebrated in the middle of the first World

UNITED GRAND LODGE FREEMASONRY

War. Nearly 8,000 freemasons then met at the Royal Alb
Hall under the presidency of the Duke of Connaught. Ev
more brethren attended the Masonic Peace Celebrations in t
same building two years later, no fewer than 500 coming fr
overseas jurisdictions and Districts and from Ireland a
Scotland.

The Royal Masonic Hospital

This extremely efficient and useful institution was fi
suggested in 1911, and the proposal was approved by Gra
Lodge in 1913. During the first World War three nursing hom
were maintained at different times for wounded soldiers (n
necessarily freemasons); these were situated in the Fulha
Road and the Bishop of London's Palace at Fulham, and
Caversham, near Reading. After the war the old Chels
Women's Hospital in Fulham Road was opened as a Fre
masons' Nursing Home, the first patient (the wife of a Ber
shire mason) being admitted in June 1920.

Its immense popularity and the fact that it could on
accommodate fifty beds produced huge waiting lists, and
became clear that a much larger building was needed. Accor
ingly, as soon as funds permitted, a five-acre site was acquir
at Ravenscourt Park; here was built at a cost of £335,000 th
present four-storied structure which so admirably fulfils th
purposes for which it was founded.

This beautiful building, equipped with every modern devic
was opened in 1933 by King George V, who was accompanie
by Queen Mary and gave permission for it to be called fro
thenceforth the Royal Masonic Hospital. It had beds for 18
patients.

Between 1940 and 1948 no fewer than 8,600 militar
patients were treated (again without distinction and withou
charge). The hospital was not affected by the National Healt
Service Act 1946 and retains its independent status.

The Foundation Stone of a considerable extension at th
back of the hospital was laid by the Grand Master in 1956 an
two years later this was opened by H.M. Queen Elizabeth th
Queen Mother, who named it the Wakefield Wing. The ne
wing, which cost about £950,000, provides room for a
additional eighty patients, making a total of 270 beds in all.
also houses the new Chapel, which was dedicated by th

THE ROYAL MASONIC HOSPITAL

bishop of London, and the Nurses' Training School, which had been started in 1949 and has more applications for entry than there are vacancies, but preference is always given to applicants from the Royal Masonic Institution for Girls.

In 1963 the remaining unopened ward of the Wakefield Wing was converted to form a Geriatric Unit. Two years later, when this rehabilitation scheme had already achieved considerable success, Grand Lodge, which supports the hospital (unlike the three Institutions) only by grants for specific objects, voted the sum of £10,000 towards the new unit. Similarly, in 1959, Grand Lodge had donated £23,131 for the purchase of X-ray equipment.

A new Intensive Care Unit was completed in 1966, its equipment including every available electronic and mechanical device for the treatment of serious heart trouble.

Of the ninety or so patients admitted to the Hospital every week, some thirty-five are emergency cases and two or three come from overseas.

In 1933 was also opened

The Masonic Peace Memorial

This was the name given to the new Freemasons' Hall and masonic Headquarters in Great Queen Street, which has many masonic traditions, although some brethren wanted to see it situated in the Adelphi, which has none. The foundation ceremony was held in 1927 at the Royal Albert Hall, whence the Duke of Connaught laid the foundation stone by electrical contact.

The architects were Bros H. V. Ashley and Winton Newman. Over the main entrance at the corner of Long Acre is a 150-foot tower (slightly higher than Nelson's Column). The Grand Temple on the first floor is 120 feet in length, 90 feet in breadth and 62 feet high, and in addition there are nineteen Temples for private lodges. There is a fine Library combined with a Museum, roughly four times as big as that in the former Hall and further extended in 1961.

The building was at first estimated to cost one million pounds, but this figure was considerably exceeded; the sum needed was raised by an ingenious scheme whereby the 1,321 lodges contributing an amount averaging ten guineas per member were declared Hall Stone Lodges, while upon every

UNITED GRAND LODGE FREEMASONRY

mason making that subscription was conferred a commemorative jewel of the Masonic Million Memorial Fund.

The Dedication Ceremony was impressive and was attended by distinguished representatives of every jurisdiction with which the United Grand Lodge is in communion, and there were present masons from all over the world, literally 'from China to Peru'.*

Grand Masters, 1939-67

When for health reasons the Duke of Connaught resigned in 1939 after a record period of thirty-eight years, H.R.H. George Duke of Kent was installed in his stead by King George VI who like his brother the Duke of Windsor (previously King Edward VIII) held the rank of Past Grand Master. Three years later the Duke of Kent died tragically on active service and thus came to an end a memorable stretch of sixty-eight years during which three Royal Grand Masters had ruled the Craft

His successor, the Earl of Harewood, did not reign much longer since he died in 1947. Again, the 10th Duke of Devonshire, who was elected in his place and was installed early in 1948, died after holding the office for only three years. Thus three successive Grand Masters had died prematurely in only eight years.

The Earl of Scarbrough was installed as Grand Master in November 1951. It is a striking fact that the 4th Baron Shuttleworth, who on that occasion took his place as Junior Grand Warden, is a direct descendant of the third Grand Master, Dr. Desaguliers (*see* p. 73), thus forging a Grand Lodge link 233 years long.

H.M. King George VI

The death of this Royal freemason on 6th February 1952 was a severe blow to the Craft. His Majesty created the precedent of an English Sovereign's actively participating in masonic ceremonies, and this before crowded assemblies. Thus on his accession he accepted (as mentioned above) the rank of Past Grand Master. He was ceremonially installed at the Royal Albert Hall before an audience of masons from all parts of the world.

Similarly he conducted in person the installation of three

* Dr. Samuel Johnson, 'Variety of Human Wishes', line 2.

KING GEORGE VI

Grand Masters — the Duke of Kent at Olympia in July 1939; the Earl of Harewood at Freemasons' Hall in June 1943; and the Duke of Devonshire at the Royal Albert Hall in March 1948. Only his last illness prevented him from installing the Earl of Scarbrough in November 1951.

King George entered Freemasonry by way of the Navy Lodge No. 2612 in December 1919, when he was Duke of York; in 1922 he was appointed Senior Grand Warden; two years later he was installed as Provincial Grand Master for Middlesex, which office he retained until coming to the Throne in 1936. He was also Grand Master Mason of Scotland for part of that year (*see* p. 196).

He himself always regarded Freemasonry as one of the strongest influences on his life.

The Order of Service to Masonry, 1945

The Earl of Harewood announced in 1945 the institution of a new distinction to be known as 'The Grand Master's Order of Service to Masonry'. The recipients, limited to twelve at any one time, were at first confined to brethren holding Grand rank, in which the distinction entitled them to rank immediately above Grand Deacons, with the prefix of Very Worshipful and the letters O.S.M. placed after the name. To the regalia was added a special jewel appended to a garter-blue collarette. The first four appointments to the Order were made in 1946.

In 1960, by which time the Order of Service to Masonry had been conferred on eighteen Grand Officers in all, the Earl of Scarbrough proposed and it was enacted that it should cease to be one of the seventy-two ranks in the masonic hierarchy of Grand Officers. The award can now accordingly be granted to any brother, depending solely on his outstandingly distinguished service to the Craft and on the limitation of the number of awards. The first ordinary brother to receive the Order was the late Bro. Reginald Easton, Secretary of Whittington Lodge No. 862, which had built up a great chain of links with overseas lodges.

'Freemasonry in the Dock,' 1951-2

An attack on Freemasonry had been launched in the Pastoral Session of the Methodist Conference of 1927 by the Rev. C. Penney Hunt. It was not very successful and the excellent

UNITED GRAND LODGE FREEMASONRY

and efficient Epworth lodges, where many Methodist divines and laymen meet 'on the level', continue to exercise a beneficial influence in several large centres of population.

It would be a fairly safe conjecture to assume that the great majority of English freemasons belong to the Church of England, whether as merely 'C. of E.' (as the Army recruit who does not claim to belong to any 'fancy religion' is conveniently labelled) or as ardent adherents. The late Lord Fisher of Lambeth, Archbishop of Canterbury from 1945 to 1961, was Grand Chaplain in 1937 and 1939 while there are numerous, devout priests who serve as Chaplains of Grand Lodges and lodges. It came, therefore, as something of a shock when an attack was launched on the Order by a group of Anglican parsons.

The trouble started with an article in *Theology* (issued under the auspices of the Society for Promoting Christian Knowledge) in January 1951; it was entitled 'Should a Christian be a Freemason?' and was from the pen of the Rev. Walton Hannah who answered his question to his own satisfaction in the negative, pointing to the secret oaths and drastic penalties implicit in Freemasonry, accusing it of being gnostic, declaring that the Order had been banned by the Roman Catholics and denounced by the Methodists and demanding that the Church should at least hold an inquiry.

There was a sequel in June, when the Church Assembly in annual session debated a motion tabled by the Rev. R. Creed Meredith,* that a commission be appointed to report on Mr. Hannah's article.

After stating that Freemasonry had been placed in the dock, Mr. Meredith defined the Order as 'a brotherhood of princes, prelates and peers, and a great body of ordinary men .... It is a brotherhood which seeks after truth, encourages members to uphold one another in the highest moral principles and in strict honesty of purpose and integrity in all matters of business.' The attack had given pain and distress to hundreds of loyal churchmen up and down the country.

The Rev. K. Healey said that, if Freemasonry could attain a measure of reform from within, its efforts would be received with joy and sympathy. The Rev. C. E. Douglas stated that in

---
*A son of Sir James Creed Meredith, Deputy Grand Master of Ireland from 1897 to 1911.

'FREEMASONRY IN THE DOCK'

the last 250 years Freemasonry had been one of the greatest factors in the building of modern civilization. 'You cannot understand Freemasonry except in a lodge. Its real secret is fellowship.'

The *then* Archbishop of York then rose; after stating that he was not a freemason and had never been one, he said: 'Freemasonry in this country has always avoided the anticlericalism which makes it offensive on the continent. It has never made any attack on Christianity and the Church.' Dr. Garbett then asked whom would the proposed Commission reassure? 'I am reassured [turning to Archbishop Fisher of Canterbury, who was presiding] by your Grace's being a member of the Order and by the fact that a distinguished layman, Lord Scarbrough, is Grand Master of the Order . . .'

The Assembly then rejected the motion with only one dissentient, a result which the mover explained he welcomed and had hoped for.

Like Mr. Hunt before him, Mr. Hannah saw fit to expand his attack into book form, which was given some publicity, unfortunately, by the more sensation-loving press of the day. As in the case of all its predecessors — a too long and wearisome line stretching back to the days *before* Grand Lodge — the attack was quite unsuccessful. More recently (and insidiously) the British Broadcasting Corporation joined in the fray, televising in March 1965 its glaringly inaccurate version of certain ceremonies. The producer, James Dewar (a nonmason), invoked also the testimony of such notable antagonists of the Order as Walton Hannah (who had been received into the Roman Catholic Church and who died shortly after appearing in the programme) and Lord Soper. To its credit, Independent Television deliberately refrained then from producing a similar programme. Mr. Dewar likewise published his researches in (illustrated) book form.

Masonic ceremonies in some detail have since been included, from time to time, in televised plays, serious and humorous, giving alas a very false impression of the purposes of the Craft and of the quality of the vast majority of its members.

The Duke of Edinburgh

H.R.H. the Duke of Edinburgh was initiated in the Navy

UNITED GRAND LODGE FREEMASONRY

Lodge No. 2612, on the 5th December 1952, being passed and raised the next year.

This was the lodge in which His Majesty King George VI, then Duke of York, was initiated in 1919, and H.R.H. the Duke of Kent in 1928.

Sir Sydney White

In 1958 there died 'a great Grand Secretary' — to quote M. W. Bro. the Earl of Scarbrough — in the person of R. W. Bro. Sir Sydney White, K.C.V.O., P.J.G.W., who had served Grand Lodge for forty years, having joined the Staff as Chief Clerk in 1918 and been appointed Assistant Grand Secretary in 1934 and Grand Secretary three years later. He was succeeded by W. Bro. J. W. Stubbs* who had been Deputy Grand Secretary since 1955.

Masonry and Religion

The relationships between English Freemasonry and religion were defined by Grand Lodge in 1961. The resulting cessation of some old practices has perhaps not met with universal acclaim. A report of the Board of General Purposes, all but one clause of which was adopted, starts by strongly asserting that 'Masonry is neither a religion nor a substitute for religion ... nor a competitor with religion, though in the sphere of human conduct it may be hoped that its teaching will be complementary to that of religion.' But it both requires a man to have some form of religious belief before he can be admitted as a mason and expects him thereafter to go on practising his religion.

It was decided that masonic rites, prayers and ceremonies should in future be confined to the lodge room and that there should be no active participation by masons as such in any part of the burial service or cremation of a brother. It was further agreed that only in rare cases should dispensations be granted for wearing regalia at acts of corporate worship and 'moreover that the order of service should in all cases be such as the officiating minister considers to be appropriate to the occasion'.

In 1963 it was decided that care must be taken that no

---

*In 1964 V. W. Bro. Stubbs was appointed to the rank of Past Junior Grand Warden.

vocal music is used in lodge that is identified exclusively with a particular form of divine worship, or lacks the sanction of the Grand Master (in respect of London lodges) or of the Provincial Grand Master concerned.

Courts of Appeal established, 1963

It having become evident that Grand Lodge was too unwieldy a body for the proper consideration of appeals from decisions of Provincial and District Grand Masters and the Board of General Purposes, its powers in this respect were delegated to a Commission consisting of five distinguished legal brethren nominated by the Grand Master and twenty-four brethren (half from the Provinces and half from London lodges) elected by Grand Lodge. In the event of an appeal, the Grand Master nominates one of the five to preside and the latter selects not fewer than six other members of the Commission to sit with him as a Court of Appeal whose decisions, arrived at by a majority vote, are final. It can *recommend* expulsion or erasure, but these sentences can still be ordered only by Grand Lodge.

The Obligation Penalties

There had arisen among English freemasons a growing dislike of the barbarous wording of the Penalties, which had already been modified (compulsorily) in Ireland and (permissively) in Scotland (*see* pp. 170 and 197). The Penalties had long formed the basis of most of the external attacks on Freemasonry. When the subject[*] was debated by Grand Lodge in December, 1964, so intense was the interest that there was not even standing room for latecomers to the Grand Temple.

R. W. Bro. Bishop Herbert, Provincial Grand Master for Norfolk, then moved that 'The Grand Lodge hereby approves the following permissive variation in each of the three degrees, viz.: in place of the words "under no less a penalty on the violation of any of them than that of having . . ." the words "ever bearing in mind the traditional penalty on the violation of any of them, that of having . . .".' In the original motion the

---

[*] Critical attention to the Penalties had been focused by an admirable paper, read before the Quatuor Coronati Lodge earlier in the year (*A.Q.C.* 77) by W. Bro. J. Rylands, P.J.G.D. With the many comments, this was at once printed and was widely circulated well before the debate in Grand Lodge.

word before 'penalty' in the wording to be substituted had been 'ancient' but this was amended to 'traditional' on the suggestion (accepted by Bishop Herbert) of the seconder, W. Bro. Harry Carr, who pointed out that the phrase 'ancient penalty' might be interpreted as implying that the fearsome mutilations had in fact been carried out in time gone by. On a show of hands, the Grand Master declared the motion, as thus amended, to have been carried by a large majority.

The changed wording resembles what has been used throughout Irish lodges since 1894; the option for lodges to adopt it is more like the Scottish practice.

Edward George, Duke of Kent, Grand Master, 1967

On June 14th M. W. Bro. the Earl of Scarbrough, who had himself been installed Grand Master for the 17th time in March, proposed the election of H.R.H. the Duke of Kent, thus bringing to an end the twenty-five years interregnum (as it were) when — since the death of his father, George, Duke of Kent — there had been no royal ruler of the Craft. The new Grand Master's first act after his election was to appoint his predecessor as Pro Grand Master. The third masonic Duke of Kent — his great-great-great grandfather had been in 1813 the last Grand Master of the Antients and the last Deputy Grand Master of the Moderns (*see* p. 106) — this personable young soldier prince (b. 1935), who had been initiated in the unique Royal Alpha Lodge No. 16 in 1963 and passed and raised in the same lodge the following year, had been appointed Senior Grand Warden in 1966. He was installed as Grand Master at an Especial Grand Lodge held at the Royal Albert Hall on 27th June 1967, to celebrate

Grand Lodge's 250th Anniversary

As already recorded (*see* p. 125), it had been possible to celebrate the Bicentenary only in a comparatively modest manner because at that time the world was at war. But no such inhibition marred the honouring of the 250th Anniversary, which was arrayed with all the colourful pomp and impressive precision that mark every British occasion of high ceremony. The meeting was held on the nearest convenient date to St. John Baptist's Day (June 24th), when the first Grand Lodge had met 250 years before.

THE 250TH ANNIVERSARY

No fewer than sixty-seven Grand Lodges were represented by high dignitaries — all but three by their Grand Masters themselves — thus making the great assembly the most representative gathering of freemasons ever held. So great was the keenness among the brethren at home to attend that tickets had to be limited to one per lodge (for the ruling Master) and even these had to be balloted-for.

When the new Grand Master had been obligated and inducted by the Pro Grand Master into the great golden throne — originally constructed during the Grand Mastership of George, Prince of Wales (later King George IV), and used for the installation of every Grand Master save the Earl of Harewood since 1813 — and had been proclaimed by his many styles and titles and had been homaged, addresses of congratulation were delivered by the Grand Masters of the next two senior Grand Lodges. Here two remarkable coincidences arose. Both the 7th Earl of Donoughmore for Ireland and Sir Ronald Orr Ewing (the 5th Baronet of that ilk), Grand Master Mason of Scotland, recalled that *their* fathers had ruled their respective Constitutions in 1939 when the present Duke of Kent's own father, Prince George, had been installed Grand Master, and that to both the 6th Earl of Donoughmore and Brigadier-General Sir Norman Orr Ewing, 4th Baronet, had befallen a similar honour of addressing the then Royal Solomon.

The superb organization of this inspiring occasion and the entertainment of the numerous important visitors from overseas throughout their stay must be credited to a special Grand Lodge Committee and notably to its Chairman, Major-General Sir Allan Adair, then the Assistant Grand Master. It was they also who decided: (1) to produce and publish *Grand Lodge, 1717-1967* (see next section); (2) to replace a small window in the tower of Freemasons' Hall with a clock and the dates '1717-1967'; (3) to hold an exhibition, which was arranged by Bro. A. R. Hewitt, at that time the Librarian and Curator, and was widely appreciated, of items illustrative of the 250 years' history.

'Grand Lodge, 1717-1967'

The publication of any book under the authority of the United Grand Lodge of England is a comparatively rare event and the only other recent one that can be recalled, apart from

UNITED GRAND LODGE FREEMASONRY

Books of Constitutions and the annual *Year Books* is a *Guide for Masonic Librarians* by Bro. A. R. Hewitt (1965). The beautifully produced *Grand Lodge, 1717-1967* is the sole official history* of the English Craft. The Foreword was by R. W. Bro. A. S. Frere, President of the Board of General Purposes (1959-72), who may be regarded as having been the general editor, and the team of experts who contributed the various chapters included Bro. Harry Carr on 'Freemasonry before Grand Lodge' and R. W. Bro. J. W. Stubbs, the Grand Secretary, on 'The Last Fifty Years'. One useful appendix supplied brief biographies of all the Grand Masters, compiled by Bro. A. R. Hewitt, and topics dealt with in the others included 'The English Provincial Grand Lodge', 'The Supreme Grand Chapter of England', and 'Overseas Development'. From the last named, by Bro. A. J. B. Milborne (a Canadian), the following notable sentence deserves quotation:

> Of all the institutions that man has created for his advancement, Masonry would seem to be the only one where 'good Men and true', irrespective of rank, creed, or colour can meet anywhere in the world upon common ground.

The Surgical Research Fund

To mark the 250th Anniversary, the Earl of Scarbrough had two years before outlined to Grand Lodge his plan that the whole English Constitution should make some useful contribution to the welfare of the country outside normal masonic activities, and in this way should 'point out to the world the happy and beneficial results of our antient and honourable Institution'.

A trust fund was accordingly established, the income of which is administered by the Royal College of Surgeons for further research, particularly through the provision of Fellowships. The fund was financed by an appeal to lodges to subscribe at the rate of one pound per head of membership. By this means it was hoped to raise at least a quarter of a million pounds. In fact, when the fund was closed on the first day of 1970, no less a sum than £594,850 had been contributed.

---

*Grand Lodge, however, emphasize that it is designed rather as a broad survey of the story of the Craft and that the views expressed are those of the writers themselves.

THE SURGICAL RESEARCH FUND

The Earl of Scarbrough stressed more than once the benefit the fund would bring to non-masons. Not that this is any new thing. It will be recalled that during both World Wars the Royal Masonic Hospital treated wounded soldiers without discrimination (*see* p. 126).

Again, no fewer than 107 special grants by Grand Lodge since 1825 are listed in the *Masonic Year Book* for 1975, with further sixteen by Grand Chapter since 1870, although none was on such a scale as the 250th Anniversary and never before have lodges been invited to contribute cash.* The beneficiaries have included: Lancashire cotton districts, 1863; The Royal National Lifeboat Institution, 1877, 1919 and 1940; the Prince of Wales's Hospital Fund, 1897; Mansion House funds, 1886, 1929, 1940, 1950 and 1952; The Red Cross, 1914, 1941 and 1943; the victims of cyclones and hurricanes, earthquakes and volcanic eruptions, famines, floods, tempests and tidal waves, and wars, in many countries; and numerous other worthy causes all over the world.

Recent instances leap to the mind; 1,000 guineas to the Winston Churchill Memorial in 1965; 500 guineas to sufferers from the Aberfan disaster in 1966; £2,000 to St. Paul's Cathedral Appeal in 1971-2 and £500,000 to the Royal National Lifeboat Institution for the purchase of a new boat.

The Earl of Scarbrough

Lawrence Roger Lumley, the 11th Earl of Scarbrough, served for only two years in the office of Pro Grand Master for which his many devoted years at the head of the Craft had so perfectly fitted him. To the great sorrow of his brethren, he died on 29th June 1969 in his 73rd year. A great Yorkshireman, it was appropriate that his last great masonic function was to install the new Provincial Grand Master for Yorkshire, West Riding, less than a month before his death.

As an Oxford undergraduate, he was initiated in the Apollo University Lodge No. 357 in 1920. While Governor of Bombay, he was appointed its District Grand Master in 1940 and greatly influenced Indian Freemasonry.

He succeeded to the earldom in 1945 and was in 1947

* From 1940 to 1945 (World War II) brethren were asked to surrender unwanted jewels and from the proceeds of their being melted down Grand Lodge was able to donate to H.M. Treasury the munificent sum of £28,131 for the relief of distress occasioned by the War.

appointed Deputy Grand Master by the Duke of Devonshire being elected Grand Master in 1951. The 250th anniversary celebrations (*see* p. 134) marked the climax of his masonic career. He will be remembered as a very great Grand Master to whom, in the words of his successor, 'English Freemasonry owes a very great debt for all that he did to maintain its standards and prestige'.

In 1963, H.M. the Queen conferred upon him the Royal Victorian Chain, an honour usually reserved for members of the Royal Family, and appointed him a Permanent Lord-in-Waiting on his relinquishing the office of Lord Chamberlain which he had held since 1952.

Grand Lodge donated a sum of £2,000 to the York Minster Restoration Fund in memory of Lord Scarbrough and this was devoted to the work on the lovely rose window of the cathedral.

Roman Catholics and Freemasonry

English Freemasonry has never opposed the admission of Roman Catholics as such. The boot was on the other foot. The Roman Church had first showed its official hostility to the Order in 1738 with the famous Bull *In Eminenti Apostolatus Specula* of Pope Clement XII. But neither this nor a further Bull *Providas* (1751) of Benedict XIV were greatly heeded in England — in Ireland they were still a dead letter at the end of that century — so that the 9th Baron Petre (1742-1801) was throughout his Grand Mastership (1772-6) regarded as the head of the Catholic community in England.

Next came an edict of Pope Pius VII in 1814 (a year after the Union), confirming the Bulls of 1738 and 1751 and prohibiting participation in meetings of freemasons and the like 'INSTITUTED UNDER THE DENOMINATIONS OF ANCIENTS, MODERNS OR THOSE OF THE RECENTLY STYLED CARBONARI . . .' (the capital letters are taken from the original text). It is possible that the last word holds the clue to the papal perseverance in its former attitude towards Freemasonry. The *Carbonari*, or 'charcoal-burners', were an Italian secret society that flourished in the early 19th century; it aimed at getting rid of certain of the Italian rulers; its ritual was a compound of Christianity, Freemasonry and the practices of the charcoal-burners.

It must be admitted that, despite the obvious innocuity of

ROMAN CATHOLICS AND FREEMASONRY

British Grand Lodges, the Roman Church has had a certain
tification for the intransigent attitude it has until quite
ently adopted towards Freemasonry. Many Continental
emasons and indeed several of the Continental Grand
ients themselves were, and still are, definitely anti-clerical
e Chapter XIX).

The next move on the part of the Vatican took the form of
e Bull *Quo Graviora* of Leo XII, prohibiting 'for ever all
cret Societies ... against the Church'. In 1865 Pius IX
livered his Allocution *Multiplices Inter*, proscribing 'that
rverse society of men called masonic', which 'had not been
nquished nor overthrown' but at whose doors lay 'the many
litious movements, the many incendiary wars which have
the whole of Europe in flames'.

There followed the Encyclicals *Humanum Genus* (1884)
d *Ab Apostolici* (1890) and a pastoral letter *Annum Ingressi*
902). All three denunciations came from Leo XIII.

The Vatican's objections to Freemasonry were based on,
stly, the fact that the Order admitted men of all religions;
condly, its secrecy — but the Roman Church has long had
own secret societies, such as the well-known Knights of
Columba ('of Columbus' in the United States); and, thirdly,
e nature of the oaths in its ritual.

Then, with the oecumenical reign of Pope John XXIII
958-63) came a gradual softening of the Catholic attitude
wards the *regular* Grand Lodges, and this has been continued
der the present Pope Paul VI. Part of the credit for this
ppier state of affairs is due to four people in particular:
ather Ferrer Benimeli, a Jesuit priest who in 1968 published
Spain *La Masoneria depuis del Concilio* (Masonry since the
Vatican] Council), showing that a regular Freemasonry based
pon belief in God does not and should not stand condemned
der the Papal Bulls; Monsieur Alec Mellor, a devoted French
atholic layman and the author of *Our Separated Brethren,
e Freemasons* (1961), who in 1969 obtained the permission
f his priest 'as a matter of conscience' to be initiated into a
gular lodge under the *Grande Loge National Française*;
rother Harry Carr of the Quatuor Coronati Lodge of London
ho, himself a member of the Jewish faith, strove for years
or a reconciliation between Church and Order; and His
minence, the late John, Cardinal Heenan, Archbishop of

Westminster, who was persuaded by Harry Carr to withdraw anti-masonic pamphlets from sale in his Cathedral.

Cardinal Heenan told Brother Carr that he had long been greatly interested in the subject of Freemasonry and that he had been much impressed by a saying of the 1st Marquess of Ripon (*see* p. 124) after he had resigned from the Grand Mastership in 1874 that 'throughout his career in Freemasonry he had never heard a single word uttered against altar or throne'. When Brother Carr said that what the freemasons really needed was an intermediary with Rome the Cardinal, who was on the eve of a visit to the Vatican, exclaimed: 'I am your intermediary!'

Although 'the mills of God grind slowly', several favourable signs have occurred to indicate that walls and fences are already being broken down: a Vatican commission has proposed that Article 1240 of the Canon Law, which forbids Catholic burial for 'suicides, heretics, freemasons and people who have been killed in duels', shall be abolished. Again, in a conference of Catholic clergy in Scandinavia in 1966, it was ruled that freemasons who desired to join the Roman Catholic Church should not be required on that account to renounce their Freemasonry. The present position appears to be that any Roman Catholic who is desirous of being initiated into a regular lodge without fear of excommunication has simply to obtain the consent of his bishop.

The Christian rites among the additional degrees present a greater problem than the Craft Masonry since it could be argued that some of them teach a type of Christianity not altogether in accordance with the principles of the Roman Catholic Church.

London Masonic Area

We referred, in describing the introduction of London (Grand) Rank in 1908 (*see* p. 125), to the problem of honours for worthy members of London lodges. The London 'masonic area', within which lodges may each recommend a Past Master at two-yearly intervals to receive London Grand Rank, was until 1971 defined as being bounded by a circle with a radius of ten miles and with Freemasons' Hall at its centre. In June 1971 it was enacted that the radius of that circle be reduced to five miles and that those existing lodges which regularly met

BOUNDARY CHANGES

tween the five and ten-mile boundaries would be permitted e choice of remaining under 'London' or of being entered the roll of the Province to which their places of meeting uld henceforth be allocated. One effect of this arrangement s to make potentially available to quite a number of London ethren an entitlement to be considered for Provincial Grand ank. London has (December 1981) 1,690 lodges and it can adily be seen that the annual investiture of Holders of ndon Grand Rank involves the presentation of as many as 5 recipients to the investing officer, a very considerable remony!

ovincial Boundary Changes

It is possible that it was partly as the result of the London teration that the Grand Master decided in 1973 to split the ljoining Province of Kent into two: the Provinces of East ent and West Kent. In having more than one Provincial rand Lodge, Kent thus joins Lancashire and Yorkshire, hich have two apiece. The Province of West Lancashire, owever, remains easily at the head of the 'league table' with 20 lodges to its credit. East Lancashire is the runner-up with 87 lodges (December 1981 figures).

he Bagnall Report

In 1971, the Grand Master appointed a Committee of iquiry charged with the task of looking into the whole ques- on of masonic charity. This Committee was chaired by R. W. ro. the Hon. Sir Arthur Bagnall (Mr. Justice Bagnall), P.J.G.W. promoted in 1974 to P.S.G.W.). On 24 April 1974, at the nnual Festival of Grand Lodge, the Grand Master announced hat their report had been laid before him. This was published n the following day, in full and summary forms, so that it ould be made available to a large number of brethren.

Among its recommendations were the following:

(1) Masonic charity should become more outward-looking and should not be confined to freemasons and their dependants.

(2) The Royal Masonic Institutions for Girls and Boys should be amalgamated into one charity as 'The Royal Masonic Education Trust'.

(3) The Royal Masonic Benevolent Institution and the

UNITED GRAND LODGE FREEMASONRY

Royal Masonic Hospital should be brought together form a single charity, which the Grand Master had mind to call 'The Foundation'. This would additional discharge the functions of the existing Board Benevolence.

(4) A Central Charity should be established (the title preferred by the Grand Master was 'The Grand Charity This would include among its functions the receipt an channelling of funds to where they were neede within and outside the context of Freemasonry.

(5) The President of each of these three Charities shou be annually appointed by the Grand Master ar invested as such within the hierarchy of Grand Lodg

(6) An additional permissive officer should be appointe (if the Master so desires) in each private lodge ar should be designated the 'Charity Steward'.

There were in all sixty recommendations; only a very fe failed to survive the first deliberations which followed the pu lication of the report.

One of the Grand Master's earliest actions on the report w to create a Steering Committee, to be presided over by th Assistant Grand Master and to co-ordinate and implement th changes which would be taking place.

One recommendation which engendered a great deal c discussion among masons and, regrettably, also in the Pres was that the Boys' School should close and that the boy should join the girls at Rickmansworth in what would becom a co-educational establishment. As has already been show (p. 119), the school at Bushey *is* closing but the Rickman worth school will remain as it is, a very fine place of learnin for girls alone.

Very great interest was aroused throughout the Englis Craft by the recommendations and many points of view wer expressed, some with marked emphasis. The London Gran Rank Association made a most useful contribution by devotin their Quarterly Meeting in November 1974 to a visit from th Assistant Grand Master and R. W. Bro. Bagnall. *The Bagnal Report* (so called at the direction of the Grand Master) wa explained to the assembled brethren and questions were ably dealt with.

The Steering Committee, which soon became known a

THE BAGNALL REPORT

The Grand Master's Committee', set to work with a will and after a very great deal of discussion, reported to Grand Lodge at intervals, all the major changes in all essentials were approved. The Grand Charity was established by trust deed and came into formal existence on 1 January 1981, the President and members of a previously expanded Board of Benevolence becoming the President and members of the Council of the Grand Charity. On the same date the offices of the Presidents of the Masonic Foundation for the Aged and Sick and the Masonic Trust for Girls and Boys (the titles originally proposed having been thus amended) came into being. From 1986 the annual charity festivals will be organized in relation to the new structure.

Charity Stewards

In September 1975, the Report of the Board of General Purposes at the Quarterly Communication of Grand Lodge referred to the 'Bagnall' recommendation that the office of Charity Steward should be instituted. It was proposed that the office should be appointive rather than elective, that the holder (if any) should take precedence after the Junior Deacon (and so be followed by the Almoner), and that he should concern himself with the masonic charities, leaving the Almoner — as has usually been the case — to welfare work, pastoral and financial, among the membership of the lodge and their widows. Finally, the Board recommended that the jewel of this office should be a Trowel, a long accepted symbol of Benevolence and Charity. All this was formally approved by Grand Lodge in December 1975.

The State of the English Craft, 1981

The annual statistical report to Grand Lodge in March 1981 recorded a total of 8,074 lodges on the Register, 1,675 being in London, 5,620 in the Provinces and 764 overseas. At each Quarterly Communication since we have learned of further additions to the number. The twenty-three Warrants for new lodges issued in the second quarter of 1981 included that for the Old Exonian Lodge No. 9000, marking a significant milestone in the onward march of Freemasonry.

Enquiries are sometimes made as to the actual membership of the English Craft. An official estimate is that there are perhaps half a million brethren owing allegiance to the United Grand Lodge. We know that no fewer than 179,401 Grand Lodge Certificates were issued from January 1971 to December 1980.

Distinguished visitors from other Constitutions are frequently welcomed to our own Grand Lodge, regalia ranging from the plain white aprons of some of the American Constitutions (though others are quite ornate) to the distinctive aprons and sashes of Scandinavia. The splendid variety of colours in the insignia to be seen on these occasions includes rich purples, yellows, crimson, thistle-green and blues of every shade, many encrusted with gold bullion.

CHAPTER VIII

IRISH FREEMASONRY

The Origins of Irish Masonry

One of the traditional heroes of Celtic mythology was the Gobhan Saor, the 'free smith', of whom many legends are told. It is perhaps significant, as Lepper and Crossle point out,* that 'saor' in the Irish tongue denotes both 'free' and 'a mason'.

That the ancient Irish possessed able masons is proved by their famous round towers, some of which still stand after existing well over a thousand years; some students have attributed the building of these towers to the Comacines (*see* p. 15), but the theory is not very widely supported today.

Links with operative masonry can be traced back to the early twelfth century as the exquisite Cormac's Chapel at Cashel, built by a Munster King in 1130, still bears witness. Prior to the Anglo-Norman invasion of that century there was evolving a 'Hiberno-Romanesque' architecture of which the surviving chancel arch at St. Mary's Cathedral, Tuam, built in 1152, affords a fine example. As further evidence of the skill of the Irish masons at this time, consider the stately high crosses with their intricate carving in the stubborn native stone.

While there is a complete absence of any Irish counterpart of the English Old Charges, as described in Chapter III, we know that the gild system flourished at any rate from the fifteenth century in the sister kingdom.

A Charter was granted to the Dublin masons, in company with the carpenters, millers and heliers (or tilers) in 1508, and it is interesting to note that people who were not craftsmen or operative masons were accepted in the Gild. Although the masons were few in number compared with the other craftsmen in the Gild, William Dougan, a mason, was its Master in 1558-60.

*History of the Grand Lodge of Free and Accepted Masons of Ireland, Vol. 1 (1925). For much of the information in this chapter the present Authors are indebted to that erudite work. The equally useful Vol. 2 by R. E. Parkinson, was published in 1957.

IRISH FREEMASONRY

Like the gild system, in all probability then Craft Masonry was imported from England.

Pre-Grand Lodge Freemasonry

From 1602 to at least 1818 there was a Freemason's Stone, a well-known landmark in the Coombe district of Dublin.

In Limerick a still more ancient relic exists and now forms one of the treasures of the Ancient Union Lodge, No. 13. This is the nearly 470-years-old Baal's Bridge Square, which was discovered in excavating the foundations of the bridge of that name over the River Shannon.

The wording on it runs:

I WILL STRIUE TO LIUE WITH LOUE AND CARE
UPON THE LEUEL, BY THE SQUARE
1507

This shows that Freemasonry was established in Ireland in the early part of the sixteenth century, and while we cannot be certain that it was then partly speculative, yet it had already an ethical symbolism for its working tools.

In the pages of *Ars Quatuor Coronatorum* (Vol. 82, pp. 255-7), Lt.-Col. Eric Ward, in support of his theory that moralising upon the working tools was one of the distinctive features of speculative Freemasonry since 'there is not the slightest evidence that operative masons moralized upon the tools of their trade', questioned the authenticity of the date 1507. He maintained that the square could have been inserted in the *foundations* (the italics our ours) of the bridge 'during one of the major repairs at any time prior to demolition' in 1830. He further claimed that Roman type did not come into general use until the 17th century and that the faked antique was probably the product of 'some 18th century kindred spirit of the boy Chatterton who had sought less successfully to create spurious antiquity by substituting "Us" for "Vs".'

His point of view was challenged by Norman Knight, who pointed out that Roman type had first been used about 1465 and thereafter spread rapidly; he suggested that in the absence of 'the slightest evidence' that the square had actually been inserted in the bridge's foundations at some later time, we must accept the wording on it at its face value, date and all.

The diary of the first Earl of Cork, who came to Ireland in

PRE-GRAND LODGE FREEMASONRY

1588, shows that he had stones specially prepared in Bristol and thence shipped to Ireland, revealing an early connexion between the operative masons of the two countries. In later speculative Freemasonry as we know the relationship between the Bristol working and that of the Irish freemasons was so close that in 1793 (when no fraternal communication existed between the two Grand Lodges) a Cork brother who visited a Moderns' (or rather Traditioners') lodge in Bristol could scarcely detect any difference in the ritual from that of his own lodge. It may easily have originated in the association of the operative masons over two hundred years before.

A Speculative Lodge in Trinity College, 1688

The first reference to a speculative masonic lodge occurs in 1688 and is in the form of a *jeu d'esprit* on the part of John Jones, a Bachelor of Arts at Trinity College, Dublin, which for several preceding years had been overrun by operative masons who were putting up new buildings. John Jones, a friend of Dean Swift, that year delivered the 'Commencements harrangue', which contains the following passage (translated from mongrel Latin by Bro. Chetwode Crawley who called the attention of the Craft to the *'Tripos' MS* in his introduction to Henry Sadler's *Masonic Reprints and Revelations* (1898)). It had previously been included in Bro. Sir Walter Scott's edition of the *Works of Jonathan Swift* in nineteen volumes [1814]) relating to an imaginary new college.

> It was lately ordered that for the honour and dignity of the University there should be introduced a society of freemasons, consisting of gentlemen, mechanics, porters (etc. etc.), who shall bind themselves by an oath never to reveal their no-secret, and to relieve whatsoever strolling distressed brethren they meet with, after the example of the fraternity of freemasons in and about Trinity College, by whom a collection was lately made for, and the purse of charity well stuffed for, a reduced brother.

Then followed a ridiculous list of gifts including 'From Sir Warren, for being Freemasonized the new way five shillings.'
The orator further announces that on the corpse of one Ridley (a notorious informer) was the 'Freemasons' Mark'. It must be remembered that this address was delivered to a well-

informed audience who were clearly expected to understand the various allusions. It indicates the existence of a society known to be secret, benevolent and of mixed membership, and postulates a recent change of procedure.

The Lady Freemason

The initiation of the Hon. Elizabeth St. Leger (afterwards the Hon. Mrs. Aldworth) in about 1710, now generally accepted as authentic, makes an interesting story.

According to the most reliable account* this lady, who was the daughter of the 1st Viscount Doneraile, had fallen asleep one afternoon in her father's library. When she awoke she sensed that something important was going forward in the large adjoining room. Although she knew that her father was wont to hold lodge meetings in the house, she was unaware that one was to take place that evening. Some repairs were being made in the house and bricks between the two rooms had been loosely replaced, making it easy for Elizabeth to remove one or two and thus get a clear view of the initiation that was being performed next door.

At first her curiosity held her spellbound; it was not until the solemn responsibilities undertaken by the candidate were reached that she realized the seriousness of her action. Now she longed only to flee and rushed out into the hall, where she found her escape cut off by the Tyler, who happened to be the family butler. She thereupon screamed and fainted; the butler-tyler's loyalties were divided between his young mistress and his lodge; the latter prevailed and he entered to bring out Elizabeth's father and brothers who, when she was restored to consciousness, learned what had happened.

They then retired into the lodge-room and anxiously considered what had best be done. The only course seemed to them to initiate in turn the fair eavesdropper, and with her consent this was done.

Elizabeth became a patroness of the Craft and a subscriber to Dr. Dassigny's famous *Impartial Enquiry* (see p. 55). After her death in 1773 the memory of 'our sister Aldworth' was

---

*By Brother Edward Conder, *A.Q.C.* Vol. 8, 1895, *p.* 16. The 1927 *Transactions of the Lodge of Research, Dublin,* contain an extensive bibliography for the Hon. Mrs. Aldworth from the pen of the late Philip Crossle.

toasted by the freemasons of Ireland. Her masonic apron exists to this day. The Colonel and brother, who in 1776 instituted the St. Leger Stakes, run at Doncaster, was her cousin. He joined the Prince of Wales's Lodge, now No. 259 (E.C.), in 1789.

There have been one or two other instances, more or less well authenticated, of women admitted into Freemasonry — one in England (d. 1802), one in the United States (b. 1815) and one in Hungary (b. 1833, init. 1875). As a result of the last case numerous expulsions and suspensions were ordered by the Grand Orient of Hungary, who promptly declared the admission of the Countess in question to be void. (For 'Co-Masonry' and women's Masonry, *see* Chapter XIX.)

'A Letter from the Grand Mistress', 1724

The first masonic pamphlet, entitled *A Letter from the Grand Mistress of the Female Free-Masons*, was published in Dublin in 1724. This skit, of which only one original copy is known to exist but which has been extensively reprinted, was believed by that great authority, Dr. Chetwode Crawley, to have been from the pen of Dean Swift himself but this authorship was frowned upon by Brother Heron Lepper, who regarded the pamphlet as altogether lacking the weight of the Master's style and as more resembling a catchpenny parody.

Be that as it may, since a second edition was called for in 1731, this publication provides evidence of the interest in and popularity of the Craft in Ireland in the seventeen-twenties. These are evinced also by the wide sales in Dublin and Cork of Anderson's *Constitutions* of 1723.

Beginnings of Grand Lodge, 1725

The exact year of the formation of the Irish Grand Lodge — the second oldest in the world — unfortunately cannot be determined, since none of its official records exists prior to 1760. Some scholars put it at 1723 or 1724, but the generally recognized date is 1725 and that year was accepted for the Bicentenary celebrations of 1925.

It is to a newspaper account — the first to mention an Irish Grand Lodge — that the ascribed year is due. On Saturday, 26th June, 1725, *The Dublin Weekly Journal* contained an informed and lively account of a meeting of the Grand Lodge

IRISH FREEMASONRY

at the King's Inns, Dublin, on St. John's Day, two days before, when 'they proceeded to the election of a *new* Grand Master',* who was Richard, 1st Earl of Rosse.

Six lodges of 'gentlemen freemasons' (all, probably of Dublin) were represented, of which the present Nos. 2 & 6 still exist today; in addition to those representatives, consisting of all the Masters and Wardens, there were numerous 'private brothers' in attendance, who were not present at the Grand Lodge ceremonies and did not vote at the election of the Grand Master and the Grand Wardens. Two things are noteworthy; first that the Grand Officers, except the Deputy Grand Master, the Hon. Humphrey Butler, were directly elected and not nominated by the Grand Master as in England; and secondly that this meeting affords the first recorded occasion of a public masonic procession by coach, the second being on the installation of the Duke of Norfolk as Grand Master of England in 1730.

The Earl of Rosse, Grand Master, 1725 and 1730

This nobleman, who was noted for his wit and wild habits, was 29 when he was first elected Grand Master. He is said to have inherited nearly a million pounds from his grandmother, the great Duchess of Tyrconnel. His Dublin townhouse was on the site of the present Freemasons Hall. He died in 1741.

He was undoubtedly Grand Master again in 1730 and it is quite likely that he held his Grand office throughout. On the other hand, the Grand Mastership may have been occupied during one or more of those years by Lord Southwell, who was referred to in the London press of 1732 as 'late Grand Master of Ireland' and next year was installed as proxy for the Earl of Strathmore, Grand Master of England. At any rate the years from 1725 to 1729 were dark and desolate ones for Ireland, other than Munster, and very little is heard of Freemasonry during that period.

Thomas Griffith, Grand Secretary, 1725-32

This first Irish Grand Secretary had a colourful personality. He was apt to mock his own small stature in his playbills, as thus: 'The part of Alexander the Great is to be played by little

*The italics are ours; the words 'new Grand Master' seem to indicate that Grand Lodge had already been in existence for at least a year.

Griffith.' We first hear of him masonically in the *Dublin Weekly Journal* already quoted, where it was reported that after the banquet following the installation of the Earl of Rosse the members of Grand Lodge and other brethren

> all went to the Play, with their Aprons, &c . . . Mr. *Griffith* The Player, who is a Brother, sung the Free Mason's Apprentices Song, the *Grand Master* and the whole Brotherhood joyning in the Chorus.

The words of this very familiar song may well have been written by Brother Griffith, who was a poet as well as an actor; the music, although attributed by Anderson to 'Dr. Birkhead, deceased', is almost certainly Irish.

Lord Southwell (Grand Master, 1743 and probably also during this period) gave him the official appointment of Tide Waiter (or Customs Officer) and as such it was his duty to keep an eye on the comings and goings of the 'Wild Geese' and other Jacobite sympathizers, of whom Lord Rosse was rumoured to be one.

It was the custom of the Irish Grand Lodge (like the English) at this time to patronize the theatre officially (particularly in the cause of charity), but one occasion on which they did so landed poor Brother Griffith in trouble, for in 1734 he chose Wycherley's *The Country Wife* for his benefit performance. According to the *Dublin Evening Post* the Grand Lodge considered this a 'great and public Affront . . . in chusing so vile and obscene a play for their Entertainment.'

He was later forgiven his trespass. Masonic historians find it less easy to forgive him his failure to record or preserve the Minutes of Grand Lodge.

Minutes are, however, fortunately available for

The Grand Lodge of Munster, 1726-33

These are mixed with records of the transactions of Lodge No. 1 of Cork, a 'time immemorial' lodge. There is every indication that the Grand Lodge was already in existence at the time of the first entry in 1726, which records the election of the Hon. James O'Bryen, a brother of the 4th Earl of Inchiquin, ruler of the English Craft in 1727, as Grand Master and of Springett Penn, a grandson of the famous Quaker, William Penn, as his deputy.

IRISH FREEMASONRY

Grand Master O'Bryen continued in office until 1730, in which year, too, Springett Penn died at the early age of 29. The latter is perhaps best remembered for having added the following verse to the celebrated 'Entered Apprentice's Song':

> We're true and sincere,
> And just to the Fair,
> Who will trust us on ev'ry occasion;
> No mortal can more
> The ladies adore
> Than a Free and Accepted Mason.

Although applications for warrants from brethren in Waterford and Clonmel are recorded, there is no mention of any lodge's having actually been constituted by the Grand Lodge of Munster. Since, however, General Regulations were formulated by it in 1728, there must have been local lodges acknowledging its jurisdiction.

With the installation as Grand Master of Munster in 1731 of that great mason, Lord Kingston, who was already Grand Master of Ireland — he had held the same office in England in 1729 — the Grand Lodge of Munster really became extinct, although efforts to preserve its independence persevered until 1733.

Irish Warrants

In 1727 the present Lodge No. 2 of Dublin and other ancient Irish lodges came under the jurisdiction of Grand Lodge, although their warrants were not issued for another five years.

In 1730 John Pennell, who was to succeed Griffith as Grand Secretary two years later, published his *Constitutions* 'for the use of the lodges' of Ireland. This volume is partly, but not exclusively, based on Anderson.

The oldest Grand Lodge warrant in the world, that now held by Lodge No. 1, Cork, was issued in 1731-2 to a lodge at Mitchelstown, Co. Cork, most probably for the household of Lord Kingston. This vellum document ante-dates by twenty-three years the first warrant known to have been issued by the Grand Lodge of England. In fact the practice of issuing lodge warrants, now adopted by every Grand Lodge in the world, certainly started with the Grand Lodge of Ireland.

IRISH WARRANTS

Thomas Griffith in 1731 inserted a notice in the Dublin press ordering that all lodges in Ireland without a warrant under the hand and seal of Lord Kingston or of Lord Netterville, the Deputy Grand Master, must immediately 'take out true and perfect Warrants and pay the Fees for the same, or they will not be deem'd true Lodges'. A similar notice was issued by John Baldwin, Grand Secretary in 1740, this time stating that all lodges which failed to apply would be proceeded against as Rebel Masons'.

Ulster in particular had numerous lodges of 'non-regular' or 'hedge Masons' which had never taken out a warrant, while Belfast itself had no regular lodge until 1748. Most of the Munster lodges came in from the beginning of the amalgamation, but the premier lodge of Ireland, the present No. 1 of Cork, remained (with immunity) without a warrant until 1761. When it did apply for one, however, it set an example that was generally copied, so that Ireland can now show no example of a 'time immemorial' lodge working without a warrant, whereas there are at least four in England, including the three surviving Old Lodges.

The difficulty was for Grand Lodge to induce its nominally submissive lodges to acknowledge its authority, especially those at a distance from Dublin; in the early days, even when they had obtained warrants, many lodges would calmly continue working for years without again getting into contact with Grand Lodge. In 1750 and again in 1759 Edward Spratt and John Calder, the respective Grand Secretaries in those years, found it necessary to remind lodges through the press that it would be as well to discharge their dues and make returns of their members.

Apart from 'private lodges' such as that at Mitchelstown (p. 152), and military lodges of the British Army, to which the Grand Lodge of Ireland issued the first ambulatory warrants, all lodge meetings were held in taverns, as in England. There was one other exception — from 1754 to 1801 there was a warranted lodge of debtor masons confined in the Dublin Marshalsea.

The Earl of Middlesex, Carolus Sackville Magister

Eldest son of the Duke of Dorset, who had been appointed

Viceroy in 1730, this nobleman founded a lodge in Florence* in 1733, when he was 22 years of age, from which it may be deduced that he was an Irish freemason, since he was too young then to have been initiated in England.†

A finely designed medal was struck to commemorate his mastership, and by his express desire it gave as his only title Carolus Sackville Magister Florentinus.

Irish Charity Founded, 1738

In 1739 under the rule of Viscount Mountjoy, who as Earl of Blesington was to be first noble Grand Master of the Antients in England (*see* p. 92), were drawn up the Regulations of the Committee of Charity, which had come into being the year before; individual lodges had always been generous in affording relief. Lodge certificates must have been in existence at this time, since the regulations imply the production of such a document** by any applicant for relief.

In 1777 a lottery scheme was started from which the promoters hoped to net a profit of £1,767. They were, however over-optimistic, since tickets were sold but it was found difficult to collect the sums due, hence the receipts amounted to less than the advertised prize money. The latter had to be paid *pro rata*, causing much heart burning among the winners.

Despite this set-back Grand Lodge and the lodges were able to give succour to all their own brethren needing relief and what is more to help distressed brethren from Turkey, Algeria and Morocco, as well as prisoners of war in France.

The Charity funds were often replenished by means of theatrical performances, and the great Sarah Siddons herself subscribed five guineas to the Masonic Female Orphan School in 1802. The idea of this school was started in 1792 by some brethren who had been inspired by the English project of the Chevalier Ruspini (*see* p. 102). They came mainly from the Royal Arch Lodge No. 190, Dublin. To start with, the children

---

*Lepper and Crossle (*op. cit. p.* 92). But although he does not dispute the Earl's early Mastership. Bro. Lepper was later to maintain (*A.Q.C.* 58, 1945) that this lodge might have been self-constituted.

†In 1741 Ireland copied England in fixing the earliest age on admission at 25, reverting with her to 21 in 1813.

**The earliest Certificate in the world still in existence today occurs (as a standard form and not an individual certificate) in the 1754 Minutes of the St. John Lodge, Lurgan, No. 134.

IRISH CHARITY FOUNDED

re not housed or fed by the sponsoring society, which rely paid for their education in a modest way.

In 1799 the scheme was adopted by Grand Lodge, a committee of which took over the management of the school from dge No. 190 in 1800. At this time many of the children ucated there were brought up as Catholics.

Disputed Election, 1740

A curious incident happened in this year. Grand Secretary ratt in his *Constitutions* of 1751 (the historical side of ich has, however, been found to be sometimes astonishingly accurate) states that, on the resignation of Viscount Mount-, of three nominees Viscount Doneraile, a nephew of the ly freemason, was unanimously elected Grand Master, and s is confirmed in *Faulkner's Dublin Journal* of the 1st July 40, but a rival advertisement in the same issue announces e installation of the Earl of Anglesey, and each notice entions a different Grand Secretary. Whatever the trouble, the atter was adjusted the following year, when Lord Tullamore, e third nominee, was installed in the presence of Lord ountjoy.

This incident may have deterred noble candidates from ming forward for the Grand Mastership; in 1745 Lord Allen ed suddenly during his term of office as a result of being ounded by some drunken dragoons in the streets of Dublin d it became necessary for the veteran Lord Kingston to step to the breach for the ensuing two years.

The 'Impartial Enquiry,' 1744

In 1744 was published *A Serious and Impartial Enquiry to the Cause of the Present Decay of Free-Masonry in the ngdom of Ireland*, by Dr. Fifield Dassigny. This book, which as bound up with the first edition of Spratt's Book of onstitutions, contains the earliest but one* known reference the Royal Arch in a passage which starts as follows: 'I am formed in that city [York] is held an assembly of Master asons under the title of Royal Arch Masons.'

Again, complaining of the poor quality of some of the ethren of his time, the author made a suggestion which

*The earliest reference is here assumed to be the report of the oughal procession (*see* p. 208 and *n.*).

155

twenty-four years later Grand Lodge put into practice when set up County Committees of Inspection. These were t forerunners of the Provincial Grand Lodges.

The Grand Master's Lodge Formed, 1749

This highly privileged lodge, which continues at the head the list without a number, was founded by Lord Kingsboroug then Grand Master, and a number of Grand Officers and d tinguished brethren 'to consult the Good of the Craft, and, far as in their Power lies, promote the welfare of the Fraterni in general'. It was at once directed by Grand Lodge that t new lodge should be known as the Grand Master's and th any member who visited Grand Lodge should 'take place every other lodge on the Registry . . . of this Kingdom'.

Up to 1837 every Master Mason raised in this lodge had vote in the Grand Lodge and up to 1856 it had the right recommending the names of new Grand Officers, their advi being almost always taken.

Grand Secretary and his Deputy

The Grand Secretary was disqualified throughout t eighteenth century from voting for Grand Officers, althou from 1767 onwards his duties and emoluments (which tend to increase considerably) were both taken over by the Depu Grand Secretary.

John Calder succeeded Edward Spratt as Grand Secreta in 1757, but ten years later we find him suddenly becomi unpopular with the Grand Master's Lodge and reverting Deputy — a post which had not been fillled since 1743. Broth Calder was succeeded in 1768 by Thomas Corker who held t office for the next thirty years. It was abolished in 1923.

Provincial Grand Masters

The first of these was appointed as Provincial *Deputy* Gran Master for Munster in 1754. He was authorized to 'receive Charity Contributions and regulate all Matters and Affai relative to the Craft, in as full and ample Manner as the Nece sity of the Business requires'. A few weeks later we fir Brother John Reilly, the appointee, busy at work constitutin a lodge at Mallow, No. 253, which number was oddly enoug also issued to the 'True Blue' Lodge of Carrickfergus, C

PROVINCIAL GRAND MASTERS

trim, constituted on the same day at the other end of [Ire]land.

A Provincial Deputy Grand Master for Ulster (possibly not [the] first) was similarly appointed in 1768 and one for Con[na]ught in 1776. Provincial (Deputy) Grand Masters have [al]ways been appointed solely by the Grand Master of Ireland, [wh]o are his representatives in their respective Provinces, [alt]hough the word 'Deputy' is now dropped from the title.

In 1790 the Provincial Grand Master of Munster was re[bu]ked for improperly suspending the Warrant of Lodge No. [7]2 without consulting Grand Lodge, and next year he was [re]moved from office for insulting the Master of No. 44.

In the thirties of the next century the organization of Pro[vin]cial Grand Lodges was, as we shall see, taken in hand, a [co]de of regulations having been adopted in 1829.

The Wesleys and the Wellesleys

These two distinguished families are really of one and the [sa]me Anglo-Irish stock.

It was for some time believed that the Rev. John Wesley, [th]e famous founder of Methodism, was a mason the supposi[ti]on being based on an entry in the lodge-book of the Union [Lo]dge of Downpatrick, which records the entering and raising [of] an initiate of that name on the 3rd October 1788. But this [m]ust have been another John Wesley, for although (by a [co]incidence) the religious pioneer's *Journals* show him to have [vi]sited Downpatrick in the course of his multitudinous travels [in] *June* of that year, yet they also prove that during the whole [of] the first week in *October* he was journeying in Norfolk.

On the other hand, his nephew, Samuel Wesley, the cele[br]ated hymn writer, was undoubtedly admitted by the Lodge [of] Antiquity, then No. 1 (E.C.) and he rose to the high rank of [G]rand Organist in the Moderns' Grand Lodge. In 1813 he com[po]sed and conducted a Grand Anthem for Freemasons in [ho]nour of the Union. A few years after he composed a Grand [M]ass for Pope Pius VI, while he also wrote the music of a [co]mplete set of Matins and Evensong which are still favourites [in] the Church of England. It does not fall to everyone to [re]ceive the commendations of the United Grand Lodge of Free[m]asons, the Roman Church and the Church of England.

The Duke of Wellington was also certainly a freemason,

157

having been initiated in 1790 in the family lodge, No. 494 Trim, as 'A. Wesley' and continuing as a subscribing mem until 1795, when he left Trim for his Indian campaign. T Duke admitted this in 1838 when Dublin Lodge No. 2, wh had acquired the Trim Warrant, sought his permission to itself by his name. Curiously enough, however, in 1851, at end of his life, when pestered by an importunate corresp dent, the Duke denied any 'recollection of having be admitted a freemason'.

His distinguished elder brother, Richard (later the Marquess Wellesley), was in 1782 elected Grand Master Ireland, as had been their father, Garret Wesley, Earl Mornington, before him (1776).

The 1st Earl of Donoughmore, Grand Master, 1789-1813

The new era begun by the installation of this brilliant a beloved young nobleman was one of exceptional difficult for the Irish Grand Lodge and of intense and successful effo on the part of the Grand Master to cope with them. It a marked the peak of Irish Freemasonry's influence, there bei scarcely a village that had not its meeting of masons. Lo Donoughmore, who was the first head of the Irish Craft hold office for more than a year or two, made it a practice travel extensively throughout the Provinces, popularizing t Order and reconciling its differences.

The first of his problems was connected with the Fren Revolution, which caused political feeling to run high Ireland. In particular the Society of United Irishmen, who influence was strongest in the north, had been barred fro meeting as an open political organization; they took refuge their masonic lodges, some of which were unwise enough publish resolutions of a political character, whereupon Gra Lodge sent out in 1793 a circular letter, which lays down t true law so clearly that one paragraph merits quotation her

FREE MASONS have sufficient opportunities of expre sing their Religious and Political Opinions in *other* Societi and in *other* Capacities, and should not, under any preten whatsoever, suffer such Topics to invade the *sacred retir ment* of a LODGE, which is peculiarly appropriated improve Moral Duties — correct Human Frailties, — ar inculcate Social Happiness.

THE 1ST EARL OF DONOUGHMORE

Another great problem that confronted Lord Donoughmore towards the end of his reign and taxed all his gifts of reconciliation was the Seton breakaway, the story of which will shortly be told.

Throughout his career this worthy Grand Master proved a doughty champion of the cause of Catholic emancipation. The outbreak of the Revolutionary War of 1793 roused his martial ardour into raising a Regiment called the Masonic, or Royal Irish, Volunteers.

The First Masonic Journal

In 1792 was started the first masonic journal in the British Isles, the monthly *Sentimental and Masonic Magazine* of Dublin. It ran for three years, after which its place was taken by the *Freemason's Journal: or Pasley's Universal Intelligence*, which appeared twice a week.

The Seton Breakaway

The story of this discreditable episode, which culminated in a violent struggle between two rival parties in Grand Lodge and eventually in the (temporary) formation of a separate Grand Lodge in Ulster, can be told quite simply.

In 1801 D'Arcy Irvine, the Grand Secretary, had appointed as his deputy his friend, Alexander Seton, an able and energetic but dishonest barrister. This Seton was the villain of the piece. As soon as he was appointed, he went to the house of his predecessor and carried off a 'hackney coach full' of books, MSS and other articles belonging to Grand Lodge some of which have never since been recovered.

Disappointed at not receiving the additional emoluments of Deputy Grand Treasurer, which his predecessor for thirty years, Thomas Corker, had enjoyed for many of them, he recouped himself by pocketing some of the lodge dues paid to him, and by re-issuing lapsed warrant numbers for a consideration, to the dismay of old lodges which found their seniority thus menaced.

Scurrilous anonymous pamphlets, aimed against the Grand Treasurer, John Boardman, and his newly appointed deputy, now began to fly about in an effort to secure the support of the lodges and particularly those of Ulster (which had certain legitimate grievances) for the Seton party.

IRISH FREEMASONRY

In 1806 Alexander Seton, who had horsewhipped the Grand Treasurer outside the Grand Lodge room, was dismissed from his office by a new Grand Secretary, and battle was joined. For the next twenty months a state of chaos prevailed with two masonic bodies in Dublin each claiming to be the Grand Lodge. In 1807 the true Grand Lodge, which had been ousted by the opposition faction from their premises in Tailors' Hall, expelled Seton from Masonry and they were encouraged by receiving the support of the Antients' Grand Lodge in England.

The Grand Master, the Earl of Donoughmore, intervened in 1808 by calling a meeting of both sides, and a reconciliation followed. On Seton's undertaking to hand over the books, to recover which a Chancery action had been started, his expulsion was on the motion of the Grand Master himself unanimously revoked. But he refused to return the more recent books (which would have exposed his own misfeasances) and the revocation was cancelled.

The Grand East of Ulster, 1808-14

Meanwhile opposition in Ulster was far from dead, and the representatives of 311 lodges (62 from Belfast district and 7 from Armagh) met at Dungannon, where they set up a Grand Lodge under the above title, with Col. W. Irvine as its first head and Seton as Deputy Grand Secretary. It was to last for six years. Four at least of the Belfast lodges, however, throughout the trouble remained faithful to the Dublin Grand Lodge; it further received the support of the Grand Lodge of Scotland (which might perhaps have been thought likely to back its Ulster brethren) and the Moderns' Grand Lodge of England which for fifty years had been cut off from fraternal intercourse with Ireland. Both assurances came from the pen of Lord Moira (*see* pp. 104 *and* 192) who was an Irish peer, taking his title from a village on the borders of Counties Down and Armagh; he spoke sometimes in the Irish House of Lords.*

The Grand East proceeded to elect officers without asking their consent as, for instance, as their second Grand Master the Earl of Belmore, who was already serving as Junior Grand Warden of the Grand Lodge of Ireland, and as Senior Grand Warden Lord Blayney (grandson of the 'Traditioner' English

*Grattan's Parliament, until the Act of Union in 1800 under which the separate kingdom of Ireland ceased to exist.

THE GRAND EAST OF ULSTER

Grand Master, 1764 — *see* p. 98), who resigned when he found it was not a Provincial Grand Lodge under the Grand Lodge of Ireland, but was nevertheless re-elected.

By 1810 the tide had already begun to turn against the upstart Grand Lodge and thirty-seven Belfast lodges reverted to their rightful allegiance, while the Armagh Committee passed an anti-Seton resolution.

In 1811 the Grand East moved to Belfast. Twenty-two lodges in County Tyrone — Seton's own county — had passed over to the Grand Lodge, which now felt strong enough to assert its authority, issuing a threat to 'suspend or cancell all lodges and expel all masons persisting in rebellious defiance'.

The following year Seton's own adherents seem to have become suspicious of his ways, for all Grand East subscriptions were ordered to be paid to the Grand Treasurer.

By 1813 the revolt had been thoroughly trounced. The protracted lawsuit came to an end with a judgment against Seton, and lodges and masons were tumbling over each other to make their submission to Grand Lodge. The last meeting of the Grand East took place in 1814; Seton himself survived in obscurity until 1844.

Ahiman Rezon, 1804

There had been previously published three privately produced Irish sets of *Constitutions*:

(1) William Smith, a Dublin bookseller of Scottish extraction had in 1735 compiled his *Pocket Companion and History of Freemasons,* which included a 'Constitution of Freemasonry Universal';

(2) John Pennell, who was to be Grand Secretary from 1732 to 1739, had in 1730 published his *Constitutions of the Freemasons,* 'containing the History, Charges, Regulations, etc., of that Ancient and Right Worshipful Fraternity';

(3) in 1751, Edward Spratt (Grand Secretary, 1743-56) had produced his *Book of Constitutions* in which he blindly followed Anderson, even to the extent of writing a highly embellished and misleading account of the laying of the foundation stone of the Irish Houses of Parliament in College Green in 1728-9.

Editions of Laurence Dermott's quaintly named *Ahiman*

IRISH FREEMASONRY

Rezon (*see* p. 91) had been published in Dublin since 1760. In 1804 Bro. Downes, printer to Grand Lodge, published under this title the first official Irish Book of Constitutions, embodying laws that had been added since 1768 and a valuable list of lodges. The third edition, published in 1817, formed the basis of all subsequent Books of Constitutions. The title was retained until the edition of 1858.

Daniel O'Connell

This famous Irish Statesman was not only Master of Lodge No. 198, Dublin, in which he had been initiated in 1799, and affiliated to the well-known No. 13, Limerick, but also acted as counsel for Grand Lodge in the litigation over Seton already mentioned.

At this time the Papal Bulls of 1738 and 1751 were ignored in Ireland, in which at the beginning of the nineteenth century the Roman Catholic freemasons far outnumbered the Protestant. The tightening up of the ban, however, by the priests* resulted in a great decline in the number of lodges and accounted for the resignation of Daniel O'Connell.

In 1837, when taunted by political opponents with still being a member of the Order, he stated in *The Pilot* that many years before he had unequivocally renounced Freemasonry, urging as his objections to it the tendency to counteract the exertions of the temperance societies and 'the wanton and multiplied taking of oaths'. On this being reported to Grand Lodge, he was by resolution excluded (*not* expelled); ironically the presiding Deputy Grand Master had himself been made a mason by Bro. Daniel O'Connell.

The 3rd Duke of Leinster, Grand Master, 1813-74

In 1813 (the year of the Union of the two English Grand Lodges and two years before the Battle of Waterloo) the oft-expressed wish of the Earl of Donoughmore to retire was at last allowed to take effect, the young Duke of Leinster whom he had proposed as his successor being duly elected in his stead. The Duke's father had served in the same capacity in 1770-1 and 1777.

---

*The Papal Bulls of 1738 and 1751 against Freemasonry were first given formal effect in Ireland by Archbishop Troy of Dublin after the French Revolution, and the screw was tightened by Cardinal Cullen, who was horrified by the revolutionary excesses of 1848.

DANIEL O'CONNELL

Although he did not often attend meetings of Grand Lodge during the sixty years of his reign, the Duke was no mere figurehead, and he was ably served by John Fowler first as his Deputy from 1818 to 1824 and then as Deputy Grand Secretary from 1827 till his death in 1856.

The Duke's term of office was mainly a period of organization and progressive legislation and, although during this time the Craft suffered a considerable decline in numbers owing to the withdrawal of the Roman Catholics, the temporary banning of masonic meetings in 1823 (*see* p. 165) and the economic state of the country — as witness the enormous volume of emigration to the United States between 1840 and 1860 — yet he left Irish Freemasonry in a sounder and healthier condition than it had ever experienced previously.

Grand Lodge of Instruction

John Fowler in 1814 presided over a meeting held in his Dublin house to standardize the Irish ritual, and six years later Grand Lodge sanctioned the formation of a lodge of instruction, which was the direct ancestor of the present Grand Lodge of Instruction, first warranted in 1860. It was reconstituted with a new Warrant in 1876 and its new Code of Laws, by which it is still governed, was adopted by Grand Lodge. There have only been eight Grand Secretaries for Instruction, who have included that scholar of international fame, W. J. Chetwode Crawley (1893-1905). Thus, in the words of V. W. Bro. R. E. Parkinson:*

> Ireland [unlike its two sister Constitutions] has an official and permanent body to preserve and promulgate its ritual as handed down by John Fowler, who, in turn, derived it from the ritualists of the last quarter of the eighteenth century. The boast of the Grand Lodge of Ireland that its ritual is older, and has suffered less at the hands of well-meaning but over enthusiastic revisers than any other in the world is no empty one.

The decisions of the Grand Lodge of Instruction, when approved by Grand Lodge, are binding on all lodges under the Irish Constitution.

*History of the Grand Lodge of Free and Accepted Masons of Ireland, Vol. 2 (1957), p. 184.

IRISH FREEMASONRY

The International Compact, 1814

At the end of 1814 the Duke of Leinster, accompanied (at the special request of Grand Lodge) by the Earl of Donoughmore, met the Grand Masters of Scotland and the United Grand Lodge of England at the Freemasons' Hall in London, in order to ascertain 'that the three Grand Lodges were perfectly in unison in all the great and essential points of the Mystery and Craft'. The outcome was the signing of the International Compact, the only full original copy of which is to be found in the Irish Grand Lodge Minutes.

Trouble in Munster, 1814-28

A Brother Miles Edwards, who called himself 'Deputy Provincial Grand Secretary' and seems to have been a sort of Munster Seton, told a number of lodges that they were 'exonerated from all demands of the National Grand Lodge' and himself collected dues and arrears from Cork lodges on behalf of the 'Grand Lodge of Munster'.

The revolt was even less successful than had been that in Ulster six years before. Grand Lodge promptly gave credit to the lodges for any payments and called on Edwards to furnish an account of them. The movement thus collapsed ignominiously.

In 1819, however, the Provincial Grand Lodge of Munster protested to the Grand Lodge against the erasure of certain old lodges, such as No. 28 of Cork and No. 31, Kinsale, and refused to recognize a lapsed warrant, No. 125, which had been re-issued to a new lodge at Ballincollig. Grand Lodge was patient, and in 1823 several of the rebellious lodges submitted, including No. 3 of Cork, but it was not until 1828 that No. 1 Cork, which had been placed on the list of erased warrants two years before, made its peace and was reinstated.

A New Form of Warrant, 1817

The original form of Irish Warrant, which had remained unchanged since 1732, had conferred upon lodges an absolute grant without providing for any power of revocation. The 1817 version, on the other hand, is a grant *quamdiu se bene gesserint* — during good behaviour.

Freemasonry Stops Working, 1823

Ireland at this time was full of secret societies, religious and political; we need only mention the Orangemen and the Ribbonmen. It was against these, rather than the Freemasons, that the Unlawful Oaths in Ireland Act, 1823, was directed, but no express exemption was made, as had been arranged in the case of the Unlawful Societies Act of 1799 (*see* p. 105), and after carefully considering the matter Grand Lodge called on all lodges throughout the country to cease meeting. This was loyally carried out, but the Duke of Leinster and Grand Lodge were not willing to lie down under the interdict, and a widely signed Petition was presented to the United Kingdom House of Commons.

This pointed out that 'the Freemasons have from time immemorial existed as a charitable, benevolent and peaceable institution, disclaiming all religious or political differences', which they were not even allowed to discuss in lodge; that the King and all the male members of his family had been enrolled among their members; and that they had been exempted from the provisions of the Unlawful Societies Act. They therefore prayed for similar exemption. Ten months later the Duke of Leinster was able to announce that the Government had declard that in framing the Act they had not contemplated Freemasonry.

This was satisfactory, but unfortunately many country lodges, having obeyed Grand Lodge's ban, never met again, to the great loss of the Craft. Further, from this time dates the increased hostility of the Roman Church, which before had looked on Freemasonry as the lesser of two evils, as compared with the other secret societies.

The ban also gave occasion for the last case of any friction with the United Grand Lodge of England. The (English) Provincial Grand Master for Upper Canada attempted to compel the Duke of Leinster's Lodge No. 283, there to accept an English warrant. The matter came before the Duke of Sussex (Grand Master of England), who in 1826 wrote to the Duke of Leinster suggesting that Irish overseas lodges would be better protected if placed under the control of the United Grand Lodge. The Irish Grand Lodge, realizing that this would mean abandoning their rights under the International Compact, reacted strongly. In their reply they characterized the Duke of Sussex's conduct as unmasonic, and a duplicate warrant was issued for Lodge No. 283. John Fowler, however, had taken a different view proposing that all overseas lodges, English and Irish, should be under the jurisdiction of the Constitution having a Provincial Grand Lodge in that particular country.*

Provincial Grand Lodges

We have already seen that a Provincial Grand Lodge was working in Munster in 1819. In 1829 Grand Lodge decided to extend this system throughout their jurisdiction, the Provincial Grand Lodges thus formed taking the place of the County Committees of Inspection,† which had existed with similar functions since 1790.

There was a final arrangement of the masonic Provinces covering all Ireland and continuing to the present day, in 1868.

Irish Freemasonry Overseas

Ireland had the honour of sponsoring the mother lodge of Australia. This was in 1820, when a warrant was granted to some citizens of Sydney who had been initiated by an Irish military lodge, No. 218, held in the 48th Foot (Northamptonshire Regt.). A warrant had already been applied for by the New South Wales Corps twenty years before, but had not then been granted. An early lodge in New Zealand was also founded by the Grand Lodge of Ireland and is still on the Irish Register — No. 348, founded in 1843.

About the same time (1800) a Provincial Grand Lodge was established in Barbados and flourished for many years but ultimately transferred its allegiance to the English Constitution.

There have been many Irish masonic Provinces established overseas, some of which have disappeared with the constitution of local sovereign Grand Lodges, but not a few survive from earlier days. The liveliness of the Irish fraternity abroad can be gauged from the fact that it is still necessary to erect Provincial Grand Lodges from time to time, and the most recently set up were those for Nigeria and Ghana in 1973.

* R. E. Parkinson, *History of the Grand Lodge of Ireland*, Vol. II (1957), pp. 62-7, quoted in the Prestonian Lecture for 1962.
† The first such Committee was created by Grand Lodge for County Armagh, and Tyrone. Monaghan and Down and other counties soon followed suit. But not all were equally successful, perhaps through size, and between 1804 and 1817 they lost their most important power — deciding upon the eligibility of candidates.

Military Lodges

As related in the chapter on Freemasonry in the Forces, the Grand Lodge of Ireland was the first to issue ambulatory warrants to regiments of the British Army, and 'in all the great campaigns which extended throughout the British Empire in the eighteenth century somewhere among the baggage of the army there was sure to be a lodge chest containing an Irish warrant.' (Lepper and Crossle, *op. cit.*)

In 1768 Army lodges were exempted from payment of annual dues, but in 1813 they came forward voluntarily with an offer to pay 10s. 10d. each while serving in the British Isles, and this offer was accepted.

Later, in 1825, they were subjected to the same dues as other lodges.

From about this time the military lodges gradually diminished in number and there remain only two still working, both being under the Irish Constitution. One of these, Glittering Star No. 322 in the Worcestershire Regiment, held a meeting in 1938 in the Tower of London, and was the only lodge ever to do so. Its bicentenary celebrations in 1959 were attended by over 350 brethren. The other surviving lodge is Waterloo No. 571, dating from 1923, in the Queen's Dragoon Guards and this has an attached Royal Arch Chapter.

Leswarree No. 646 was the last military lodge to be constituted. Uniquely, in 1932 the Grand Lodge of Ireland met on English soil in Hampshire and Lord Donoughmore performed the ceremony. This lodge and its Royal Arch Chapter have recently closed.

The Irish Charities

We have already mentioned on p. 154 the foundation of the Female Orphan School, which was provided with a home in Charlemont Street, Dublin, by John Boardman, the Grand Treasurer (1791-1813) whom Seton saw fit to horsewhip. After various moves the school was built in 1880 at Ballsbridge.

The Girls' School had been in existence for nearly three-quarters of a century before similar provision was made for the sons of deceased masons. After subscriptions had been received for this purpose, a start was made in 1869 by placing four orphans in a suitable school. Three years later the number ha[s] increased to fifteen. In 1878 the Governors bought Adelaid[e] Hall, which was used for the first separate Masonic Boy[s'] School until 1895, when a far better site was found [at] Richview, where the present school stands. £10,000 wa[s] quickly subscribed for converting and adding to the buildin[g]. A service was held in St. Patrick's, Dublin, in 1967 to celebra[te] its centenary and an extension of the school was begun i[n] commemoration of the event and was opened in 1969 as th[e] 'Raymond Brooke Memorial Building'.

How efficiently the schools* served the country's educ[a]tional requirements is shown by the fact that the form[er] Grand Secretary, Bro. James Harte, is himself a product of th[e] Irish Masonic Boys' School, while another (among a host o[f] distinguished Old Boys) is Rt. Rev. Alan Buchanan, Bishop o[f] Clogher and Provincial Grand Chaplain of Antrim, who serve[d] in the Parachute Regiment in World War II, was one of th[e] first to jump into Sicily and was captured at Arnhem, wher[e] he had remained behind with the wounded. As regards th[e] girls' school, some years ago a senior brother who was a gove[r]nor of one of the big Dublin hospitals was able to fill [a] vacancy for a teenage school-leaver on the secretarial sta[ff] with a girl fresh from the Masonic School. So efficient, indee[d] indispensable, did she prove that another governor, a devou[t] Roman Catholic who detested Masonry, asked and was tol[d] whence she had come. He exclaimed, 'Well, if she is a[n] example of how you look after your orphans, you are doin[g] the Lord's work!'

Alas, times have changed. Recent educational reform i[n] Northern Ireland led to a marked diminution in the number o[f] applicants for vacancies at the schools. It was found to b[e] economically impossible to keep them open and decision[s] were reluctantly reached that, after long and distinguishe[d] periods of service to the orphans of deceased brethren, the[y] had to be closed. It is scarcely necessary to add that th[e] Charities themselves remain open to provide for the 'out [of] education' of girls and boys at other schools.

*A fascinating account of the fine role of the Schools is given i[n] *Shop Window to the World*, by J. F. Burns (Dublin, 1967), a copy o[f] which is available in the United Grand Lodge Library. Bro. Burns, himself an Irish 'Old Masonian', has been since 1956 the editor of 'Hansard' for Northern Ireland.

IRISH MASONIC CHARITIES

Freemasons Hall Built, 1865

The Dublin Masonic Hall Company of Ireland (Ltd.) which was formed by Grand Lodge with a capital of £8,000, bought 17 & 18, Molesworth Street, the Duke of Leinster contributing £200 towards the purchase of a third house.

On this site was erected the present Freemasons' Hall, 73 feet high, the lower part of the front elevation being of the Doric order, the centre of the Ionic and the upper of the Corinthian.

Grand Lodge took over the Hall from the company in 1869 and thirty years later became sole owners, having paid off all debentures. As already mentioned on page 150, the Hall stands on the site of the town house of the first recorded Grand Master. It has recently undergone internal reconstruction to adapt it to the needs of today.

The Dukes of Abercorn, Grand Masters, 1874-1913

After his sixty-one years' reign — a record for any Grand Master — the Duke of Leinster was succeeded by the Duke of Abercorn, who continued in office until 1885, when his son ruled in his stead. During this time Irish Freemasonry made good progress and the number of lodges increased steadily.

In 1877 Grand Lodge broke with the Grand Orient of France (being the first Grand Lodge to do so) on the French freemasons' discarding the Volume of the Sacred Law.

The Victoria Jubilee Masonic Annuity Fund Founded, 1887

The third Charity was begun by a young doctor, Bro. Joseph Graham Burne, who on the death of an old patient in a Dublin Poor Law Hospital had found a Grand Lodge certificate under his pillow. The old man had made no attempt to trade on his membership. Bro. Burne vowed then that so far as he could help it no brother should ever be buried in a pauper's grave. He was assisted by members of Lodge No. 250, and at present there are some 320 old Brethren and widows in receipt of modest annuities.

In 1901 Bro. J. G. Burne installed his son as Master of Lodge No. 2, his own father, Bro. John Burne being present.

The golden Jubilee of the fund was marked in 1937 by a service in St. Patrick's Cathedral.

There are a number of Provincial charities doing excellent

IRISH FREEMASONRY

work in addition to the 'Three Jewels'. Thus Cork had had its own girls' school for nearly fifty years, before it was merged with the Dublin one in 1871.

Relaxation of the Penalties, 1893

The Irish was the first Constitution to recognize that the archaic penalties of the various obligations, based as they were upon the savage punishments inflicted under the medieval penal codes, could not be accepted literally. As early as 1893 a strong three-brother committee was set up by Grand Lodge. This comprised the Deputy Grand Master, R. W. Bro. Robert Shekleton, Q.C., and Bros. Chetwode Crawley and Lord Justice Fitzgibbon; as a result of their recommendations every candidate has since pledged himself merely to bear in mind the ancient and symbolic penalty and to bind himself by the real and no less effective penalty of being branded as false and faithless. Far more recently Scotland and England (in that order), with slight modifications, followed suit (*see* pp. 197 *and* 133).

The 6th Earl of Donoughmore, Grand Master, 1913-48

The sixth Earl of Donoughmore, descended from a brother of the Grand Master from 1789 to 1813, succeeded the 2nd Duke of Abercorn on the latter's death.

In 1919 the Grand Lodge met for the first time outside Dublin; since this Belfast meeting the October communication has been held each year in some external centre. This is possibly an example that might usefully be copied by other Grand Lodges.

Up to 1922 the Grand Secretary was practically an honorary Officer, the actual work being mainly carried out by his Deputy. On the retirement of Lord Dunalley in that year his deputy, V. W. Bro. Henry Charles Shellard, was promoted to be Grand Secretary, since when no deputy has been appointed. Brother Shellard, who had served the Irish Craft since 1898 as Clerk, Deputy Grand Secretary and Grand Secretary, retired from 'active service' in 1951, but continued to read the Minutes as Grand Secretary Emeritus till his death in 1955. He was succeeded by R.W. Bro. James O. Harte.

In 1924 the Prince of Wales (later the Duke of Windsor) was appointed Past Senior Grand Warden.

1913-1948

Deputations attended from the Grand Lodges of England, Scotland, the United States, Denmark, Canada and Australia to mark the celebration of the Bicentenary of the Grand Lodge of Ireland in 1925. The then Deputy Grand Master from 1920 to 1930 was an English mason, R. W. Bro. Col. Claude Cane ('The O'Cahan'). As a member of one of the oldest families in Ireland he formed a direct link with Lord Kingston (Grand Master, 1731), whose mother had also been an O'Cahan.

Two years later honorary Past Grand Rank, which had previously been confined to a few outstanding brethren of the Irish Constitution overseas, was extended to members at home. In 1928 the Duke of Connaught accepted the rank of Past Grand Master.

In 1933 it was decreed that all Grand Officers should wear the gold chain of office, which had hitherto been confined to the Grand Master and his Deputy.

Grand Lodge issued in 1938 an important Declaration setting forth its relations *vis-à-vis* Continental Grand Lodges, reaffirming, *inter alia*, its refusal to participate in conferences with so-called international associations which admit to membership bodies that fail to recognize the fundamental principles of Freemasonry.

Irish lodges in New Zealand presented three officers' chairs to the Irish lodge in Malta in 1944 to replace those lost in the 'Blitz'.

Freemasonry and 'the Troubles'

In the Easter Rising of 1916 the Grand Master himself (Lord Donoughmore) was among the non-belligerent casualties, being slightly wounded by a stray bullet. More serious results followed the treaty of December, 1921. In a few places, says Parkinson, masonic halls were sacked and destroyed and, on 24th April 1922, Freemasons' Hall, Dublin, was itself seized by irregulars, who held it for six weeks; fortunately no wanton damage was done.

Raymond Brooke, Grand Master, 1948-64

When the 6th Earl of Donoughmore, known and loved throughout the masonic world, died in 1948 he was succeeded by M. W. Bro. Raymond Brooke, who had served as his deputy during the preceding 18 years. The new Grand Master, who had been initiated in Meridian Lodge No. XII, Dublin, as long ago as 1909, was 'outstanding not only for his skill as a presiding officer, but for his unparalleled knowledge of Masonry in all its aspects'.*

Shortly after his being elected a political change occurred which might have been disastrous to the unity of Freemasonry in Ireland. Eire — the Irish Republic — withdrew from the Commonwealth in 1949, but Ulster retained its close association with the British Crown, remaining a part of the United Kingdom. Thus the Grand Lodge of Ireland had to administer daughter lodges in two entirely separated nations. This it succeeded in doing (one notable feature has been to hold certain of its Quarterly Communications in Ulster) and it was Brother Brooke who set the right course. His successor described him as 'undoubtedly one of the greatest Grand Masters that Ireland has ever had'.

Ireland and India

The Grand Master was unable to travel to India in 1961 for the formation of the new Grand Lodge there, but was represented by the Deputy Grand Master, R. W. Bro. George S. Gamble, who performed the ceremony of Constitution. All the preliminary arrangements for the foundation had been carried out by a Steering Committee which was presided over by R. W. Bro. Lieut-Gen. Sir Harold Williams,† the Irish Grand Inspector for Northern India and Pakistan. It is noteworthy that out of sixteen Irish lodges in India no fewer than ten opted to remain under their old constitution — a far larger proportion than in the case of either of the other two old Constitutions of England and Scotland.

The 7th Earl of Donoughmore, Grand Master, 1964—81

Lord Donoughmore, who succeeded M. W. Bro. Raymond Brooke on the latter's death, belonged to a family with a number

*V. W. Bro. R. E. Parkinson, P.S.G.D. (Ireland), in *A.Q.C.*, Vol. 78 1965, p. 226. Bro. Parkinson tells the story of a conference in London, at which a Scottish member saw fit to make remarks disparaging to the Grand Lodge of Ireland. Bro. Brooke reproved him in his own inimitable way, whereupon the presiding officer smilingly remarked: 'Now you know, Brethren, why they are called 'the Fighting Brookes'!'

†Already Past Grand Warden of England, Ireland and Scotland, and Past Deputy Grand Master of India, the Order of Service to Masonry was conferred upon him in September 1968. He died in 1971.

THE 7TH EARL OF DONOUGHMORE

of associations with the Irish Grand Lodge. His father had been the penultimate Grand Master and he was also collaterally descended from the 1st Earl (Grand Master, 1789-1813, *see* p. 158), whose brother the Hon. Abraham Hely-Hutchinson, was Deputy Grand Master from 1807 to 1818, while the 2nd Earl had served as Senior Grand Warden from 1791 to 1823 and the 4th Earl from 1846 to 1866.

At the Royal Albert Hall, London, celebration of the 250th anniversary of the Grand Lodge of England in June 1967*, it behoved Lord Donoughmore, as representing the next senior Grand Lodge, to deliver the opening speech of congratulation to the newly installed Duke of Kent. In doing so he recalled that *his* father had acted in a similar capacity at the installation of the present Duke of Kent's own father by King George VI in 1939. He also spoke of the singular longevity of Irish Grand Masters — during the 175 years between 1789 and 1964 his predecessors had numbered but six — and trusted that the Duke would similarly still be on the grand throne when the 300th anniversary should come to be celebrated.

On 4 June 1974, the Earl and Countess of Donoughmore were kidnapped from their home in Clonmel, Co. Tipperary, presumably by the Irish Republican Army. This atrocious act is believed to have been a pro-republican rather than an anti-masonic gesture. None the less there was great relief when they were restored, unharmed, to their home a few days later. That they bore themselves so bravely during their ordeal is only in accordance with the family motto: *Fortiter gerit crucem* (He bears the cross courageously). Lord Donoughmore died on 12 August 1981. He was succeeded by the 7th Marquess of Donegall.

The 250th Anniversary of Grand Lodge

The celebrations in Dublin on 22-24 June 1975 of this great event in Irish Freemasonry included a Service of Thanksgiving in St. Patrick's Cathedral, special meetings of the Grand Lodge of Instruction and the Lodge of Research No. 200, and of course an Especial Communication of the Grand Lodge itself. The Pro Grand Master, Earl Cadogan, and the Deputy Grand Master, Sir Allan Adair (himself an Irishman), headed the Deputation from the United Grand Lodge of England. The

see also p. 135.

Grand Master Mason of Scotland, Captain R. W. Gordon of Esselmont, and his predecessor led the representation from Edinburgh, and four other Grand Masters were among the leaders of the world-wide Craft who met to honour the occasion. Irish freemasons had travelled from many overseas Provinces and lodges.

The Grand Master, the Earl of Donoughmore, presided and there was unanimous satisfaction at his recovery from the ordeal to which he had been subjected in the previous year.

The meeting of the Lodge of Research was devoted to the reading of a paper by V. W. Bro. R. E. Parkinson entitled 'The Grand Lodge of Ireland and the World of Freemasonry'. This, with a report of all the Anniversary proceedings, was published in a booklet which was later made available from the Grand Secretary's office, an excellent and valuable record of a significant milestone in masonic history.

Differences from English Working

By 1760 at latest the Irish ritual had assumed very much the same form as is still in use today.

For as long a period as till 1875 Irish lodges always installed their Masters on two occasions each year, the two days of St. John. Since that year there has been only one installation a year, on or after 27th December, after the Installation of Officers in Grand Lodge at High Noon.

The beautiful Chair degree has always been practised in Ireland, whereas it was largely dropped by most Modern lodges in England and was only fully re-adopted in 1813.

Other points of difference in the two Constitutions (although the substance of the systems is of course the same) include:*

(1) In Ireland *all* offices in Grand Lodge (save the Deputy Grand Master), Provincial Grand Lodges (save the Provincial Deputy Grand Master and the Provincial Grand Inspectors — an office unknown in England), and in lodges are filled by election, not appointment; (2) England has nothing at all resembling the Irish Grand Lodge of Instruction (*see* p. 163);

*The authors' sources are mainly twofold: 'The Masonic Visitor in Ireland' by Bro. R. E. Parkinson, *A.Q.C.* Vol. 78, pp. 222-6, and *The Three Constitutions*, by Bro. A. Holmes-Dallimore (*The Masonic Record*, 1927).

DIFFERENCES FROM ENGLISH WORKING

(3) All Irish Grand Officers are either Right Worshipful or Very Worshipful; (4) Ireland still retains overseas 'Provinces' (in England, 'Districts' since 1865); (5) Irish private lodges mostly have nine to eleven regular meetings a year. A formal dinner rarely follows, except on installation nights, held usually in January.

(6) By-laws of all Irish lodges state not only the place and date but also the time of each regular meeting; (7) the term 'Installation' applies in Ireland not only to the Master but to both Wardens, the other officers being 'proclaimed'; (8) With the exception of the instructions to the new Master, which are restricted to a 'Conclave' of Installed Masters, the entire Installation is carried out in open lodge, working in the first degree; (9) No brother can be installed, if elected to an office, without the written approval of Grand Lodge; (10) No one under the rank of M.M. can vote in lodge or be elected to office; traditionally a Fellow Craft has the right —seldom exercised — to *speak* but not to vote; (11) in the absence of both Worshipful Master and Immediate Past Master the *junior* Past Master presides; (12) No one who is maimed or lame or defective can be admitted as a candidate except by dispensation.

(13) No more than one candidate may be taken at a time in the 1° and 3°; (14) When the initiate is restored to light his attention is directed to the brethren round the Altar. On the one hand he sees hands outstretched in welcome and fellowship; on the other, backs turned in indifference, working tools snatched up as weapons and drawn swords — a warning of what he might (symbolically) expect if he were to fail to keep his undertaking; (15) The 'steps' or distinctive modes of progression, likened by Laurence Dermott to 'a convivial soul at Donnybrook Fair', are quite unknown in Ireland.

(16) The English 'joining' brother is in Ireland 'affiliated'; (17) An affiliating Past Master takes precedence immediately after the Worshipful Master of the year in which he is affiliated, and is not placed at the bottom of the roll as in England; (18) An Irish lodge Secretary must be a Past Master, except by special exemptions; (19) Minutes, when confirmed, are signed by Secretary as well as Master and they must also be sealed, the seal to bear the device of a hand and trowel with the name and number of the lodge; (20) The Irish Tyler is 'not deemed an officer of the lodge'; (21) A 'Tyler's obligation' may be

IRISH FREEMASONRY

administered to Irish lodge visitors.

(22) Tracing Boards are not used in Irish working; (23) Ireland forbids the printing of books of ritual; (24) 'Masonic funerals' are permitted in Ireland to the extent that brethren may march in front of the coffin of a deceased brother wearing sprigs of 'acacia', which are deposited in the open grave; (25) No Royal Arch jewels may be worn in a Craft lodge nor Craft jewels in a chapter; (26) Irish aprons are invariably worn under the jacket — this is because candidates are 'clothed' while still clad for the ceremony; (27) Finally traces of Christianity have persisted in Irish Freemasonry, and Christian forms of prayer are still printed in the *Book of Constitutions* (1965) for use when no brother was present to whom they could be offensive; the Lord's Prayer is often used as part of the ordinary Craft ritual.

And so we must leave Irish Freemasonry, which has the second oldest Grand Lodge in the world and the only one to have ever held a regular meeting in another country; which has the honour of having introduced the Charge to the newly initiated candidate as well as certificates of membership, lodge warrants, military lodges and masonic journalism; and which has the earliest known references to the Royal Arch and much else of which it can justly be extremely proud.

CHAPTER IX

SCOTTISH FREEMASONRY

The study of Freemasonry in Scotland involves a return to medieval times as the development via the Mason Word followed lines very different from those of England. Then, though material is very plentiful, it is less easily digested, the histories of the Grand Lodge of Scotland by the two Lauries being out of date and not altogether reliable. There is among many magnificent lodge histories the monumental tercentenary edition of Murray Lyon's *History of the Lodge of Edinburgh* (*Mary's Chapel*) *No. 1,* and it may be briefly stated here that Scotland is rich in records of the operative and the pre-Grand Lodge speculative Craft.

Down to the close of the thirteenth century, the development of the two countries followed much the same lines but the Anglo-Scottish Wars and the Franco-Scottish alliance resulted in a divergence of those lines.

What was a Freemason?

We have encountered diversity of interpretation of the word 'freemason' in England. In Scotland it first appears in its modern significance in 1725 when the Lodge of Edinburgh is described as 'the Society of Free Masons'. The words 'frie mesones' used in the same lodge a century earlier clearly relate to the Freedom of a Burgh — the right to practise the Craft. In 1483 we have in Aberdeen 'Masonreys of the leige', here meaning the body of workmen who used the room or lodge.

Much has been claimed on behalf of the Gild organization in England, but we have shown how tenuous was the thread of continuity. North of the Border, the disruption of war meant poverty and the Mason Gilds were forced to amalgamate with the organizations of other Crafts.

SCOTTISH FREEMASONRY

Organization

The general medieval organization ran on similar lines to the English, though direct labour tended to give place to the contract system. The term *'Master Mason'* is constantly met with sometimes describing the chief technical official, sometimes a grade of employee – a master tradesman working on a job with his own servants.

The duties are nowhere clearly defined and examples of the second form are found at Holyrood House in 1735-6 where two master masons are engaged on the same job, one at 18s. a week and one at 16s. (Scots). Then, it is not easy to sub-divide the Scottish building craft; indeed no less an authority than Douglas Knoop divides them into three groups and admits some overlapping. These were *quarriers* who hewed and roughly prepared the stone, *cowans*, or builders of drystone walls, a craft not yet extinct in the north of England (or, alternatively and more commonly, masons without the Word) and *masons*, there being no distinction in Scotland between hewers and layers.

The Edinburgh Seal of Cause, 1475

We have seen that in England there was little or no sign of organization among the masons before the latter part of the fourteenth century, also that the Gilds tended to develop on oligarchic lines. In Scotland the excluded humbler brethren did not supinely accept their lost status but built up their own organization which grew in power as the Merchant Gilds declined, despite attempts to 'supress' leagues and bands of craftsmen. A statute of 1424 placed each craft under a Deacon (for the sake of simplicity we are omitting many delightfully medieval Scots ways of spelling and expression). Two years later the Deacon's powers were restricted to a testing of the craftsman's proficiency while the fixing of wages was vested in the council of the local burgh.

Within half a century the Masons and Wrights of Edinburgh were strong enough to obtain from the Burgh a *Charter of Incorporation of the Freemen-Masons and Wrights of Edinburgh,* the 'Seal of Cause' of 1475 (*see* p. 181). Trade Regulations were drawn up.

No Old Charges

It is remarkable that Scotland produced no traditional

THE SCHAW STATUTES

history such as England had from about 1400 in the Old Charges. The few copies associated with Scotland are obviously copied from English sources; indeed one or two naïvely require the Craftsman to be true to the King of *England*. The Edinburgh Incorporation already mentioned eventually became known as the *Incorporation of Mary's Chapel*. Other trades joined and the movement spread to other parts of Scotland.

Apprenticeship

It may be well here to consider the Apprenticeship system. Records are found in the fifteenth century and some youths were apprenticed to monasteries. The period varied — 5, 6, 7, 9 years. In Edinburgh, the Seal of Cause provided for a term of seven years after which the apprentice was to be examined by four searchers and, if found proficient, admitted to membership of the Craft.

The Schaw Statutes

Two documents of especial importance have survived. They contain Statutes drawn up in 1598 and 1599 by William Schaw who had been appointed Master of Work and General Warden of the Masons by James VI in 1583. He was a trusted official and enjoyed the confidence of the King and Queen. The earlier document was circularized to all lodges and a copy in Schaw's own hand is to be seen in the earliest minute book of the Lodge of Edinburgh (Mary's Chapel) No. 1. Another copy is preserved in the important minutes of the defunct Lodge of Aitchison's Haven, while the originals of both sets of Statutes are preserved in the Library of the Grand Lodge of Scotland. They were presented in 1952 by the 17th Earl of Eglinton and Winton (Grand Master Mason 1957-61), in whose family's possession they had remained for two centuries or more.

These documents are far too long to transcribe here and it may merely be said that they provided an elaborate code of organization and procedure, the 1599 portion providing a more intimate (what we would today call a Provincial) structure, especial powers being given to Kilwinning as the second Lodge in Scotland.

Mother Kilwinning

We have just introduced a name more hallowed among

masons in Scotland than is the name of York among the English Craft. In fact, *Mother Kilwinning* has her followers in every part of Scotland (and abroad) in the multitude of lodges that have adopted the word as part of their name.

The Abbey of Kilwinning was founded in 1140 and dedicated to St. Winning. It is situated three miles north of Irving near the Irish Sea, and was probably of unusual magnificence. Traditions which will hardly bear investigation have attached themselves to the building and its builders but is is confidently claimed that a lodge existed as early as the fifteenth century.

The second Schaw Statutes of 1599 very definitely ascribe to the Lodge of Kilwinning the second place on the roll and oversight was given to four districts. She has claimed a seniority over which she was prepared to go into the wilderness from 1744 to 1807 and now appears at the head of the Scottish Roll of Lodges, with the number 0 and precedency 'before 1598'.

The Lodge of Edinburgh (Mary's Chapel) No. 1

Although this appears on the Roll as No. 1, below Kilwinning, there can be no doubt that it holds real pride of place, its oldest surviving (though probably not earliest) minute following Schaw's entry of a copy of his own Statutes of 1598 (*see* p. 179). It is dated 'Ultimo Julii 1599' and deals with a complaint against one George Patoun who had offended by employing 'ane cowane' in his work but, as he made submission, no penalty was imposed though a general warning was issued. The minute is attested with the mark of Thomas Weir, the Warden.

We shall have more to say about this lodge later.

The St. Clair Charters

Two other documents of great interest and value are the St. Clair Charters of 1601 and 1628. In the first, the claim is made on behalf of the Lairds of Roslin that they had been for ages patrons and protectors of the mason craft in Scotland, that this patronage had been allowed to fall into abeyance and that, with the express permission of William Schaw, William St. Clair of Roslin was to purchase of the King, 'liberty, freedom and jurisdiction' over all masons in burgh and sheriffdoms. This was agreed to by the representatives of the lodges of Edinburgh, St. Andrews, Haddington, Aitchison's Haven and Dunfermline

– that is, five widely scattered lodges united in the common interest.

The second charter of 1628 confirms and elaborates the former and is signed by representatives of the lodges at Edinburgh, Dundee, Glasgow, Stirling, Dunfermline, Ayr and St. Andrews, seven in all and partly overlapping the previous list. The attempt to secure the recognition of the Crown was unsuccessful for in 1629 Charles I appointed Sir Anthony Alexander as Master of Work and Warden General and summarily brushed aside the prompt objection of Sir William Sinclair [sic], son of the William of the 1601 Charter.

The Incorporations

Incorporations existed among various crafts in various burghs and were generally established by 'seal of cause' which confirmed and approved on behalf of the municipality, rules drawn up by the craftsmen. By the end of the seventeenth century at least six had been granted.

The Masons and Wrights of Edinburgh, 1475.

The Coopers, Wrights and Masons of Aberdeen, 1527, ratified in 1541, when the Carvers, Slaters and Painters were added.

Glasgow, 1551.

Canongate. Date unknown but a list of Deacons and admissions from 1585. This included the Wrights, Coopers and Masons from 1630.

Lanark. A new seal of cause granted in 1674 to replace an earlier one destroyed in process of disinfection after the death of the holder from plague in 1645.

Ayr. The Squaremen Incorporation (Masons and Wrights) in 1556.

The Mason Word

We now come to the great feature of Scottish Freemasonry. England had in its Old Charges the traditional history but Scotland had the Mason Word. Douglas Knoop said in a paper before the Quatuor Coronati Lodge that the bridge between operative and speculative masonry rested mainly on Scotland at the operative end and on England at the speculative end. Like many of his statements this was hotly attacked by his fellow students, but it is more than probable that he was right.

SCOTTISH FREEMASONRY

We have briefly reviewed the operative development and some evidence of combination among the lodges. They certainly had the Word, which was something more than a mere expression. The Rev. Robert Kirk, Minister of Aberfoyle, said in 1691 that the Mason Word 'is like a Rabbinical Tradition, in the way of comment on Jachin and Boaz, the two pillars erected in Solomon's Temple. (1 Kings, 7. 21) with ane Addition of some secret Signe delyvered from Hand to Hand by which they know and become familiar ane with another'

The discovery of the catechisms described elsewhere (Chapter IV) has confirmed that, at the conclusion of the ceremony of admission, the word was circulated amongst the brethren and that there were two distinct degrees, the Entered Apprentice and the Fellow-Craft or Master.

The earliest known printed reference is the celebrated passage in Henry Adamson's *The Muses Threnodie*, printed in Edinburgh in 1638:

> For we be brethren of the Rosie Cross;
> We have the Mason Word and second sight,
> Things for to come we can foretell aright.

What was an Entered Apprentice?

Bro. Harry Carr, after a thorough examination of the Edinburgh Register of Apprentices and the Burgess Rolls, has come to the conclusion that there were four stages in the process of the operative mason: Booking (town); Entered Apprentice (lodge), about 2½ years later; Fellow-Craft (lodge), a further 7½ years on average; Freeman Burgess (town), after about one more year (*The Mason and the Burgh*, 1954). The Schaw Statutes required the presence of six masters and two apprentices at the reception of a master or fellow craft, so the entered apprentice had a share in government.

The term is not found in pre-Andersonian Masonry other than in Scotland.

Custom of Admission

In primitive times, candidates for admission to the adult body of the tribe were often subjected to ordeals ranging from the sublime to the ridiculous. As the *Edinburgh Register House MS* of 1696 indicates, racial memories were not dormant and the decorum now associated with Freemasonry was conpicuous by its absence. It also indicates the existence of two separate degrees or ceremonies, one conferred on entered apprentices, the other on fellow-crafts or masters. Knoop goes so far as to suggest that there may have been two sets of secrets as early as 1598, though he admits that in the Schaw Statutes of that year there was no requirement that the mark of the entered apprentice was to be booked (presumably he had none, although in Aberdeen in 1670 the names and marks of the entered apprentices were recorded in the Mark Book).

At least a few of the old Scottish lodges were in possession of copies of the Old Charges, though regard must be paid to the caution given earlier in this chapter. The Lodge of Aberdeen in 1670 admitted its apprentices with considerable ceremony. Not only did they impart the Mason Word; they also read over the lodge version of the Old Charges and the Laws and Statutes of the lodge.

The *Edinburgh Register House MS* indicates that the person to be admitted to the fellowship was introduced to a version of the five points of fellowship differing only in detail from our own. These points are more fully dealt with in the *Graham MS* of 1726 (*see* Chapter IV) which, though discovered in Yorkshire in 1936, very probably related to Scotland or the Border country. It introduces also a counterpart of the Hiramic legend, the central figure being Noah, not Hiram.

Appearance of the Speculative Element

Very early in Scottish Masonic history, the non-operative makes his appearance. On 8th June, 1600, the Lodge of Edinburgh met at Holyrood House* and the minutes are attested by *all present* including John Boswell, Laird of Auchinleck, a prominent landowner. Incidentally he was an ancestor of another famous brother, James Boswell† the biographer of Dr. Johnson. The same lodge, in 1634, admitted as Fellows of the Craft Lord Alexander, Sir Antony Alexander and Sir Alexander Strachan. The admission of Sir Robert Moray has already been mentioned.

The presbytery of Kelso ruled in 1652 'there is neither sinne nor scandale in that' (the Mason) 'word, because in the purest

---

*Bro. Harry Carr believes this meeting to have been called only to try' an offending office-bearer, and that Boswell (not a lodge member) was there in either a municipal or a legal capacity.

† 1740-1795. Depute Grand Master of Scotland, 1776-1778.

SCOTTISH FREEMASONRY

tymes of this Kirke, maisons haveing that word have bee ministers;...'

The position of these non-operatives improved slowly an at variable speed. It is possible that they were looked upon i some places for patronage and support, rather like the honorar vice-president of a village cricket club today, expected to b 'forthcoming' when necessary but to take no part in th government of the lodge. In Aberdeen and Kilwinning ther was no bar, but in Edinburgh it was not until 1727 that a nor operative was chosen as Warden and that the operative elemen lost its hold. This state of affairs is not found in England wher the operative lodge is almost unknown owing to the loss o all early records.

The Hiving Process

Towards the end of the seventeenth century there began a expansion among the lodges similar to that which *followed* th establishment of the Grand Lodge of England. In earlier times lodges had been few and widely separated but economic con ditions had their repercussions — the demand for the masons services increased and the tight little oligarchies began to mee rivals. The Lodge of Edinburgh had for upwards of a couple o centuries exercised control in and around Edinburgh, but sud denly in 1677 found a new lodge in the Canongate. Th 'interlopers' evaded the wrath of Edinburgh by producing document from Kilwinning acknowledging the new lodge to b a branch of itself. Of course Canongate Kilwinning was i effect an independent lodge from the beginning but what coulc Edinburgh do about it? In any event the Burgh of the Canor gate was then a quite separate entity.

Eleven years later another lodge, Canongate and Leith Leith and Canongate,* set up its own authority without the pretence of authority from Kilwinning — and without assen from the Crown or Warden-General. Edinburgh countered thi move by banning the new movement but their 'sanctions' were quite unsuccessful and the position was not accepted until 1736

Then, in 1709, schism struck within the Lodge of Edinburgl itself. Opposition to the management of lodge funds by the Master Masons, without reference to other grades, culminatec

*This curious title was intended to demonstrate the equal status o the two burghs.

THE HIVING PROCESS

in the formation of the Lodge of Journeymen Masons who, after a period of legal process, secured for themselves a Decreet Arbital in 1715, which empowered them to communicate the Mason Word.

A third method, successful in more isolated places, was the mere assemblage of a number of masons into a lodge without pretence of authority, though there was a tendency to adopt the 'blessed word' Kilwinning as part of the title. The Lodge of Holyrood House (St. Luke) came into being in this manner in 1734, two years before the formation of the Grand Lodge of Scotland.

The fourth method anticipated the Grand Lodge system. The new lodge applied to and accepted a warrant from some established body; for example, in 1729, Kilwinning granted one to the Lodge of Torphichen at Bathgate.

Visit of Dr. Desaguliers

By this time the Grand Lodge of England was in being and, as we have seen, was making good use of the Scottish material imported by Dr. Anderson. During 1721, Dr. Desaguliers happened to be in Edinburgh on business when he visited the Lodge of Edinburgh where he was 'received as a brother'. Within a few days, the lodge admitted as Entered Apprentices and Fellowcrafts the Lord Provost, several members of the Council and other distinguished Scotsmen, as well as a couple of ordinary operative apprentices.

The Third Degree

That mystery of mysteries, the origin of the third degree, again appears here. We know it was in full operation in England before 1730 and was almost certainly introduced into Scotland from England yet, by some extraordinary chance, the earliest known record of its operation is found in what is now Dumbarton Kilwinning Lodge No. 18 (S.C.), whose opening Minute of the 29th January 1726 refers to 'Masters, fellows of craft and Entered prentices'. At the following meeting on the 25th March a Fellow Craft was 'unanimously admitted and received a Master of the Fraternity and renewed his oath and gave his entry money in the terms of the Constitution.'*

*See H. Carr, *The Conjoint Theory*, A.Q.C., 66, 1953.

SCOTTISH FREEMASONRY

The Grand Lodge Projected

By this time it must have been well known in Scotland that the establishment of a Grand Lodge in England had proved successful and had been followed by similar action in Ireland. In 1735 there were six lodges in Edinburgh:

> Lodge of Edinburgh (Mary's Chapel) — pre 1598.
> Canongate Kilwinning, 1677.
> Canongate and Leith, Leith and Canongate, 1688.
> Journeymen Masons, 1709.
> Kilwinning Scots Arms, 1729.
> Holyrood House (St. Luke), 1734.

Canongate Kilwinning took the initiative and three others joined, namely Mary's Chapel, Kilwinning Scots Arms and a newly-formed addition, Leith Kilwinning.†

At this point the St. Clairs of Roslin re-enter the story for, probably in order to suggest a link with the ancient brethren, Canongate Kilwinning initiated William St. Clair. He was initiated in the ordinary way and paid his fee.

There were further cautious preliminary movements after which a proposal was circulated that a Grand Master Mason should be appointed. Canongate Kilwinning agreed and added that a proper Secretary was also essential.

The Four Lodges Meet

As in England, so in Scotland, four old lodges were associated in the formation of Grand Lodge. Canongate Kilwinning, Mary's Chapel, Kilwinning Scots Arms and Leith Kilwinning were all represented by their Masters and Wardens on 15th October 1736, the delegates taking their places without precedence but in the order of entry into the room. A series of resolutions formed the first regulations and these were transmitted to the Masters of all the known regular lodges in Scotland.

Progress at first was slow and the lodges hesitated before joining the movement. Among the candidates with an eye on the throne were William St. Clair of Roslin, the Earl of Home and Lord Crawford. The Grand Election was held on 30th November 1736, when thirty-three lodges were represented,

† Kilwinning Scots Arms and Leith Kilwinning are extinct and their records have been lost. The other lodges are still on the Roll.

GRAND LODGE FORMED

their Masters and Wardens producing their authorities. After they had disposed of a difficulty caused by the presence of two sets of representatives of the Lodge of Falkirk, the wily St. Clair produced a written resignation of powers which in fact he and his family did not possess over speculative Freemasonry. This handsome (though meaningless) gesture captured the assembly and William St. Clair was elected first Grand Master Mason* of Scotland though it is believed that a substantial number of brethren had intended to vote for the Earl of Home.

Establishment of Precedency

This was a most difficult matter in Scotland where many lodges, some of long standing, were in existence at the time of the formation of Grand Lodge. England, so far as its Roll was concerned, had but the four old lodges to consider. Murray Lyon tells us that the thirty-three lodges attending the Grand Election were placed on the roll in the order in which they entered the hall. (This was but a temporary arrangement and on St. Andrew's Day, 1737, the Grand Lodge decided to enrol its lodges according to seniority of foundation, those producing no documents to be placed at the end of the Roll.)

There was a prompt objection to the presence of Canongate and Leith, Leith and Canongate, as a schismatic body, but this was smoothed over.

The first quarterly meeting of the new Grand Lodge was held on 12th January 1737, when the minutes of the four associated lodges and of the Grand Election were approved. Kilwinning submitted complaints -- especially about the meeting place being always Edinburgh, very properly pointing out that it was as easy for the Master and Wardens of that city to go elsewhere as for the rural brethren to come to town. It was also submitted that the registration fee of half a crown bore unfairly on the operative brethren who were hard put to it to meet their lodge dues. This was overruled and Grand Lodge decreed that those who failed to pay the entry fee should not benefit from the charity fund.

Earl of Cromartie

William St. Clair was succeeded by the Earl of Cromartie

*The Head of the Scottish Craft has always been so entitled. This stems from the fact that the Master of a lodge in the early days was known as the Master Mason.

on 30th November 1737, Grand Lodge having patriotically adopted St. Andrew's Day as that of the Grand Election. It was also decided that the Grand Secretary and Grand Clerk should not be elected annually but should hold office 'during good behaviour'. Grand Lodge lost little time in emerging into public view for the foundation stone of the new Royal Infirmary of Edinburgh was laid with masonic honours on 2nd August 1738.

Until 1756 the Grand Master Mason was elected annually but was probably something of a figure-head for it is observed that the Depute Grand Master and the Substitute Grand Master held continuous office during most of this time. Thus regularity was maintained while the tenure of the principal Office by a succession of persons of distinction must have conduced to the public regard for Freemasonry.

Relations established with England

It was agreed in 1740, under the Earl of Strathmore, that a correspondence should be opened with the Grand Lodge of England.

The Kilwinning Secession

We have already seen that Kilwinning was not too happy about the new state of affairs. When the precedence of the lodges was decided by Grand Lodge, the Lodge of Edinburgh minute of 'Ultimo Julii, 1599' was older by forty-three years than anything that could be produced by Kilwinning. For some years this situation seems to have been accepted, but there were evidently mental reservations and in 1743, having failed in an attempt to secure promotion to the head of the list, Kilwinning quietly resumed its independence. This it maintained for the next seventy years, granting charters on its own authority not only in Scotland but also in North America.

The Jacobite Rebellions

It is probably true to say that Anglo-Scottish military strife had a more noticeable effect on the Scottish Craft than it had on the brethren south of the border. It has already been stated that the earliest recorded initiation in England was carried out by members of the Lodge of Edinburgh who were at

THE JACOBITE REBELLIONS

Newcastle with the Scottish army in 1641. The English Grand Lodge was set up two years after the collapse of the 'Fifteen', the Scottish nine years before the 'Forty-five'. The only effect of the latter in England was a short sharp panic as the Jacobites advanced to Derby and as swiftly withdrew. Very different was the story in Scotland where the contending armies marched and counter-marched and where most of the fighting took place.

There were brethren serving on both sides though, once again, the lodges generally steered clear of politics. Murray Lyon tells us that, in the Lodge of Dunblane, many of the brethren were non-operatives and some of these were Jacobites; some took part in each of the rebellions. Canongate Kilwinning is said to have been markedly Jacobite but, though it ceased to meet for a year, it is not true that it was 'closed'. Some of the members of Holyrood House were 'out' and one or two were transported and others pardoned, Robert Seton (one of the latter class) serving as Master of the lodge in 1747-8.

There was more trouble in Inverness, where some of the members of St. John's Kilwinning were said to have taken up arms on behalf of the Government in the 'independent companies'. When Charles Edward occupied the town in 1746 these withdrew into Ross and Sutherland. St. Andrew's Kilwinning, of the same town, complained that the Duke of Cumberland's troops broke into the lodge chest and carried off everything but the charter. This may be discounted by the fact that in 1750 an investigation was held into the conduct of the Treasurer at the time of the alleged losses.

However, peace eventually prevailed and Scottish Freemasonry settled down to a couple of centuries of uninterrupted working before the Royal Arch Chapter at Gretna Green was dispersed in tragic and untimely fashion by a German bomb on 7th April 1941.

Anti-Masonry appears

We have already referred briefly to curiosity about the Mason Word. In England the earliest known of a long series of attacks appeared in 1678. The Associate Synod of Stirling considered in 1745 the propriety of the mason oath and allowed the various kirk sessions to act as they thought proper. There was only a moderate reaction to this and in 1775 the kirk sessions were ordered to be more searching in their inquiries; a further stiffening took place in 1757 when the interrogation of masons was ordered, those refusing information to be excommunicated. A confession of participation in Freemasonry involved public penance and a sessional rebuke. The Grand Lodge of Scotland took no cognizance of this attack, the effect of which was hardly noticeable.

Grand Lodge continues

For some years little of note occurred; each Grand Master Mason nominated his successor, who was duly elected, until 1752 when Lord Boyd took no action and a committee selected as his successor Mr. George Drummond, remarkable as being the first person recorded as *raised* in Mary's Chapel Lodge. It is curious that at the same time it was necessary to find replacements for the Depute and Substitute Grand Masters and the Grand Clerk, each of whom had held his office since Grand Lodge's establishment.

Is it possible that we have here a repercussion of the Jacobite troubles? The new Grand Master Mason had, by raising and leading volunteers, done much towards the defeat of the 1745 Rebellion yet the retiring Depute Grand Master, John Young, had also a very active military career.

The earliest instance of the *re-election* of a person as Grand Master came in 1756 when Sholto, Lord Aberdour*, was again chosen. During this nobleman's first year it was unanimously resolved that the Grand Master Mason for the time being be affiliated and recorded as a member of every daughter lodge in Scotland. There was also some extension of the system of appointing Provincial Grand Masters. Colonel Young, former Depute Grand Master, was appointed Provincial Grand Master for America and the West Indies.

It now became customary for the Grand Master Mason to serve a second year, but at the end of the first he nominated his successor who was known for twelve months as Grand Master elect. This system prevailed until 1827.

Innovations Resisted

Grand Lodge forbade in 1759 the use by lodges of painted floor cloths; in 1760 they attempted to restrict the practice of

*later the 15th Earl of Morton, Grand Master of England (Moderns), 1757-61.

giving 'vails' or drink money to servants, and in 1762 declined to issue a warrant to some brethren in London who were desirous of setting up a Scottish lodge there.*

More progressively, the Grand Chaplain was made a member of Grand Lodge in 1758. In 1765 it was ordered that proper clothing and jewels should be procured for the Grand Officers and in 1770 Grand Lodge, by advertisement, threatened to call in the charters of lodges who failed to render their dues to the Grand Secretary.

In 1778 lodges were forbidden to offer bounties to military recruits. (Freemasonry, though abstaining from politics, was always interested in the welfare of the Services and lodges in Scotland and England occasionally joined the recruiting parades.)

The Lodges are numbered

It has already been mentioned that attempts were made at a very early date to decide the precedence of lodges. From about 1760 onwards they were distinguished by numbers and were re-numbered in 1809, 1816, 1822 and 1826.

Robert Burns

No account of Scottish Freemasonry would be complete without some reference to that most famous of national poets, Robert Burns. He was initiated in St. David's Lodge, Tarbolton, in 1781 though a year later he and others seceded and formed the Lodge of Tarbolton Kilwinning, St. James, which possesses a fine collection of his relics. He served as Deputy Master and took an active part in the social side, many poems about the lodge or its brethren being found among his works. Perhaps the best is 'Adieu! a heart-warm fond adieu!' written when, having failed as a farmer, he was about to emigrate. This course was avoided at the last minute and he visited Edinburgh, proving a favourite at Canongate Kilwinning, though it must be recorded with regret that the famous picture of his inauguration as Poet-Laureate of the lodge was painted many years after his time and the genuineness of the incident has been disputed. The first reference to his having *held* the office occurs only in 1815!

*They nevertheless formed an Antients' Lodge, which is today the Caledonian Lodge No. 134 (E.C.). Scotland did warrant lodges in Carlisle (1786) and Douglas, Isle of Man (1843), which are represented today by Nos. 310 and 1004 on the English Register.

He died in 1796, leaving the Craft the poorer for the loss of this wayward but lovable genius.

The Additional Degrees

Grand Lodge disapproved of the participation of the brethren in additional degrees and in 1799 formally prohibited its lodges from holding 'any other Meetings than those of the Three Great Orders of Masonry'. It was necessary to repeat this a year later as some lodges were so closely identified with the Royal Arch and Knights Templar.

The Earl of Moira

In 1805, the Prince of Wales (Grand Master of England (Moderns) from 1790 to 1813), although not a Scottish freemason, was elected 'Grand Master and Patron' and remained so — by re-election — until his succession to the throne in 1820. A series of seven 'Acting Grand Masters' ruled the Scottish Craft during this period, the first being the Earl of Moira (1806-1808) who was also Acting Grand Master of England (1790-1813). Lord Moira was notable both for eloquent orations and for his success in reconciling dissident masonic authorities. In addition to his leading role in the negotiations leading to the English Union of 1813 there will be remembered his creation of the ties which have since closely linked the Scottish and English jurisdictions. It was during his Scottish Acting Grand Mastership that the reconciliation between Grand Lodge and Mother Kilwinning was brought about.

Dissension

Upon the reconciliation of Kilwinning with Grand Lodge, Kilwinning was given a new position at the head of the list without a number. This was certainly unfair to the Lodge of Edinburgh (Mary's Chapel) No. 1, which had its minutes complete from 1599. Edinburgh was willing to stand aside if Kilwinning could only produce the proof. This resulted in the temporary secession of several lodges who set up an organization styling itself 'The Associated Lodges seceding from the present Grand Lodge of Scotland'. Masters of the seceding lodges occupied the chair of the provisional body in rotation at its annual festivals. Another rebellion at the time was led by a Dr. John Mitchell, Master of Lodge Caledonian, who moved

DISSENTION

a Grand Lodge in 1807 that an address be presented to the King thanking him for supporting the established religion of the country. This was lost by a majority of one vote. The following year, Dr. Mitchell was found guilty by Grand Lodge of having proposed at a meeting of Caledonian Lodge that it should secede from Grand Lodge. He was suspended but, three days later, his lodge re-installed him in the chair and the lodge *did* secede! After consultation with the Grand Lodges of England and Ireland, the Grand Lodge of Scotland expelled Dr. Mitchell in 1808 and suspended several members of Mary's Chapel and *their* associates. The lodge promptly backed Dr. Mitchell, and the majority of its office bearers and those of the Lodge of St. Andrew, which had taken similar action, were suspended.

There ensued a long and bitter struggle but happily in 1813 peace was achieved, Grand Lodge having to give way on most matters with the exception of the expulsion of Dr. Mitchell.

The Laws Revised

Despite, or perhaps because of, the antiquity of Freemasonry in Scotland Grand Lodge managed to get along without their own Book of Constitutions for nearly a century. A Committee was set up in 1829 to revise the Laws and their first code was published in 1836 since when there have been several revisions.

The Centenary of Grand Lodge

On St. Andrew's Day, 1836, the Centenary of Grand Lodge was celebrated, the Grand Master Mason being Lord Ramsay, afterwards Marquess of Dalhousie. Gold medals struck in commemoration were presented to the Grand Lodges of England and Ireland.

Benefit Societies

Before the day of organized masonic benevolence, there existed in many lodges an element now associated more nearly with the Friendly Society movement. This was not peculiar to Scotland, being found in many parts of the north of England; indeed the benefit side of the Travelling Mark Lodge of Ashton-under-Lyne was still in operation until very nearly the end of the nineteenth century. In 1844 the Grand Lodge of Scotland ordered an inquiry into the effects, good or bad, of benefit societies on the prosperity of Freemasonry. It was reported that in some lodges it was explained to candidates that their fees would be so much for the Craft and so much (more) for the benefit society, and it appeared that the person who did not take up membership of the society was debarred from office in the lodge. It was admitted that the societies were often conducted with great care and were beneficial to the parties concerned.

On 6th May 1844, it was resolved 'that all lodges who may hereafter form benefit societies are hereby prohibited from depriving any of the members of their lodges of the right of voting at the election of office-bearers, or being chosen office-bearers; and those lodges who already have benefit societies connected therewith, are instructed to make such alterations upon their bye-laws and practice as will admit every duly constituted member of the lodge, not lying under any masonic disability, to vote, or to be eligible for office, at the elections of office-bearers. The Grand Lodge also recommends all lodges having benefit societies to be very careful in keeping the funds of the lodge perfectly distinct and separate from those of the society.'

Two years later the Fund of Masonic Benevolence was established.

Interval between Degrees

It was ordained in 1844 that an interval of two weeks should elapse between each of the Craft degrees. This met the convenience of lodges meeting bi-monthly but was designed to stop the practice of hurrying candidates through all three in one night. There was a proviso permitting the ban to be overridden by the Master or Wardens 'in any particular case of emergency' but this no longer applies. A further condition more recently imposed is that intrants (a Scottish term) may *not* be initiated at the meeting at which the ballot is taken. At one time, seven candidates could receive their degrees (first, second or third) together but the maximum is now five.

Installed Masters

In 1846 it was declared: '. . . The Grand Lodge further considers every Master Mason qualified to be elected to and fill he chair as R. W. Masters without receiving any additional secrets whatever.'

It was not until 1870 that Grand Lodge, under the Earl of Rosslyn, recognized and adopted from England the Installed Master's degree.

Grand Temple and Library

The foundations of what is now a fine masonic library were laid in 1849 when the widow of Dr. Charles Morison of Greenfield (founder of the Supreme Council 33° for Scotland) presented to Grand Lodge his fine collection of masonic books and manuscripts. This was catalogued by the great historian, Murray Lyon, and has since been very considerably augmented. From 1950 to 1960 it was in the energetic hands of Brother George Draffen of Newington,* another distinguished masonic scholar.

In 1857 a committee was appointed to consider the propriety and practicability of providing a Masonic Hall. A year later the foundation stone was laid by the 6th Duke of Atholl, Grand Master Mason, and on 24th February 1859 the hall, in George Street, Edinburgh, was consecrated and inaugurated. The corner stone of the present hall, on the same site, was laid by the Marquess of Tullibardine, Grand Master Mason, on 20th April 1911 and Grand Lodge met therein for the first time on 7th November 1912 when the Temple was consecrated.

Scottish Masonic Charity

Scotland's efforts for masonic charity have ever taken a practical form. We read of the taking of a collection of £10 in Grand Lodge in 1737 and, the same year, Grand Lodge agreed to pay the wages of a number of operative masons engaged on the building of the Edinburgh Infirmary. Provision was also made for the apprenticing to their fathers' trade of a number of orphans of operative masons; during the apprenticeship of eight years Grand Lodge provided clothing and other necessaries. Widows and distressed brethren were not forgotten and donations quickly came in from distant lodges, some of them overseas.

In 1759, ten guineas was voted towards the relief of French

---

*Substitute Grand Master, Scotland 1966-7. Depute Grand Master, 1974-6.

prisoners of war in Edinburgh Castle, priority being given to brother masons.

The Grand Lodge Charity Fund covered all benevolent work for more than a century until, in 1846, the Fund of Scottish Masonic Benevolence was established to which office-bearers of Grand Lodge were required to contribute. An Annuity Fund was established in 1888 and in 1917 the Orphan Annuity Fund was established. Law 171 of the Constitutions requires every daughter lodge to take a collection at the annual Installation for the benevolent funds of Grand Lodge.

A significant development was the acquisition of a house called 'Ault Wharrie' in Dunblane, Perthshire, which was opened in 1951 by H.R.H. the Princess Royal for use as an old people's home. In 1959, 'Randolph Hill' (in the same city and burgh) was adapted as an extension to 'Ault Wharrie'. Subsequently, in 1967, a further new building was commenced to accommodate married couples.

Bi-Centenary of Grand Lodge

The Bi-Centenary of Grand Lodge was celebrated with great *éclat* on 30th November 1936, when Sir Iain Colquhoun of Luss was succeeded as Grand Master Mason by H.R.H. the Duke of York, who was already Provincial Grand Master for Middlesex under the English Constitution. His Royal Highness made his entry into Scottish Freemasonry by affiliation with the lodge at Glamis, of which his father-in-law, the Earl of Strathmore, was a Past Master. On his accession to the Throne as King George VI he resigned his office.

Overseas Visitations

A marked feature of Scottish Freemasonry in recent years has been the admirable tendency for Grand Master Masons, the Grand Secretary and other dignitaries to travel widely abroad to visit Scottish Masonic Districts and isolated daughter lodges. In 1965 Bro. Lord Bruce (then ruling the Scottish Craft), while on an extensive tour of this nature formally consecrated the Grand Lodge of Turkey which had been in existence for some ten years. An amusing anecdote is recorded that when, on the morning of the ceremony, Lord Bruce was being shown around the seraglio in the old Sultan's palace at Istanbul he heard the guide say

OVERSEAS VISITATIONS

'And here we had a better collection of Hellenic treasures even than that collected by Lord Elgin.'

The great-great-grandson of the collector did not acknowledge the implied compliment!

The Year Book

In 1952 Grand Lodge issued its first *Year Book* and for many years George Draffen (*see* p. 195 *n.*) was the editor of this most effective and valuable publication. Each issue includes several well-chosen papers on various aspects of the Craft and a yearly 'Progressive Index' makes the series a useful work of reference to the student. A great deal of information about Grand Lodge and daughter lodges is given, the latest statistics reporting 1,094 lodges — 441 being outwith Scotland.

The Penalties

On 3rd November 1966, Grand Lodge recommended that 'all daughter lodges within the Scottish Constitution should omit the "ancient" penalties from all the obligations given in their Lodges'. This, it will be seen, goes further than the comparable resolution in the United Grand Lodge of England (*see* p. 133).

Differences from English Working

As was done in the chapter on Irish Masonry, we list some of the Scottish practices which vary so interestingly from the English:

(1) The *office-bearers* (not officers) of a lodge and their jewels are:

Master: square, compasses, arc of 90° and the sun; Past Master: the same without the sun; Depute Master: the square and compasses; Substitute Master: the square; Wardens, Secretary, Treasurer (in that order): as in England; Almoner: level and compasses; Chaplain: a triangle with the All-Seeing Eye; Senior Deacon: a mason's mell (maul); Junior Deacon: a trowel; Director of Ceremonies: as in England; Architect: a Corinthian column on an arc of 90°; Jeweller: a goldsmith's hammer; Bible-Bearer (abroad this title is varied in accordance with the book(s) in use): an open Bible (Koran, etc.); Sword Bearer: two swords in saltire; Director of Music: two trumpets

SCOTTISH FREEMASONRY

in saltire; Steward: cornucopia and cup; Inner Guard and Tyler as in England. A Piper (bagpipes between square and compasses) and an Organist (lyre) may also appear in the list, as may a Bard and a Standard Bearer (jewels unspecified).

Any member of the lodge admitted at least fourteen days before nomination can be nominated and *elected* (not appointed) to any office. The lodge committee usually recommends brethren for office but they must be proposed and seconded.

The nominee for Master does not *have* to be a Past Warden. The offices of Depute and Substitute Master do not imply installation in the English sense but all office-bearers are said to be 'installed' as such.

The Master is 'Right Worshipful' and the Wardens 'Worshipful' during their tenure of office. All Scottish masons are known as 'Brother A.B.'; the prefixes of acting Grand and Provincial or District office-bearers are attached to the office and not the person (e.g. Bro. A.B., Most Worshipful Grand Master Mason).

(2) There are no Lodges of Instruction. Rehearsals, where necessary, should take place in open lodge and in the usual lodge room.

(3) Craft jewels only may be worn in lodge; Royal Arch and other jewels are therefore forbidden.

(4) The aprons and sashes (the latter are optional) of a lodge will be trimmed in the colour(s) adopted by the lodge at its constitution. The widest possible variety can be seen, including many different tartans. The full dress apron can be richly ornamented with gold. Aprons are worn *under* the coat except where the coat (e.g. in uniform) has to be buttoned close.

(5) A Lewis (the son of a mason) may seek initiation, without special Grand Lodge approval, after attaining the age of 18 years.

(6) There is no standard ceremonial for degree work and many printed formularies are popular. Typical points are the darkened Temple for initiation, the removal of a shoe before taking an obligation, reference to the Holy St. John in the $1°$ obligation, and an extremely dramatic $3°$ where – in some rituals – the participants are left to 'ad lib' rather than follow printed wording.

(7) It is the exception for a formal dinner to follow a

DIFFERENCES FROM ENGLISH WORKING

meeting. 'Harmony' — a very simple repast accompanied by songs and good fellowship — is the usual practice.

(8) Meetings are advertised in special columns in the local press and summonses (called 'billets') are often printed only for the annual Installation meeting. (Overseas, the Scottish lodges generally follow local masonic custom in this.)

Kilwinning

Several references have already been made to this lodge, properly described as 'Mother Kilwinning No. 0 (nought). One of the conditions under which the reconciliation with Grand Lodge took place in 1807 was that the Right Worshipful Master of Kilwinning should automatically hold the office of Provincial Grand Master of Ayrshire. This condition had been faithfully observed.

A special committee of Grand Lodge has recently been discussing with representatives of the lodge a proposed further change in the special status so accorded. By this a new masonic Province of Kilwinning would be established to have jurisdiction over the lodge and any future lodge erected within the parish of Kilwinning. The Province would be the senior under the Scottish Constitution. The appointment of its ruler would rest with Mother Kilwinning Lodge and the brother elected to the office was, *ipso facto*, to be 'Kilwinning Depute Grand Master of Scotland', ranking immediately after the Depute Grand Master. Any new lodge erected in the new Province was to be specially numbered '01', '02', etc.

Although Grand Lodge in 1981 approved all these arrangements, it seems that some residual doubts remained with Mother Kilwinning and it is possible that the proposed remarkable changes will not be put into effect.

CHAPTER X

THE HOLY ROYAL ARCH

Origins

Whence came the Royal Arch? For that matter, how did we acquire any of our masonic degrees? For some sort of answer we must delve into that shadowy background from which the three degrees of Craft Masonry evolved in the years before and after the foundation of the first Grand Lodge.

Some students believe that the Royal Arch was born in France as one of many degrees created after the spread of Freemasonry to the Continent and that it was 'exported' to England. It is true that — in the years after the establishment of the first Grand Lodge — there were those who found themselves dissatisfied with the simple teachings of the Craft and embellished it with all kinds of additional degrees.

Craft ritual was, as we have seen, more or less settled into the three degrees by 1730 by which time the Hiramic legend had come to stay; yet there are scattered indications of other stories of loss and recovery of vital secrets. In the Old Charges of the operative masons much attention was paid to two pillars — not those of King Solomon's Temple but two pillars designed to carry the knowledge of mankind over an impending catastrophe; this proved to be Noah's flood. Early speculative Freemasonry *may* have known three distinct third degree legends: the building of the Ark and the flood; the death of Noah; and the building of the Tower of Babel.

The *Graham MS* of 1726, which bases its legend of the loss of knowledge on the (natural) death of Noah, indicates that *faith* supplies the want. Quite early in the century there are indications that there was something further — possibly a secret learning imparted only to Masters. In 1725 a skit on Freemasonry — many were published — refers to a mysterious hocus-pocus word which belonged to the anathema pro-

ORIGINS

ounced against Ananias and Sapphira, and a catechism of the ame year includes a word known to Royal Arch masons today lus a flood of gibberish and a reference to the first chapter of t. John's Gospel.

This reference links up with deputations to constitute lodges t Exeter, Bath and Bury in 1732, each containing the motto n Greek, 'In the beginning was the Word', and the same (in nglish) has been added by a later hand to the *Grand Lodge No. 1 MS* of the Old Charges. The idea of a Being so dread that is name was not to be mentioned was widespread in sixteenth- nd seventeenth-century literature and, although no specific eference to this name can be found in Freemasonry before 1725, the idea is possibly much older.

The Rule of Three

Also appearing in the evidence of those times is another detail now particularly associated with the Royal Arch — the Rule of Three. An advertisement of 1726, almost certainly a parody, refers to 'the necessity there is for a Master to understand well the Rule of Three' and the *Graham MS* explains how Bezaleel agreed to instruct the two sons of King Alboyn in the theoretical and practical part of Masonry on condition they never disclosed it without another to themselves to make 'a trible voice'. After his death the secrets were lost because there was no third person to make this 'trible voice'. An early rhyme reads:

> If a Master Mason you would be
> Observe you well the Rule of Three

Two Continental Publications

There are to be found in the catechisms of the 1720s slight indications of the esoteric knowledge now communicated to Installed Masters. Some confirmation of this may be sought in two documents, unfortunately neither very satisfactory. A French work of 1740 entitled the *Rite Ancien de Bouillon* professes to be a third degree ritual in which is mixed up esoteric knowledge now associated with the Royal Arch and in another early continental publication, *L'Ordre des Francs Maçons Trahi* (1745), a tracing board suggests a combination of the two. It must, however, be remembered that in those early days the tracing board was only beginning to develop and

THE HOLY ROYAL ARCH

it is quite often found that emblems of more than one degree appeared in the same design without any suggestion that the degrees were fused. We have no evidence that the legend now associated with the third degree was ever associated with that of the Royal Arch and we do not know when the latter legend was joined to the teaching.

It must be admitted that early references to Royal Arch Masonry are vague and it is difficult to say when a completely separate degree was established with its present-day ritual and ceremonial. It is worthy of note that in other countries the Royal Arch itself became much more elaborate than in Great Britain and some details split off and were themselves expanded into degrees. Members of the Cryptic Degrees and, in England, the Allied Degrees will be especially aware of this.

Dassigny's Serious and Impartial Inquiry

One of the earliest references to the existence of Royal Arch Freemasonry is found in Fifield Dassigny's *Serious and Impartial Inquiry*, published in Dublin in 1744. Only two copies of this book are now known to exist. It tells us that, some few years before, a brother was made a Royal Arch mason in London.

Early Working

It is believed that the oldest Royal Arch Chapter is at Stirling (now No. 2 of Scotland), acknowledged to have met since 1743. Though its earliest minutes are missing, its bylaws of 1745 included 'No. 8. Exalting Excellent and Super Excellent, 5s. 0d.'

The oldest Royal Arch *minute* in existence is to be found in the United States, a fact of which that country is rightly proud. On 22nd December 1753, three brethren were 'raised to the Degree of Royal Arch Mason' in Fredericksburg, Virginia. At home, an early reference is to be discovered in Bristol in 1758 when we find 'Bros, Gordon and John Thompson Raised to the Degree of Royal Arch Masons'.

The earliest minutes of the Antients' Grand Lodge show that the Royal Arch degree was practised from the start. Indeed, 'Antient' lodges frequently worked Craft, Mark, Royal Arch and Knight Templar ceremonies under the authority of one warrant.

EARLY WORKING

Under the Grand Lodge of All England at York the Royal Arch was conferred from the time of the 'revival' of the Grand Lodge in 1761 to that of its collapse in the early 1790s.

The Grand Chapter

The original (Moderns') Grand Lodge of England would for some time have nothing to do with Royal Arch Freemasonry. In 1758 we have the famous letter from the Grand Secretary: 'Our Society is neither Arch, Royal Arch, or Antient'. As late as 1792 it was resolved that 'the Grand Lodge of England has nothing to do with the proceedings of the Society of Royal Arch Masons'. But the Royal Arch was certainly not neglected by individual brethren and on 22nd July 1766* the Charter of Compact of the Grand and Royal Chapter of the Royal Arch of Jerusalem was signed by Lord Blayney, Grand Master of the Moderns, and others including Dunckerley. Hughan agrees in his *Origin of the English Rite* that even if the Antients had not taken the strong line they did in promulgating the degree it would nevertheless have spread, but we must admit we have the Antients to thank for its almost universal adoption before it received a very belated blessing from the premier Grand Lodge.

It is of some importance to realize that the Antients' Royal Arch organization was controlled virtually from within their Grand Lodge. The mention of a 'Grand Chapter' appears in 1771 but, in fact, Chapter regulations were considered in Grand Lodge and were issued in print as part of the rules for lodges right up to 1813.†

The Union in the Royal Arch

We have thus seen the rise and spread of the Royal Arch during the second half of the eighteenth century. By the end of the century the Grand Lodge of All England at York had faded away and steps were being taken to unite the two remaining rival Grand Lodges, success being reached in the Union of 1813.

The second Article of Union has already been mentioned. Its full text was:

*A curious falsification of this date was discovered by J. R. Dashwood, late Secretary of the Quatuor Coronati Lodge, and is discussed in *A.Q.C.* 62 and 64.
†A. R. Hewitt's excellent paper before Supreme Grand Chapter at its Bi-Centenary Convocation in 1966 (published by Grand Chapter and also reprinted in *A.Q.C.* 78) is essential reading on this subject.

THE HOLY ROYAL ARCH

It is declared and pronounced that pure Antient Masonry consists of three degrees and no more, *viz* those of the Entered Apprentice, the Fellow Craft, and the Master Mason, including the Supreme Order of the Holy Royal Arch. But this article is not intended to prevent any Lodge or Chapter from holding a Meeting in any of the Degrees of the Orders of Chivalry, according to the constitutions of the said Orders.

(The final sentence has for a long time been omitted from the reprint of the Article in the *Book of Constitutions*.)

Royal Arch Masonry, Antient and Modern, remained on a separate footing for another four years, being united on 18 August 1817 and a Chapter of Promulgation completed its rather sketchy labours in 1835. The United Grand Lodge was lukewarm at first and, following the union of the two Grand Chapters,

> Resolved, Unanimously, That the Grand Lodge will, at all times, be disposed to acknowledge the proceedings of the Grand Chapter, and, so long as their arrangements do not interfere with the Regulations of the Grand Lodge, and are in conformity with the Act of Union, they will be ready to recognize, facilitate, and uphold the same.

There is no reference to the Royal Arch in the early post Union Books of Constitutions of Grand Craft Lodge.

Ritual

There is in the Grand Lodge Library a MS copy of the ritual of exaltation 'Approved by the Duke of Sussex, Grand Master Z', dated 2nd November 1834; some of the printed rituals used today claim to be copies of this. The English Royal Arch has an advantage over the Craft in that there *is* something to which reference can be made whereas nobody can say just what ritual was adopted by the United Grand Lodge after the Lodge of Reconciliation had done its work. There are also copies of old rituals and lectures dating back into the eighteenth century, probably 1780-90, in the form of catechisms.

One detail 'appeared' quite suddenly in the ritual in about 1825. Before that date one finds no trace of 'the mysterious triple tau', the emblem of the Royal Arch then being the

RITUAL

monogram T. over H. This was described by Thomas Duncker-ly as the Templum Hierosolyma (Temple of Jerusalem). After the Union, when regalia tended to become standardized, the T. became joined with the H. and some enterprising manufacturer, eliminating the serifs, found he had the equivalent of three taus or levels and an entirely fanciful explanation was grafted on to the ritual. This may be compared with some of the explanations of the Craft apron occasionally heard today.

H and J

As far as is known, the Royal Arch Masons of England have always followed the Zerubbabel legend and there is a hint of this in Dermott's *Ahiman Rezon* of 1756 (*see* p. 91) in the toast:

To the memory of P.H., Z.L., and J.A.

This has been interpreted as Principal Haggai, Zerubbabel and Joshua (or Joshua Armiger).

Under the American system, it is J — known as the High Priest — who is the equivalent of our M.E.Z., but the legend is basically the same as the English. In Scotland, the Royal Arch Chapter also has a strong similarity to our own.

It is in Ireland that the most marked differences are found. There the legend is that of the repair of the Temple* — at an earlier date than Zerubbabel's rebuilding — and Josiah, Hilkiah and Shaphan are represented by the Principals who are, in fact, entitled the Excellent King, the High Priest and the Chief Scribe. The story has the merit of being the only one founded upon Holy Writ. It has been suggested that this and other references indicate a divergence between two rival Royal Arch legends of the early days, just as we have seen that there could have been alternative third degree legends, but there is as yet no evidence available.

Rather curiously, evidence exists of early Irish working of the Zerubbabel legend, often — it seems — in parallel with the Josiah version, with separate sets of officers for each within the same lodge or chapter. Two or three attempts to supplant the Josiah legend with that of Zerubbabel, one of them early in this century, came to naught.

*II Chronicles, Chapter 34.

THE HOLY ROYAL ARCH

Although we propose to mention in chapters XIII to XVII as appropriate, the practice of the Royal Arch abroad it relevant to add here that the Zerubbabel story – in English Scottish or American form – is common to all regular juri dictions. Only in chapters owing allegiance to Dublin will b found the ritual based on Josiah and his contemporarie

The Royal Arch and the Craft Installation Ceremony

For many years there was a close connexion between th Royal Arch and the Craft Installation ceremony. Down to th 1840s it was customary for a candidate for exaltation, if h had not served as Master of a lodge, to be placed formally 'i the chair' and rule the lodge for a moment or two. Th minutes of many old English lodges of the time record th 'passing of the chair' by several brethren at a time – generally but not invariably, at the regular Installation meeting. Ther does not appear to have been any conferment of secrets o these occasions.

Today, in England, Ireland and Scotland, a Master Mason* may seek exaltation in a Royal Arch chapter but – under th first two Constitutions – no one can be installed into either o the three principal offices of a chapter unless he has already been installed as the Master of a Craft lodge. Under Scotland no such restriction applies. American practice (*see* chapter XV demands 'passing the chair' as a prior qualification for exaltation

There is a suggestion that the early Royal Arch may have been associated with what were described as 'Masters' lodges' these met on Sundays, whereas ordinary lodges did not Chapters very frequently met on that day until, in 1811, Grand Chapter discouraged the custom.

The Royal Arch Installation Ceremony

The companion, in English Royal Arch Masonry, who has not yet been installed in a Principal's chair has – from the early days – been subjected to certain restrictions within the chapter. From 1817 until 1902 he was excluded from the ceremony of opening his chapter, the Principals and Past Principals alone being permitted to be present. At the annual installation convocation it was, until 1961, the fate of the same unfor-

* Under the English Constitution, of four weeks' standing; under the Irish, twelve months (except in overseas and military chapters were one month will suffice); under Scotland no period is specified.

INSTALLATION

companion to remain outside the door of the Chapter for the greater part of the proceedings. In that year, after very lengthy consideration by the Committee of General Purposes and by Grand Chapter, a *permissive* variation of the sequence of the Installation ceremonies was agreed. When adopted, this permits all companions to be present for all but the esoteric working and requires their absence from the chapter for only a fairly brief period. Not surprisingly the variation has found wide favour.

The Penalty of the Obligation

As a consequence of the careful deliberations in Grand Lodge as to the Craft penalties (*see* p. 133) and of the permissive changes in wording which were thereafter approved, a similar resolution came before Grand Chapter in 1967. As the Earl of Scarbrough said, it was scarcely necessary for 'another full dress debate to take place on the subject' and Grand Chapter readily agreed that chapters should have the same rights in the matter as Craft lodges.

Bicentenary of Supreme Grand Chapter, 1966

On 1st July 1966, in the Grand Temple at Freemasons' Hall, London, an Especial Convocation was held to celebrate the two hundredth anniversary of the signing of the Charter of Compact and the constitution of the first Grand Chapter of the Order. The Grand Chapters of Scotland, Ireland, New Zealand, British Columbia, Manitoba, Queensland, France, the Netherlands and India were officially represented by delegations of their most eminent companions; in several instances one or more of the Grand Principals themselves headed their delegations. The First Grand Principals of Scotland, France and India replied to the address of welcome from M.E. Comp. the Earl of Scarbrough, then First Grand Principal of England. There followed the reading by by E.Comp. A. R. Hewitt of his most valuable paper (*see* p. 203n) and the proceedings closed after a solemn prayer especially written by the Third Grand Principal, M.E. Comp. Bishop Herbert.

Emphasis was laid by visiting speakers on the debt owed to the Supreme Grand Chapter of England for its part in the erection of their own Grand Chapters. It is worthy of note that, in addition to its obvious connexions with the histories

THE HOLY ROYAL ARCH

of the sovereign jurisdictions of the Commonwealth, English Royal Arch Masonry has been the progenitor of the Supreme Degree in France, Finland, the Netherlands and Switzerland

The State of the Royal Arch, 1981

At the end of 1981 it was reported that there were 3,050 chapters on the English Roll, 706 being in London, 2,025 in the Provinces and 319 overseas.

Irish Royal Arch Masonry

The earliest printed reference in Ireland is in 1743 when a newspaper reports that the Master of a lodge was preceded by 'the Royall Arch carried by two Excellent Masons' in a procession at Youghal.* It will have been observed that Dassigny's book (*see* p. 155) of 1744 was published in Dublin and there are Craft lodge minutes recording Royal Arch activity from the 1750s onwards. Later there were formed 'Lodges, Assemblies or Chapters' for the conferment of the degree (the first two words being far more common than the third). On 11th June 1829, no fewer than fifty-three of these constituted themselves into a Supreme Grand Royal Arch Chapter.

Although this event had the 'blessing and approval' of the Irish Grand Lodge it is strange to note that not until 1931 was formal recognition accorded in the Craft *Laws and Constitutions.* The present Law No. 3 reads:

> Pure Ancient Masonry consists of the following Degrees and no others, viz. — The Entered Apprentice, the Fellow Craft, the Master Mason and the Installed Master, but the Degrees of Royal Arch and Mark Master Mason shall also be recognized so long as the Supreme Grand Royal Arch Chapter shall work only those two Degrees in the form in which they are worked at the passing of this Law.

Despite the apparent lack of warmth in the situation here recorded, it is significant that from 1829 to 1874 the offices of Grand Master of the Craft and Grand King of the Royal Arch were filled by the 3rd Duke of Leinster and a similar dual role was played by the 2nd Duke of Abercorn between 1891 and 1913. Since the last date the two bodies have been ruled by

---

*It can only be assumed that what was carried was something relating to the degree. The mention of 'Excellent Masons' lends some weight to the assumption.

different persons but from the same address and administered by one eminent brother and companion as Grand Secretary and Grand Registrar (the latter being the equivalent of the English Grand Scribe E and not a legal office). Another unmistakable tie is that a chapter is allotted the same number as the Craft lodge with which it is most closely associated although the lodge plays no part in sponsoring the companions' petition for a Warrant.

A candidate for exaltation is automatically a candidate for the Mark degree to which he is advanced in a Mark lodge opened under the chapter warrant before being admitted to the chapter itself. We have already referred to the Josiah legend on which the Irish Royal Arch ceremony is based. This ceremony includes a version of 'passing the veils' and any Royal Arch mason hailing from a regular jurisdiction is permitted to be present despite the fact that certain secrets are communicated during the passage.

Scottish Royal Arch Masonry

The position of Royal Arch Masonry in Scotland in the early nineteenth century was chaotic. At the time of the formation of the Supreme Grand Royal Arch Chapter of Scotland in 1816 there were at least five species of chapter (the working of the degree under Craft warrants had by this time been discontinued):

1. Chapters working under warrants from the Grand Chapter of England.
2. Chapters which had worked without warrants since the eighteenth century.
3. Chapters working under the authority of Knight Templar warrants.
4. Chapters working under various forms of authority from Ireland.
5. Chapters of recent formation working without warrant from any source.

Grand Lodge was antipathetic, insisting even after the formation of Grand Chapter that no recognition be accorded to degrees and Orders beyond the Craft (which, in Scotland, includes the Mark*), whereas England, at the Union of 1813,

*See Chapter XI.

THE HOLY ROYAL ARCH

had formally recognized the Royal Arch. On 4th August 1817, it was decreed that lodges admitting persons to their processions or meetings wearing 'regalia, insignia, badges or crosses' other than those belonging to St. John's Masonry would be proceeded against. On 3rd November an overwhelming majority voted that no person holding an official position in any body sanctioning higher degrees should be entitled to sit, act or vote in Grand Lodge

A very dignified protest from Grand Chapter — signed by two Past Grand Masters, the Earls of Moray* and Aboyne† — was not even considered but, though the Royal Arch and other masonic degrees have never formally been acknowledged, the prohibitions quickly fell into disuse.

In 1845 Grand Chapter announced that its Chapters were entitled to confer the Mark, Past, Excellent and Royal Arch, the Royal Ark Mariner and the Babylonish Pass degrees.

The degrees now controlled by Grand Chapter are:

Mark Master
Excellent Master
Royal Arch
Royal Ark Mariner
Babylonish Pass or Red Cross
Royal Master
Select Master
Super Excellent Master

and the relevant 'chair' degrees. The last five are worked in lodges and councils *attached* to and bearing the same numbers as Royal Arch chapters; the first three are conferred under the Charters of chapters themselves.

The degrees of Mark Master and Excellent Master are prerequisites to exaltation as a Royal Arch mason but the former may have been obtained in a Scottish Craft lodge (*see* chapter XI) or from a Mark lodge under a sister Constitution. The Excellent Master degree is concerned with 'passing the veils' but only those who have been 'received' into the degree may be present at its working (cf. Irish Royal Arch practice, p. 208).

---

* 5th Earl (later 9th Marquis of Huntly), G.M.M., 1802-4.
† 9th Earl, G.M.M., 1796-8, as Lord Doune.

CHAPTER XI

THE ORDER OF MARK MASONRY AND THE ROYAL ARK MARINERS' DEGREE

THE MARK DEGREE

The use of marks as means of identification is not peculiar to Masonry and has literally existed from time immemorial. Masons' marks are found on buildings in almost every country and an interesting reference to the feared infringement of the rights of the nobility is to be found in Andrew Favine's *The Theater of Honour and Knighthood* published in London in 1623:

> The Honour of bearing Shieldes, that is to say Armes, belongeth to none but Noblemen by extraction, or by calling and creation. And yet it is not an hundred yeares, since such as were not of noble condition, were punished with great fines and amercements, if they but attempted to beare any. It was permitted to them, to have only Markes, or notes, of those Trades and Professions which they used: As a Tailor to have his Sheares, a Mason his Trowell, and the Compasse and Square, and so of other Merchants (for their more honour) might beare the first Letters of their names and surnames, enterlaced with a Crosse . . .

Functions of the Mark

Masons' marks are found in buildings of all ages and all countries, sometimes painted, but more often cut or scratched. Probably they were first imposed on the workmen by their superiors and, as time went on, the former took pride in their work and were proud to carve their marks upon the finished stone. Incidentally, it is often forgotten today that the bare stonework to which we are accustomed was not the intention of the original builder and the mark, having served its purpose, disappeared beneath a coating of lime and plaster.

It has been suggested more than once that there was some esoteric significance attaching to the use of masons' marks but this theory has comparatively little following today. The function was utilitarian and the late Dr. G. G. Coulton and the late

Bro. H. Poole independently traced the migration of individual masons from job to job in Norfolk and the north-west of England.

The Torgau Statutes

We hear of the ceremonial adoption of the mark in Germany. 'The first definite and explicit evidence comes from the Torgau Statutes of 1462. The journeyman took his mark at a solemn admission-feast, partly at the master's cost and partly at his own. In the lodge he was forbidden to engrave it on his work until the stone had been inspected and passed by the master or lodge warden.' (George Coulton's *Art and the Reformation*, 1928, p. 157.)

Scotland

We find it provided in the Schaw Statutes of 1598 that, on the admission of a Fellow of Craft, his name and mark were to be registered and the oldest minute of the Lodge of Edinburgh (Mary's Chapel) of Ultimo Julii 1599 is signed by the warden and attested by his mark. The Lodge of Aberdeen possesses a beautiful record of the names of its members and their marks from 1670 onwards and it will be remembered that in these early days these were predominantly but by no means exclusively lodges of operative masons. In the Kilwinning Lodge two apprentices 'paid their binding money and got their marks' on 20th December 1678. Many such examples can be quoted from Scottish sources. These provisions are not to be found in the Old Charges, which were of English origin.

Some early documents

When we turn from operative Masonry to speculative Freemasonry we are on less sure ground. It was not until comparatively recent times that the Mark degree was standardized and there exist fragments of a good many obsolete degrees which include the name Mark without being recognizable by the present-day Mark mason, but also sometimes contain teaching now associated with the Mark.

There are significant passages in some of the early documents. For instance, from 'A Mason's Examination' — an exposure printed in *The Flying Post* of 11-13 April 1723 — we have two quotations:

SOME EARLY DOCUMENTS

> If a Master Mason you would be
> Observe you well the *Rule of Three*;
> And what you want in Masonry
> Thy *Mark* and *Maughbin* make thee free.

Where does the Master place his Mark upon the work? Upon the S.E. Corner.

(The italics are from the original.)

The *Graham MS* of 1726, discovered in 1936, contains a short passage on the payment of workmen which is of interest to Mark masons, especially in Ireland and some of the Canadian and American jurisdictions.

> ... now it is holden fforth by tradition that there was a tumult at this Errection (the Temple) which should hapened betwext the Labourours and masons about wages and ffor to call me all and to make all things easier the wise king should have had said be all of you contented ffor you shall be payed all alike yet give a signe to the Masons not known to the Labourours, and who could make that signe at the paying place was to be payed as masons the Labourours not knowing thereof was payed as fforesaid.

In 'A Mason's Confession', said to relate to the working of a Scottish operative lodge of about 1727, but printed in *The Scots Magazine* of 1755-6, we have this passage on the choosing of the mark:

> The day that a prentice comes under the oath, he gets his choice of a mark to be put upon his tools, by which to discern them. So I did chuse this —— which cost one merk Scots. Hereby one is taught to say to such as ask the question, Where got you this mark? A. — I laid down one, and took up another.

There is a hint of rejection rite in the preface to Robert Samber's *Long Livers* of 1722:

> Ye are living Stones, built up a spiritual House, who believe and rely on the chief *Lapis Angularis*, which the refractory and disobedient Builders disallowed, you are called from Darkness to Light, you are a chosen Generation, a royal Priesthood.

MARK AND ROYAL ARK MARINER DEGREES

In the satirical poem, 'The Free-Masons', of 1722-3 we have
> They then resolv'd no more to rome,
> But to return to their own Home;
> Tho' first they Signs and Marks did frame,
> To Signify from whence they came;

Chapter of Friendship, Portsmouth

The examples just quoted date from that shadowy period when Freemasonry was emerging from its uncharted past to the Institution to which we are so proud to belong today. It was not until comparatively recent times that the Mark degree was standardized. The earliest record of Mark Masonry in a speculative body is dated 1st September 1769 and occurs in the opening minutes of the Chapter of Friendship, now No. 257, of Portsmouth. It is written in cipher and is thus translated:

> At a Royal Arch Chapter held at the George Tavern, Portsmouth, on First Septr. Seventeen hundred and sixty-nine *Present* Thomas Dunckerley, Esq., William Cook, 'Z,' Samuel Palmer, 'H,' Thomas Scanville, 'J,' Henry Dean, Philip Joyes and Thomas Webb -- The 'Pro. G.M.' Thomas Dunckerley, bro't the Warrant of the Chapter and having lately rec'd the 'Mark' he made the bre'n 'Mark Masons' and 'Mark Masters.' And each chuse their 'Mark' . . .
>
> He also told us of the mann'r of writing w'ch we may give to others so they be F.C. for 'Mark Masons' and MASTER M for 'Mark Masters'

The importance of this short passage cannot be exaggerated. Dunckerley, who claimed elsewhere to have been exalted into the Royal Arch in 1754, here refers to the Mark degree as a going concern. It was introduced into a Royal Arch Chapter and a version of the masonic cipher, now obsolete but for many years associated with Mark Masonry, was used. Incidentally this cipher was by no means exclusively masonic and may be found today in any elementary work on ciphers. The two degrees were conferred, as they are today, the Mark Man being then reserved for the Fellow Craft and the Mark Master for the Master Mason.

In Scotland, as in England, the earliest record of the mark in connection with speculative Freemasonry is in the Royal Arch. The Journeyman Lodge of Dumfries (now the Thistle

EARLY WORKINGS

Lodge, No. 62) records (on 8th October 1770) the 'elevation' of a brother to the degree of Royal Arch mason and, in the course of a form of certificate, mentions his qualifications as Entered Apprentice, Fellow-craft, Master and Mark Master Mason, Master of the Chair, Sublime Degree, of Excellent, Super-Excellent and Royal Arch Mason. This is *not* the record of an innovation.

Other examples are to be found in the Marquis of Granby Lodge, Durham, in 1773, and St. Thomas's Lodge, London, in 1777, and the minute books of the Lodge of Friendship, 277, Oldham, contain records of the making of Mark masons from 1795 to 1838.* The earliest-known Irish record is a certificate of 27th August 1775 granted by the 'Knight Templars' of Kinsale, County Cork.

The Post-Union Position

The effect of the Union of 1813 on the additional degrees, many of which had been worked under Craft warrants, was disastrous. Some continued for a few years to be performed until they wilted under the cold eye of that peculiar autocrat, the Duke of Sussex. It was many years before Grand Lodges, Councils, etc., were constituted and the shattered remains of many rites reconstructed. In Scotland and Ireland the position differed from England, the Mark being a prerequisite to the Royal Arch, which was recognized officially by neither Grand Lodge.

In England, the story of the Mark in the mid-nineteenth century is complicated. The degree was being conferred under the banners of Craft lodges as well as by such bodies as the Travelling Mark Lodge of Cheshire. This curious organization — which partook of many of the functions of a friendly society — met on a Sunday afternoon, the brethren travelling from their headquarters at Dukinfield, Cheshire, to some place within a few miles. Here one of the local Craft lodges opened up to the third degree; the Mark brethren then entered and took over the principal offices before opening in the Mark degree, advancing any candidates who presented themselves. As there were at one time or another some twenty-four Craft lodges on the 'circuit', visits to a particular place were few and

*The recently discovered records of the Lodge of Fortitude (Grand Lodge of All England at York) indicate the working of the Mark degree at Hollinwood, Oldham, between 1790 and 1793.

MARK AND ROYAL ARK MARINER DEGREES

far between.

The ritual was different from that to which we are accustomed and included an exercise in the lifting and carrying of a stone of a peculiar shape and instruction in the Mark alphabet and the paper missive, neither of which was peculiar to Mark Masonry, the latter being referred to in *The Free-Masons: An Hudibrastick Poem,* of 1722-3:

> A Mason, when he needs must drink
> Sends letter without Pen and Ink
> Unto some Brother, whos at hand
> And does the message understand;
> The Paper's the Shape that's square,
> Thrice-folded with the nicest care.

Bon Accord Mark Lodge

Some lodges claimed that, under the terms of the Union, Mark Masonry was not excluded but by the middle of the century Mark Masonry had become nobody's child. It was then that six brethren of the Bon Accord Chapter of Aberdeen, who were resident in London, applied to their Chapter for a 'commission' to make Mark masons. The Chapter granted a warrant for a London Mark lodge which was disavowed by the Supreme Grand Royal Arch Chapter of Scotland and eventually Bon Accord Chapter was suspended with all its members in 1855. It never met again.

Formation of Grand Mark Lodge

The Bon Accord affair precipitated action by the United Grand Lodge of England. A joint committee, consisting of seven members each from Grand Lodge and Grand Chapter, was set up and reported on 5th March 1856 that the Mark masons' degree did not form part of Royal Arch Masonry and was not essential to Craft Masonry, but it might be considered as forming a graceful addition to the Fellow Crafts' degree. It was thereon unanimously resolved:

That the Degree of Mark Mason or Mark Master is not at variance with the ancient landmarks of the Order, and that the Degree be an addition to and form part of Craft Masonry; and consequently may be conferred by all regular Warranted Lodges, under such regulations as shall be prepared by the Board of General Purposes, approved and

FORMATION OF GRAND MARK LODGE

sanctioned by the Grand Lodge.

Opposition forces quickly rallied and at the next Quarterly Communication of Grand Lodge the non-confirmation of the minute was moved by Bro. John Henderson, a former President of the Board of General Purposes, and carried by a majority. It is a curious fact that the majority of speakers on this occasion were themselves Mark Master Masons, according to the *Freemason's Monthly Magazine* of September 1st 1856, being members of rival Mark lodges. That journal recognized the difficulty under which English brethren laboured when they desired admission into Royal Arch Chapters elsewhere. A severe blow to Mark Masonry, the rebuff was met by the establishment of Grand Mark Lodge in 1856. Bro. Lord Leigh, the first Grand Master, called a general meeting of Mark masons in London, expressing the hope that the brethren would abstain from discussing the validity of their various authorities and keep in view solely the course to be pursued for the future well-being of the Craft. The fact that this interesting portion of Freemasonry had been omitted since 1813 was deplored and it was pointed out that there were brethren living with sixty years' experience of Mark Masonry.

The formation of Grand Mark Lodge by no means ended the difficulty. Its parent, the Bon Accord Mark Lodge, was far from legitimate — 'Born in sin and shapen in iniquity' it was described — and the Supreme Grand Royal Arch Chapter of Scotland issued at least fifteen warrants between 1856 and 1858 for new Mark lodges in many parts of England and one in Canada, and even constituted a Mark Province of Lancashire. Happily, a concordat was entered into by the two authorities and since 1878 the Grand Lodge of Mark Master Masons of England and Wales and the Dominions and Dependencies of the British Crown has been sole ruler of the Mark degree in the 'territory' embraced by English Masonry.

The Present Position

By the end of the century the Mark degree had ceased to be worked in England except under the warrant of Grand Mark Lodge, the Travelling Mark Lodge of Cheshire, which had assumed Grand Lodge status, coming into the fold as recently as February 1900. An official form of ritual is now worked by the majority of lodges though a few of the older ones retain traditional features which one hopes they will never discard.

The most recent statistics show that there are over 1,300 Mark lodges of the English Constitution, not a few of them being overseas. The Provincial and District organization in the Mark degree closely follows that of Craft and Royal Arch Masonry, and London and Overseas Grand Ranks have in recent years been introduced.

The status of the Mark degree in English Freemasonry has been emphasized by its royal Grand Masters: Albert Edward, Prince of Wales (1886—1901), the Duke of Connaught (1901-39), George, Duke of Kent (1939—42) — all of whom had during the same periods presided over the Craft and Royal Arch. In June 1982, H.R.H. Prince Michael of Kent, brother to the Craft's Grand Master, was installed as the successor to the 4th Earl of Stradbroke, ruler of the Mark degree from 1973.

We have referred in the previous Chapter to the place of the Mark degree in modern Irish and Scottish Freemasonry. It is perhaps pertinent to add that there are strong similarities in the rituals used by all three Constitutions and that, between the Grand Lodge and Grand Chapter of Scotland, a Concordat of 1860 establishes a common ceremonial for the conferment of the Mark degree.

The practice of the degree abroad will be dealt with under the relevant headings but it is appropriate to mention here that, in the American system and in those jurisdictions which have followed Scottish Royal Arch practice, Mark Masonry is controlled by Grand Royal Arch Chapters. Only in South Australia, Victoria, Queensland, India and Finland are there Grand Mark Lodges on the English model, and these enjoy the official recognition of the Craft and Royal Arch governing bodies.

The Mark Benevolent Fund

We have dealt at some length in chapters VI and VII with the Craft charities. The Mark Benevolent Fund is comparatively simple to describe. Established in 1869, it was designed to assist brethren of the Order, their widows and their children in distressed circumstances. There are three branches — Benevolent, Educational and Annuity — the objects of which are self-explanatory. An Annual Festival has been held since the

THE ROYAL ARK MARINER'S DEGREE

and began, always with excellent results.

It is important to add that, although Grand Mark Lodge does not enjoy the official recognition of the United Grand Lodge, the former contributes very liberally to the latter's charities! A notable instance was the donation of £500,000 towards the building of one of the residential homes of the Royal Masonic Benevolent Institution. This was the one at Sindlesham, near Reading, and is named 'Lord Harris Court' after George St. Vincent, 5th Lord Harris, who ruled Grand Mark Lodge from 1954 to 1973.

THE ROYAL ARK MARINER'S DEGREE

It is possible that this degree has a more intimate association with early operative masonry than is generally realized, the woodworkers being at one time much more closely allied with the stoneworkers than is the case today. In the eighteenth-century speculative Craft there are many legendary details which are now present in Royal Ark Masonry, details which did not reappear in the Craft after the Union of 1813.

Noah's Ark is found as a masonic emblem from about the middle of the 1700s; there is a picture of one on the Stirling Brass of 1743 and some beautiful Royal Ark jewels of the same period, painted on ivory and set in brilliants, are to be seen in United Grand Lodge Museum, London.

It was said in a 'history' in 1871 that the Grand Lodge of Ark Mariners was *reconstituted* in London in 1772 but little is known of this body. There is a clear suggestion of an earlier existence but no evidence whatsoever. But we do know that the degree was being performed at Portsmouth under the auspices of the ubiquitous Thomas Dunckerley in 1780 and in Cornwall at about the same time. In 1790 it was being worked in Bath and there were indications that it was then nothing new. In the Kent Lodge of London* it was being conferred in 1794, in conjunction with the Mark and Cryptic degrees.

Ebenezer Sibly — also known as Noah Sibly — introduced Ark Masonry at Ipswich; a reference of 1790 shows that it was by then already established. We hear of Brother Dunckerley again in 1794 as Grand Commander of the *Society of Antient Masons of the Diluvian Order, or Royal Ark and Mark Mariners.* The headquarters of this body, which was somewhat oddly

*Now No. 15.

MARK AND ROYAL ARK MARINER DEGREES

united with the Knights Templar (Dunckerley was their Gra Master too), were at the Surrey Tavern in the Strand and Sit was Deputy Grand Noah. The first Lord Rancliffe succeed Dunckerley in both Orders in 1796.

The last Grand Masters of the two rival Grand Craft Lodg (the Dukes of Sussex and Kent) were both members of t Grand Lodge of Royal Ark Mariners but, after the Union 1813, the Duke of Sussex looked with anything but a frienc eye on all masonic work beyond the three Craft degrees a the Royal Arch and the Order, like many others, almost fad out of existence.

The Revival of 1870

On 13th May 1870, John F. Dorrington, a very elder mason, who had been Grand Commander of the Order in 181 appointed Morton A. Edwards as his Deputy, nominating hi as his successor and handing over a warrant dated 1793. Sever Ark Mariners joined or were elevated and by the followi year, although there were only twenty-eight lodges on the Rc (some still in course of formation), a great effort was bei made to organize the Order.

Grand Mark Lodge disputed this action, claiming the rig to confer the degree by the ancient usages of the Time Imm morial lodges on its Roll, but in 1871 the Mark Grand Mast agreed officially to protect the Ark Mariner degree and set u what is now called the Grand Master's Royal Ark Council. Th degree has since prospered and spread throughout the worl

The Present Position

A lodge of Royal Ark Mariners is 'attached' to a Mark lodg from which it takes its number and a candidate must be Mark Master Mason. Recent returns record about 500 Lodge under the English Constitution. A recent development is th institution of 'Grand Rank' and 'London, Provincial and Ove seas Grand Ranks' for members of the Order; this was pr viously the only regular masonic organization with no highe honour than that of having occupied the presiding chair.

As will have been noted, the degree under Scotland is con trolled by the Grand Royal Arch Chapter. A candidate fo admission will already have taken the Mark, Excellent Maste and Royal Arch degrees and, since every Scottish Royal Ar Mariner lodge is 'paired' with a Council of Red Cross Knights

THE ROYAL ARK MARINER'S DEGREE

elevation will be followed by his reception into that [Cou]ncil.

The degree is not worked in Ireland. In the United States it [is] one of the Allied Masonic Degrees and in Canada the Royal [Ar]k Mariner lodges are 'moored' to Councils of Royal and [Se]lect Masters. In New Zealand and Australia, the degree is [co]ntrolled by Grand Mark Lodges or Grand Royal Arch [Ch]apters.

[M]ark Masons' Hall

In 1979 the headquarters of the Grand Lodge of Mark [M]aster Masons moved to a new address, the former home of [th]e Constitutional Club at the southern end of St. James's [St]reet, London. In the Grand Lodge's 123 years successive [Gr]and Secretaries had worked in several different buildings: a [sm]all office at 40 Leicester Square (1857–61); 16a Great Queen [St]reet (1861–7); 2 Red Lion Square (1867–81); 8a Red Lion [Sq]uare (1881–90); 64–5 Great Queen Street (1890–1938); [ ] Kingsway (1938–54); 40 Upper Brook Street (1954–79).

8a Red Lion Square had a large hall suited to ceremonial [oc]casions, space for lodge rooms and a modest rental but the [op]portunity of moving to the masonic centre of London was [no]t to be missed. The lease of Bacon's Hotel, next door to the [Cr]aft Freemasons' Hall of those days, fell vacant and it proved [ca]pable of conversion with an imposing Grand Temple, lodge [ro]oms, a dining hall and administrative offices, the cost – [in]cluding furnishings (many of which survive) – being £7,237! [O]n the expiry of the lease that Mark Masons' Hall was [de]molished and its site is now occupied by part of the [Co]nnaught Rooms. The Kingsway office was a somewhat [ex]tended stop-gap but the building at Upper Brook Street, [al]though it offered very little room for meetings and no [di]ning facilities, had much dignity and charm.

The present Mark Masons' Hall, being on a 99-year lease, [se]ems likely to be the most permanent home of all and it [pr]ovides a meeting and dining-place for a very large number of [m]asonic bodies. Large though it is, the Grand Temple there [ca]nnot accommodate the Quarterly Communications of Grand [M]ark Lodge and these, as they have been for many years past, [ar]e held in the Grand Temple at Freemasons' Hall, Great [Q]ueen Street, where the Great Priories of the Temple and [M]alta also meet.

CHAPTER XII

OTHER DEGREES AND ORDERS

We have given special prominence in this book to Roy Arch and Mark Masonry — the former because of its clo association with and full recognition by the Craft in Englar and elsewhere and the latter for its wide popularity, either c its own or as a step towards the Royal Arch. There is, too, th important factor that the Mark and Royal Arch are regarde by many as completing the Fellow Craft and Master Masc degrees respectively.

But one overhears, with increasing frequency, the casu reference among freemasons of the Craft to meetings of th other degrees and Orders and, so often, curiosity is arouse and left unsatisfied.

Origins

What are these degrees, and whence came they? Did a fev brethren assemble one day and say 'Let us be Emperors of th Sun and Moon', or something equally fantastic? In a fev instances this could almost be true but many of the ritua now used in these 'additional' degrees provide evidence tha they are perpetuating — perhaps in a much more elaborat form — features that were discontinued from early Craft an Royal Arch workings. A notable example (already mentione in chapter X) is the 'Passing of the Veils'. Once a part of th English Royal Arch ceremony, it is now found only withii Bristol Chapters and those governed from Dublin; unde Scottish and certain Commonwealth Constitutions it forms separate degree, that of *Excellent Master*. Again, certain dis carded details of old Royal Arch Masonry in America are nov preserved in the *Red Cross of Babylon,* a degree worked unde several titles in various countries but highly regarded b; members of the Allied Masonic Degrees of England (q.v.).

'SCOTTISH' RITES

We have seen how Craft Freemasonry developed into the familiar three degree system in the years following the foundation of the Grand Lodge in 1717. A few decades later there came, by addition or separation, the Royal Arch. The 'Antient' Masons pursued matters further but, at the Union of 1813, the pattern was firmly set by Article 2 (*see* p. 204).

Continental Developments

But when Freemasonry spread beyond our islands it fell into hands not content with the plain, unvarnished story taught in its original home. The links with the homely operative past were not appreciated by the more modish followers of what was proving a fashionable cult, so a host of brilliant ceremonies was quickly developed, many of which proved ephemeral while others have lasted to the present day and are accepted and respected throughout the world.

'Scottish' Rites

Among the earliest continental freemasons were several adherents of the Stuarts who had a curious tendency to father every innovation on Scotland or Ireland, especially the former country. A great impetus was given to all this expansion by an oration prepared for delivery in 1737 by the Chevalier Ramsay, a Jacobite exile, who had been initiated in England in March 1730 and who had been associated with many prominent freemasons both in the Royal Society and in the Gentlemen's Club, Spalding. His part in Freemasonry ceased in 1737 at the orders of Cardinal Fleury, King Louis XV of France's minister.

With the probable exception of the *Royal Order of Scotland* none of these early degrees took its rise in or was connected with Scotland. The so-called Scots degrees appeared in France during the 1740s and such was their diversity that they defy classification into any clear sequence. A secret vault was common to many, also a legend of descent from the Templars; one factor they all had, the autocratic direction of a head rather than an elective body.

The Scots Philosophic Rite

A number of hermetic schools were established at Avignon about 1740, becoming organized under this title as a pseudo-masonic rite. It was dissolved by order of the Inquisition but

OTHER DEGREES AND ORDERS

appeared in Paris in 1766, changing its name later to *Social Contract*. The Mother Lodge ceased to work on the outbreak of the Revolution, the Chapter continuing a chequered existence until about 1826.

The Strict Observance

This is another body which has been attributed to Jacobite influence. Beginning in a small way it flared into prominence *after* any Jacobite influence had waned, when it swept Europe for several years. A Baron von Hund was appointed Provincial Grand Master for Germany and, with the assistance of one or two colleagues, revised the rituals and organization. In the Apprentice degree an oath of unquestioning obedience to unknown superiors was exacted; the Master of a lodge, who had to be a Knight of the 5° of the Rite, was not elected by the members but appointed by Grand Chapter. These Knights were originally chosen from among the nobility but persons of lower station were later appointed. There was some confusion and difficulty caused by one Johnson who disputed von Hund's authority to the point of splitting the Order. In 1767 another member, von Starck, engrafted on the Order a new branch of so-called Knight Templary and von Hund's influence began to wane. He died in 1776 and the Strict Observance did not long survive him.

Degrees and Orders of Today

One analysis of the recognized masonic Orders in England today claims that, beginning with the Entered Apprentice there are 112* degrees to which — with the necessary time, finance, persistence and acceptance — the aspiring freemason could conceivably advance. To these could be added at least fifteen more as 'chair' degrees, where the elected ruler is placed in his seat in the *absence* of the rank and file. It is as well to stress that many of the 112 are never 'worked'; they are 'communicated by name' to candidates. It is also important to add that they are, in almost every case, grouped into Rites and Orders (to be hereafter described).

We have already mentioned the term 'additional degrees'; commonly used also are the words 'higher' and 'side degrees'. None of these descriptions is wholly justified. It can fairly be said (in the light of the *Book of Constitutions*) that there can

* There are other possible ways of carrying out this survey!

ROYAL AND SELECT MASTERS

be nothing *additional* to or *higher* than pure, Antient Masonry. We shall discuss genuine 'side degrees' in due course. The late Bro. A. Langdon Coburn employed, with telling effect, the phrase 'beyond the Craft' in speaking and writing of the Masonic domain we are about to explore.

The Royal Arch, Mark and Royal Ark Mariner degrees have already been examined. Let us now firstly consider the other degrees and Orders which draw their inspiration from the Old Testament and are thus open to brethren of many faiths.

The Royal and Select Masters

This title officially describes a series of four related degrees familiarly called 'Cryptic', but this is a misnomer because not all are concerned with a crypt or vault): *Most Excellent Master, Royal Master, Select Master* and *Super-Excellent Master*. They are controlled in England by a Grand Council constituted in 1873 by four Councils chartered two years earlier by the Grand Council of New York†. The formation of these Councils was facilitated by the visit to England of R. Puissant Comp. Jackson H. Chase, an officer of that Grand Council, armed with authority to confer the three last-named degrees at sight. That of Most Excellent Master, a prerequisite to the Royal Arch in America, was added subsequently to the three. All four precede the English Royal Arch ceremony in historical sequence and relate to various events beginning with the completion and dedication of the first Temple at Jerusalem.

A recent official report records eighty-eight active councils. In 1972, twenty-one councils in New South Wales were formed into a Sovereign Grand Council (but *see* p. 301) but thirteen remain in Victoria under a District Grand Council under the English Constitution. There is also a District of South Africa.

Candidates for the degrees must be Mark Master and Royal Arch masons. The regalia is unique in English Freemasonry since it includes a *triangular* apron.

Under Scotland, Cryptic Councils working the Royal, Select and Super-Excellent degrees only have been attached to Royal Arch Chapters since 1915 and bear the same numbers. The earlier history is not unlike that of English Cryptic Masonry since the Grand Council of Illinois in 1877 appointed Comp.

†The origins of the degrees in America are referred to in chapter XV.

OTHER DEGREES AND ORDERS

R. S. Brown of Edinburgh — he was Grand Scribe E of the Royal Arch — as Deputy Grand Master in Scotland for Illinois. A Scottish Grand Council was soon formed by three daughter Councils but it made little progress and it was the surviving members who were instrumental in placing the remnants of the Order under Royal Arch control.

The degrees are not worked in Ireland.

The Allied Masonic Degrees*

In 1880, the Grand Council of the Allied Masonic Degrees was established in London and Rule 1 of the original Constitutions stated:

> In view of the rapid increase of lodges of various Orders recognizing no central authority and acknowledging no common form of government, a ruling body has been formed to take under its direction all lodges of such various Orders in England and Wales and the Colonies and Dependencies of the British Crown as may be willing to join it.

The degrees which, from the outset, acknowledged the supremacy of the Grand Council were: *St. Lawrence the Martyr, Knight of Constantinople, Red Cross of Babylon,* and *Grand High Priest.* The revised constitutions of 1902 added to these the degrees of *Grand Tiler of Solomon* and *Secret Monitor,* plus the thirty-three degrees of the *Holy Royal Arch Knight Templar Priests* (q.v.) (and four other degrees formerly but no longer conferred). In addition, rule 1 was extended to read:

> ... and the superintendence of all such degrees or Orders as may hereafter be established in England and Wales with and by the consent of, The Supreme Council 33°, Great Priory, Grand Lodge of Mark Master Masons, Grand Council of Royal and Select Masters and Grand Imperial Conclave of the Red Cross of Constantine, but not under the superintendence of such governing bodies.

In 1925 the Knight Templar Priest degrees were returned to the Grand College at Newcastle, which had been in abeyance, and in 1931 the single degree of Secret Monitor (an American

---

*An interesting MS paper by the late M. W. Bro. Captain A. G. Rumbelow, Grand Master of the Allied Masonic Degrees (1964-69), is the source of much of the information in this section.

ALLIED MASONIC DEGREES

version) was 'surrendered' to the independent Order of that name. Five therefore remain alive under Grand Council.

The formation of Grand Mark Lodge in 1856 had directed attention to the other degrees, some of great interest and importance, which had from 1813 onwards only just managed to survive in a masterless and slightly furtive way. The new Grand Council offered a form of legitimacy and so was able to preserve for masonic posterity some very valuable and worthwhile tributaries of the main stream.

The five degrees hereafter briefly described in no sense form a sequence and can be conferred in any order. Two have a Royal Arch qualification and the Mark is also a prior condition of membership. Although complicated and colourful regalia is prescribed for each degree the brethren are required only to wear five jewels, usually in miniature form. The Council is opened, the business conducted and the Master installed in the St. Lawrence degree for which orange and blue collars are worn by the officers. Full fraternal communication is maintained with the present Grand Council of Allied Masonic Degrees of the United States.

There are at present over eighty Councils under the English Constitution, many being overseas.

St. Lawrence the Martyr. The legend has very little to do with Freemasonry generally; indeed it has nothing to do with the Old Testament. It is claimed that the degree was worked in Lancashire and Yorkshire over two centuries ago and it is thought that it is a piece of old operative ritual intended to distinguish a genuine craftsman from the (then) new-fangled speculatives.

Knight of Constantinople. This is a real 'side' degree in the sense that, many years ago, it was customary for one brother to confer it on another. He would take him *aside* at the end of a lodge meeting, for instance, administer a simple obligation and entrust him with the secrets. The origin of the degree is not known (there is a strong flavour of operative influence in its ritual) but it was being worked in America in 1831. It first came to England in 1865, brought to Plymouth from Malta by a military brother, and three councils were erected there to work it in full form. Although these councils accepted the control of Grand Council in London in 1910 they still present the degree in an extended ceremony unknown elsewhere in the Order and they restrict membership therein to Christian breth-

OTHER DEGREES AND ORDERS

ren, a limitation not applied in any other Council. (They also wear curious aprons of dark green and red.)

Red Cross of Babylon. Here is another degree of considerable antiquity with plenty of evidence of its working in early Craft and Royal Arch minutes. It relates — among other incidents — to the building of the second Temple at Jerusalem and Zerubbabel figures prominently.

Its Scottish counterpart is the Babylonish Pass or Red Cross (*see* p. 210), uneasily associated with the Royal Ark Mariner under Royal Arch control. As in Ireland, where the Grand Council of Knight Masons (q.v.) now governs the Red Cross, there are in fact three 'points' within the degree: Knight of the Sword, Knight of the East and Knight of the East and West. To add to these complications, there is a strong relationship to the 15° and 16° of the Ancient and Accepted (Scottish) Rite but — perhaps fortunately — these are not *worked* in England, Ireland and Scotland!

The American entanglements are even worse but will be dealt with in their proper place.

Grand Tiler of Solomon. This has a most interesting ancestry with very early evidence (1790) of its existence, as 'Select Mason of Twenty-Seven', in America and in Scotland in about 1803. In 1892 it was brought into the newly-formed American Sovereign College of Allied Degrees whose first Grand Master, in the same year, conferred it upon the Earl of Euston and C. F. Matier 'with power to propagate it', which they did! Both were prominent in the English Grand Council and the degree, as we have seen, was formally added to the Constitutions at the next revision.

It has much in common with the Cryptic degree of Select Master already referred to and with the 6° of the Ancient and Accepted Rite, all three being concerned with the accidental intrusion of a Craftsman into a certain subterranean council chamber.

Order of the Grand High Priest. One authority states that this Order was being conferred in Berlin in 1780. There is ample evidence of its existence in America by 1802 where it became — and still is — the perquisite of a present or past High Priest (First Principal) of a Royal Arch Chapter. The title of 'High Priest' appears also in the list of degrees to be divided between the Grand Royal Arch Chapter and the Knights Templar of

ORDER OF THE SECRET MONITOR

Scotland when the former was established in the early nineteenth century. This title, however, may indicate merely the secrets of a Principal's chair and early references in England arouse similar doubts. How the Order of the *Grand* High Priest came to England is not known; we know only that it was here when the Grand Council of the Allied Degrees was formed in 1884.

Until 1934, only Past Principals Z were eligible for admission. In that year the qualification was amended to include all Royal Arch masons. The singularly beautiful and interesting ceremony may be performed in each subordinate council not more than once in each year.

The Order of the Secret Monitor

This Order has an alternative title, the *Brotherhood of David and Jonathan*, and this relates to its legendary history which has been derived from the Book of Samuel. Particular emphasis is laid upon the value of true friendship and loyalty.

There are many early traces of degrees with obvious similarities to the present workings. *The Order of Brotherly Love*, for instance, appears in a Rite once active in Scotland. An *Order of Jonathan and David and Jesus Christ*, with seven degrees, existed in the Netherlands in 1773; the first three of these are clearly an ancestral form of the modern ritual. It is possible that Dutch emigrants took some or all of them to America for there are many references there in the mid-nineteenth century, usually as a 'side degree' and often under the modern name of *Secret Monitor*.

A Doctor I. Zacharie (of English birth) served as a surgeon in the American Civil War and settled for a while thereafter in California, where he became closely involved with Freemasonry. In about 1875 he returned to England where he found a number of brethren who, like himself, had informally received the degree of Secret Monitor.

A Conclave was formed in 1887 by Zacharie and these and other brethren (including the Grand Secretaries of the Craft and Mark Grand Lodges) and, in the same year, a Grand Council to control and propagate the Order, with Zacharie as Grand Supreme Ruler. Two more degrees were formulated and added in the following year, the second of these being attached to the office of Supreme Ruler of a conclave.

OTHER DEGREES AND ORDERS

In 1895 some unfortunate events involving the Grand Master of the Sovereign College of the American Allied Degrees, the Order of the Secret Monitor and the English Grand Council of the Allied Masonic Degrees resulted in a breach between the two London bodies. This was so serious that members of the Allied Degrees were ordered by their Grand Master to withdraw from the other Order. Furthermore, the Allied Degrees acquired from their American counterpart their one Secret Monitor degree and added it to the English series. There was, happily, a Concordat in 1898 but the Allied Masonic Degrees continued to work the one Secret Monitor degree (American version) until 1931 when a further agreement (signed on both sides by Colonel C. W. Napier-Clavering, the head of both Orders!) left the Order of the Secret Monitor in undisputed control.

Although it has never spread to Scotland or Ireland, the Order has grown rapidly at home and has proved especially popular overseas. In Australia three sovereign Grand Conclaves have been formed by conclaves originally chartered from London. Needless to say, the warmest ties are retained between the mother Grand Conclave and her offspring.

Membership of the Order requires a Craft qualification only. The brethren wear a very simple jewel until they progress to District or Grand Rank when a sash is added.

The Ancient and Accepted Rite

Here we have the first of several Orders which, under the English, Irish and Scottish, and certain other Constitutions, demand of their members a Trinitarian Christian faith. It is known in almost every other jurisdiction as the Ancient and Accepted *Scottish* Rite on the very slender basis mentioned earlier in this Chapter. In England the Order is often referred to as the *Rose Croix*, the brief title of the degree common to all its members.

In 1754, the Chevalier de Bonneville established a Chapter at Clermont in France to confer twenty-five ultra-Craft degrees. The Rite spread to Germany where it was adopted by the Grand Lodge of the Three Globes in 1758. Some dissension gave rise to a new governing body named the *Council of the East and West* to control what it now called the *Rite of Perfection*.

ANCIENT AND ACCEPTED RITE

In 1761, one Stephen Morin was empowered to carry this Rite to America. (Copies of his Patent exist; the original has disappeared.) He succeeded in establishing it in the West Indies whence it spread to the mainland. Until 1801, the twenty-five degrees sufficed but, when the first Supreme Council for the Ancient and Accepted Scottish Rite was formed at Charleston, South Carolina, in that year eight more degrees were imported from Europe to make the number up to thirty-three. It is from this Supreme Council, now based at Washington, that all other Supreme Councils directly or indirectly derive their authority.

The Rite in this form travelled to many countries and, in some, has had rather a chequered career.

The first Supreme Council for England and Wales was established in 1819 but, although the Duke of Sussex became a member and accepted the 33°, he discouraged masonic activity of every kind that did not come strictly within 'Article 2'. And so the Rite quietly faded away, to be reborn in 1845 after the inflexible Duke had been gathered to his fathers. The moving spirits in the revival were Doctors Crucefix* and Leeson. Leeson took the first step and applied to France for authority but, meanwhile, Crucefix obtained a warrant from the second American Supreme Council (of 1813) at New York (now at Boston) and it is through this document that the present Supreme Council for England claims kinship with the older body of 1801.

Of the thirty-three degrees controlled by the Rite only a few are worked in full in this country. The 1° to the 3° are equivalent to the Craft degrees and a candidate for the Rite must therefore be (in England and Scotland) a Master Mason — and one year's standing is now required. The 4° to the 17° are communicated by name only; one or two of these are *demonstrated* at length each year at widely attended meetings, one in London and one in the provinces. It is the 18°, the *Knight of the Pelican and Eagle and Sovereign Prince Rose Croix of Heredom*, which is rightly the central feature of the Order. It is always worked at length and is regarded by many as the most beautiful and satisfying of all masonic degrees. It is in Chapters Rose Croix that the members of the Rite assemble to transact their business and choose their officers and they have the right to recommend those of their number who have served as

*See Chapter VII.

OTHER DEGREES AND ORDERS

Most Wise Sovereign (ruler) of a Chapter to Supreme Council for advancement to the 30°. The 19° to the 29° are quickly given by name only but the 30° is worked in England only by the nine members of the Supreme Council themselves, and very impressive it is. (In countries abroad where Chapters owe allegiance to London, it requires not less than three Inspector General 33° – the rulers of 'Districts' of the Rite – to assemble before the 30° can be conducted.) The degrees above the 30° are sparingly conferred in London by the Supreme Council as distinctions for service to the Rite.

There are about 850 Chapters Rose Croix under the English Constitution, some 250 being overseas.

The Supreme Council for Scotland obtained its charter from the French Supreme Council in 1846. Although, in many respects, the subsequent development resembles that of the Rite in England its scale is quite different, there being very few 'Sovereign Chapters' in Scotland but many more overseas 'Sovereign Councils' exist (two at home and several abroad) in which the 30° can be rather more freely conferred than in England since not only Past Sovereigns but other brethren who have held the 18° for more than five years can be invited to seek advancement. The higher degrees (here is a correct use of this term) are treated, as they are south of the Border, as the reward of merit.

Some extremely interesting differences appear in Ireland. There the Supreme Council dates from 1824 when it was chartered directly from Charleston. The degree elsewhere known as Rose Croix has long been worked in Chapters of *Prince Masons*,* controlled by a Grand Chapter, and limited to thirty-three members each, and admission requires prior membership of a Preceptory of Knights Templar. Advancement is governed by the Supreme Council itself and is to the 28°, 30°, 31°, 32° and 33° but the fact that less than a hundred Irish brethren (and these include members of the higher degrees) are entitled to attend meetings in the 28° gives some idea of how highly prized such promotion must be.

Although we have so far described the rise of the present governing bodies of the Ancient and Accepted (Scottish) Rite, it must not be overlooked that certain degrees within the Order

*The two oldest chapters have been working since 1782 and are therefore the oldest in the world conferring the Rose Croix degree.

were well known in these islands long before Rites of Perfection and Supreme Councils were heard of. In particular, the Rose Croix appears as an avenue for advancement for the Knight Templar and this feature has been preserved in Ireland. Bristol and Bath are noted for their distinctive Freemasonry; there is evidence of a Rose Croix ceremony at Bath in 1793. The Antiquity Encampment of Knights Templar there continued to confer the degree until 1866 when its Rose Croix members accepted a warrant from the Supreme Council. The story of Bristol, where — to the present day — admission to the Rose Croix requires the Knight Templar qualification, is told later under the heading of *The Baldwyn Rite*.

Although there are still many Supreme Councils 33° in the world (and there are many which have not survived), only a few are recognized by those of England, Scotland and Ireland. These are the two in the United States and those for Canada, the Netherlands and Finland. The special links with Scandinavian degrees will be mentioned in chapter XIV.

Knights Templar

The familiar title is properly extended into *The United Religious, Military and Masonic Orders of the Temple and of St. John of Jerusalem, Palestine, Rhodes and Malta in England and Wales, etc.* As can be seen it actually embraces two Orders and these are quite separately conferred, the second being necessarily preceded by a short degree named *Knight of St. Paul and Mediterranean Pass*.

It is important to discount at once any theories (and there have been several) which claim an historical or ritual connexion with the medieval Military Orders with similar titles. The masonic degrees of the Templar Rite grew — like the Rite of Perfection — from the desire of continental brethren to graft colourful ceremonies, often with a Christian content, upon the Craft Freemasonry which — so Anderson's *Constitutions* tell us (*see* p. 77) — had become open to many faiths. Traces of these European degrees are found in the British Isles from the middle 1760s onwards. Our old friend Thomas Dunckerley, in 1778 authorized the Royal Arch Chapter of Friendship at Portsmouth 'to make Knights Templars [*sic*] if we wanted to'. A year later the Templar degree was being worked under the York Grand Lodge and, by 1780, not only was there a *Supreme*

OTHER DEGREES AND ORDERS

Grand Royal Encampment at Bristol but both Templar and Malta degrees were in fashion in Ireland. The Bristol attempt at a national organization failed but Dunckerley succeeded in 1791 in presiding over a *Grand Conclave* representing several Encampments and so counts as the first Grand Master. (It will be recalled that this Grand Conclave was associated with the Ark Mariners (*see* p. 219)).

Early progress was slow and during the (Templar) Grand Mastership of the Duke of Sussex (1812-1843) suffered the usual opposition from the die-hards and Grand Conclave was not assembled. Oddly enough the Duke himself, rather surreptitiously, helped matters along by allowing dispensations and, later, personally warranting a few Encampments and erecting a Province for Dorset. Normal conditions were restored after his death and the United Orders made better progress. Until after 1850, the rituals in use were many and varied but a standard working was then produced.

In the 1870s a *Convent-General*, designed to embrace the Orders in England, Scotland and Ireland, but leaving domestic control to each, came into being with the Prince of Wales as Sovereign. Scotland, however, remained outside it; they had troubles of their own! Under this arrangement the English Grand Conclave changed its name to the *National Great Priory* and, when the Convent-General ceased to exist in 1895, made the final amendment to *Great Priory of England and Wales, etc.* and resumed complete independence. The Duke of Connaught was Grand Master of the Orders in England from 1907 to 1939, a long reign by any standards, but his Grand Mastership in Ireland stretched from 1878 to his death in 1942!

There are now 430 or more Preceptories (the modern equivalent of Encampments) of Knights Templar on the English Roll (about 125 overseas), each entitled to hold Priories of the Order of Malta. Admission, by invitation, is restricted to Royal Arch masons. The regalia is elaborate and is based on the costume of the medieval Templars and Knights of Malta.

The Great Priory of Ireland claims its descent from the *Early Grand Encampment of High Knights Templar* for which it quotes a date 'ante A.D. 1770'. But the earliest records of this body cannot be traced. A printed pamphlet of rules of

RED CROSS OF CONSTANTINE

1788 refers back to the dubbing of a knight in 1765; this is not contemporary evidence, of course, but it is — if true — the earliest known date anywhere for the conferment of the degree. The modern Irish Great Priory governs some ninety Preceptories, only three being abroad.

The history of the Order in Scotland is very involved.* In all probability, the first Encampment was that at Aberdeen, chartered by the Early Grand Encampment of Ireland. The date of 1794 is open to some doubt but from 1798 others followed. A *Royal Grand Conclave* for Scotland was authorized by the Duke of Kent, Royal Grand Patron for England, in 1809 and most of the existing Encampments transferred their allegiance to it. There were subsequent disputes, dissensions and difficulties; one effect was the chartering by Ireland of the *Early Grand Encampment of Scotland* in 1826. After much more trouble there was, happily, an amalgamation in 1909 and the *Great Priory of the Temple and Malta* is now the sole authority. About a hundred Preceptories (many in New Zealand and Australia) are currently on the Roll.

Cordial relationships are maintained by all three Great Priories with the Templar jurisdictions in Canada, the United States and Switzerland, and the Scandinavian Grand Lodges are also in amity (*see* Chapter XIV).

The Red Cross of Constantine

Here again a much fuller title reveals that there is more than one degree. *The Masonic and Military Order of the Red Cross of Constantine and the Orders of the Holy Sepulchre and St. John the Evangelist* are governed by a *Grand Imperial Conclave* which dates from 1865. In that year a group of prominent Freemasons, including W. H. White (Past Grand Secretary of the Craft), W. J. Hughan (the distinguished masonic historian) and R. W. Little (later Secretary of the Royal Masonic Institution for Girls and a senior Middlesex mason), assembled and 'having reconstituted the Grand Council and elected the venerable Sir Knight William Henry White, Past Grand Chancellor, as Grand Sovereign, proceeded to re-establish the Order upon a working basis'. Thus wrote Little; there was, in fact, no previous Order to re-establish! Even Hughan, usually a most careful student before he put pen to paper, wrote an

---
*An excellent account is given in *Pour la Foy* by G. S. Draffen.

OTHER DEGREES AND ORDERS

article which tried to show that the Order existed in 181

Confusion can quite easily arise and for several reasons. Pe haps the foremost is that, from the earliest days of speculativ Masonry, we find degrees and Orders with the title of 'Re Cross'. We have dealt already with the Red Cross of Babylo there was, too, the Red Cross of Daniel and a Red Cross o Palestine. The many other degrees including a reference to th Rose Croix, the *Rosae Crucis*, the Rosy Cross or the Rosy an Triple Cross amply demonstrate the difficulty of tracing genuine line of descent to a modern Order.

True it is that the *degree* of the Red Cross of Constantin was among those worked in the Royal Grand Conclave o Scotland (described in the previous section) and it is a reasor able supposition that it was derived from the parent Earl Grand Encampment of Ireland, although there is no evidenc of this. In Scotland the 'extra' degrees fell largely into disus in the Templar bodies leaving only the Orders of the Templ and Malta and the Mediterranean Pass alive. The last recor under the Royal Grand Conclave of the conferment of the Re Cross of Constantine is in 1857. It is probable that the degre was also worked in England within a Templar context. There i no direct evidence and there was certainly no 'Grand Council The claims of the revivalists of 1865 may therefore be dis counted. The late Brother G. E. W. Bridge (Grand Librarian t Grand Mark Lodge for many years) made it clear that thei 'history' related to the Red Cross of *Palestine* and could not b invoked as ante-dating their entirely new Order.

Having said that, it remains to add that the 'new Order' pro ceeded to establish itself and now flourishes. Its present muste of over 215 Conclaves (over 70 of them abroad) is the balance of over 360 which have been constituted. Many of the 'missing Conclaves are now on the Registers of the sovereign Granc Imperial Conclaves or Councils of Canada, Scotland and 'The United States of America, Mexico and the Philippines'.

To each Conclave is attached a Commandery in which the appendant Orders are conferred. Candidates for admission to the Conclave must be Royal Arch masons.

The Orders were re-introduced into Scotland in 1871 by the grant of a charter from England to form a Conclave at Edinburgh Others followed and a Grand Imperial Council was constituted in 1876. Scotland, too, has established the Orders overseas.

KNIGHT TEMPLAR PRIESTS, ETC.

In 1942, a charter was prepared by Scotland for the erection of a Conclave at Belfast but representations from the Grand Lodge of Ireland resulted in its cancellation.

The Holy Royal Arch Knight Templar Priests and Appendant Degrees

Earliest references to the Order are in Ireland and date back to 1806, and there are many certificates preserved. John Yarker (1833-1913), who was associated with many Masonic activities, creditable and otherwise, organized a Tabernacle of the Order at Newcastle and a governing Grand College. Thirty-three degrees are controlled but all save one are 'communicated by name'.

The Order was for some time taken under the protective wing of the Allied Masonic Degrees but the Grand College was happily re-established at Newcastle in the 1920s and recent years have seen a considerable expansion, Tabernacle No. 80 having been warranted in 1980. Others have been erected in Australia and New Zealand and, from the latter country, the degrees were carried to America in 1933 and a sovereign Grand College was constituted there in amity with the one at Newcastle.

Candidates for admission under England must be Knights Templar and Installed Masters of the Craft.

Societas Rosicruciana in Anglia

This was formed in 1866 by Hughan and Little and other zealous brethren who claimed to have discovered some ancient rituals in the archives of Grand Lodge. The English society consists of twenty-eight colleges, six of which meet beyond the shores of 'Anglia', the whole governed by a High Council in London, and is in communion with similar societies in Scotland and the United States.

There are nine grades or degrees, the two highest being conferred only by the Supreme Magus, the ruler of the society.

As papers are read and discussions follow at the meetings of the Colleges, membership is sought in particular by more studious brethren and no other qualification is required save that of Master Mason.

The Order of Eri

John Yarker was head of the *English Revived Order of the*

OTHER DEGREES AND ORDERS

Red Branch of which the Order of Eri is the descendant. Admission in this country is by invitation only and is restricted to members of the 5th grade of the Societas Rosicruciana.

The Order now confers three degrees and the ritual includes a good deal of Irish bardic verse. As far as is known, only one *Faislart* (chapter) meets in London under the name of 'Brian Boru'.

In America the Grand Council of the Allied Masonic Degrees controls the *Order of the Red Branch of Eri*, working the same ritual.

The August Order of Light

This was founded at Bradford in Yorkshire in 1902, and, at the time, its membership was drawn from that of the Societas Rosicruciana. To qualify for admission, however, the candidate needs only to be a Master Mason. The Order moved to York in 1971 and a second *Temple* was consecrated in London in 1972.

Its ritual is oriental in character and teaches a spiritual outlook on life; membership is therefore of advantage only to those who are likely to appreciate its deep significance.

The Worshipful Society of Free Masons, Rough Masons, Slaters, Paviors, Plasterers and Bricklayers

This society is popularly known as 'The Operatives' because it preserves the old operative rituals in its ceremonies. An interesting paper on the society appeared in the *Transactions of the Lodge of Research No. 2429, Leicester for 1911-12* revealing, with permission, much of the inner working. Perhaps the most significant detail is that, of the Three Masters who jointly rule an operative lodge or Assembly, the first and second hold office for life or until they retire but the third is ritually 'slain' each year and another brother elected in his place.

The Channel Row and Abbey Assemblages (with the appropriate superior lodges) meet in London to carry on the work of the society and, in recent years, there has been expansion outside the metropolis. Candidates for Apprenticeship must be Mark Master and Royal Arch masons of the speculative sort. There are seven degrees in all and, for admission to the sixth — Passed Master — there is a further condition that the applicant must be an Installed Master in the Craft and Mark.

The Baldwyn Rite

At Bristol there is a unique survival from the early days of speculative Freemasonry in a 'Time Immemorial' Rite of Seven Degrees. We mentioned in connexion with the story of Knights Templar that a Supreme Grand Royal Encampment was set up in that city in 1780. (It is fair to admit that both the date and the charter on which it stands are subject to elements of doubt). We have also seen that Encampments of the Templar Orders often had under their wing the control and propagation of other masonic and chivalric degrees.

Since space forbids the logical development of the story let us merely say that, despite the pressures of highly organized sovereign authorities in London, there still exists such an Encampment working degrees otherwise obsolete.

The Rite consists of:

I° Craft (the three Craft degrees, taken in any convenient lodge)
II° The Supreme Order of the Holy Royal Arch (by exaltation — inclusive of passing the veils — in a Bristol chapter)

THE CAMP OF BALDWYN
(The Five Royal Orders of Knighthood)

III° Knights of the Nine Elected Masters
IV° The Ancient Order of Scots Knights Grand Architect and the Royal Order of Scots Knights of Kilwinning
V° Knights of the East, the Sword and Eagle
VI° Knights of St. John of Jerusalem, Palestine, Rhodes and Malta and Knights Templar
VII° Knights of the Rose Croix of Mount Carmel

The Camp of Baldwyn is under the rule of a Most Eminent Grand Superintendent. In 1862, by agreement, the VI° came under the banner of Great Priory in London with a particular proviso that the *Baldwyn Commandery and Preceptory* should continue to work its own rituals. In 1881, by a similar treaty, the VII° accepted the jurisdiction of the Supreme Council 33°, the *Baldwyn Chapter Rosae et Crucis* retaining its own traditional ceremonies and the right to require that its candidates should be Knights Templar and, indeed, should appear for advancement in Templar habit. The Grand Superintendent

OTHER DEGREES AND ORDERS

ranks as Provincial Prior in Great Priory with but the one Preceptory in his Province. Similarly, he is an Inspector General 33° of the Ancient and Accepted Rite with the one Chapter Rose Croix under his control.

The Royal Order of Scotland

There is but one Grand Lodge of the Order in the regular masonic world and that, of course, is stationed in Edinburgh. It spreads its influence through Provincial Grand Lodges, there being now no lesser bodies, and these are also found outwith Scotland in many countries. Several are in England where invitation to membership is highly prized. Two degrees are conferred: *Heredom of Kilwinning* in the Provincial Grand Lodge itself and *Rosy Cross* in an attached Provincial Grand Chapter.

Tradition associates the former with David I and the latter with Robert Bruce. It is said to have been among the degrees established in France by Ramsay and there certainly was a *Royal Order of Heredom of Kilwinning* there in the early years of Grand Lodge Freemasonry. There are references to lodges of the Order in London between 1743 and 1750 and of a Provincial Grand Master for South Britain in the latter year.

The earliest record book in Scotland itself mentions a candidate in 1754. The first minute of a *meeting* of the Order in Edinburgh is in 1766 and postulates the existence of an established body. Grand Lodge was formed in the following year and the interesting tradition was born that the King of Scots shall be the hereditary Grand Master, a place being reserved for him at every meeting. The burden of rule falls upon an elected Deputy Grand Master and Governor.

The Order passed through a lean period and was in abeyance from 1819 to 1839 when two brethren succeeded in reviving the Grand Lodge. None of the earlier subordinate bodies remained but the establishment of the Provincial Grand Lodges began in 1859.

Knight Masons

The last masonic Order to claim our attention was, until 1967, controlled wholly from Dublin but in that year its Province for the United States was constituted into a sovereign jurisdiction.

The Knight Masons of Ireland — sometimes referred to as

ROYAL ORDER OF SCOTLAND

the 'green degrees' (as, similarly, the 'blue degrees' are the Craft) — came into existence as a separate Order in 1923 when the Great Priory of Ireland relinquished control over the 'Red Cross' degrees of *Knight of the Sword, Knight of the East* and *Knight of the East and West*. We have already touched upon the origin of these degrees and their control in England and Scotland (*see* p. 228).

In recent years Councils of the Order have been established in several countries overseas.

CHAPTER XIII

FREEMASONRY IN THE FORCES

'Masonry hath always been injured by War, Bloodshed, and Confusion,' says the second Charge in Anderson's *Constitutions* of 1723, but we propose to shew how our Craft derived great, though indirect, benefits from the wars of the eighteenth century and how Freemasonry, in its turn, proved beneficial to many members of many armed forces.

Pre-Grand Lodge days

Among the characters associated by legend or in history with the building craft we may mention briefly St. Alban and the Quatuor Coronati, all military martyrs under Rome. The first initiation in England of which we have any record was that of Sir Robert Moray, Quartermaster-General to the Army of Scotland, which took place at Newcastle in 1641, the brethren concerned being members of the famous Edinburgh lodge already described. In 1646 we have the initiation of Elias Ashmole at Warrington and, among those present, was his father-in-law, Colonel Mainwaring. Thus, of the three names just quoted we find a covenanter, a royalist and a parliamentarian. The earliest-known initiation of a naval officer is that of Admiral Robert Fairfax, admitted at York in 1713.

Early Grand Lodge Days

War was endemic during the eighteenth century but total war, as we know it only too well today, was yet unknown, so travel through enemy territory was by no means impossible and a certain amount of trade persisted. On the expansion of Freemasonry, the Craft came to the notice of many who followed the drum. The first noble Grand Master, the Duke of Montagu, was Master-General of the Ordnance. His successor, the Duke of Wharton, the black sheep of the Craft, founded in 1728 the first lodge in Spain to appear on the Register of

EARLY WARRANTS

Grand Lodge, but in the year before he was found engaged in the siege of Gibraltar — on the enemy side!

The first purely military lodge of which we know was established in Gibraltar in 1728 but this was a stationary body and not of the ambulatory type which later travelled from place to place with the Regiment to which it was attached. The first *travelling* warrant was issued by the Grand Lodge of Ireland to the lodge in the First Foot (Royal Scots) in 1732. By 1734 four further lodges were warranted, in the 33rd Foot (now part of the Duke of Wellington's Regiment), 27th (now part of the Royal Irish Fusiliers), 21st (now part of the Royal Highland Fusiliers) and 28th (the 'Glorious Gloucesters'). In 1747 the Grand Lodge of Scotland issued a warrant to a lodge in the Duke of Norfolk's 12th Foot (now part of the Royal Anglian Regiment), and it was claimed in the petition that this lodge had been established about the same time as the formation of the regiment in 1685.

England lagged behind in the issue of military warrants and, by the time the first was issued, Ireland had warranted twenty-nine and Scotland five military lodges, a fact that had important bearing on the spread of influence of the Antients; their working was more nearly akin to those of Ireland and Scotland.

The Minden Lodge

One cannot better exemplify the vicissitudes of a military lodge than by following the story of one of the older lodges through the first century of its existence. The Minden Lodge, No. 63 on the Register of the Grand Lodge of Ireland, was warranted in the 20th Regiment of Foot (now part of the Royal Regiment of Fusiliers) in 1748, its first Master being Colonel George, Lord Saville; the name *Minden* was later adopted after the victory of that name. At the time of the lodge's formation the regiment was employed in the pacification of the Highlands after the 1745 rebellion; in 1756 it was ordered to Germany, where an army order of 1759 directed it out of action owing to its severe losses — an order countermanded two days later *at the regiment's own request*. From 1762 to 1775 it served at home, this being followed by General Burgoyne's disastrous campaign in America, the surrender at Saratoga and imprisonment from 1777 to 1783. Although the early records of the lodge were lost the warrant was preserved

FREEMASONRY IN THE FORCES

by some providential, though unknown, means.

Six years' service in England was followed by four in the then dreaded West Indies, from which a skeleton force of survivors landed at Plymouth in April, 1796. Recruitment soon brought the regiment up to a strength of two battalions and there followed a period of intense activity — Holland, Ireland, an attempt to invade Brittany and, in 1801, to Egypt whence — after a successful engagement — the regiment sailed to Malta. Here is found the earliest recorded meeting of the lodge, Charles Whitton (rank unknown) being installed, and by 1804 a membership of forty had been attained.

Naples, 1805; Sicily, 1806; Gibraltar, 1807; these tours of duty were followed by a brief trip home in 1808. Then came the Peninsular campaign and a longer spell in Britain after Corunna in 1812. It was then found that the Grand Lodge regarded the lodge as defunct, no returns having been rendered for the past forty years (a fact at which we need hardly wonder), but the lodge was permitted to resume work under the old warrant without payment of fees. Duty then recalled the regiment to the Peninsula and 1819 found it mounting guard over Napoleon at St. Helena, where lodge work was quite impossible owing to lack of facilities.

The lodge resumed its labours in India in 1821 though death, disease and discharge had reduced the roll to four but, with the assistance of brethren of other lodges, the Minden Lodge was revived. Membership soon increased, charitable duties were resumed and the brethren participated in many masonic functions. After twenty years' service in India the regiment and the lodge returned to England, the latter ravaged once again by the 'the exigencies of the Service'; once again it built up its strength and this time established a masonic library!

'The end of the tale,' in the words of Brother R. E. Parkinson,* 'is contained in a letter to Grand Lodge, 8th December 1868, that the warrant, jewels, etc., had been lost in India during the Mutiny.' The lodge name is now honoured by the Minden Lodge, 464, which was founded in Calcutta in 1920 and has worked there as an Irish Masters' lodge but is (in 1975) finding it difficult to survive when only two other Irish lodges remain

*See p. 145n.

THE MINDEN LODGE

in Eastern India (the remainder having transferred their allegiance to the Grand Lodge of India).

The Last English Warrants

The last English military warrants were surrendered as recently as 1947 and 1949. In the former year the warrant of Social Friendship Lodge, 497, attached to the old 89th Foot (now part of the Royal Irish Rangers) was surrendered, the lodge receiving a renewed warrant authorizing it to meet as a stationary lodge. In 1949, similar action was taken by the Lodge of Unity, Peace and Concord, 316, belonging to the Royal Scots.

The Board of General Purposes commented on these events:

> This brings to a close an important chapter in English Freemasonry, for there can be no doubt that the spread of the Craft overseas was largely due to the enthusiasm and pertinacity of the members of the military lodges, who carried with them the seeds of Freemasonry to many distant garrison towns and cantonments, where stationary lodges were established and still flourish.
>
> The Board would not wish this change of status of these famous old lodges to pass unnoticed by the Craft.

Surviving Ambulatory Lodges

Of no less than 419 Lodges granted travelling warrants from London, Dublin or Edinburgh, there remain with their regiments only the two Irish lodges referred to in chapter VIII (p.167). It will have been noted there that one lodge has an attached Royal Arch chapter, also with an ambulatory Warrant. Some of the companions, incidentally, meet regularly as members of the Military Lodges Preceptory of Knights Templar, No. 300, under a stationary charter from the Great Priory of *England!*

Lodges in the Fleet

Only three regular lodges are known to have been warranted in men-of-war and Thomas Dunckerley is believed to have had a hand in all of them. The first, in H.M.S. *Vanguard* in which Dunckerley was serving as gunner, was warranted in 1760. It became a shore lodge in 1768 and is now the London Lodge, 108. Dunckerley was posted to H.M.S. *Prince* in 1761 and the following year obtained for it a warrant, which he appears to have transferred (with himself) to H.M.S. *Guadeloupe*. On his retirement from the Navy, in 1766, he used it for the Somerset House Lodge which, with the Old Horn Lodge, is now the Royal Somerset House and Inverness Lodge, No. 4. A third lodge, 'to be held in the most convenient place adjacent' to H.M.S. *Canceaux*, at Quebec, in 1762, was also probably founded by Dunckerley. It was erased in 1792. There was further an attempt in 1810 to form Naval Kilwinning Lodge in H.M.S. *Ardent*, but the petition was refused by the Grand Lodge of Scotland.

French Military Lodges

Military lodges are to be found or traced under many jurisdictions but, after our British lodges, no country seems to have had as many as France. Seventy-six are known to have been founded down to 1787 but, after that, expansion was slower and stopped with the Revolution. Though the lodges established under the Bourbon Monarchy generally went out of existence, there were sixty-nine French military lodges in 1812, which at that time used to open and close with the cry, 'Vive l'Empereur!' They fell on hard times with Napoleon's defeat and by 1821 the last of them had gone out of existence.

Freemasonry among Prisoners-of-War

In the days before total war, Freemasonry provided a great solace for fellow-members of the Craft who found themselves occupying the same prisoner-of-war establishments. In particular the French formed many masonic associations, especially in this country. These lodges, for they met as such, were first formed during the Seven Years' War of 1756-63 and many more came into being during the Napoleonic wars. There were many instances of donations by British lodges to alleviate the privations of these French brethren, while in Montrose a number of prisoners were removed from the local jail to the house of a local mason. There are many recorded instances of French prisoners on parole having been received as visitors in lodges in the British Isles.

The French brethren often established lodges* of their own; probably the majority were unauthorized but in four cases.

---

*There is a charming little reference, fictional of course, in Sir Arthur Quiller-Couch's novel, *The Westcotes*.

PRISONERS-OF-WAR

at Ashby-de-la-Zouch, Chesterfield, Leek and Northampton, permission to hold lodges was sanctioned by the Earl of Moira, Acting Grand Master of England, though, of course, the working of the Grand Orient was followed.

The prisoners generally restricted their activity to the admission of their own countrymen, yet hospitality was exchanged with local lodges. Many degrees were worked, including Scots Master, Knight of the East and Rose Croix, and lodges have been traced in five of the eight prisons and even six of the fifty-one hulks. Certificates were issued and most of our masonic museums contain pathetic relics in the form of jewels of tinsel and coloured material carefully cut into tiny emblems and mounted between watch glasses.

There were also many British prisoners in France, but the only lodge known to have met there was No. 183 of the Antients, established in the 9th Foot (now part of the Royal Anglian Regiment) in 1813. A detachment of this regiment was wrecked on the French coast and during its captivity the lodge met regularly. A charge was actually brought against the French freemasons of Verdun that they connived at the escape of British prisoners-of-war.

There is evidence that lodges were formed by prisoners-of-war of various nationalities in other countries; two surviving examples are described in the immediately following paragraph.

Internees in Holland

Holland was the scene of some remarkable masonic activity in the first World War. There the Lodges Gastvrijheid (Hospitality) and Willem van Oranje were warranted by the Grand East of the Netherlands in 1915 and 1918 respectively. These were for British naval and military personnel interned in the country, the second lodge being founded by prisoners-of-war transferred from Germany under the Hague Convention. English working was followed and initiation was restricted to British internees. After the war, both lodges were transferred to London under special warrants and charters of dedication issued by the Duke of Connaught. The ceremonies of Dedication were performed by the Pro Grand Master, Lord Ampthill, in 1919 and the two lodges were given the number 3970 and 3976 on the English Register. They are still very much alive and the former has since formed a Royal Arch Chapter.

FREEMASONRY IN THE FORCES

Under similar conditions, a Gastvrijheid Rose Croix Chapter was founded under Netherlandic authority in 1916 and moved to London in 1919, where it still works as the Royal Naval Volunteer Reserve Chapter, No. 207, under the Supreme Council for England.

Masonic 'Passports'

It is interesting to note that during the 1914-18 War the Ailwyn Lodge, 3535, among others, provided any of its members entering the armed forces with a card of introduction for use *outside* the United Kingdom. This was printed in English, French, Italian, German and Arabic.

World War Two

An astonishing amount of masonic activity is recorded as having occurred in the very difficult conditions of German, Italian and Japanese prison camps.* The incredible hazards of holding and tyling meetings 'of instruction' to rehearse degrees without arousing the suspicions of the guards, of making and concealing equipment, of retaining possession of such printed rituals as were available and those written from memory, of obtaining any form of official sanction from a relevant masonic authority, and of writing and preserving records: the mind boggles at the problems and one is lost in admiration for the courage and tenacity of those who solved them.

Examples of the jewels and working tools which were made and of the minutes which were kept can be seen in masonic museums. Small-sized emblems were essential so that they could be slipped into pockets in any emergency.

Charitable work ranged from the giving up of treasured 'comforts' to even less fortunate brethren in the camp hospitals to a 'deed of gift' of 150 guineas in favour of the Royal Masonic Institution for Boys.

Even under the outstandingly oppressive conditions in Changi Camp (military) and Changi Gaol (civilian) at Singapore it was found possible to hold meetings, and at one time these were quite frequent and extremely well-attended. Extra precautions included the appointment of additional Tylers (twenty-four on one occasion!) to warn of approaching danger

---

*An excellent account will be found in *Craftsmen in Captivity* by A. R. Hewitt (*A.Q.C.* 77 or the *Year Books* of the Grand Lodge of Scotland for 1965, 1966 and 1967).

and carefully rehearsed rapid conversions of 'lodge rooms' to innocent appearance.

Forces of Occupation

Modern developments in the practice of their Craft by military brethren far from home deserve some mention.

After the first World War, there was formed in Cologne (in 1923) a Lodge of Instruction under the authority of the Lodge of Honor and Generosity No. 165, London. Here freemasons of the forces occupying the Rhineland could meet, rehearse the ceremonies and hear and discuss papers, but they could not make masons. There were undoubtedly similar gatherings in other cities and in other countries.

The aftermath of the second World War left the Forces of several of the allied nations serving in considerable numbers in Europe, Asia and Africa. In many theatres the presence or revival of established masonic authority permitted full-scale activity by the brethren in uniform. In Germany, however, national Freemasonry had been crushed by Hitler and the efforts to re-create the old or set up new jurisdictions gave no promise of early recognition by the Grand Lodges of the United Kingdom. The British military brethren and those in the Control Commission formed at various centres small but vigorous groups — often with the blessing of the Grand Secretary in London, sometimes without — to rehearse and learn. After some years, several of these federated as the Association of British Freemasons (Germany) under the presidency of a senior member of the Craft and, eventually, all save the Berlin 'Circle' adhered to this Association and accepted the general guidance of its Central Committee. Upon the formal recognition by the British Grand Lodges of the new German Grand Lodge, the association was dissolved and many of its branches (with full approval from all concerned) were granted German warrants for lodges to work in English according to English ritual. These lodges were placed in the charge of a Provincial Grand Master of British birth, the first to hold such office being the last President of the old association. There are now twelve lodges in this Province (now styled a 'Land Grand Lodge') (one being for Canadian brethren) and English-style Royal Arch chapters and Mark and Royal Ark Mariner lodges have lodges have recently been established.

FREEMASONRY IN THE FORCES

Certain American Grand Lodges chartered lodges from the outset to work in Germany and it was quite possible for British brethren to visit and join, for instance, Lodge No. 46 of the Rhode Island Constitution in Berlin. In more recent times, warrants have been sought from the German Grand Lodge and there is now an American-Canadian Land Grand Lodge

Occupied Austria — on a somewhat smaller scale — also saw the formation of masonic groups and the very lively Trieste Masonic Association was evidence of the fraternity among British and American forces in that most interesting city. The withdrawal of troops naturally brought about the closure of these outposts of the Craft.

Services Lodges

It must not be overlooked that a very large number of stationary lodges have been formed by members of the armed forces. Most of these are associated with particular regiments or corps of the army, both regular and volunteer; there is one for the Royal Navy generally and there are a few connected with present or past divisions of the senior Service; similarly, there is a Royal Air Force Lodge and there are others formed by members of special groups within the R.A.F. Other lodges welcome members from all three Services.

This category of 'class' lodge is by no means restricted to English Freemasonry. Irish, Scottish and Commonwealth jurisdictions have also warranted lodges of like character and leading examples of the practice in the United States are the Major General Henry Knox Lodge at Boston, Massachusetts and the United Services Lodge No. 1118 at New York.

Some Masonic encounters

From the earliest days of the Craft, there have been occasions in war when freemasons have been able to assist 'enemy' brethren or their families. Many such incidents have been recorded; a few are here repeated.

America

The earliest-known military lodge in America was formed in 1738 under authority from Boston. After the French War (1755) the existing influence of the Moderns was greatly modified by the arrival of many military lodges, the majority

SOME MASONIC ENCOUNTERS

olding warrants from Ireland, Scotland or the Antients. We shall refer elsewhere to the part played by American freemasons in such episodes as the Boston Tea Party. The majority of the leaders of the revolution were freemasons and, with the outbreak of the revolutionary war, military lodges were active in both sides. There is evidence that George Washington visited the lodge in the 46th Foot (now incorporated in the Light Infantry Regiment) but claims that he was initiated therein have been proved untrue. During the war the masonic chest of the lodge in the 46th Regiment was captured by the Americans and Washington directed its return under a flag of truce, with an escort of honour under the command of a distinguished officer. Some years later, in 1805, the chest of the same lodge was captured by the French in Dominica and was returned three years later by the French Government.

During the war of 1812, one Lieutenant Colonel Tytler was thrown to the ground and was on the point of being bayoneted. He managed to give a masonic appeal whereon the American stayed his hand and gave the colonel not only life but liberty.

General John Corson Smith, who was an honorary member of the Lodge of Unity, Peace and Concord, 316, attached to the 2nd Battalion, the Royal Scots, told many stories of the American Civil War. At one time he was in charge of a camp of Confederate prisoners and observed the adjutant of an Alabama regiment wearing a masonic emblem. Verifying his masonic status, the general accepted his parole within the lines until it was possible to arrange an exchange.

During the Atlanta campaign, an Illinois general saw a small white apron nailed to a cabin door. The woman of the house told him it was her husband's, that he was away with the forces but had said that if she let the Federals know she was the wife of a mason she would be protected.

Joseph Brant was a Mohawk chief, said to have been initiated in London in 1776. He commanded some Indian allies of the British by whom Captain McKisty of the U.S. Army was captured. McKisty was about to be burned at the stake when Brant recognized a masonic appeal, intervened and saved his life, afterwards handing him over to some Quebec masons, who arranged for his repatriation. Brant's sister, Mary, married Sir William Johnson.

FREEMASONRY IN THE FORCES

Europe

The story that, in 1812, the life of a French army captain was spared when he gave a masonic sign as a Russian lancer was about to pierce him was deemed incredible by the Editor of the *Freemasons' Quarterly Review*. The incident has, however, been independently vouched for, the original narrator, Sir Robert Wilson, having actively intervened at the time.

In the Crimean War, an English officer, whose men were wiped out during the attack on the Redan, was on the point of being killed when he, happening to catch the hand of a Russian officer, gave him a masonic grip. The Russian immediately struck up the bayonets of his men, led the Englishman to the rear and treated him with all kindness.

More than one story is told of incidents in the heat of the battle of Waterloo, members of both sides being spared by others who recognized them as masons.

The benefits of Freemasonry worked both ways in the case of one French officer. On entering the town of Genappe, his men were engaged in taking prisoners when they were infuriated by losses inflicted by fire from a house. They stormed the house and were about to put to death nine wounded men who were lying there when one of these made the appropriate sign. The French officer immediately interposed and spared the life of the enemy. The following day he was, in his turn, wounded and captured by the Prussians, one of whom recognized him as a mason, attended to his wants and restored the money of which he had been plundered.

At Sea

We have no stories of the adventures of the few naval lodges but many sea-faring brethren derived benefit from their connexion with Freemasonry.

In 1795 a ship from Maine, U.S.A., was captured by pirates from Tripoli and the captain and crew were imprisoned in that port. While engaged on slave labour the captain was recognized as a freemason by an Arab officer who had been initiated in France. He took steps to ensure his comfort and eventual liberation. Despite furious personal attacks, the American in later years refused to bow down before the anti masonic storm that followed the Morgan affair.

A story was related at Stability Lodge of Instruction in

845 that, fifteen years previously, a merchant vessel bound for Cuba was captured by pirates who looted the ship, tied up captain and crew and prepared to burn the vessel. In his extremity the captain made the sign of an Entered Apprentice to which a pirate responded with that of a Fellow Craft. The latter interceded with his captain, who spared the lives of the crew and, when he again encountered the ship the following day, left her unmolested. We are not surprised to hear that the mate lost no time in seeking admission to the Craft on his return to England. Commenting on this incident the *Freemasons' Quarterly Review* said, 'we have a remarkable instance of a man who, though he disregarded every law both human and divine, had yet remained faithful to his masonic obligation.'

In 1844 the crew of an English brig were attacked on the west coast of Africa by some natives urged on by Spanish slavers. The Englishmen were on the point of being exterminated when the captain noticed a masonic emblem in the neckerchief of one of the Spaniards. He gave a masonic appeal on which the Spaniard hurriedly proved him (in the heat of battle!) and brought over his men, dispersing the natives.

The brethren of Poole, Dorset, have preserved records of their part in the Napoleonic wars. They raised funds for British prisoners in France and at least once entertained a French brother, a prisoner-of-war. One of their members, a captain, was taken by a French privateer, whose commander discovered the Englishman's masonic certificate among his papers. It was then too late to release him but he made arrangements for his favourable treatment in France and eventually he was accommodated in the house of a brother at Verdun. During his captivity, which lasted from 1803 to 1814, Napoleon personally ordered the provision of a Christmas dinner for the English Freemasons.

The Amity Biscuit

The story of the Amity biscuit has often been told. Captain Jacques le Bon, a noted French privateer, captured the brig *Oak* in 1813. Discovering that the Captain was a freemason he not only released him but sent with him a little dog, the property of a freemason recently captured, with a biscuit suspended from its neck, signifying that he would not keep a brother's dog in bondage nor see it want food, much less a

FREEMASONRY IN THE FORCES

brother himself. The biscuit, mounted and framed, is st[ill] preserved and prized by the Lodge of Amity No. 137, Pool[e].

The same lodge welcomed in 1917 an Australian broth[er] rescued from the torpedoed hospital ship *Lanfranc*. Man[y] survivors of this disaster were taken into the port.

* * * * *

Finally, we tell of an unusual military investiture. At [a] meeting of the Lodge of Amity on 8th October 1917, Br[o.] W. J. Telfer, of Boston, U.S.A., who was serving with th[e] British Army, was presented with the Military Medal by th[e] Provincial Grand Secretary of Dorset.

So far, therefore, from masonry having 'always bee[n] injured by War and bloodshed', we have seen that its principle[s] learnt in peace, prevailed in conflict, that in the heat of batt[le] freemasons have been willing to spare their enemies who[m] they found to be in the Craft, and that prisoners of war i[n] their captivity have found their greatest solace in the memories of Masonry and the rehearsal of its ritual.

CHAPTER XIV

FREEMASONRY IN EUROPE

The object of this and the following four chapters is to indicate very briefly the progress of Freemasonry in many countries near and far. In the space available we can give no more than an indication of the lines on which the Craft has developed. It may also serve as a warning, for in many places the brethren have wandered to such an extent from the strict line ever observed by the United Grand Lodge of England (and supported by the sister Constitutions of Ireland and Scotland) that masonic intercourse has had to be suspended. In more than one country religious and political controversies have arisen within and with respect to Freemasonry.

Conscious that this book is designed to be a 'pocket' history we have with one exception omitted special mention of countries where the political situation has made the effective practice of Freemasonry impossible. We would direct the student to any good masonic library to pursue research in such a field. In Spain, Portugal, Czechoslovakia, Poland, Hungary, Rumania, Bulgaria and Russia the Order has ceased to exist.

Portugal does, however, deserve notice here. The persecution, under a royal edict of 1743, of the small number of freemasons who then existed in the country has indirectly provided the masonic student of today with some most interesting and valuable material. The best-known brother of those days is John Coustos, who had been initiated in England before settling in Lisbon. There he was arrested under the edict and, after a long drawn out ordeal under the Inquisition, was claimed by the British Ambassador as one of King George II's subjects and released. In 1746, Coustos published an account of his sufferings in which he stated that, despite torture, he had revealed neither the names of his brethren nor any information about the Craft. His reputation suffered a belated blow more than two centuries later when the relevant records of the Inquisition were published in translation in *A.Q.C.* 66. Brother Dr. Sidney Vatcher's subsequent work on Coustos and his fellow-freemasons in Lisbon in *A.Q.C.* 81 and 84 has made excellent use of those records and reveals among other things a good deal about Craft practice at the time.

AUSTRIA

The first lodge in the Austrian Empire was founded at Prague in 1726 by a Count de Spork whose own masonic origins are not quite clear. An important event for the Craft in Austria was the initiation and passing of Francis, Duke of Lorraine, at a lodge at The Hague in 1731 by six English brethren headed by Doctor Desaguliers, Past Grand Master together with one Dutch brother — presumably the first Netherlandic freemason as this meeting was the first recorded on Dutch soil. Later the same year, at an 'emergency' lodge held at Houghton Hall, Norfolk, under the gavel of the reigning Grand Master of England, Lord Lovel, a Brother Lothringen — otherwise Duke Francis — appears in the minutes as having been raised to the degree of a Master Mason. He married in 1736 Maria Theresia the heiress to the Imperial Throne, and in 1740 became joint ruler with his wife of the vast dominions of the Austrian crown.

The Papal Bull of 1738 against Freemasonry was not published in Vienna, very probably owing to Francis's influence with his father-in-law and to the fact that, while there were undoubtedly several masons living in the city, there was no lodge there. This deficiency was quickly repaired for, on 17th September 1742, the Lodge *zur den drei kanonen* (Three Principles) was constituted by a lodge from Breslau under its ruling Master, the Catholic Prince-Bishop of that city, with Francis as its most exalted founder-member. Unfortunately his wife, the Empress, was strongly averse to the Craft and all his good offices were powerless to prevent the occasional outburst of anti-masonic activity on her part. For instance, on 7th March 1743, she ordered the lodge meeting-place to be surrounded and had eighteen brethren — chiefly of the nobility — arrested and put under lock and key for twelve days. It is said that Francis himself, being present, was put to the indignity of escaping at the rear of the building to avoid

AUSTRIA

direct marital complications! The lodge continued to meet in secret for some time but was soon able to come into the open when Francis, through his election in 1745 as Emperor of Germany, acquired rather more influence in Austrian affairs. There was, in fact, an uneasy sort of peace until 1764 when the Empress tried again, forbidding the practice of Freemasonry throughout Austria by Imperial Decree. It seems, however, that no one took much notice of this effort.

In the following year, the Emperor Francis died and his son became joint ruler, as Joseph II, with his mother. He was not himself a mason but showed a considerable and benign interest in the Order. When Maria Theresia died in 1780 he ruled alone and then began the brief but fruitful and prosperous era in Austrian Freemasonry. In 1784, with a view to curtailing external political influence in the lodges, the Emperor decreed that they should transfer their allegiance from the foreign Grand Lodges which had constituted them to an Austrian National Grand Lodge which he ordered to be erected under the Grand Mastership of Count Dietrichstein. Forty-five lodges were thus nationalized, of which eight worked in Vienna itself. On 17th December 1785, under great pressure from the clergy, he unwillingly decreed further that the number of lodges, and their memberships, should be reduced within eleven days. This drastic and most unpopular edict meant that no more than three lodges could exist in Vienna. It was obeyed, at the cost of many resignations of influential brethren and the immediate closure of two lodges, but the limitation of membership proved a serious blow and the vitality of the Order began to wane. Joseph's death in 1790 was the beginning of the end. His brother, Leopold II, staunchly promasonic (and, indeed, thought by many to have been a member of the Craft) ruled for only two years. Leopold's son and heir, Francis, was as staunchly *anti*-masonic — living constantly in fear for the safety of his throne and person and believing that *any* secret society must be working against him. In such an atmosphere, the lodges voluntarily closed in 1794 and Freemasonry was formally suppressed in the following year. There followed a long and difficult period for Austrian Freemasonry with virtually complete darkness until 1867 when Hungary became a separate kingdom within the Empire. It then became possible for Austrian brethren to form

FREEMASONRY IN EUROPE

lodges across the border under a Hungarian Grand lodge which came into being in 1870. But it was not until after World War I that a Grand Lodge could again be formed in Vienna and, in 1930, this was recognized by the Grand Lodge of England. Of its twenty-six lodges one was consecrated in the Far East by the English District Grand Master of Northern China, with permission from London! But the invasion of Austria by the Nazis in 1938 brought masonic activity to an end once more.

When the second Great War ended the Grand Lodge (*Grossloge von Österreich*) was revived, with several of the old lodges, and gained recognition again from regular jurisdictions. One of the Vienna lodges is named 'Mozart' after one of the most distinguished brethren of early Austrian Freemasonry. Mozart's music, not a little of which was specially written for the Craft, is a lasting memorial to the spirit of those times.

There is also an irregular *Grand Orient* and a *Supreme Council* 33° not so far in amity with the British Supreme Councils. A co-masonic Order exists in Vienna under the title of *Osterreichischer Universaler Freimaurer-Orden 'Humanitas'*.

BELGIUM

The earliest Freemasonry in what is now the Kingdom of Belgium was furnished by English lodges, the first on record being No. 341 at Alost in Flanders in the Austrian Netherlands. Others followed and there is evidence of a Provincial Grand Lodge from 1769 to 1787 by which time the events which we have recorded for Austria itself were having repercussions in its detached dominions. From 1795 to 1814 the country was under French governance and Freemasonry revived under the French Grand Orient. Between 1817 and 1830 Belgium was a part of the Kingdom of the Netherlands and came under a Grand Lodge of Administration with Dutch authority.

The next stage begins with Belgium's independence as a Kingdom, closely followed by masonic independence, when some of the former Dutch lodges constituted the *Grand Orient*. King Leopold I, who had been initiated in Switzerland, became its Protector although he never visited its meetings. The later development of political and anti-clerical tendencies led to the rupture of relationships with regular Grand Lodges, including that of England. Within the Grand Orient itself there was schism, some lodges ranging themselves under a Supreme

BELGIUM & DENMARK

Council for the Scottish Rite. The Grand Orient copied its French counterpart in withdrawing insistence on the presence of the Volume of the Sacred Law at all meetings and has not since amended its views.

In 1959, five lodges, realizing that there was little possibility of general acceptance as regular masons while this policy remained unaltered, broke away and were constituted by the Grand East of the Netherlands into a *Grand Lodge of Belgium*. This Grand Lodge was recognized by the United Grand Lodge of England in 1965. Unfortunately a recent Grand Master sought to return to Grand Orient practices and English relationships were severed in June 1979. But some of the Belgian Lodges and brethren at once broke away and formed the *Regular Grand Lodge of Belgium*. By December 1979, this comprised ten lodges and the English Grand Lodge gladly extended recognition.

The Royal Arch has been introduced from the Netherlands but the *Supreme Council 33° for Belgium* has not for many years been recognized as regular.

DENMARK

A lodge was established in Copenhagen in 1743 by Baron von Munnich, a member of the *Three Globes* of Berlin, seemingly without authority. Other lodges followed — some warranted from England — but from 1765 onwards the Scandinavian Rite (*see* p. 265) progressively 'took over' Danish Freemasonry. Over a long period, from 1792 to 1950, the *National Grand Lodge* (*Den Danske Store Landsloge*), which continues to work this rite, was ruled by a member of the Royal Family — often the King himself.

Another Grand Lodge (*Storlogen af Danmark af gamle, frie og antagne Murer*), sometimes styling itself 'Grand Orient', drew its authority from Italian and French sources and was not recognised by regular masonic authorities. Until 1960 it worked under a Supreme Council 33° (*det højeste Råd af 33° af Danmark*) but, in that year, its lodges voted for affiliation with the National Grand Lodge, changing their organization's name to 'The Guild of Freemasons of Ancient, Free and Accepted Masons' (*Frimurerlauget af Gamle og Frie Antagne Murer*). This did not please all the members and some withdrew, forming a new *Storlogen af Danmark* under the old

Italian and French documents and placing it under the Supreme Council 33°. The latter body has never achieved international recognition.

FINLAND

In 1756, when Finland was under the Swedish Crown, the first masonic lodge was erected in Helsingfors (now Helsinki) under Swedish authority (from 1759 the National Grand Lodge of Sweden). The Strict Observance having come to Stockholm, a St. Andrew's lodge was founded in Helsingfors to confer the higher degrees. Both lodges remained active until after the Russo-Swedish War of 1808-1809, as a result of which Finland became a Grand Duchy within the Russian Empire with the Czar as its Grand Duke. It is not clear as to how the two lodges fared in the immediate aftermath; there was a Grand Lodge or Grand Directory in Russia but they may have remained under Swedish control. In any event, 1822 saw their closure for in that year Freemasonry was suppressed by the Czar throughout his dominions.

When Finland became a sovereign state after the first World War, the Swedish lodges were revived, the St. John's (Craft) lodge in 1923 and the St. Andrew's in 1934. Two more Craft lodges followed and a Stewart lodge to confer the 7° and 8° was founded in 1953 (The system of degrees is described under **SWEDEN.**).

In 1922, under the authority of the Grand Lodge of New York, a Craft lodge was consecrated in Helsinki to satisfy the desire of Finnish-speaking citizens for Freemasonry. (The Swedish lodges cater largely for the Swedish-speaking minority.) One of the first initiates was Sibelius, the eminent composer, who — as Grand Organist — later wrote masonic music for the lodge. In 1924, similar lodges having come into being, a Grand Lodge (*Suomen Suur-Loosi*) was formed and this has grown to a strength of over seventy lodges. Royal Arch Masonry was introduced from England in 1930 and a Grand Chapter was erected in 1961 with the aid of a deputation from London. Mark Masonry is practised in a growing number of lodges formerly holding English warrants but now constituted into a Grand Mark Lodge. The Ancient and Accepted Rite has been similarly sponsored from London and the Chapters Rose Croix are now governed by a Finnish Supreme Council.

FINLAND & FRANCE

Thus in one small country there are two masonic systems, both regular in every sense and widely recognized as such.

FRANCE

There are many stories about lodges being formed in France in the latter part of the 17th century by expatriate Scots; these however are incapable of proof. What we do know is that Charles Radcliff (the self-styled Earl of Derwentwater), James Hector McLean, Squire Heguarty and others established a lodge in Paris in 1725. We also know that Freemasonry spread to France in the very early days of our own Grand Lodge and that the country proved a prolific breeding-ground for the additional degrees. The *Grand Lodge of France* flourished until, under the Duc d'Orleans (Citizen Egalité) it was, to all external appearances, swept away during the revolution. But 1795 saw the rise of a new *Grand Orient* (one had been set up in 1773), sanctioned in 1798 by the Paris police, which quickly absorbed the surviving elements of its predecessors.

There were renewed attacks on the Craft during the troubles of 1848 and, to counteract these, the Grand Orient in 1852 elected as its Grand Master Prince Lucien Murat, an active ruler until his resignation in 1861. Relations with the Grand Lodge of England were not harmonious and, in 1877, the Grand Orient having removed from its Constitutions the affirmation of the existence of T.G.A.O.T.U., Ireland and then England withdrew recognition and similar action was taken by many other Grand Lodges.

Scottish Rite Freemasonry had also established itself, a *Supreme Council* 33° being set up in 1804 under de Grasse-Tilly who, so to speak, brought back from America the line of authority taken west by Morin (*see* p. 231). In 1880, arising from disagreements with the Grand Orient, the Supreme Council sponsored a *Grand Lodge of France* to govern the Craft degrees. Like the Grand Orient, it is still in existence but is not recognized by England since it has many of the agnostic principles which were acquired by the older obedience. In 1913 a National Grand Lodge (*Grande Loge Nationale Française*) was founded on a regular basis and has since received a good deal of active cooperation from English brethren. A Grand Royal Arch Chapter is attached. (The Mark lodges are governed from London.) It is important to emphasize that these two wholly regular bodies are administered from a headquarters at Boulevard Bineau, Neuilly, Paris, since an *irregular* Grand Lodge using the same name was established a few years ago in the Avenue de l'Opéra.

Remnants of earlier 'high degree' systems still linger under such names as *Rite de Memphis et Misraim, Grand Collège des Rites* and *L'Ordre Martiniste*.

GERMANY

After one or two abortive attempts a German lodge was established at Hamburg in 1737. A year later, the future Frederick the Great was initiated and opened a King's Lodge at his Castle of Rheinsberg. There was a temporary interruption following his departure to war after which a new lodge was established in Berlin in 1740 and out of this was formed the *Grand National Mother Lodge of the Three Globes*.

Lodges were quickly erected in many towns and one became the *Grand Lodge Royal York*. Additional degrees also became popular and conflicting loyalties led to much confusion; von Hund's Strict Observance was one of the disturbing elements.

The *Grand National Lodge of German Freemasons in Berlin* was established by von Zinnendorf to unite most of the German lodges (Frankfurt excepted) and was recognized by England. In all nine Grand Lodges were formed in Germany, in addition to five independent lodges which, though acknowledged as regular, owed no allegiance to anybody. During the 1914-18 War and for some years thereafter, masonic intercourse between England and Germany ceased. It was happily restored but under Hitler's rule Freemasonry was ruthlessly suppressed, its Temples pillaged and some members murdered or sent to concentration camps.

In 1956, after careful examination, England recognized the *United Grand Lodge of Germany* which had revived the lodges working in the normal Craft system. There was also a *Grosse Landesloge* which was governing lodges of the Scandinavian Rite. By 1960 the two authorities had come together as the *United Grand Lodges of Germany, Brotherhood of German Freemasons (Vereinigte Grosslogen von Deutschland)*.

The Royal Arch, Royal and Select Masters and Knight Templar degrees have been introduced by the American Forces and a Grand Chapter, a Grand Council and a Grand Commandery have been constituted with allegiance to the 'General Grand' organizations mentioned in chapter XV.

GREECE

The first lodge in Greece was founded at Corfu in the Ionian Islands by the Grand Orient of France in 1809 and a second was established there in the following year. An English lodge (and, later, a Royal Arch Chapter) was consecrated in the same place in 1837 and remained active until 1894. In 1861 England warranted the Star of the East Lodge (now No. 880, E.C.) at Zante, farther south in the Islands, and it still works there.

On the Greek mainland there was in 1866 a Provincial Grand Lodge governing eight lodges under the Grand Orient of Italy and in 1868 it became, with Italian agreement, the *Grand Orient of Greece*. The present regular *Grand Lodge of Greece* is the same authority, as reconstituted after the second World War. Among its many lodges is one, Parthenon No. 112, which works in Athens in the English language.

A *Supreme Council 33° for Greece*, dating from 1872, is not at present in amity with England.

ICELAND

Freemasonry in Iceland was until 1951 controlled by the *National Grand Lodge of Denmark* but, when Iceland became politically separate, it desired masonic independence also. Accordingly the Grand Master of Denmark, on 23rd July 1951, constituted the *National Grand Lodge of Iceland* (*Storstuka Frimurareglunnar a Islandi*) which is as regular as its parent Constitution. It works in the Scandinavian Rite.

ITALY

Before its unification in the middle of the last century, Italy was a geographical expression rather than a political entity and its masonic history is thereby the more difficult to unravel. The Craft is said to have been introduced by Charles Sackville, Earl of Middlesex in 1733 and met with varying success in the different sovereign states. Of some significance was the part played by Garibaldi, the Grand Master of one of several 'Grand Bodies' of the 1860s. Largely as a result of his efforts a single authority, the *Grand Orient of Italy*, emerged from the chaos in 1873 to control both the Craft and the Scottish Rite Masonry.

FREEMASONRY IN EUROPE

This Grand Orient, as recently as in 1972, was recognised as regular by the United Grand Lodge of England. It governs upwards of 500 lodges, including at least one (in Rome) which works in English. In 1981 much unpleasant publicity was given to the activities of the Rome lodge known as 'P.2' but the Grand Orient had suspended this lodge five years previously and it had acted quite independently.

A Grand Royal Arch Chapter of the American pattern was established some years ago and more recently a chapter on English lines has been consecrated at Florence.

There is a Supreme Council 33° operating from the same headquarters (in the Via Giustiniani, Rome) as the Grand Orient but *not* in fraternal communication with the English Supreme Council. It is important for regular masonic visitors to Italy to note that address because, administered from other headquarters, there are several *irregular* bodies, including the *Gran Loggia Nazionale Italiana* with an associated Supreme Council 33°, and the *Gran Loggia d'Italia* (admitting descent from the *Nazionale* but separately ruled) with its own linked Scottish Rite system.

LUXEMBURG

In 1969, the United Grand Lodge of England accorded recognition to the *Grand Lodge of Luxemburg*. In this tiny country, where the vast majority of the population are Catholics, there is clearly a limit to the number of lodges and there had been for some time a question as to the authenticity of the Grand Lodge itself. This was resolved with the help of the Grand Lodge of Belgium. There is also an irregular *Grand Orient of Luxemburg*.

The first lodge in the country was formed in 1776 under a Belgian warrant but it did not survive beyond 1793. Other lodges were later established under German and French authorities but a Grand Lodge (later the Grand Orient) was illegally constituted by only one private lodge and this fell under the influence of the Grand Orient at Paris.

THE NETHERLANDS

The initiation at the Hague of the Duke of Lorraine in 1731

eems to have been in a lodge specially convened for the occasion under English authority. The first genuine record of a local lodge dates from 1734 but it is not known whence it derived its origin. Several more lodges were formed under English warrants and in 1756 a *Grand Lodge of the Netherlands* was established. This amended its title in the nineteenth century to the *Grand East of the Netherlands* (*Grootosten der Nederlanden*). A few years ago, with the help of the Anglo-Dutch Chapter No. 5862, London, the Royal Arch was introduced into the country and a Grand Chapter now governs the Order there. The first Mark lodge was constituted, under the English Grand Lodge, in 1957 and others have since been established as has a Lodge of Royal Ark Mariners, all under a District Grand Lodge formed in 1972. *The Supreme Council 33° for the Netherlands* is also in amity with its English counterpart, but there is also an irregular *Supreme Council of the A. and A. Rite* and an equally suspect *Grootloge der Nederlanden*.

NORWAY

Norway's masonic history is that of Sweden until 1891 when, well in advance of complete political separation, the *Grand Lodge of Norway* (*Den Norske Store Landsloge*) was formed from the appropriate division of the Swedish obedience. It is significant that King Gustav V of Sweden (and Norway until 1905) headed the list of Honorary Members of the Norwegian Grand Lodge and he remained on it until his death in 1950.

The Scandinavian Rite is worked (to be described in the following section).

SWEDEN

Den Nordiska Första, the first lodge in Sweden, was founded in 1735 and was one of several which constituted the *National Grand Lodge* (*Svenska Stora Landslogen*) in 1759. In 1756 some higher degrees, based upon the French Clermont Rite (*see* p. 230), were brought to Stockholm and a St. Andrew's lodge (still in existence) was formed to promote them. This was affiliated to the new Grand Lodge and so the foundations of the Swedish or Scandinavian Rite were laid. Other degrees were added and for a very long time the system (embracing Denmark, Norway and Iceland as well) has consisted of the following:

FREEMASONRY IN EUROPE

1° to 3° The Craft degrees, conferred in St. John's lodge
4° to 6° The Scots degrees, conferred in St. Andrew's lodge
      4° Scottish Apprentice
      5° Fellow of St. Andrew
      6° Scottish Master of St. Andrew
7° to 10° The Chapter degrees, conferred in Grand Lodge
           Provincial Grand Lodges or Stewart lodges
      7° Stewart Brother
      8° Confidant of Solomon
      9° Confidant of St. John
    10° Confidant of St. Andrew

The highest degree, 11°, Knights Commander of the Red Cross, is in Sweden an Order of Chivalry known as the Order of King Charles XIII. It is conferred by the King, who (if a member of the Craft — which he usually is) is always the Grand Master of Masonry, and its holders must wear its insignia on appropriate occasions in public.

By agreement, Royal Arch and Rose Croix masons from regular jurisdictions may be present at Scandinavian workings up to the 6th degree. Similar arrangements cover the 30th to 33rd degrees of the Ancient and Accepted Rite whose members can be admitted, respectively, to assemblies in the 7th to 19th degrees in Scandinavia. The concordats operate reciprocally. For Knights Templar no formal ruling exists but visits may be possible after seeking and obtaining prior approval through the appropriate channels.

SWITZERLAND

A number of English freemasons established a lodge at Geneva in 1736 and it is said that, in the following year, an English Provincial Grand Master was appointed but this does not seem to be confirmed by the archives of the Grand Lodge of England. The political situation in the Switzerland of those days and the cantonal form of government made the formation of a federal masonic authority a virtual impossibility but an *Independent Grand Lodge of Geneva* was formed in 1769 by ten lodges working in that city. After a later period of great difficulty the Grand Lodge became the *Grand Orient of Geneva* in 1786. The Grand Orient of France was busily warranting lodges as well and as many as seventy-two are reported in a

SWEDEN – SWITZERLAND

newspaper of 1787. The Rite of Strict Observance also entered the field and, at a Congress at Basel in 1777, two obediences were set up, one for German-speaking Switzerland and one for the area where French is most widely used.

The post-Napoleonic period presents a confusing history but, bringing together all but six lodges, the *Grand Lodge Alpina of Switzerland* emerged in 1844 as a central authority, which it remains to this day.

Unfortunately, relationships between the United Grand Lodge of England and Grand Lodge Alpina were temporarily severed in 1971, after a period of warning, because irregular masons were being permitted to attend meetings of Swiss lodges. More positive action by Alpina led, happily, to the full restoration of fraternal communion in 1972.

With English assistance – a Royal Arch Chapter Von Tavel was first consecrated for the Helvetica Lodge in London then moved to Berne – a Swiss Grand Royal Arch Chapter has been constituted.

Although the *Supreme Council 33° for Switzerland* is not recognized, the Great Priory of England is in communion with its counterpart at Geneva. There is also in Switzerland the *Grand Priory of the Rectified Scottish Rite*, more often referred to as the *Knights Beneficent of the Holy City*. This is, in effect, the old Rite of Strict Observance of Baron von Hund. It is regarded as an exalted pinnacle of Freemasonry and its Swiss members have the privilege of attending meetings of the 33° of the Scottish Rite. Great Priories of the Order have been established in France, the United States and England, the last of these being dormant.

There is an irregular *Grand Orient of Switzerland* and the French Grand Orient and Grand Lodge also have lodges.

GIBRALTA AND MALTA

To complete this survey of active European Freemasonry it is important to add that very active lodges, chapters, etc., of the principal masonic Orders have long been established in these small but extremely important outposts of the British Commonwealth. All are governed from London, Dublin or Edinburgh and can trace their origins to the soldiers and sailors of the early years of the speculative Craft.

CHAPTER XV

FREEMASONRY IN AMERICA

CANADA

There is a tradition that a French lodge met in Quebec in 1720 but no evidence has been found to support it. The facts are that the earliest lodges appeared in Nova Scotia, at Annapolis Royal and Halifax in 1749 and 1750. Earlier dates have been quoted but it has been established that the 'St. John's Grand Lodge of Massachusetts' (a Provincial Grand Lodge at this time) issued the necessary authorities. As is the case elsewhere, it was the military lodges who were primarily responsible for the spread of Freemasonry in the country. In Wolfe's army, which fought at Quebec in 1759, there were at least nine regiments with travelling lodges and their Masters and Wardens met in the winter of that year to form a Grand Lodge. The transfer of some of the regiments prevented this but some civilian lodges in Quebec applied to London for a Provincial warrant. The one sent in 1762 did not arrive; a second attempt was successful in 1767.

After the American War of Independence there were those who preferred to remain under the British Crown. These naturally moved to Canada and the masons among them formed lodges. Provincial Grand Lodges of Upper and Lower Canada were constituted and a significant appointment was that of Prince Edward (later Duke of Kent) to the charge of the latter.

The strength of the Craft grew and in the middle of the nineteenth century — partly because of unbearable delays in obtaining certificates from London and partly because of the confusion between the English, Irish and Scottish procedures — Canada sought masonic independence. Two separate and sovereign authorities were at first established but they soon merged, in 1858, as the *Grand Lodge of Canada.* It was established at Hamilton in the Province of Ontario but, at that

CANADA

time, claimed jurisdiction over the whole of Canada, then comprising Ontario and Quebec. With the formation of the Dominion of Canada in 1867, and after various 'growing pains' had been cured, the original Constitution became the *Grand Lodge of Canada in the Province of Ontario* and eight more Grand Lodges came into being as the country developed. These, and the dates of their erection, are as follows: *Nova Scotia*, 1866; *New Brunswick*, 1867; *Quebec*, 1869; *British Columbia*, 1871; *Prince Edward Island*, 1875; *Manitoba*, 1875; *Alberta*, 1905; *Saskatchewan*, 1906.

Newfoundland's Craft Masonry is still governed from London and Edinburgh, there being eighteen English and nine Scottish lodges with a Distrct Grand Lodge in each case. This stems, of course, from the rather curious political history of the island which joined the Dominion of Canada only in recent years.

The Royal Arch in Canada has grown on rather similar lines and there are Grand Chapters for all the Provinces save Prince Edward Island and Newfoundland where the subordinate Chapters answer to Nova Scotia. The workings are a mixture of English, Scottish and American, three of the Grand Chapters owning allegiance to the General Grand Chapter centred in the United States (q.v.).

The Supreme Council $33°$ *for Canada* was chartered in 1874 from London. The *Great Priory of Knights Templar* and the *Grand Conclave of the Red Cross of Constantine* are also of British origin and there are Eastern and Western *Grand Councils of Royal and Select Masters* controlling the Royal Ark Mariner as well as the Cryptic degrees. Many of the United States' masonic and quasi-masonic organizations have active branches in Canada.

One final point: on the mainland of Canada there remain a few sturdy outposts of English Freemasonry, retaining with great pride their London warrants. These are the Lodges of St. Paul No. 374 (1770) and St. George No. 440 (1829) at Montreal and the Royal Standard Lodge No. 398 (1815) at Halifax. These are under the care of a Grand Inspector. St. Paul's Lodge has a Royal Arch Chapter attached, dating from 1827, and in 1952 a Chapter was consecrated at Halifax for the Royal Standard Lodge, but this closed in 1976. In 1871, a Mark Lodge of St. Paul No 131 completed the Montreal

THE UNITED STATES OF AMERICA

The late Bro. Fred Pick aptly wrote that 'the discussion of Freemasonry in the United States within a short chapter combines all the difficulty of getting a quart into a pint pot with the representation of the treasures of Aladdin's cave within the resources of a provincial pantomime'. His successor in the attempted task has come to the conclusion that Fred Pick was given to understatement! In fact, since this book is 'a pocket history' and since much of American Masonic history is for the connoisseur, it has been decided that a 'tabloid' approach might be more serviceable in dealing with the multiplicity of salient dates and factors.

But there are many names and many incidents that are quite inseparable even from the briefest story.

The Earliest Traces

Eminent students of the Craft believe that the earliest lodges working in the North American colonies were established by immigrants from Great Britain without the sanction of warrants. Naturally enough no dates can be given but the first decades of the eighteenth century can fairly be deemed to have seen something of the sort in the new world on the eastern coasts of the continent.

It is known that Lord Alexander, who became a member of the Lodge of Edinburgh in 1634, was shortly afterwards forming a colony on the St. Lawrence river but we have no *record* of masonic activity by him. A tale about the introduction of the *three* Craft degrees into Newport, Rhode Island, in 1658 must be apocryphal! But one piece of evidence is important — the *Tho. Carmick MS* of the Old Charges, copied in 1727. In 1756 this document was in the hands of a leading Pennsylvanian freemason named P. Frazer.

It is said that the earliest known American member of the Craft was Jonathan Belcher, born in Boston and educated at Harvard and 'made' in an English lodge in about 1704. Returning to Boston in the next year he became a prosperous merchant and obtained from George II in 1730 the Governorship of Massachusetts and New Hampshire. The date, 1704, derives from a letter which he wrote in 1741 when he claimed to have been a freemason for 37 years. There is, of course, no confirmatory record in England.

Daniel Coxe

Here is an important name. In 1730 Daniel Coxe was appointed Provincial Grand Master for New York, New Jersey and Pennsylvania. He was empowered 'for two years to nominate and appoint his Deputy Grand Master and Grand Wardens and to constitute with strict care regular lodges within his Province, the members of which were, after the expiry of his commission, to elect every other year a Provincial Grand Master for themselves.' Absolute freedom, financial and otherwise, was accorded to Bro. Coxe but he was required to see that the *Book of Constitutions* was strictly adhered to and that the names of the lodges and their members were sent to the Grand Master. He was also asked to recommend the establishment of a General Charity for the benefit of poor brethren. And so, at this early date, began the magnificent record of masonic benevolence in the United States, a heart-warming story which will continue until the end of time.

He attended Grand Lodge in London in 1731 but we have, alas, no document describing his activities for the Craft in his Province; there is indeed a suspicion that he did very little.

Benjamin Franklin

This very famous freemason, later one of the leading spirits in America's struggle for freedom, was born at Boston in 1706. After some years in London he settled in Philadelphia as a printer, founding the *Pennsylvania Gazette* in 1729. He formed a 'Leather Apron Club' in 1728, possibly in rivalry to a St. John's Lodge of freemasons said to have been established in the city the previous year. On 8th December 1730 his newspaper published what is now the earliest printed notice about the Craft in America:

> As there are several Lodges of FREE MASONS erected in this Province; and People have lately been much amus'd with Conjectures concerning them; we think the following Account of *Free-Masonry* from *London* will not be unacceptable to our readers.

There then followed a reprint of an alleged exposure. Despite this statement, there is no evidence of any lodge in Philadelphia other than St. John's, the earliest records of which are contained in a ledger giving the names of members from 1731 to 1738. This is 'Libre B'; one assumes a previous volume.

Franklin himself became a mason — probably in February 1731 — and his previous apparent cynicism changed to the greatest possible interest. Within a year and a half he became Master of his lodge and produced the oldest draft of American lodge by-laws still in existence. In 1732 he was Junior Grand Warden of the Provincial Grand Lodge of Pennsylvania and by 1734 had been appointed Provincial Grand Master by Henry Price, (Provincial) 'Grand Master of His Majesty's Dominions in North America' (recorded in London as 'for New England'). In the same year he reprinted the 1723 edition of Anderson's *Constitutions*. His career of public service is well known and included travels to England and France, where he spent some years. Outstanding in his subsequent masonic life is his presence at a communication of the Grand Lodge of England in 1760, in whose minutes he is then recorded as 'Provincial Grand Master'. He assisted at the initiation of the aged Voltaire in the Lodge of the Nine Sisters in Paris in 1778 and afterwards became an affiliated member and its Master. He died at Philadelphia in 1790.

Henry Price

Henry Price was born in London in 1697, went to New England about 1723 and returned later to his native city. In 1730 he was a member of a lodge meeting at the Rainbow Coffee House and in 1733 received a deputation appointing him Provincial Grand Master for New England. Almost immediately he sailed to Boston and there appeared with the rank of Major conferred by Governor Belcher.

He is recorded by the United Grand Lodge of England as having been in office four times: 1733-6; 1740-2; 1754-5; 1767-8.

A St. John's (Provincial) Grand Lodge and a private St. John's Lodge were established at Boston by Henry Price in 1733.* By 1734 it was rumoured that Price's powers had been

---
*The Boston records of these events date from 1751 but there is collateral and conclusive evidence that the private lodge was founded on 31st August 1733.

HENRY PRICE

extended over all America and we have already seen that Benjamin Franklin's appointment in that year supported this idea. Price's Boston lodge appeared on the roll of the Grand Lodge of England in 1734 where No. 126 is shown as meeting at Boston in New England.

On February 5th, 1736, a petition was addressed to Henry Price by six brethren 'of the holy and exquisite Lodge of St. John' of Portsmouth, New Hampshire, asking for power to hold a lodge though they declared they had their 'Constitutions both in print and manuscript as good and as ancient as any that England can afford'. 'Constitutions in manuscript' seem to indicate the possession of a copy of the Old Charges and this may indicate that the lodge had been in existence some time previously. 'Constitutions in print' no doubt refers to a copy of Anderson's *Constitutions* or Franklin's reprint.

On the 7th December 1736, Robert Tomlinson was appointed Provincial Grand Master for New England. The reason for his succession is not explained and in 1738 Tomlinson went to London via Antigua where he found some Boston Brethren and 'went to work making the Governor and other gentlemen of distinction Masons', thus founding Freemasonry in the West Indies.

Tomlinson died in 1740 and the vacancy was filled by Henry Price.

Thomas Oxnard

Thomas Oxnard was a merchant of some importance and was appointed Provincial Grand Master for *North America* on 23rd September, 1743. In 1749 he issued a Provincial Commission to Benjamin Franklin and in 1750 the second lodge in Boston was founded. We thus have the position that, both at Boston and Philadelphia, freemasons were meeting, sometimes as a Provincial Grand and at other times as a private lodge. This state of affairs was also found in England long after this period where it was no uncommon thing for the Provincial Grand Master to select his officers from a single lodge which, to all intents and purposes, carried out the functions of Provincial Grand Lodge.

Henry Price appears to have held the position of Master of the lodges at Boston, the first in 1738 and the second in 1750, The first lodge conferred two degrees only until 1794 when the third appears.

A separate set of minutes was kept for the Masters' (*i.e.* third degree) lodge, another factor commonly found in England at this period and it is obvious that, as in Scotland, many were content with the first two degrees until late in the eighteenth century. Thomas Oxnard himself, who was Master of the lodge in 1736 and again in 1737, was not raised to the degree of Master Mason until 1739.

Oxnard went to England in 1751 and the same year a 'Humble Remonstrance' signed by all the lodges of Boston was addressed to the Grand Master of England in which it was requested that he be granted a 'full and plenary commission as Grand Master over all the Lodges in North America.' He died in 1754 and Henry Price, on the request of the Deputy Provincial Grand Master, resumed his old office.

Jeremy Gridley

On October 11th 1754 a committee was elected to obtain the appointment of Jeremy Gridley, Counsellor at Law. Henry Price wrote the following year in support of the petition, describing his own services as Provincial Grand Master and how, on the death of Tomlinson and Oxnard, the chair had reverted to him again. He pointed out with pardonable pride that over forty lodges had sprung from his first lodge in Boston. Gridley was duly appointed in 1755, his Deputation reading 'for all Such Provinces and Places in North America and the Territories thereof, of which no Provincial Grand Master is at present appointed'. He was installed by Henry Price on 1st October 1755 with great pomp and ceremony. At the time of his death in 1767 he was Attorney-General, a member of the General Court and a Justice of the Province. Once again, Henry Price stepped into the breach.

Further South

We have so far seen something of the development of the Craft in the northerly provinces of the Atlantic seaboard. But the south was not masonically neglected for the Grand Lodge of England started subscription in 1733 for 'sending to the new colony of Georgia in America' distressed brethren 'where they may be comfortably provided for'. A lodge was formed at Savannah in 1735 and appears in the Engraved List of 1736, this being the second American Lodge of which we have official

GEORGE WASHINGTON

record. Quickly the Craft spread into South Carolina and in 1736 a Deputation was issued to John Hammerton as Provincial Grand Master for South Carolina. (Hammerton had been made a mason at the Horn Lodge in Westminster and was one of the first to offer his services as a Steward at the Annual Feast.)

He attended Grand Lodge in 1738 when there were present such early stalwarts as Desaguliers, Payne and Anderson, and in 1739 was accompanied there by Robert Tomlinson, Provincial Grand Master of New England. But by this time Hammerton had been succeeded by James Graeme (1737) who was in turn replaced by Peter Legh in 1754.

George Washington

We turn from the earliest rulers of the American Craft to one of the most notable of all American brethren.

George Washington was born in Virginia in 1732 and carved out a career for himself as a surveyor. He was also a 'part-time' soldier and was appointed in 1754 by the Governor to be the Colonel in command of the Virginia Regiment in the wars against the French and the Indians. It is scarcely necessary to add that he became a politician, by election to the House of Burgesses at Williamsburg in 1759, and that in 1775 he took command of the American army and so directed the forces of the thirteen Colonies in the long struggle for independence.

He was initiated into Freemasonry in 1752 in the lodge at Fredericksburg, Virginia, and was passed and raised in the following year. In 1777, when the lodges of the Colony were in the process of forming a Grand Lodge, Washington was proposed for Grand Master but he declined, reminding his brethren that he was a mere Master Mason and not qualified for the high office. But in 1788 he willingly became the Master of the lodge at Alexandria (just across the River Potomac from the capital city which bears Washington's name) when it changed its Pennsylvanian warrant for one from Virginia. In honour of his mastership that same lodge is now the Alexandria Washington No. 22 and it meets within a truly magnificent masonic building dedicated to his memory and built and furnished with the aid of donations from brethren, Grand Lodges and masonic Orders world-wide.

In 1789, Washington became the first President of the United States of America and he was still Master of his lodge.

FREEMASONRY IN AMERICA

He repeatedly expressed and demonstrated his affection for the Craft and it is not only our American brethren who remember him with pride as one of the truly great men of all time who were also notable freemasons.

The Boston Tea Party

On 16th December 1773, three cargoes of tea were thrown overboard from three East Indiamen in the Port of Boston by a party of persons in the disguise of 'redskins'. Somewhat suspiciously, the Lodge of St. Andrew closed early that night 'on account of the few members in attendance' and the relevant page in its minute book is several times embellished with the letter T writ large.

The War of Independence

To the name of Washington could be added a long and distinguished list of other freemasons who furthered their country's cause. Richard Caswell, Mordecai Gist, James Jackson, Morgan Lewis, John Sullivan: these were great men who all became Grand Masters of their State Grand Lodges and three of them governed their States as well. Paul Revere is a particularly noteworthy example of the splendid and independent breed which our American colonies produced. Born in Boston in 1735, initiated in St. Andrew's Lodge there in 1760 and its Master in 1770, he was a leader of the Tea Party which has already received mention. It is perhaps his ride from Charlestown to Lexington in 1775 which has best captured the imagination of posterity and has been honoured in prose, verse and song. Revere became one of the Grand Masters of Massachusetts.

Paul Jones began life at Kirkcudbright in Scotland in 1747 as John Paul and later added the famous surname. It was in the Lodge of St. Bernard in his birthplace that his raising took place in 1770 and he emigrated soon after that date to America. There he gained distinction as a naval officer and afterwards served in the French and Russian navies. He is best known for his part in the fight off Scarborough against H.M.S. *Serapis*.

In the war which led to the separation of the American colonies from the British Crown, as in later wars elsewhere, there were repeated instances of brotherhood surmounting the rivalries of battle and masonic courtesies being extended when the parties might have been forgiven for overlooking them. One such case occurred during General Grey's expedition into Massachusetts in 1778 when the masonic chest of the military lodge in the 46th Foot (now incorporated in the Light Infantry Regiment) was captured. Brother General Washington directed that it be returned under the escort of a guard of honour.

It is not generally realized that the independence of the United States owes quite a lot to Freemasonry. Many of the leading men of spirit in the Colonies met together in their lodges and the close ties of brotherhood were, in many instances, easily and naturally employed to band them together in the common cause of freedom. Many signatories to the Declaration of Independence were members of the Craft as were many of those who, at the successful conclusion of their military efforts, were selected to guide the new nation through its first years.

A political severance from Britain led to the desire for masonic autonomy. Existing Provincial Grand Lodges assumed the character of sovereign and self-governing Grand Lodges. We have already noted a tendency for early Provincial rulers to extend their influence over the then known continent — to a Province of North America. With the idealism of the day, there was in 1780 a move to elect a General Grand Master for all Craft Masonry in the country. Pennsylvania was in favour; Massachusetts had doubts; and so the idea was laid aside, never to be seriously revived.

The Morgan Affair

This all too frequently misquoted incident in American masonic history produced the strongest attacks ever known on a largely innocent Craft. The man at the centre of it — William Morgan — was born in 1774. It is not known whether he was ever regularly initiated but he succeeded in visiting some lodges. He was, however, refused admission in his home town of Batavia and it was here that he conspired in 1826 with one Miller, a journalist, to publish an attack upon Freemasonry in the form of an exposure. Some ineffective attempts were made to procure his silence; he was then removed (accounts vary as to whether he went willingly or not) to Fort Niagara. The rest is silence, but a rumour of his murder gave rise to an anti-masonic movement. Newspapers were founded within it and anti-masonic candidates ran for public office. Three of the alleged assassins received sentences of imprisonment.

The attacks grew to such strength that — throughout the United States of the day — countless lodges closed down. Lodge rooms were attacked and their contents destroyed; families were divided; public disavowals of guilt by the fraternity were discounted. The pace of the movement did not materially slacken for ten years and it was not until the middle of the century that the Order was again making progress. But it is a comment on human nature that the enemies of Freemasonry are still using the Morgan affair as a plank for argument.

The exposure was in fact published by Miller and went through many editions. The whole affair seems rather odd if one recalls that at least twelve editions of an English exposure (*Jachin & Boaz*) had been published in America between 1762 and 1818 without any effect on the Craft. It was, of course, Morgan's supposed abduction, rather than his book, that caused most of the excitement!

What Happened to Morgan?

There were numerous theories: he became a hermit or an Indian chief; he was hanged as a pirate; these and many more. A body in Lake Ontario was identified by his wife but proved to be someone else. The most plausible tale is of a William Morgan who was shipwrecked in the Caribbean in 1827 and settled there, marrying (or re-marrying!) in 1829. Having raised nine children, *this* Morgan died in 1864 at the age of 89 (which corresponds with what is known of *the* William Morgan's birth date).

Apart from name and age, the other relevant factors are that he was rumoured to have betrayed masonic secrets; that some of his descendants were married to people in the Batavia incident or *their* descendants; that he was buried in masonic regalia. Taking these points together it seems likely that this sojourner in the Caribbean was *the* Morgan and that he must have been persuaded to keep silence. One possible advantage of his situation was that he could have welcomed separation from the wife who so readily recognized his 'corpse' and who re-married in 1830!

THE GRAND LODGES OF THE UNITED STATES OF AMERICA

	First Recorded Lodge	Source of earliest Warrants	Grand Lodge Founded
Alabama	1812	Kentucky	1821
Alaska	1868	Washington	1981
Arizona	1865	California	1882
Arkansas	1819	Kentucky	1838
California	1848	Missouri and others	1850
Colorado	1859	Kansas	1861
Connecticut	1750	Massachusetts (St. John's Prov.G.L.)	1789
Delaware	1765	Pennsylvania (Antients) and Maryland	1806
District of Columbia	1789	Maryland	1811
Florida	1768	Scotland and Pennsylvania	1830
Georgia	1735	England	1786
Idaho	1864	Oregon and Washington	1867
Illinois	1806	Pennsylvania	1823 re-const. 1840
Indiana	1807	Kentucky	1818
Iowa	1841	Missouri	1844
Kansas	1854	Missouri	1856
Kentucky	1788	Virginia	1800
Louisiana	1793	South Carolina, France, etc.	1812
Maine	1769	Massachusetts (St. John's Prov.G.L.)	1820
Maryland	1750	Massachusetts (St. John's Prov.G.L.), England and Pennsylvania	1783
Massachusetts	1733	England	P.G.L. 1733 G.L. 1792
Michigan	1764	New York (Prov.G.L.)	1826 re-const. 1840
Minnesota	1849	Ohio	1853
Mississippi	1801	Kentucky	1818
Missouri	1807	Pennsylvania	1821
Montana	1863	Nebraska, Kansas, etc.	1866
Nebraska	1855	Illinois	1857
Nevada	1862	California	1865
New Hampshire	1736	Massachusetts (St. John's Prov.G.L.)	1789
New Jersey	1761	New York (Prov.G.L.)	1786
New Mexico	1851	Missouri	1877
New York	pre-1737	England	P.G.L. 1738 G.L. 1787
North Carolina	1755	England	1787
North Dakota	1863	Minnesota	1889
Ohio	1776	Massachusetts (St. John's Prov.G.L.)	1808
Oklahoma	1848	Arkansas	1874*
Oregon	1846	Missouri	1851

*The Grand Lodge of Indian Territory was formed in 1874 and the Grand Lodge of Oklahoma in 1892, the two being united in 1909.

FREEMASONRY IN AMERICA

	First Recorded Lodge	Source of earliest Warrants	Grand Lodge Founded
Pennsylvania	1731	England	P.G.L. 1731
			P.G.L. (Ant) 1761
			G.L. 1786
Rhode Island	1749	Massachusetts (St.John's Prov.G.L.)	1791
South Carolina	1735	England	G.L.(Mod) 1776
			G.L.(Ant) 1787
			Union 1817
South Dakota	1863	Iowa	Dakota 1875
			S. Dakota 1889
Tennessee	1789	North Carolina	1813
Texas	1835	Louisiana	1837
Utah	1858	Missouri, Kansas, etc.	1872
Vermont	1788	Massachusetts (St. Andrew's Prov.G.L.)	1794
Virginia	1733	England	1778
Washington	1852	Oregon	1858
West Virginia	1796	Virginia	1865
Wisconsin	1824	New York	1843
Wyoming	1868	Colorado	1874

The Development of the Modern Craft

We here present a list (with some important relevant data) of no less than fifty regular Grand Lodges, one for each of forty-nine States† which — until fairly recent times — constituted the nation, and one for the federal capital in the District of Columbia. The growth of the States and the establishment of their Grand Lodges very largely follow the expansion of the population and its movement westwards in search of land and living, and perhaps of gold. We have only to see a 'western' film to be reminded that communications in those days were difficult and hazardous and that dangers from Indians and outlaws were ever-present. Among the gallant pioneers were many freemasons and strong ties of brotherhood were added to the natural tendency to form close-knit communities. When sufficient brethren had settled in a new town they would seek a charter for a lodge, sometimes seeking it from the the nearest established Grand Lodge and, in other cases, writing back to the States from which they had set out on their travels.

With at least three lodges founded in a territory, it was accepted that a Grand Lodge could be formed and many of

†The fiftieth State is Hawaii, where York Rite Freemasonry is dependent upon the Grand Lodge of California.

DEVELOPMENT OF THE MODERN CRAFT

the now firmly rooted jurisdictions of the west began their existence on such a slender basis.

Political changes sometimes necessitated the division of one Grand Lodge into two. Virginia and West Virginia, North Carolina and Tennessee and the two Dakotas are instances of this. In other cases the present sovereign body arose from the fusion of two predecessors.

As we have seen, an early attempt to federate the State Grand Lodges under a General Grand Master met with no success. There are then forty-nine autonomous and entirely separate jurisdictions, many of them cordially disagreeing about comparatively minor points and not all of them necessarily in communion with the same Grand Lodges in other parts of the masonic world. Happily and naturally they are — usually — in harmony with each other (and with London, Dublin and Edinburgh) and an annual Grand Masters' Conference enables an exchange of views to be made. There is a fascinating variety of regalia to be seen in the different states, ranging from a plain white lambskin apron to a richly embellished counterpart with royal purple trimming.

There are also many different rituals in use but it is generally true to say (except perhaps of Louisiana and other places where a continental influence exists) that there is much in the Craft working that stems from British pre-Union ceremonial.

One more factor must be mentioned since it partially accounts for the spread of other masonic activities. This is the numerical strength of lodges. A statistical exercise a few years ago revealed that under New York, with well over a thousand lodges, the average membership was about 280. This was the largest jurisdiction (again numerically speaking) but twelve others could show higher averages, the records at the time being headed by the Grand Lodge of the District of Columbia (Washington, D.C.) where its forty-eight lodges averaged 482 members per lodge. Averages of necessity conceal some remarkable extremes, there being in Texas forty-three lodges over a thousand strong, some of them in fact of double or treble that figure.

The very strength of lodges — hitherto often regarded as a barometer of success — has caused concern to leading American masons. A few years ago a Grand Master of New York gave his opinion, at his Installation, that lodges of 600 or more brethren were unduly large and restricted active participation to a small proportion of the membership. He added that consideration should be given to the placing of a limit of 300 founder members upon new lodges!

It is indeed membership participation which exercises the attention, and indeed the ingenuity, of lodge committees and there are many skilful plans by which brethren not in office can be brought into the active work of the degrees. But, of course, in the larger lodges the prospects of advancement to the Master's chair are proportionately limited. It is, therefore, understandable that a high percentage of the brethren enter the degrees and Orders beyond the Craft and it is to these that we turn our attention.

The Royal Arch

Although there are previous indirect references, the earliest Royal Arch minute in the world is found in Washington's mother lodge at Fredericksburg, Virginia:

Decemb^r. 22^d. 5753* Which Night the Lodge being Assembled was present

Right Worshipfull Simon Frazier G M } of
    D°   John Neilson S Ward^n } Royall
    D°   Robert Armistead } Arch
                   Ju^n Ward^n } Lodge

Transactions of the night
   Daniel Campbell   } Raised to the Degree
   Robert Halkerston } of Royall Arch
   Alez^r Wodrow   } Mason

Royal Arch Lodge being Shutt Enterd aprentices Lodge Opend present

Right Worshipfull   Danl Campbell G M
    D°   John Neilson S.W.
    D°   Robert Halkerston J.W.
                   Alex^r Wodrow Secretary
                   Robert Armistead Treas^r
                     pro Temp
                 Robert Spotswood
                 Simon Frazier   Visiting Bro^r.

John Benger was admitted as a Member of this Lodge...

*A.D. 1753.

THE ROYAL ARCH

It is interesting to find the Master, Junior Warden and Secretary of the Craft lodge candidates for what we now call 'exaltation'.

Fascinating as it is, we dare not yield space to recount the history of this supremely important part of Freemasonry in the United States. Suffice it to say that a Grand Chapter for North America was constituted in 1797 at Boston by seven companions from three chapters, and that — although State Grand Chapters have been formed at various dates from 1797 onwards — that original Grand Chapter survives under the modern title of the *General Grand Chapter Royal Arch Masons International*. Adhering to this comprehensive authority are the Grand Chapters of forty-seven jurisdictions in the United States, of three Canadian Provinces, and of Germany, Mexico, the Philippines and Italy.

The forty-seven referred to correspond to the Grand Lodges listed on pp.279-80, other than the States of Pennsylvania and Virginia whose Grand Chapters have always been independent and Texas whose Grand Chapter withdrew from the General Grand Chapter in 1861.

The *General* Royal Arch system consists of four degrees: *Mark Master*, (*Virtual*) *Past Master*, *Most Excellent Master* and *Royal Arch Mason*. They are taken in that sequence. An additional degree, the *Anointed Order of High Priesthood*, is restricted to those who rule, or have ruled, a subordinate chapter and is conferred annually in a *Convention* which is held at the same time as the communication of the State Grand Chapter (*see* also p. 228).

We have referred elsewhere to the place of the Mark degree in relation to the Royal Arch. An interesting survival in Pennsylvania is that two independent Mark lodges remain under the State Grand Chapter. We have also seen how, in the early days in England, only brethren 'past the chair' could be exalted. In America generally, this tradition is preserved by the institution of a special degree of Past Master. The exceptions are in Pennsylvania and West Virginia where the secrets of an Installed Master are customarily revealed to Master Masons at their raising. The Most Excellent Master's degree is similar to that which English Royal and Select Masters practise.

The Royal Arch degree itself presents several interesting differences from English, Irish and Scottish practices. We have already mentioned in Chapter X the titles of the three Principals — the High Priest (J), the King (Z) and the Scribe (H). Ezra and Nehemiah are not present. It will also have been observed that the ceremony of Passing the Veils is an integral part of the ritual of exaltation. What may not be so widely known is that American chapters frequently present the degrees in full costume, with the benefit of lighting, make-up and music, and that great numbers of the companions will sometimes assemble to see a 'Class' of candidates take the degrees under such conditions.

The Royal and Select Masters

Again, it is impossible to do justice to the early history of Cryptic Masonry in the United States. Following the pattern set by the Craft and Royal Arch, councils were formed by brethren who had taken the degrees — probably within old Royal Arch chapters — and the councils came together to constitute Grand Councils within State boundaries. The earliest of these was in Connecticut in 1819 and now there exist forty-seven. These correspond to the list of Grand Lodges of the Craft, less Virginia and West Virginia where the old custom of controlling the Cryptic degrees from within the Royal Arch system still applies, and Wyoming whose three Councils have not yet formed a governing body.

A *General Grand Council* was set up after a series of meetings between 1872 and 1881 and forty State Grand Councils now acknowledge its authority. As with the Royal Arch, certain Grand or subordinate Councils elsewhere also accept its control. The degrees of *Royal Master, Select Master* and *Super-Excellent Master* are conferred.

Knights Templar

The Order of the Temple came to America at an early date and, as was the case in the Old World, was practised within lodges and Royal Arch chapters. The first *Grand Encampment* to control the Order was established in Pennsylvania in 1797 and, some years later, Knights from other States joined in reconstructing it on a general basis. Another 'General' authority grew up in Rhode Island in 1805 and later met in New York to enlarge their jurisdiction. A good deal of con-

THE YORK RITE

sion ensued and it was not until 1856 that a *Grand Encampment of Knights Templar of the United States of America* was created from a merger of the two bodies. This now holds undisputed sway over forty-seven *Grand Commanderies* within the United States. (There is none for Delaware and there is one for Massachusetts and Rhode Island combined.) As with the degrees already described, there are some Grand and subordinate Commanderies outside the United States which adhere to the Grand Encampment.

The degrees worked are: the *Order of the Red Cross*, the *Order of Malta* and the *Order of the Temple*, in that sequence — thus presenting at once an interesting difference from English practice. Although a profession of the Christian faith is essential to membership, the Red Cross (similar to the Red Cross of Babylon in the Allied Degrees of England) is based on an Old Testament incident.

The American knights wear an impressive 19th century military uniform of black with gold trimming, and cocked hats with plumes (which are usually white but, in a few jurisdictions, are black), and carry swords with which — in public as well as within their commanderies — they perform intricate drills often on a competitive basis.

The York Rite

The Craft, Royal Arch, Royal and Select Masters and Knights Templar together constitute what is called the York Rite (sometimes the American Rite) and are regarded as a sequence in which only the Cryptic degrees are optional. Some encouragement is given to this co-ordination by planning Festivals of the York Rite at which candidates from the 'blue lodges' can — over the course of a few days — be admitted to the four Royal Arch degrees, the three of the Cryptic series and those within the Commandery of Knights Templar.

A further stimulus to the linking of the degrees has been the creation in 1930 of the *Convent General of the York Cross of Honour* and in 1957 of the *York Rite Sovereign College of North America.* Through *Priories* of the former (usually one to each State) and *Colleges* of the latter, each with special degrees, particular emphasis is laid on co-operation between the established Orders of Freemasonry.

FREEMASONRY IN AMERICA

The Scottish Rite

This is the other (not necessarily an alternative) mai[n] stream of masonic advancement beyond the Craft. We hav[e] already seen how the first Supreme Council 33° came int[o] being in 1801 and a second in 1813. These two between the[m] divide the United States into Southern and Northern Juris[-] dictions, entirely autonomous but in great harmony. There ar[e] many differences in detail in the way that they organize an[d] present their degrees but it may be said of both that they wor[k] all from the 4° to the 32° in full and that most candidate[s] advance through them all in a short period. The 33° is fairl[y] liberally conferred on an honorary basis for services to the Rite[.] Among the curious features of their procedure (curious, tha[t] is, to the members of the Ancient and Accepted Rite i[n] England with whom the Americans are in complete amity) i[s] the fact that there is no bar to the admission of candidate[s] of other than the Christian faith, and this requires that muc[h] of the ritual (the 18° in particular) has to have a differen[t] interpretation. Another point of statistical interest is that with very few exceptions and however large the city, only on[e] Scottish Rite *Valley* can be established in each place. Thi[s] leads, in some instances, to astronomical memberships o[f] 30,000 or more – a Secretary's nightmare, demanding ful[l] time salaried staff to make effective administration possible[.] Candidates are usually received twice yearly, in some case[s] three or four hundred at a time. One is selected to participate i[n] the ceremonial – often performed on the stage of an audi[-] torium within the *Scottish Rite Cathedral,* with all the colour which costume, lighting and production can offer – and the others form part of the audience. In the larger Valleys, sufficient talent is available for an orchestra and chorus to provide incidental music.

Other Masonic Degrees

It will be sufficient to list the following regular Orders, Rites and Degrees which the keen American freemason will not overlook:

    The Red Cross of Constantine
    The Holy Royal Arch Knight Templar Priests
    The Societas Rosicruciana in Civitatibus Foederatis
    The Knights Beneficent of the Holy City

DEGREES AND ORDERS

these have been described already in earlier pages and, in America, the ruling bodies are in nearly every case in fraternal communion with their counterparts in the Old World. *The Allied Masonic Degrees for the United States* are also in amity with the Grand Council for England (*see* p. 227) but it may be of interest to add that the present American Grand Council* — which was set up in 1932 after the introduction of the Scottish Excellent Master and Royal Ark Mariner degrees by the Grand Royal Arch Chapter of Scotland — controls the following: *Royal Ark Mariner, Secret Monitor, Knight of Constantinople, St. Lawrence, Architect, Grand Architect, Superintendent, Grand Tiler of Solomon, Master of Tyre, Excellent Master, Red Branch of Eri*, and *Ye Antient Order of Corks*. The last-named is entirely humorous and was brought to America from Scotland in 1933 by the Marquis of Ailsa, then First Grand Principal of the Grand Royal Arch Chapter there. With the exception of the Cork degree — which is a completely separate concern — none of the Allied Degrees is actually conferred. A candidate (who must be a Royal Arch mason) takes a general obligation on joining a council and is then presented with the complete set of rituals. The ceremonies are worked for demonstration purposes from time to time but a feature of meetings of most councils is the reading and discussion of a paper of masonic interest.

To complete the tally, it is necessary to add that a *Grand Council of Knight Masons* was formed in 1967 by several councils who originally held their charters from Dublin. And, lastly, there is a Provincial Grand Lodge of the *Royal Order of Scotland* in which membership is sought by 32° masons from all parts of the country.

Degrees and Orders with Masonic Connexions

It is quite impossible to avoid, in discussing American Freemasonry, the mention of the *Eastern Star* and the *Shrine* since they are so often the subject of query. They are, in fact, two of many organizations which — in America and elsewhere — have been established in the context of Freemasonry without forming any part of it. A list of the more important of them, with a few comments on each, may remove certain misunder-

---

*The earlier *Sovereign College* (mentioned on p. 228) was practically dormant and it amalgamated with the new Grand Council.

FREEMASONRY IN AMERICA

standings. **Membership in most is strictly forbidden for English freemasons.**

For Masons only

The Ancient Arabic Order of the Nobles of the Mystic Shrine dates from 1872 and works in a humorous ritual with an oriental content. Admission is restricted to Knights Templar or 32° Scottish Rite masons. An extremely extrovert society with *Temples* in Canada as well as in every State of the Union, it serves the community splendidly through its many hospitals for crippled children where neither race nor the absence of masonic connexion affects the availability of entirely free treatment.

The Royal Order of Jesters, formed in 1917, finds its membership — by invitation only — from 'Shriners'. *Courts* are related to most Shrine Temples.

The Mystic Order of Veiled Prophets of the Enchanted Realm, popularly referred to as 'The Grotto', began simply in 1889 in New York and has grown into a vast organization over 80,000 strong. Its ritual is said to be founded on an old Persian MS and it admits Master Masons to membership. Again its good humour conceals great charitable acts, the especial object being the establishment and support of clinics for those who suffer from cerebral palsy.

The Tall Cedars of Lebanon meets in *Forests* with a Supreme Tall Cedar at its head. Its charitable purpose is to finance research into and the treatment of muscular distrophy.

For Masons and their Ladies

The Order of the Eastern Star, entirely serious in its teaching and ceremonial, is the largest by far. It dates from 1850 and is now controlled by a *General Grand Chapter* (1876) to which most State Grand Chapters pay allegiance including those of Canada. The ritual has no masonic content but the male members must be Master Masons. In Pennsylvania, the Craft Grand Lodge forbids entry to this Order. In New York, *any* Master Mason (not a member of the Order) can attend meetings after taking a simple obligation of secrecy only. (The Order in Scotland is entirely independent of America and has removed any masonic requirement from its regulations.)

The Order of the Amaranth began about 1860 and its Sup-

THE EASTERN STAR, ETC.

reme Council was formed in 1873. It earlier offered advancement from the Eastern Star but subsequently became independent of it and direct admission is now possible for Master Masons and their ladies.

The Order of the White Shrine of Jerusalem, wholly Christian in character and teaching, also began (1894) as a degree above the Eastern Star and is now quite separate.

The Supreme Conclave True Kindred and the *Order of the Golden Chain* are other organizations of the same category but smaller in scale.

For the Masonic Family

The ladies have Orders, serious and humorous, related to many of those in which their menfolk meet. The *Royal Arch Widows*, the *Social Order of the Beauceant*, the *Daughters of the Nile*; these titles are self-evident, and there are several others which offer both social and ritual activity to the neglected wives while affording opportunities of supporting the relevant charities.

The Order of de Molay is for boys and each of its many Chapters is masonically sponsored. It is made clear that membership offers no guarantee for future admission to the Craft. The *Order of Rainbow* and the *Order of Job's Daughters* are similary organized for girls. Many of these societies have spread beyond America and can be found in Australia and other countries where the Craft is firmly established.

The Charities

In laying some stress on the charitable role played by the quasi-masonic organizations, it must equally be made plain that the Craft, Royal Arch, Knight Templar and Scottish Rite bodies in no sense lag behind in their care for the less fortunate. Splendid hospitals and homes for the elderly brother and his wife or for his widow have been established in every part of the country. In addition, particular support is given to special fields of medical care and research, the Knight Templars' Eye Foundation being an excellent example of this. Under this heading also it is proper to mention that, in a community where blood donours usually receive payment in cash for their services, the Blood Banks which many lodges run for the good of all amply demonstrate that *giving* is not restricted to the dollar. The greatest possible emphasis is laid upon personal service, including the visitation of the sick and lonely.

Masonic Research and Literature

The Masonic Press in the United States runs to many hundreds of different publications. Not a few excellent magazines are put out by Grand Lodges themselves and one of the best – *The Royal Arch Mason* – is issued quarterly by the General Grand Chapter for a modest subscription. There are many weekly newspapers for freemasons and individual lodges, or local 'families' of lodges, chapters. etc., produce pleasant little periodicals wich often serve the additional purpose of giving notice of coming meetings and obviate the issue of a separate summons (which the Americans like to call a 'trestle board'). All these papers include articles designed to assist the brother wishing to make his daily advancement.

More specifically directed to this last purpose are the lodges and other masonic bodies who have dedicated themselves to research. The *Allied Degree Councils* and the *Societas Rosicruciana* have excellent annual booklets; the *Philalethes Society* holds no meetings but sends out to its large membership a most interesting magazine; the *Grand College of Rites* has, for its prime purpose, the preservation and publication of the rituals of degrees and Orders no longer in existence and its annual volume, *Collectanea*, is eagerly awaited.

There are several Lodges of Research, the most influential being the American Lodge of Research of New York and the Missouri Lodge of Research. There is a Royal Arch Chapter of Research for Ohio. The Transactions of many of these bodies are extremely well produced and printed and furnish information on many aspects of Freemasonry. There is, understandably, a preponderance of American masonic history but this is, in itself, a fascinating subject.

Finally, in this section devoted to the subject of masonic research and literature, two unique organisations deserve special attention. The *Society of Blue Friars* was founded in North Carolina in 1932 for the stated purpose of recognising masonic authors. Each year one such author is selected by the Grand Abbot of the society from nominations submitted to him by the members. For twelve years, until the numbers grew, the society was conducted by correspondence but, since 1944, an annual Consistory has been held in Washington, D.C., at which the new Friar for the year (if present) is introduced and usually presents a short paper. It is worthy of note that, although the majority of the members, present and past, have understandably been from the western side of the Atlantic, the following brethren from the United Kingdom have been honoured by appointment: 1939, A.E. Waite; 1951, George Draffen of Newington; 1955, Fred Pick; 1963, Harry Carr; 1964, Bernard Jones; 1970, Frederick Smyth.

The *Masonic Book Club* was promoted, in 1970, by distinguished brethren including Louis Williams and Alphonse Cerza of Illinois, for the purpose of publishing masonic 'classics' and out-of-print masonic books. Its membership, consisting both of individuals and lodges, libraries, etc., was originally restricted to 333, so that the first editions of its earlier annual publications have something of the value of collector's items. It has recently been decided, in response to an overwhelming demand from would-be members and also in the light of economic circumstances, to extend the membership. So far, the volumes have included facsimiles of *The Regius MS*, Franklin's reprint of Anderson's 1723 *Book of Constitutions*, Dermott's *Ahiman Rezon*, Preston's *Illustrations* and Dassigny's extremely rare *Serious and Impartial Enquiry* with other pamphlets. The most recent issues have been, fairly enough, related to the Bicentenary of the constitution of the United States and the freemasons who were involved in that historical event. For 1977, Harry Carr is preparing a study of Prichard's *Masonry Dissected*. It can readily be seen that the members of the Book Club have the tremendous advantage of having on their own bookshelves valuable works of reference which, without being extremely fortunate or extremely rich, they could not possibly have expected to own.

Negro Freemasonry

Before leaving this complex and colourful display of Freemasonry, in all its aspects, in the United States it is important to describe briefly the place of the negro *vis-à-vis* his white brother.

Directly arising from the initiation of several negroes in 1775 in an Irish regimental lodge at Boston, and from the leading role subsequently played by one of them named Prince

Hall, there is now a vast organization, scarcely less complex than that we have described, which offers to the worthy coloured man counterparts of all the important degrees and Orders, masonic and quasi-masonic, which have been already introduced for the man of European descent. Craft, Royal Arch, Knights Templar, Scottish Rite, Eastern Star: these and other Orders have General or State Grand Lodges, Chapters, Supreme Councils, etc., which seem to be admirably run. There are probably at least 5,000 Craft lodges within the system and its influence has spread to Canada, Hawaii, parts of the West Indies and, as we shall see in the next chapter, to Liberia.

White freemasons are officially forbidden to visit Prince Hall lodges but it is clear that, in many of the American States, a much more sympathetic view is being taken of the coloured brethren and less is being said about the doubtful descent of their masonic degrees from Prince Hall.

An interesting and little-known fact is that the regular and recognized Alpha Lodge No. 116 of Newark, New Jersey, consists entirely of negro freemasons and is much visited by the brethren of other races. The story of this lodge is too long to tell here but it was founded by white masons in 1871 with the clear intention of initiating thereafter gentlemen of colour if they otherwise met the high standards set by the Craft. At the time, and for many years afterwards, there was friction between other Grand Lodges and that of New Jersey but the lodge has survived many difficulties to earn the great respect it now has. A Past Master of the lodge was in 1965 appointed to the office of Grand Chaplain in the Grand Lodge of New Jersey. At least one distinguished white freemason is an honorary member and he has said that he holds this fact in high esteem.

A Warning Note

It would be as well to add that, apart from the regular masonic bodies and their associated organisations and the Prince Hall structure just described, other fraternal societies in great variety can be found in the United States. Many of these in no way conflict with masonic membership; The Elks, the Oddfellows and the Knights of Malta (no connexion with the Knights Templar) are in this category. Others are blatantly imitative of the Craft and generally incorporate a grandiose reference to it in the titles under which they operate. Some care is advisable on the part of a brother from the United Kingdom visiting America to ensure that he makes contact with *regular* authorities only and he will be well advised to consult his Grand Lodge Year Book where he will find the names and addresses of Grand Secretaries of all recognised Craft jurisdictions.

CENTRAL AND SOUTH AMERICA

The masonic, and indeed the political complications 'South of the Border' are endless and we can do no more than sketch in a few historical and contemporary details. Some of these details are subject to sudden obsolescence in countries where political changes tend to occur at rather short notice.

Mexico, according to the late Bro. Ray Denslow, could muster in 1953 no fewer than twenty-two different Grand Lodges, most of them related to State boundaries and some of them very weak in numbers. Twelve have met together in a Congress but that seems to be as far as federation has gone. The Craft entered the country in the early nineteenth century but political upheaval and religious antagonism have done very little to smooth its path. The only jurisdiction widely recognized outside Mexico is the *York Grand Lodge*, until 1910 named *Grand Lodge Valle de Mexico* but that description is now used by one of the other bodies. The York Grand Lodge controls only English-speaking lodges. There is a recent *Grand Royal Arch Chapter* under the General Grand Chapter International.

Honduras. The colony of British Honduras (now Belize) at one time had some English lodges but the last of these ceased to work in 1862. Scotland warranted four lodges in the Republic of Honduras between 1919 and 1923 but these have been erased. There is a Grand Lodge of Honduras, formed in 1922, which is of Scottish Rite origin and is not generally recognized. Masonic philatelists will have observed that a pictorial stamp was issued by the Republic in 1938 depicting the 'Templo Masonico de Tegucigalpa'. Few postal authorities in other countries have done likewise!*

*In very recent times Cuba and Surinam have issued stamps of a similar character.

FREEMASONRY IN AMERICA

Guatemala. Here Craft lodges were established from 1887 onwards by the Scottish Rite Supreme Council for Central America with the intention of furnishing the nucleus for a Grand Craft Lodge. In 1903, eight lodges were ready to take such action and, despite political difficulties, the *Gran Logia de la Republica de Guatemala* survives and is in amity with most regular jurisdictions.

El Salvador. This is the smallest of the Central American States. There were several early attempts to establish Freemasonry but the significant date is 1912 when, from the fusion of two contending bodies, the *Gran Logia Cuscatlan de El Salvador* was established and gained the recognition of regular Grand Lodges in many countries. It recorded nine lodges in 1974.

Nicaragua. There is a story of a lodge in the country with an English warrant in the early nineteenth century but no evidence to support it. Later years found lodges warranted by authorities in neighbouring countries and a *Grand Lodge of Nicaragua* came into being in 1907. This is fairly widely recognized by American Grand Lodges and a Royal Arch chapter has been established in the country by the General Grand Chapter International. But none of the British Grand Lodges exchange representatives with Nicaragua.

Costa Rica. Freemasonry in the 'rich coast' was sponsored by the Central American Scottish Rite system and four lodges then met in 1899 to found an independent Grand Lodge. The latest report is of nine lodges, one of which works in the English language. It is a regular jurisdiction.

Panama. This republic also boasts a regular masonic authority. The early history is obscure, lodges having been chartered from Massachusetts, Texas, Spain, France and Colombia. The present day Freemasonry seems to be multi-racial for a contemporary writer reports that only one lodge (of the nine) in the country does not have negro members and that lodge is composed entirely of Chinese! There are also two Scottish lodges and a Scottish chapter.

Canal Zone. A broad strip of land bordering the Panama Canal and therefore cutting right through the Republic of Panama is under the United States Government. Here the Craft Masonry is chartered from Massachusetts and is accompanied by 'York Rite' bodies and other masonic Orders.

CENTRAL AND SOUTH AMERICA

Dominican Republic. Freemasonry is said to have come to the island in the 1830s, before the Republic was established in 1844. A Grand Lodge was formed in 1891 but it was not until 1970 that the United Grand Lodge of England granted it recognition.

The Caribbean. The British territories are well furnished with Craft lodges and many of the other degrees and Orders of Freemasonry and the numbers borne by them are evidence of the early dates on some of the warrants. Barbados has had an English Provincial or District Grand Master since 1740 and Jamaica since 1742. There are Scottish Districts for both islands. Bermuda has Grand Inspectors for English, Irish and Scottish lodges. Trinidad has Scottish and English District Grand Masters. Many of the other islands, Leeward and Windward, have lodges dating from the early nineteenth century and there is even an old English lodge at Curaçao in the Netherlands Antilles working happily with the lodges warranted from The Hague. Puerto Rico is now American territory and its Grand Lodge, dating from 1885, is fully regular. Cuba is something of a masonic enigma at present although it still has an official place among the recognized Grand Lodges of the world.

Guyana has English and Scottish lodges under their respective District Grand Masters.

French Guiana has Grand Orient lodges and two governed by the irregular Grand Lodge of France. *Dutch Guiana* has a Netherlandic lodge dating from 1773.

Venezuela has a typically confused masonic history. There is a regular *Grand Lodge of the Republic of Venezuela* with (in 1974) eighty-one subordinate lodges, some of which work in English.

Colombia has five Grand Lodges, three of which are regular. The multiplicity in this comparatively small country appears to be justified by terrain, communications being hampered by mountain ranges.

Brazil presents a masonic problem in that the Grand Lodges of England, Scotland and Ireland accord recognition to the *Grand Orient* while the North American jurisdictions on the whole discountenance the Grand Orient and prefer one or more of the rival Grand Lodges, most of which seem to be related to the larger States of the Brazilian nation. The earliest

FREEMASONRY IN AMERICA

lodges in the country were set up at the end of the 18th century but were mostly political. The Grand Orient of Brazil was formed in 1822 under Emperor Dom Pedro but was at once suspended by him and subsequent schisms, and masonic invasions from Belgium and elsewhere, make its progress difficult to record. A most unusual change of sovereignty took place in 1935, under the friendliest circumstances, when ten English-speaking lodges under the Grand Orient accepted new warrants from the Grand Lodge of England and were formed into an English District Grand Lodge.

Paraguay has a regular Grand Lodge which, until 1923, was called the Grand Orient. Most of its membership is found from foreign nationals residing in the republic.

Peru. Freemasonry here dates from 1821 and was originally derived from Colombia. A Grand Lodge seems to have been set up in 1831 but turned into a Grand Orient. Other Grand Lodges appeared and one, in 1882, was reinforced by the addition of five Scottish lodges. This has enjoyed general recognition and works in harmony with three lodges still working under warrants from Edinburgh. One of these shares with a Peruvian lodge the honour of regularly meeting in the highest Temple in the world, 12,270 feet above sea level. There are two Scottish Royal Arch chapters.

Ecuador. Here is another very obscure masonic history and it is best to begin in 1897 when there was a revival, with lodges being instituted from neighbouring Peru. These were strong enough to found a Grand Lodge in 1918. This Grand Lodge is still officially recognized but political difficulties in the country have prevented progress.

Bolivia. This republic is named after the liberator of South America from foreign domination, Simon Bolivar, himself a freemason. Revolutions and counter-revolutions since the State came into being in 1825 have delayed masonic development until the present century was well advanced. In 1929 a regular Grand Lodge was formed by several lodges chartered from the Grand Lodge of Chile. Others have since come into existence and it is understood that two of them work in English according to the Emulation ritual.

Uruguay. There are conflicting stories about the earliest lodges in the country, one claiming that the Grand Orient of France founded the first in 1827 and another that a Pennsyl-

SOUTH AMERICA

vanian warrant established it in 1832. Other lodges followed and there were sufficient to create a Grand Lodge in 1855. Unfortunately this Grand Lodge chose to authorize the removal of the Volume of the Sacred Law from its Temples and this led, in recent years, to the withdrawal of recognition. Two English lodges still work in Montevideo, with one Royal Arch chapter.

Argentina. Freemasonry began here in 1795 under French auspices and there were English lodges as early as 1806-7. But it was not until 1856 that a Grand Lodge was founded and a Treaty of Amity between the new jurisdiction and that of England followed in 1860, one result of which is reported as having been the exaltation to the Royal Arch of the then President of the Republic and several of his Ministers! The existence of a sovereign Grand Lodge in the country (with, in 1974 seventy-eight daughter lodges) has not prevented the establishment of quite a number of English lodges, under a District Grand Master.

Also warranted from England are Royal Arch chapters, Mark lodges and a Royal Ark Mariner lodge. A *Grand Royal Arch Chapter of Argentina* has recently been formed from three chapters founded in Buenos Aires. As far as can be ascertained, this follows the English pattern.

Chile. This oddly elongated country has had a Grand Lodge since 1862 and, despite some difficulty over the interpretation of a phrase meant to describe the Great Architect, harmonious relations with London, Dublin and Edinburgh have continued to this day. Side by side with the Chilean lodges (134 in 1974) are others holding warrants from England, Scotland and Massachusetts, and there are Scottish and American Royal Arch chapters.

CHAPTER XVI

FREEMASONRY IN AFRICA

Too long described as 'the Dark Continent', the light of Freemasonry has penetrated into many parts of this complex and multi-racial land. Although recent years have seen the independence of numerous former colonies of European powers only one sovereign Grand Lodge, enjoying full recognition from regular jurisdictions, has taken its place in the great masonic family.

Understandably, we find in former French dependencies that there are lodges under the Grand Orient or Grand Lodge of France and here and there — in the Cameroun, for instance — a National Grand Orient. At one time it was possible for masons to meet in Portuguese territory and the old *United Grand Lusitanian Orient* had lodges working in several different colonies. An interesting survival from those days is the Britannic Lodge of Madeira No. 3683 which was consecrated in 1913 in Funchal but brought its warrant back to London when conditions out there became impossible.

In Egypt, alas, Freemasonry has been proscribed and the English, Scottish and Greek lodges no longer meet. Even the National Grand Lodge of Egypt, dating from 1786 and at one time enjoying wide recognition but later 'blotting its copybook', has been dissolved.

Liberia, the remarkable republic established in 1821 by freed negro slaves, has a Grand Lodge dating from 1867. It has, however — and very naturally — allied itself with the negro brethren in the United States (the 'Prince Hall' Grand Lodges are mentioned in Chapter XV) and, while they remain outside the association of regular masonic authorities, Liberia must of necessity stay with them.

It was in 1726 that Richard Hull was given a patent as Provincial Grand Master for the Gambia on the inhospitable west coast and other brethren of those days were given the charge of the Cape Coast and other parts. But it seems that they found little scope for their undoubted talents, for the first recorded lodge was erected in West Africa in 1792. There are, of course, many nowadays and the Craft, Royal Arch, Mark and other degrees and Orders are practised in East, West and Central Africa under English, Irish and Scottish warrants although the political situation in certain countries (Uganda, for instance) has led to the closing down of all masonic activity. In Zimbabwe, also, are lodges under the Grand East of the Netherlands, working in harmony with those of the British Constitutions. There are some interesting outposts of the Craft on the islands of St. Helena (the lodge — 488 E.C. — dating from 1843) and Mauritius, where an English lodge erected in 1877 and a Scottish lodge of 1864 share not only the Masonic Temple but also the name of 'Friendship'. In both cases the present lodges are heirs to earlier masonic traditions including, in Mauritius, a close cooperation in happier days with the French Grand Orient lodge there.

SOUTH AFRICA

The Dutch were first on the scene, establishing lodges at Capetown in 1772 and 1802. The first English lodge, British No. 334, was founded in 1811 and is now the senior of no fewer than 264 holding warrants from London and working in the Republic. Scotland have 144 lodges and Ireland 49. The Grand East of the Netherlands still controls one lodge at Johannesburg but the many other lodges formerly under that jurisdiction in 1961 constituted the *Grand Lodge of Southern Africa*. Here the Dutch ritual is still used, often in English translation. The five Constitutions work in complete harmony, constantly visiting each others' lodges, and this is perhaps the point at which to mention an interesting complication which arises between lodges using a 'British type' ritual and those whose ceremonies are 'continental' in character. Because the first and second degree secrets are in some respects transposed (as an English mason would see it) in the Netherlandic working, intervisitation is not allowed until the Master Mason's degree has been taken by all concerned.

A *Grand Royal Arch Chapter of Southern Africa* has been formed recently from Netherlandic chapters and there are also

FREEMASONRY IN AFRICA

many Royal Arch chapters of the English, Scottish and Irish Constitutions.

It is sadly true that, whereas in other parts of Africa brethren of all races meet together in perfect harmony, in South Africa admission to regular Freemasonry is restricted to those of European descent.

CHAPTER XVII

FREEMASONRY IN AUSTRALASIA

In considering the development of Freemasonry in the Antipodes it is important to remember that, at one time, the whole of the continent of Australia (with Tasmania) *and* New Zealand answered to the Government of New South Wales. The former colonies became independent under the familiar titles as follows: Tasmania, 1825; Western Australia, 1829; South Australia, 1834; New Zealand, 1840; Victoria, 1851; Queensland, 1859. In 1901, the Australian Commonwealth was formed and New Zealand is also, of course, a self-governing Dominion.

NEW SOUTH WALES

Captain Cook proclaimed New South Wales a British possession in 1770 and, eight years later, the first convict ships arrived at Sydney Cove. The earliest recorded masonic meeting took place in 1803 and involved 'several officers of His Majesty's Ships, together with some respectable inhabitants of Sydney'. Because the assembly contravened the Governor's orders some of the freemasons were arrested but were later set free. The leading light, Brother Sir Henry Browne Hayes, was order to Van Diemen's Land (Tasmania) by way of punishment but it seems likely that the move was not enforced! This was not a promising beginning for the Craft but we must remember that the Governor had a very awkward collection of people in his care and, in all probability, had not heard of the exemption of Freemasonry from the Unlawful Societies Act of 1799.

Military lodges brought the first regular meetings to the country and from 1816 onwards there are records of their activity. The most important work of one of them, Irish Lodge No. 227 in the 46th Foot (now part of the Light Infantry Regiment), was to sponsor the first *stationary* lodge, the Australian Social Lodge No. 260 I.C., in 1820. (This is now Antiquity No. 1 N.S.W.) Others followed and, by 1839, there was an English Provincial Grand Lodge. Scotland and Ireland set up masonic Provinces in 1856 and 1858 respectively.

FREEMASONRY IN AUSTRALASIA

There were some local difficulties, leading to premature attempts to establish sovereign Grand Lodges. In 1877, thirteen lodges — mostly under Irish Warrants — formed themselves into a *Grand Lodge of New South Wales*, but this did not gain recognition from the home jurisdictions. It was not until 1888 that the conflicting elements resolved into harmony in the *United Grand Lodge of New South Wales* and this now has upwards of 900 lodges on its Register.

The Royal Arch in New South Wales until 1980 presented a complicated situation in that, despite the existence of a *Supreme Grand Chapter* since 1889 (with, eventually, some ninety chapters), there also existed a District Grand Chapter under Scotland whose Grand Chapter for some reason withheld recognition from the local sovereign authority. There has now been formed the *United Supreme Grand Chapter of Mark and Royal Arch Masons of New South Wales and Australian Capital Territory,* bringing together not only the two groups of chapters already mentioned but also the former *Grand Lodge of Mark Master Masons* of 1889 and the *Grand Council of Royal and Select Masters* of 1972, both modelled on the English authorities from which they had derived. There remains one Irish chapter at Sydney, dating from 1843.

In 1959, a *Grand Conclave of the Order of the Secret Monitor* was formed from the former English District Grand Conclave. Some years ago some Rose Croix masons formed a *Supreme Council 33°* for New South Wales but this remains irregular. Other degrees and Orders are very popular and hold their Charters from London or Edinburgh.

SOUTH AUSTRALIA

The first lodge here dates from 1834, when it was consecrated in *London* as the South Australian Lodge of Friendship No. 613. Its third meeting was held in Adelaide, where it continues to thrive. There are now more than 200 lodges on the Register of the *Grand Lodge of South Australia* which was established in 1884 from a happy agreement by all the English, Irish and Scottish lodges in the State, save one, to sever their old allegiances and accept new charters.

A *Supreme Grand Royal Arch Chapter* followed in 1886, very much on the English pattern, and there is also a *Grand*

SOUTH AUSTRALIA

Lodge of Mark Master Masons. Craft, Royal Arch and Mark Masonry are governed from the same headquarters with the one brother as Grand Secretary and Scribe E over all three.

With the exception of the Order of the Secret Monitor, in which the South Australian Conclaves have joined those of Victoria and Tasmania in a new sovereign Grand Conclave (1967), all other Orders are governed from England or Scotland. An Irish Craft lodge and Royal Arch chapter remain independent.

VICTORIA

The Lodge of Australia Felix No. 697* was warranted by England in 1841, the lodge having begun work the previous year. The gold rush of the 1850s brought expansion of the Craft and an interesting story is told of a meeting convened by a card nailed to a gum tree in Bendigo in 1854. Brethren of various nationalities are said to have responded and, a Bible having been found, they 'sealed their Obligations'. Stability in a somewhat fluid situation was found in a unique triple appointment. Sir William Clarke was appointed in 1883 as District Grand Master for Victoria of the English lodges and was given similar office by Scotland and Ireland. Unfortunately, at the same time, one Scottish and two Irish lodges set up a Grand Lodge for the State; it gained very little recognition. But in 1889, the *United Grand Lodge of Victoria* (now controlling over 800 lodges) came into being with Sir William Clarke as the first Grand Master. A *Supreme Grand Chapter* was established in the same year under the same ruler and a curious feature of its early days is that certain chapters who had obtained warrants from *Canada* joined the former English and Scottish chapters who had constituted the new governing body.

There is a *Grand Mark Lodge* on similar lines to that of England but for other Orders the situation is the same as in South Australia.

An English Craft lodge, Combermere No. 752 (dating from 1858), bravely survives in Melbourne.

---

*No. 474 after the 1863 re-numbering. It became No. 1 of the United Grand Lodge of Victoria.

FREEMASONRY IN AUSTRALASIA
TASMANIA

Ireland was the source of the first Freemasonry in Van Diemen's Land, and it was the military lodges who brought it. The earliest civilian lodge was founded in 1828 and another, also Irish, was warranted in 1834 and this latter now heads the Roll of the *Grand Lodge of Tasmania* as the Tasmanian Operative Lodge No. 1. The Grand Lodge was established in 1890 from English, Irish and Scottish lodges. The Royal Arch in the island is governed from Edinburgh and, rather curiously, an English Mark lodge and an attached Royal Ark Mariner lodge keep going in Hobart. Other degrees and Orders are as popular as elsewhere in the Commonwealth.

WESTERN AUSTRALIA

This part of the continent was the last to be extensively developed and its first masonic lodge, an English one, came to Perth in 1842. As elsewhere, the rush for gold stimulated the expansion of the Craft and, when the Grand Lodge of Western Australia was formed in 1899, no fewer than twenty-six of the thirty-three English lodges who constituted it were less than ten years old. The Grand Lodge of Scotland held aloof, for some reason, from the new Grand Lodge and forbade any of their daughter lodges in the State to have anything to do with it. The differences were not settled until 1907 when Scotland recognized the Western Australian jurisdiction and agreed to charter no more lodges themselves. Fifteen Scottish lodges, in two Districts, remain under Edinburgh — the survivors of twenty-three who originally held out. There is, too, the Plantagenet Lodge No. 1454 on the English Register, defying the odds at Albany. But the Western Australian Grand Lodge has (1974) 310 lodges on its roll.

A *Grand Chapter of Western Australia* was established in 1904 and has about seventy chapters under it, while ten Scottish chapters retain their home charters.

QUEENSLAND

Freemasonry came to Queensland in the year of its separation from New South Wales, 1859, with the founding of an English lodge at Brisbane. Several more followed under London warrants and the first Irish lodge was established in 1863, with Scotland issuing its first Charter in 1864. English, Irish and

QUEENSLAND – NEW ZEALAND

Scottish Provinces were set up between 1862 and 1866 and several attempts were made thereafter to create a sovereign Grand Lodge but these met with disapproval from London. Local patience having been sorely tried, a *Grand Lodge of Queensland*, modelled on that of New South Wales, was formed in 1904 with Irish blessing by forty-four lodges. But eighty lodges remained under the English District and nearly seventy under that of Scotland. Although the Grand Master of New South Wales installed the Ruler of the new jurisdiction, the United Grand Lodge of England refused recognition. In 1920, however, after an effort by all the parties, 85 English and 101 Scottish lodges formed another Grand Lodge of Queensland and, in the following year, this joined with the older Grand Lodge in the *United Grand Lodge of Queensland*. The 281 lodges on its original Roll have grown to about 500. The few English lodges which stood out for independence have dwindled to two.

The Royal Arch suffered from the unhappy Craft situation and, for a while, the brethren owing allegiance to the Grand Lodge of 1904 could be exalted only in the one Irish chapter in the State. In 1917, New South Wales granted warrants for four chapters and four Mark lodges. A *Grand Chapter* was formed from these in 1918 and a second Grand Chapter was constituted in 1922 from the English and Scottish chapters. The two were united in 1930 as the *Supreme Grand Royal Arch Chapter of Queensland* and this now works on the Scottish pattern (*see* p. 210). There is also a *Grand Lodge of Mark Master Masons* and a *Grand Conclave of the Order of the Secret Monitor* was constituted in 1968.

All the other degrees and Orders are practised under warrants from Great Britain and Ireland.

NEW ZEALAND

The first Europeans settled in the North Island in 1792 but it took many years for the colony to build up its strength. Freemasonry came in 1842 when the New Zealand Pacific Lodge No. 758 was warranted from London and an Irish lodge, Ara No. 348, was founded three months later. There were even French lodges in the early days but these have not survived. As in other colonial territories, the number of lodges grew, Provincial and District Grand Lodges arose and in 1890 a *Grand Lodge of New Zealand* was constituted. Its establishment was not achieved without internal trouble and there were instances where dissentient brethren carried away the warrants to prevent the lodges from meeting. (The English *Book of Constitutions* was thereafter amended to cover such an eventuality!) An interesting sidelight on the proceedings was that Lodge Ara 348 I.C. divided, one part remaining on the Irish Register and the other, as the Ara Lodge, 1 N.Z.C., joining the new jurisdiction. Both lodges still work very contentedly in Auckland. Many lodges chose to remain under their old obediences and forty English lodges are still in existence within two Districts. Eleven Scottish lodges, in two Districts, and four Irish lodges under a Provincial Grand Master also survive, and there are Royal Arch chapters, Mark lodges and several other masonic bodies holding Charters from London, Dublin or Edinburgh. A so-called *Grand Priory of New Zealand Incorporated* (of Knights Templar) is irregular.

The *Supreme Grand Chapter of New Zealand* was established in 1892 and elected to follow the Scottish system. provision being made for companions who had been exalted in English chapters to receive the Excellent Master and Mark degrees without charge on changing their allegiance. The Royal Ark Mariner, Red Cross and Cryptic degrees are now worked as well.

A notable feature of New Zealand Freemasonry is the great interest in the history and symbolism of the Order. Grand Lectures are appointed both by Grand Lodge and Grand Chapter to encourage this interest and no fewer than eight Lodges of Research and one Chapter of Research, with associate members in all parts of the world, are supported by annual grants.

THE PACIFIC ISLANDS

It is always a little difficult to define the boundaries of Australasia but it is convenient to mention, within this chapter, that Freemasonry exists on many of the islands in the Pacific Ocean.

Hawaii. Here the Craft lodges are chartered from California and the Royal Arch from the General Grand Chapter, and the other masonic Orders also stem directly from the United States.

Fiji and the Solomon Islands. The English lodges are locally under the care of a Grand Inspector and Scotland is rep-

THE PACIFIC ISLANDS

resented by a lodge and two Royal Arch chapters.

Guam and Okinawa. These American dependencies draw their Freemasonry from the Craft and Royal Arch jurisdictions of the Philippines.

New Guinea and Papua. Queensland has warranted all the lodges in these Australian dependencies save one. The English Lodge Rabaul No. 4468 dates from 1922.

CHAPTER XVIII

FREEMASONRY IN ASIA

INDIA, PAKISTAN AND BURMA

We may perhaps be forgiven for beginning this chapter with these countries but Norman Knight spent some time in the sub-continent and his present collaborator had the privilege of entering Freemasonry in a delightfully 'Kiplingesque' lodge in the Punjab among brethren of several different faiths.

The masonic history is closely bound up with that of the East India Company and the armed forces. In 1728, not twelve years after the founding of the Grand Lodge of England, one George Pomfret was authorized by London to 'open a new lodge in Bengal' and he appears in the record as the first Provincial Grand Master for India, but nothing further is known of him or his activities. A lodge *was* opened in 1730 but the oldest to survive to this day (Star in the East No. 67) dates officially from 1740. Pomfret's successor gained merit in Grand Lodge by sending home to them a 'chest of the best arrack' plus ten guineas for charity.

The wars of the succeeding years hindered the establishment of permanent lodges but, as in other countries, the regimental lodges offered opportunities for masons to meet. Meanwhile the Craft was coming to Madras (1752) and Bombay (1758). Some difficulties arose from the 'Antient and Modern' situation at home but news of the Union eventually reached India and the arrival of the Earl of Moira with his general Patent for the whole of the country materially assisted the restoration of harmony.

The Grand Lodge of Scotland appointed Doctor Burnes of the Indian Medical Service as its Provincial Grand Master for Western India (at Bombay) in 1836, his jurisdiction being extended to all India in 1846. There was at the time no English Province at Bombay and the Scottish Freemasonry attracted not a few English brethren from their lodges; in one case an entire lodge went over to the rival jurisdiction! Perhaps the most significant of Dr. Burnes' masonic acts was the founding in 1844 of a lodge, Rising Star No. 342, at Bombay for the general admission of Indian (including Parsi) gentlemen. The *Masonic Register for India* of 1869 shows that, twenty-five years later, the Indian brethren were well and truly established in English lodges as well as holding office in the English District and Scottish Province. A rather endearing touch is that, among the officers of the Rising Star Lodge, sandwiched between the Architect and the Inner Guard is an *Interpreter*!

In 1847, the Scottish Province became the *Grand Lodge of All Scottish Freemasonry in India*, in reality a very large District Grand Lodge, but with its Grand Master enjoying the 'local rank' of Most Worshipful.

There were, of course, several individual cases of the admission to the Craft of approved Indian candidates before Dr. Burnes' action of 1844 but from then on Freemasonry in all its branches became highly popular among Parsis, Hindus, Muslims and Sikhs, and it became necessary to furnish, in many lodges, several different forms of the Volume of the Sacred Law — including the Zend Avestas, the Bhagvad Gita, the Koran and the Granth Sahib. Many Indian princes joined the Order and rose to high masonic rank. Although some lodges up and down the country remained exclusively European it was usually the case that others, of Indian or mixed membership, met in the same hall or nearby. To not a few military or civilian Britons, there was a great attraction in meeting on the level with decent people of conflicting castes and creeds, united in their respect to the Great Architect.

After the second World War, the separation of India into three independent countries — India, Pakistan and Burma — brought great trouble to the people at the time but, in many cases, Freemasonry was able to assist.

In 1961, the Grand Lodge of India was impressively inaugurated by the Grand Master Mason of Scotland and the Deputy Grand Masters of England and Ireland. 145 lodges, English, Scottish and Irish, ranged themselves under the new banner but nearly as many chose to remain faithful to their old warrants. The first Grand Master of India was M.W. Bro. H. H. The Nawab of Rampur who had for some years been Grand Master of United Scottish Freemasonry in India and Ceylon.

In 1963 a *Grand Royal Arch Chapter* was formed by thirty-six English and two Irish chapters. The Scottish chapters remained under their Edinburgh charters, primarily because the new jurisdiction proposed to work according to English practice and this would have meant the abandonment of the related degrees.

In 1965 there followed the consecration of the *Grand Mark Lodge of India* by a deputation from London. Many Mark and Royal Ark Mariner lodges transferred their allegiance from London to the new obedience.

In all three cases, Craft, Royal Arch and Mark, the agreements between the original and the new jurisdictions allow for continuance under the old charters where desired, and also provide that no *further* warrants will be granted from London, Dublin or Edinburgh. This is the usual practice in granting masonic sovereignty.

The Order of the Secret Monitor is extremely popular in India, there being nearly fifty conclaves (in three Districts) owning allegiance to London. The Royal and Select Masters and the Allied Degrees are also well represented.

Freemasonry in Pakistan is at present in abeyance, under political pressure. In Burma there is no question of masonic independence but activity is maintained, especially in Rangoon.

An interesting feature of the withdrawal of British troops and civilians from India and Pakistan has been the removal of lodges, Royal Arch and Rose Croix chapters and a Mark lodge from various locations up and down the sub-continent to England (usually London). Well over a dozen Craft lodges have found new and active careers in this country while serving as pleasant rendezvous for the old Service members.

SRI LANKA (formerly CEYLON)

The earliest recorded meeting in the island was of an Antient military lodge in 1761. Two lodges of 1822 afterwards moved to India and the oldest surviving masonic body is St. John's Lodge of Colombo No. 454 which now meets at Kandy. There are, in all, ten English lodges (in a District formed in 1907), three Irish (founded between 1861 and 1874) and one Scottish, this last with the delightful name of Bonnie Doon and dating from 1877. There are six English Royal Arch chapters and four Mark lodges, with one or two other masonic Orders.

INDIA – SRI LANKA – FAR EAST
SINGAPORE AND MALAYA

An Antient lodge was established at Penang in 1809 but had a rather spasmodic career which formally terminated in 1862. The earliest surviving lodge is at Singapore, Zetland-in-the-East No. 508, warranted in 1845. There are now eight English lodges on the island, four of them consecrated since 1951, and they work in great harmony with two Scottish lodges and one Irish. All the other degrees and Orders are well represented.

Up-country there are lodges and chapters in all the main centres.

The English District governing the area is known as that of the Eastern Archipelago and it includes also three lodges in North Borneo and one in Brunei. The Scottish District, rather oddly, is named 'Middle East' and its jurisdiction extends to Brunei, Sarawak and Laos, and to Thailand, where there has been a Scottish lodge since 1910.

CHINA AND JAPAN

Masonically speaking, 'China' now seems synonymous with 'Hong Kong' and there is a strong element of truth in this. But it is interesting to look back two centuries and find that the Lodge of Amity was established at Canton in the then Celestial Empire in 1767, a Swedish lodge following in 1788. Both were extinct by 1813. The next was the Royal Sussex of 1844, also formed at Canton, but it later moved to Shanghai and now meets at Hong Kong. Others followed at Hong Kong and various Chinese cities, and Scotland and Massachusetts joined London in issuing warrants. Freemasonry being quite impossible within the present political climate of China, most lodges have been erased but one or two moved to Hong Kong and the Tuscan No. 1027 travelled further from Shanghai and now meets in London with its attached Royal Arch chapter.

Hong Kong is now particularly strong in lodges and other masonic bodies, English, Scottish and Irish, and the Chinese community play a very active part.

It is relevant to add that a *Grand Lodge of China* enjoys general recognition from America but not from the British jurisdictions since it governs only the island of Taiwan (Formosa).

Japan also has a Grand Lodge dating from 1957 and inspired very largely by American residents. Its founding lodges were originally chartered from the Philippines. Neither London nor Dublin seem to have accorded recognition as yet. There was at one time an English District Grand Lodge for Japan with several subordinate lodges but only one, at Kobe, has survived. Two Scottish lodges still work in the country and a third was founded in 1908 in Seoul, South Korea, and continues to meet there.

THE PHILIPPINES

In Spanish days, Freemasonry was under a royal ban which was harshly enforced, but it seems that a lodge came into existence in 1856 with a Portuguese charter. Filipinos were rigidly barred from the Order until 1889 but even then political and religious persecution made the practice of Masonry almost impossible. The Spanish-American War of 1898 brought the wind of change and leading masons of earlier days were occupying responsible positions in the New Government. Lodges were warranted from America, Spain, France and Scotland. The Americans were instrumental in forming a Grand Lodge in 1917 which now controls over 130 lodges. One Scottish lodge remains independent as does a Scottish chapter. The Philippines Grand Chapter is allied to the General Grand Chapter International. Many of the other degrees and Orders practised in America are established in the Republic of the Philippines. There are references in fairly recent times to unrecognized organizations including the *Gran Logia del Archipelago Filipino* and the *Gran Orient Filipino*.

THE MIDDLE EAST

Iran (Persia) presented an interesting masonic situation with regular Masonry introduced from Scotland, France (Grande Loge Nationale Française) and Germany, including the Royal Arch from the first two named. A sovereign Grand Lodge was constituted under Scottish sponsorship, and was accorded recognition by the United Grand Lodge of England in 1970. The changes in political climate in the country now prevent masonic activity.

Iraq, too, has forced the closure of all the English and Scottish lodges within its frontiers, and those in the Persian

Gulf have moved to England or are recorded as 'not at present meeting'.

Jordan has two lodges and a chapter, all Scottish, while the Lebanon, also with some Scottish Masonry, has the unusual distinction of having a dozen lodges warranted from New York under a District Deputy Grand Master.

The *Grand Lodge of Israel* is widely recognized and was set up in 1953 under mainly Scottish sponsorship. More recently a *Grand Royal Arch Chapter* has been constituted.

In Cyprus, English lodges come under a Grand Inspector and there are also regular Greek lodges.

In 1970, the revived *Grand Lodge of Turkey* was recognized by the United Grand Lodge of England, Scotland having earlier agreed to exchange representatives. The revival had taken place in 1948 after some years of suppression of a Grand Lodge which, since it appeared to have drawn its inspiration from the French Grand Orient, had not been regarded as regular. However, evidence was forthcoming that the old National Grand Lodge of Egypt, in the days when it was in communion with London, had been the principal sponsor.

CHAPTER XIX

UNRECOGNIZED ORDERS

Here we approach a subject which could well provide material for a very thick volume on its own. The reasons for non-recognition, by regular jurisdictions, of a sovereign masonic body — or one claiming sovereignty — are manifold.

More obviously — and we have considered some of these in their proper chapters (*see*, for example, p. 281) — there are those with fairly legitimate origins who have subsequently departed from the Landmarks or otherwise surrendered their places among the majority. A second category embraces Grand Lodges (under various titles) and organizations controlling degrees beyond the Craft who have not yet established their right to recognition. Some of these seem at times to be near such a goal but never quite reach it. Others, comparatively new, align themselves with the 'Grand Orient' schools of thought and are widely separated from regularity as we understand it.

We have referred in Chapter XV to the 'Prince Hall' Freemasonry centred in the United States of America and having associations with African countries.

A further class includes almost innumerable and ephemeral self-styled sovereign bodies which have been set up (many on paper only) either by eccentrics or by persons concerned principally with the collection of fees. Some of these may try to justify their existence by elaborate charters or wordy histories of their ancestry. A notable example in this country, towards the end of the last century, was John Yarker's *Sovereign Sanctuary, Supreme Grand Council of Rites (Scottish, Mizraim and Memphis)* which assumed control over ninety-five degrees. Many of these were, in practice, the same as the thirty-three of the Ancient and Accepted Rite and Yarker, writing as Grand Master General 33°, 90°, 96°, in his *Laws and Regulations of the Grand Mystic Temple, Council General No. 1* actually

TYPES OF UNRECOGNIZED ORDERS

admitted his object to be 'to give every reputable Master Mason a chance of acquiring the high masonic initiation *at reasonable cost*' (the italics were his). His action earned his expulsion from many regular masonic Orders. He had previously been concerned, in the 1870s, with the *Primitive and Original Rite of Freemasonry or Swedenborgian Rite* of which he was then Supreme Grand Master.

Much more recently, in 1930, a *Book of Constitutions* was published (no names or addresses of its executive were given but a Scottish flavour is clear from the text) for *The Masonic Order of Ancient Mysteries*. This gives the impression of an effective and established organization for the Craft, with recognition of the Mark and Royal Arch degrees. Nothing else can be traced in connexion with this Order and one suspects that it lived and died within the pages of its statutes — an expensive piece of eccentricity, to be sure!

In America, hundreds of such organizations have been launched, in some cases their progenitors ended up in prison.* Very rarely, one of these degrees or Orders has been found to have real merit and — unable to survive on its own — has been taken under the wing of an established sovereign body. *The Supreme Quarry of the World, Masters of Tyre* was an instance of this. Its architects designed for it an elaborate hierarchy and constitution with ceremonies not unworthy as adjuncts to Craft Masonry. But it achieved no more than local fame and, lapsing into abeyance, its rituals were preserved—and are still worked—by the *Grand Council of Allied Masonic Degrees of U.S.A.* (in amity with our own).

A division of unrecognized Freemasonry which demands fuller treatment in these pages — if only because it is so frequently misunderstood and misrepresented — is that which contains Grand Lodges, etc., which admit women to membership. As we have seen in Chapter VIII, there have been accidental admissions of the fair sex, and perhaps a few carried out on a 'once only' basis with deliberate intent.

There have been, also, from the early days of the organized Craft various forms of 'Adoptive Masonry' — not really Masonry at all — under which men and women gathered together in 'lodges' under the protection of a Craft lodge. In eighteenth

---

*A notable instance was that of Mathew McBlain Thompson, an expatriate Past Master of a lodge in Scotland. He and his associates were convicted in 1922 of 'using the mails to defraud by purveying false masonic degrees'.

UNRECOGNIZED ORDERS

century France, for instance, curious and colourful ceremonies were worked but there was no question of the ladies being brought into the Craft itself. The widespread modern Order of the Eastern Star and similar organizations (*see* Chapter XV) could be styled 'Adoptive Masonry' in this sense although, again, they are not in themselves masonic.

For the origins of women's Freemasonry we have to go back to the year 1882. In those days, in France, there was a hopeless muddle in the Craft and Scottish Rite. Dissension had led to the formation of new sovereign bodies, one of these having been set up in 1879 under the title of the *Grande Loge Symbolique Ecossaise* by twelve lodges which had broken away from the Grand Orient. These lodges resolved to change the way in which private lodges were administered and decided to govern themselves instead of being ruled from a distance by high-degree masons. Their slogan appears to have been 'a free mason in his free lodge'. One lodge of this new jurisdiction wrote into its by-laws the right to initiate women and, although there were efforts to obtain Grand Lodge approval, the end result was the withdrawal of the lodge (not inappropriately called 'The Free-thinkers') from its allegiance.

Its minutes of 14 January 1882, under the heading of *Loge Symbolique Ecossaise Mixte 'les libres Penseurs'*, record that Mademoiselle Maria Deraismes was initiated on that day. The story thereafter is involved but it will be sufficient to note for our purposes that other lodges with similar ideas were organized and there emerged, in 1899, the *Ordre de Maçonnerie Internationale Mixte* with a Supreme Council claiming control over the thirty-three degrees of the Scottish Rite. This Supreme Council still exists and its use of the term 'Internationale' has been more than justified for it has 'Federations' (equivalent in most senses to District Grand Lodges) in many parts of the world, including Great Britain.

On the 26th September 1902, it consecrated the Lodge of Human Duty No. 6 at 24 Albemarle Street, London and many more have sprung up in this country, where they are usually described as 'Co-Masonic'. In its earlier years in England Co-Masonry drew many of its adherents from the Theosophical Society and Mrs. Annie Besant — President of that Society — became the Head of the British Federation of Co-Masonry. There was also a strong link with the Liberal Catholic Church;

CO-MASONRY — WOMEN'S MASONRY

one of the bishops of that sect was a Grand Inspector General 33° of the Co-Masonic Supreme Council. The ties with Theosophy certainly still remain and the rituals used by the Order, while clearly based on those with which we are familiar, include a great deal of (to us) fanciful and mystical material.

A curious development in British and other Co-Masonic Federations is that Mark and Royal Arch Masonry have somehow found their way into the Scottish Rite system. Of the last-named, only the 18th, 30th and higher degrees are worked.

It seems clear that in Britain — and probably elsewhere — the membership is very strongly weighted in favour of the ladies.

In 1908, a group of members left the ranks of British Co-Masonry to form a sovereign British Grand Lodge on the lines of the United Grand Lodge of England. Under the title of *The Honourable Fraternity of Antient Masonry*, although its first Grand Master was an Anglican priest it rapidly developed into an Order for ladies only and this it remains under the modern title of *The Order of Women Freemasons*.

In the early 1920s, its Grand Master — Mrs. Marion Halsey — petitioned the United Grand Lodge of England for a full examination with a view to recognition. Our Board of General Purposes very properly found itself unable to make any such recommendation!

But the Order of Women Freemasons has progressed very well on its own and has (1981) over 330 Craft lodges (many overseas) on its register. It works, also, in most of the degrees and Orders with which we are familiar but, in some respects, follows Irish or Scottish practice. It publishes an excellent official magazine entitled *The Gavel* and it is fair to add that some quite outstanding charitable work is carried out by its lodges.

In 1913 several members withdrew from the Honourable Fraternity of Antient Masonry and formed their own Grand Lodge under the name of *The Honourable Fraternity of Ancient Freemasons*. This, too, has advanced (as an Order for women only) and has over thirty Craft lodges — mostly in London or the north-west of England, with the Mark, Royal Arch and Rose Croix degrees worked on a small scale.

The tally of these Orders in Britain is not quite complete for, in 1925, English Co-Masonry suffered another breakaway. *The Order of Ancient, Free and Accepted Masonry* was estab-

UNRECOGNIZED ORDERS

lished as a result and this continues to permit the initiation of men and women. It has, however, granted autonomy to its few constituent Craft lodges and this has resulted in some of them deciding to restrict admission to women.

This Order is governed by a Supreme Council controlling the thirty-three Scottish Rite degrees. Among the unrecognized bodies in Britain it is unique in that it is a member of an International Masonic Union under the name of *Catena*. This Union includes Orders for men and women (other than Co-Masons proper) in Austria, the Netherlands, Germany and Sweden.

It is, perhaps, worth adding that there are women's masonic Orders in Finland, France and Germany and that a measure of inter-visitation with the British ladies' Orders is not unknown.

Although not strictly masonic Orders in the sense so far conveyed, this is as good a place as any to mention that several attempts have been made — usually from the best of motives — to hold conferences and the like of sovereign Grand Lodges and Grand Orients where points of common interest can be discussed and differences, perhaps, cleared away. The British Grand Lodges have invariably refused to be associated with masonic conferences, meetings, unions, etc., where unrecognized jurisdictions are also to be represented.

The existence of several international organizations designed to bring together masonic jurisdictions deserves some publicity since British freemasons are forbidden to participate in their activities. The *Alliance Fraternelle des Puissancess Maçonniques* of Paris consists of Grand Orients and those Grand Lodges in sympathy with them. The Union *Catena* has already been mentioned. *C.L.I.P.S.A.S.* — the full title is unnecessary to our purpose — claims to be a liaison centre for signatories to the Strasbourg Declaration of 1961. We were not there; most of the Grand Orients were!

Perhaps the most dangerous of all these organizations are those which appeal, not to Grand Lodges and the like but to individual Brethren. The *Europäische Bruderkette* (European Brotherhood Chain) was organized from Germany, but ceased to exist in 1967. Its last President requested the members to join the *Universal League of Freemasons*, centred in Switzerland, which seeks to bring together brethren of all races, religions, political beliefs and masonic jurisdictions. This holds special meetings in Europe, often in connexion with inter-

INTERNATIONAL ORGANIZATIONS

national fairs and congresses, and British brethren sometimes receive invitations to attend. Our Grand Lodges have made it clear that we must not do so, even though the senior members of the League are frequently high in the councils of Grand Lodges which we recognize as regular. A very confusing state of affairs and the only safe solution is to leave it well alone.

'A DAILY ADVANCEMENT'

The newly-initiated brother is charged, among other things, with making a daily advancement in masonic knowledge. But perhaps only rarely will his sponsors, or other members of his lodge, suggest how this might be attempted. The owner of this book thus possesses the material for many diurnal discoveries about his Craft. We set out hereafter a list which may lead the way to further reading.

There is a valuable adjunct — possibly an alternative — to solitary study, in the lodges and associations for masonic research and in most of these the zealous Master Mason may seek corresponding or similar membership. At a very reasonable outlay he will acquire the privilege of meeting with other brethren to hear talks about every possible aspect of Freemasonry and to discuss them. In nearly every case, the proceedings will be published and will build up into a valuable library of reference. Questions can be put to the experts and answers will be given or obtained.

Beyond all doubt the oldest and most outstanding lodge of research was founded in 1884 and is the Quatuor Coronati No. 2076, London. (Its Secretary can be found at 27 Great Queen Street, London, W.C.2.) Its Correspondence Circle has in the region of 12,000 members in every part of the world and its transactions (*Ars Quatuor Coronatorum*) set an almost unapproachable standard of editing, indexing, printing and illustration.

There are many more to be heartily recommended and some are recorded below. An associate membership in an overseas lodge offers the particular advantage of opening the door to a different masonic world and of reading how the brethren of the same Craft but of other climes practise the Royal Art. Information can always be obtained from the Grand Lodges concerned and the Masonic Year Books helpfully give addresses.

The Lodge of Research No. 2429, Leicester

The Manchester Association for Masonic Research

The Merseyside Association for Masonic Research, Liverpool

The Lodge of Research No. CC, Dublin

The American Lodge of Research, New York.

The Missouri Lodge of Research, Fulton, Missouri.

The Masters' and Past Masters' Lodge No. 130, Christchurch, New Zealand

The United Masters' Lodge No. 167, Auckland, New Zealand

The Research Chapter of New Zealand No. 93, Auckland, New Zealand.

The Phoenix Lodge No. 30, Paris (works in English)

A SHORT LIST OF RECOMMENDED BOOKS

Published by the United Grand Lodge of England
Grand Lodge, 1717-1967 (1967)
Masonic Year Book (Annual)
Masonic Year Book Historical Supplement (2nd ed., 1969)

Published by the Grand Lodge of Ireland
Irish Freemasons' Calendar and Directory (Annual)

Published by the Grand Lodge of Scotland
Grand Lodge of Scotland Year Book (Annual, 1952 onwards)
These Scottish Year Books contain valuable and interesting papers and reports as well as the usual information about lodges. Unfortunately most editions are out of print; an advance order should be placed with the Grand Secretary to secure a copy of each future edition, usually published in March.

Published by the Quatuor Coronati Lodge and available only to the members of its Correspondence Circle
The Collected Prestonian Lectures 1925-60, edited by Harry Carr (1967)
The Early Masonic Catechisms by Knoop, Jones and Hamer (2nd ed., 1963)
The Early French Exposures, edited by Harry Carr (1971)
Ars Quatuor Coronatorum, Vols. 1-3 (1886-90), in facsimile
The Freemason's Book of the Royal Arch by Bernard E. Jones (revised)

Published by the Lodge of Research, CC, Dublin
History of the Grand Lodge of Ireland, Vol. II (1813-1957) by R. E. Parkinson (1957). Vol. I, by Lepper and Crossle, is out of print

Published by the Grand Lodge of Mark Master Masons
The History of Grand Mark Lodge, by J. A. Grantham (1960)

A DAILY ADVANCEMENT

Other recommended books available from bookshops or masonic suppliers (those marked * may be obtained also from the Quatuor Coronati Lodge).

*Freemasons' Guide and Compendium, by Bernard E. Jones
*The Mediaeval Mason, by Knoop and Jones (3rd ed. 1967)
*King Solomon's Temple in the Masonic Tradition, by Alex Horne (1972)
*Emulation – A Ritual to Remember, by Colin Dyer (1973)
*A Commentary on the Freemasonic Ritual, by E. H. Cartwright (2nd ed., 1973)
Coil's Masonic Encyclopedia (U.S.A., 1961)
*The Freemason at Work, by Harry Carr (1976)
*Symbolism in Craft Freemasonry, by Colin Dyer (1976)
*Rose Croix, by A. C. F. Jackson (1980)
*The Freemason's Pocket Reference Book, by F. L. Pick and G. N. Knight (3rd ed., revised F. H. Smyth, 1983)

Books which are out of print but which may be consulted in good masonic libraries. Some are likely to be available second-hand.

History of Freemasonry, by R. F. Gould (1882-7)
   The third edition, edited by the Rev. H. Poole (1951) is recommended.
The Old Charges, by the Rev. H. Poole
The Old Charges of the British Freemasons, by W. J. Hughan (2nd ed. 1895)
The Origin of the English Rite, by W. J. Hughan (3rd ed. 1925)
Masonic Facts and Fictions, by Henry Sadler (1887)
English Gilds, by Toulmin Smith
Records of the Hole Craft and Fellowship of Masons, by E. Conder (1894)
The Genesis of Freemasonry, by Knoop and Jones (1947)
The Scottish Mason and the Mason Word, by Knoop and Jones (1939)
History of the Lodge of Edinburgh (Mary's Chapel) No. 1, by D. Murray Lyon (tercentenary edition, 1900)

SOME NOTABLE MASONIC DATES

A.D.	
* 298	Martyrdom of Quatuor Coronati
c.1230	London regulation regarding Apprentices
1350	Statute of Labourers
1376	Earliest known use of word 'freemason'
c.1390	*Regius Poem*
c.1425	*Cooke MS*
1462	Torgau Statutes
1475	Edinburgh Seal of Cause
1583	*Grand Lodge, No. 1 MS*
1598	Oldest surviving Minute of Aitchison's Haven Lodge (now extinct
1598	Schaw Statutes, No. 1
1599	Earliest (Edinburgh) lodge minutes
1601	(and 1628) St. Clair Charters
1619	Earliest known books of London Masons' Company
1641	Initiation of Sir Robert Moray
1642	Earliest surviving minute of Lodge Mother Kilwinning
1646	Initiation of Elias Ashmole
*1663	General Assembly of Masons
1688	Trinity College skit, Dublin
*1691	Initiation of Sir Christopher Wren
1696	*Edinburgh Register House MS*
1698	First known anti-masonic pamphlet
1701	First rules of Alnwick Lodge
1702	Haughfoot Lodge minutes
*1710	The Lady freemason initiated in Ireland
1717	Four old lodges form Grand Lodge under Anthony Sayer
1718	George Payne, second Grand Master
1719	Dr. Desaguliers, third Grand Master
1721	Duke of Montagu, first noble Grand Master
	Dr. Desaguliers visits Edinburgh
1723	Anderson's first *Book of Constitutions*
	First minutes of Grand Lodge
1724	The Gormogons start
	Committee of Charity started
1725	Irish Grand Lodge formed
	York assumed Grand Lodge status
1726	*The Graham MS*
	Grand Lodge of Munster
1728	Grand Stewards appointed in Grand Lodge of England
1730	Samuel Prichard's *Masonry Dissected*
	Daniel Coxe made Provincial Grand Master for New York, etc.
	First lodge founded in India
1736	Grand Lodge of Scotland formed
1738	Anderson's second *Book of Constitutions*
1738	Pope Clement's Bull against Freemasonry
1743	Lodge Mother Kilwinning withdrew from Grand Lodge of Scotland
	The Stirling Brass

*Date traditionally ascribed.

SOME NOTABLE MASONIC DATES

1743	First printed reference to Royal Arch
1744	Dr. Dassigny's *Impartial Enquiry*
1746	Newfoundland – first lodge formed
1749	Canada – first lodge formed
1751	Antients' Grand Lodge formed
	Benedict XIV's Bull against Freemasonry
1752	Laurence Dermott appointed Antients' Grand Secretary
	George Washington initiated
1753	Fredericksburg (Va.) minute (R.A.)
1754	Ancient and Accepted Rite started
1756	First edition of *Ahiman Rezon*
	Entick's *Book of Constitutions*
1758	'Strict union' between Antients and Grand Lodge of Ireland
1761	York Grand Lodge revived
1766	Charter of Compact (R.A.)
1769	Charter of Incorporation proposed by Moderns' Grand Lodge
1772	William Preston's *Illustrations of Masonry*
	South Africa – first lodge formed
1773	'Strict union' between Antients and Grand Lodge of Scotland
1776	Freemasons' Hall opened in London
1779	Grand Lodge South of River Trent started
1781	Robert Burns initiated
1784	Noorthouck's *Book of Constitutions*
1788	Royal Masonic Institution for Girls started
1792	First masonic journal
1798	Royal Masonic Institution for Boys started
1799	Unlawful Societies Act
1802	Irish Masonic Female Orphan School founded
1807	Lodge Mother Kilwinning rejoined Grand Lodge
1808	The Grand East of Ulster
1809	Lodge of Promulgation formed
	First Scottish Freemasons' Hall consecrated
1813	United Grand Lodge of England formed by Union
	Lodge of Reconciliation formed
	Duke of Leinster, Grand Master of Ireland
1814	International Compact
1816	Grand Royal Arch Chapter of Scotland formed
1817	Union of Royal Arch Grand Chapters, England
1820	Australia – first lodge formed
1823	Unlawful Oaths in Ireland Act
	Grand Lodge of Wigan
1826	The Morgan affair in U.S.A.
1836	First Book of Scottish Constitutions issued.
1837	English Grand Lodge library started
1838	Royal Masonic Benevolent Institution founded
1842	New Zealand – first lodge formed
1845	Supreme Council 33° for England founded
1856	Grand Mark Lodge formed
1859	Masonic Hall inaugurated in Edinburgh
1860	Mark degree restored to the Scottish working
1865	Present Irish Freemasons' Hall built

SOME NOTABLE MASONIC DATES

1866	Second Freemasons' Hall opened in London
1869	Masonic Boys' School started in Ireland
1870	Prince of Wales installed as Grand Master
1871	Royal Ark Council set up
1877	Grand Orient of France — recognition withdrawn
1887	(Irish) Victoria Jubilee Masonic Annuity Fund founded
1891	The last independent lodge joined Grand Lodge of Scotland
1901	Duke of Connaught installed as Grand Master
1902	Boys' school at Bushey Park completed
1908	London Rank instituted
1912	Present (third) Scottish Freemasons' Hall consecrated
1913	6th Earl of Donoughmore becomes Grand Master of Ireland
	The last independent lodge (at Wigan) joined Grand Lodge of England
1917	Bicentenary of Grand Lodge of England
1925	Bicentenary of Grand Lodge of Ireland
1933	Masonic Peace Memorial opened
	Present Royal Masonic Hospital opened
1934	Girls' school buildings at Rickmansworth opened by Queen Mary
1936	Bicentenary of Grand Lodge of Scotland
	Duke of York (later King George VI) installed as Grand Master Mason of Scotland
1937	King George VI invested as Past Grand Master of England
1939	Duke of Kent installed as Grand Master by King George VI
1942	Duke of Kent, Grand Master, killed on active service
	Earl of Harewood installed as Grand Master by King George VI
1948	Duke of Devonshire installed as Grand Master by King George VI
	Raymond Brooke installed as Grand Master of Ireland
1949	The last English travelling lodge (no.316) becomes stationary
1951	Earl of Scarbrough becomes Grand Master of England
1952	Schaw Statutes gifted to Grand Lodge of Scotland by the Earl of Eglinton
1953	Sir Allan Adair appointed Assistant Grand Master
1960	Earl Cadogan appointed Deputy Grand Master
1961	Grand Lodge of India consecrated
1964	7th Earl of Donoughmore becomes Grand Master of Ireland
1966	Bicentenary of Supreme Grand Chapter, R.A.
1967	250th Anniversary of Grand Lodge of England
	H.R.H. the Duke of Kent installed as Grand Master
1969	Earl Cadogan appointed Pro Grand Master
	Sir Allan Adair appointed Deputy Grand Master
1971	Hon. Fiennes Cornwallis appointed Assistant Grand Master
1976	Hon. Fiennes Cornwallis (*later* Lord Cornwallis) appointed Deputy Grand Master
	Hon. Edward Latham Baillieu appointed Assistant Grand Master
1982	Lord Farnham appointed Assistant Grand Master
	Lord Cornwallis appointed Pro Grand Master
	Hon. Edward Latham Baillieu appointed Deputy Grand Master
	H.R.H. Prince Michael of Kent installed as Grand Master of Mark Master Masons

SOME FAMOUS FREEMASONS
MONARCHS
Britain: GEORGE IV (1762-1830); WILLIAM IV (1765-1837); EDWARD VII (1841-1910); EDWARD VIII (1894-1972); GEORGE VI (1895-1952). *Belgium:* LEOPOLD I (1790-1865). *Brazil:* Emperor PEDRO I (1798-1834). *Denmark:* FREDERICK VII (1808-63); CHRISTIAN IX (1818-1906); FREDERICK VIII (1846-1912); CHRISTIAN X (1870-1947). *Germany:* ERNEST OF Hanover (1771-1851); GEORGE V of Hanover (1819-78); FREDERICK II (the Great) of Prussia (1712-86); FREDERICK WILLIAM III of Prussia (1770-1840); FREDERICK I of Wurtemburg (1754-1816). WILLIAM I of Prussia, first German Emperor (1797-1888); Emperor FREDERICK III (1831-88). *Greece:* GEORGE I (1845-1913); CONSTANTINE I (1868-1923); GEORGE II (1890-1945); *Hawaii:* KAMEHAMEHA IV (1834-63); KAMEHAMEHA V (1830-72); DAVID KALAKAUA (1836-91). *The Netherlands:* WILLIAM II (1792-1849). *Norway:* HAAKON VII (1872-1957), 2° only. *Poland:* STANISLAUS II (1732-98). *Sweden:* ADOLPHUS FREDERICK (1710-71); GUSTAV IV (1778-1837). *Sweden and Norway:* CARL XIII (1748-1818); CARL XIV JOHANN (Marshal Bernadotte) (1763-1844); OSCAR I (1799-1859); CARL XV LUDWIG (1825-72); OSCAR II (1829-1907). *Sweden:* GUSTAV V ADOLF (1858-1950); GUSTAV VI ADOLF (1882-1973). *Holy Roman Empire:* Emperor FRANCIS I (1708-65). *Bonapartist Kings:* JEROME of Westphalia (1748-1860); JOACHIM MURAT of Naples (1767-1815); JOSEPH of Spain (1768-1844); LOUIS of the Netherlands (1778-1846).

PRINCES OF THE UNITED KINGDOM
FREDERICK LEWIS, Prince of Wales (1707-51); WILLIAM AUGUSTUS, Duke of Cumberland (1721-65); EDWARD AUGUSTUS, Duke of York (1739-67); WILLIAM HENRY, Duke of Gloucester (1743-1805); HENRY FREDERICK, Duke of Cumberland (1745-90); GEORGE AUGUSTUS FREDERICK, Prince of Wales (George IV) (1762-1830); FREDERICK AUGUSTUS, Duke of York (1763-1827); WILLIAM HENRY, Duke of Clarence (William IV) (1765-1837); EDWARD AUGUSTUS, Duke of Kent (1767-1820); ERNEST AUGUSTUS, Duke of Cumberland (King of Hanover) (1771-1851); AUGUSTUS FREDERICK, Duke of Sussex (1773-1843); WILLIAM FREDERICK, Duke of Gloucester (1776-1834); GEORGE FREDERICK, Duke of Cumberland (King of Hanover) (1819-78); ALBERT EDWARD, Prince of Wales (Edward VII) (1841-1910); ARTHUR, Duke of Connaught (1850-1942); LEOPOLD, Duke of Albany (1853-84); ALBERT, Duke of Clarence (1864-92); ARTHUR, Prince of Connaught (1883-1938); EDWARD, Prince of Wales (Edward VIII, Duke of Windsor) (1894-1972); ALBERT, Duke of York (George VI) (1895-1952); GEORGE, Duke of Kent (1902-42); PHILIP, Duke of Edinburgh (b. 1921); EDWARD GEORGE, Duke of Kent (b. 1935).

PRESIDENTS OF THE UNITED STATES OF AMERICA
1st, George WASHINGTON (1732-99); 5th, James MONROE (1758-1831); 7th, Andrew JACKSON (1767-1845); 11th, James K. POLK (1795-1849); 15th, James BUCHANAN (1791-1868); 17th,

SOME FAMOUS FREEMASONS

Andrew JOHNSON (1808-75); 20th, James A. GARFIELD (1831-81); 26th, Theodore ROOSEVELT (1858-1919); 27th, William H. TAFT (1857-1930); 29th, Warren G. HARDING (1865-1923); 32nd, Franklin D. ROOSEVELT (1882-1945); 33rd, Harry S. TRUMAN (1884-1972); 36th, Lyndon B. JOHNSON (1908-63), 1° only; 38th, Gerald R. FORD (b. 1913).

STATESMEN

AGA KHAN III (1877-1957); Leopold S. AMERY (1873-1955); Dr. Eduard BENES (1884-1948), President of Czechoslovakia; Sveinn BJÖRNSSON (1881-1951), 1st President of Iceland; Simon BOLIVAR (1783-1830), South America; William Jennings BRYAN (1860-1925), U.S.A.; Edmund BURKE (1729-97); George CANNING (1770-1827); Philip, 4th Earl of CHESTERFIELD (1694-1773); Lord Randolph CHURCHILL (1849-95); Sir Winston CHURCHILL (1874-1965); Harry Frederick, Viscount CROOKSHANK (1893-1961); Thomas DEWEY (b. 1902), U.S.A.; John DIEFENBAKER (b. 1895), Canada; Paul DOUMER (1857-1932), President of France; Félix FAURE (1841-99), President of France; Benjamin FRANKLIN (1706-90), U.S.A.; Léon GAMBETTA (1838-82), France; General Guiseppe GARIBALDI (1807-82), Italy; Barry M. GOLDWATER (b. 1909), U.S.A.; Henry GRATTAN (1746-1820), Ireland; Hardinge, 1st Earl of HALSBURY (1823-1921), Lord Chancellor; Sam HOUSTON (1793-1863), U.S.A.; Sir Thomas INSKIP, 1st Viscount Caldecote (1876-1947); Benito JUAREZ (1806-72), President of Mexico; Frank B. KELLOGG (1856-1937), U.S.A.; Alexander KERENSKY (1881-1970), Russia; Lajos KOSSUTH (1802-94), Hungary; Sir John A. MACDONALD (1815-91), 1st Prime Minister of the Dominion of Canada; Jan MASARYK (1886-1948), Czechoslovakia; Guiseppe MAZZINI (1805-72), Italy; Francis, 2nd Earl of MOIRA (*later* 1st Marquess of Hastings) (1754-1826); Daniel O'CONNELL (1775-1847), Ireland; Joel R. POINSETT (1779-1851), U.S.A., after whom was named the flowering plant, *poinsettia*. Manuel Luis QUEZON (1878-1944), President of the Philippines; Sir Thomas Stamford RAFFLES (1781-1826), Singapore; Cecil RHODES (1853-1902), South Africa; Manuel A. ROXAS (1892-1948), President of the Philippines; Manuel Ferraz de Campos SALLES (1846-1913), President of Brazil; Gustav STRESEMANN (1878-1929), Germany; Charles Maurice TALLEYRAND de Périgord (1754-1838), France; Richard Colley, 1st Marquess WELLESLEY (1760-1842).

MEN-AT-ARMS

General Sir Ralph ABERCROMBY (1734-1801); Field-Marshal Earl ALEXANDER of Tunis (1891-1969); General Benedict ARNOLD (1741-1801), U.S.A.; Field-Marshal Sir Claude AUCHINLECK (b.1884); Rear-Admiral Lord Charles BERESFORD (1846-1919); Marshal Gebhard von BLUCHER (1742-1819), Prussia; General of the Army Omar BRADLEY (b. 1893), U.S.A.; General Mark CLARK (b. 1896), U.S.A.; Admiral Sir George COCKBURN (1772-1853); Field-Marshal Sir John FRENCH, 1st Earl of Ypres (1852-1925); Field-Marshal August, Graf Neithard von GNEISENAU (1760-1831), Prussia; Field-Marshal Earl HAIG of Bemersyde (1861-1928); Admiral Earl JELLICOE (1895-1935); Marshal Jules JOFFRE (1852-1931), France;

SOME FAMOUS FREEMASONS

John Paul JONES (1747-92), 'Father' of the American Navy; Marshal François KELLERMAN (1735-1820), France; Field-Marshal Earl KITCHENER of Khartoum (1850-1916); Field-Marshal Mikhail KUTUZOV (1745-1813), Russia; General Marie Jean Motier, Marquis de LAFAYETTE (1757-1834), France; General Douglas MacARTHUR (1880-1964), U.S.A.; Marshal Etienne MacDONALD (1765-1840), France; General of the Army George MARSHALL (1880-1959), U.S.A.; Marshal André MASSENA (1758-1817), France; General Sir John MOORE (1761-1809); General Sir Charles NAPIER (1782-1853); Admiral Horatio, Viscount NELSON (1758-1805); Marshal of the Royal Air Force Lord NEWALL (1886-1963); Marshal Michel NEY (1769-1815), France; General Sir James OGLETHORPE (1696-1785), founder of Georgia; General John PERSHING (1860-1948), U.S.A.; Marshal Prince Josef PONIATOWSKI (1763-1813), Poland and France; Field-Marshal Earl ROBERTS of Kandahar (1832-1914); General José de SAN MARTIN (1778-1850), South America; General Gerhard von SCHARNHORST (1755-1813), Prussia; Admiral Sir (William) Sidney SMITH (1764-1840); Marshal Nicholas SOULT (1769-1851), France; General Joseph STILWELL (1883-1946), U.S.A.; Field-Marshal Count Alexander SUVOROV (1729-1800), Russia; Grand Admiral Alfred von TIRPITZ (1849-1930), Germany; Lieutenant-General Sir Charles WARREN (1840-1927), 1st Master of the Quatuor Coronati Lodge; Field-Marshal the Duke of WELLINGTON (1769-1852); General Sir Francis WINGATE (1861-1953); Field-Marshal Garnet, 1st Viscount WOLSELEY (1833-1913).

EXPLORERS OF LAND, SEA AND SPACE

Roald AMUNDSEN (1872-1928); Sir Richard BURTON (1821-90); Admiral Richard BYRD (1888-1957); Colonel Charles LINDBERGH (b. 1902); Robert E. PEARY (1856-1920); Captain Robert Falcon SCOTT (1868-1912); Sir Ernest SHACKLETON (1874-1922); and the following Astronauts: Colonel Edwin E. ALDRIN, L. Gordon COOPER, Donn F. EISELE, Colonel John GLENN, Virgil I. GRISSOM, Edgar D. MITCHELL, Walter M. SCHIRRA, Thomas P. STAFFORD.

MEN OF THE SCIENCES

John ARBUTHNOT (1667-1735), physician; Sir Joseph BANKS (1744-1820), botanist and founder of Kew Gardens; Alexandre Gustave EIFFEL (1832-1923), engineer and builder of the Eiffel Tower; Sir Alexander FLEMING (1881-1955), discoverer of penicillin; Edward JENNER (1749-1823), discoverer of vaccination; Friedrich Franz (or Anton) MESMER (1733-1815), physician and founder of mesmerism; John L. McADAM (1756-1836), inventor of 'macadamizing' roads; Jacques Etienne MONTGOLFIER (1745-99) and Joseph Michel MONTGOLFIER (1740-1810), inventors of the balloon; Hans Christian OERSTED (1777-1851), Danish discoverer of electro-magnetism; James SMITHSON (James Lewis Macie) (1765-1829), chemist and mineralogist, founder of the Smithsonian Institution of Washington; Sir Bernard SPILSBURY (1877-1947), pathologist.

MEN OF LETTERS

Pierre Augustin Caron de BEAUMARCHAIS (1732-99); Major-General

SOME FAMOUS FREEMASONS

Ian Hay BEITH ('Ian Hay') (1876-1952); Sir Walter BESANT (1836-1901); James BOSWELL (1740-95); Robert BURNS (1759-96); Giacomo CASANOVA de Seingalt (1725-98); Samuel L. CLEMENS ('Mark Twain') (1835-1910); Camille DESMOULINS (1760-94); Sir Arthur Conan DOYLE (1859-1930); Edward FITZGERALD (1809-93); Edward GIBBON (1734-94); Sir William S. GILBERT (1836-1911); Johann Wolfgang von GOETHE (1749-1832); Oliver GOLDSMITH (1730?-74); Sir Henry Rider HAGGARD (1856-1925); Johann Gottfried von HERDER (1744-1803); James HOGG ('The Ettrick Shepherd') (1770-1835); Theodore Edward HOOK (1788-1841); Jerome K. JEROME (1859-1927); Douglas William JERROLD (1803-57); Rudyard KIPLING (1865-1936); Mark LEMON (1809-70); Gotthold E. LESSING (1729-81); Edward Bulwer LYTTON, 1st Lord Lytton (1802-73); Captain Frederick MARRYAT (1792-1848); Charles Louis de Secondat de MONTESQUIEU (1689-1755); Sir Gilbert PARKER (1862-1932); Alexander POPE (1688-1744); Alexander PUSHKIN (1799-1837); Friedrich RUCKERT (1788-1866); Abraham Victor RYDBERG (1828-95); Richard SAVAGE (1697?-1743); Sir Walter SCOTT (1771-1832); Richard Brinsley SHERIDAN (1751-1816); Dean Jonathan SWIFT (1667-1745); James THOMSON (1700-48); Anthony TROLLOPE (1815-82); VOLTAIRE (François Marie Arouet) (1694-1778); Lewis WALLACE (1827-1905); George John WHYTE-MELVILLE (1821-78); Christoph WIELAND (1733-1813); Oscar WILDE (1856-1900); John WILSON ('Christopher North') (1785-1854); Francis YEATES-BROWN (1866-1944).

MEN OF THE ARTS

John Sell COTMAN (1782-1842), painter; John CROME (1768-1821), painter; Jean-Baptiste GREUZE (1725-1805), painter; William HOGARTH (1697-1774), painter; Jean-Antoine HOUDON (1741-1828), sculptor; Alphonse MUCHA (1860-1932), painter and illustrator; Alexander NASMYTH (1758-1840), painter; Sir Robert SMIRKE (1781-1867), architect; Sir John SOANE (1753-1837), architect; Sir James THORNHILL (1675-1734), painter; Claude Joseph VERNET (1714-89), painter; Emile Jean Horace VERNET (1789-1863), painter; John ZOFFANY (1733-1810), painter.

MEN OF MUSIC

Thomas ARNE (1710-78), composer of 'Rule Britannia' and arranger of the tune of the British national anthem; Johann Christian BACH (1735-82); Irving BERLIN (b. 1888); Sir Henry BISHOP (1786-1855), composer of Home, sweet home'; François Adrien BOIELDIEU (1775-1834); William BOYCE (1710-79); Ole BULL (1810-80), Norwegian violinist; Sir Michael COSTA (1808-84), Grand Organist, 1851-3; Charles DIBDIN (1745-1814), composer of 'Tom Bowling'; Ferde GROFE (b. 1892); Mark HAMBOURG (1879-1960), pianist; William C. HANDY (1873-1958), jazz composer; Franz Josef HAYDN (1732-1809); Johann Nepomuk HUMMEL (1778-1837); Franz LISZT (1811-86); Henry Charles LITOLFF (1818-91); Gustav Albert LORTZING (1801-51); Lauritz MELCHIOR (1890-1973), Danish operatic tenor; Giacomo MEYERBEER (1791-1864); Lionel MONCKTON (1862-1925), Past Grand Organist, 1899; Leopold

SOME FAMOUS FREEMASONS

MOZART (1719-87); Wolfgang Amadeus MOZART (1765-91); Rev. Sir Frederick OUSELEY. Bt., (1825-89), Grand Chaplain, 1864; Sigmund ROMBERG (1887-1951); Sir Landon RONALD (1873-1938), Grand Organist, 1918; Carl ROSA (1843-89), operatic impresario; Jean SIBELIUS (1865-1957), Grand Organist, Finland; Sir George SMART (1776-1867), 2nd Grand Organist, 1818-43; John Stafford SMITH (1750-1836), English composer of the tune now used for 'The star-spangled banner'; John Philip SOUSA (1854-1932); Ludwig SPOHR (1784-1859); Sir William STERNDALE BENNETT (1816-75); Sir Arthur SULLIVAN (1842-1900), Grand Organist, 1887; Samuel WESLEY (1766-1837), 1st Grand Organist, 1812-17.

MEN OF THE THEATRE

Sir George ALEXANDER (1858-1918); Sir Squire BANCROFT (1841-1926); Edwin Thomas BOOTH (U.S.A.) (1833-93); Arthur BOURCHIER (1863-1927); David GARRICK (1717-79); Sir Henry IRVING (1838-1905); Edmund KEAN (1787-1833); W. S. PENLEY (1851-1912); Sir Herbert Beerbohm TREE (1853-1917); Sir Donald WOLFIT (1902-68).

MEN OF THE CINEMA
(Producers and other executives are marked*)

Richard ARLEN (1900-76); Gene AUTRY (b. 1907); George BANCROFT (1882-1956); Leslie BANKS (1890-1952); Warner BAXTER (1889-1951); Wallace BEERY (1886-1949); John BOLES (b. 1900); Ernest BORGNINE (b. 1917); *Frank BORZAGE (1893-1962); George BRENT (b. 1904); Joe E. BROWN (1892-1975); Eddie CANTOR (1892-1964); Charlie CHASE (1893-1940); Andy CLYDE (1892-1967); Chester CONKLIN (b. 1888); Donald CRISP (b. 1882); *Cecil B. de MILLE (1881-1959); Reginald DENNY (1891-1967); Richard DIX (1894-1949); Brian DONLEVY (1901-72); Leon ERROLL (1881-1951); Douglas FAIRBANKS, senior (1883-1939); W. C. FIELDS (1879-1946); Clark GABLE (1901-60); John GILBERT (1895-1936); *D. W. GRIFFITH (1880-1948); Oliver HARDY (1892-1957); *Will H. HAYS (1879-1954); Jean HERSHOLT (1886-1956); Al JOLSON (1888-1950); Otto KRUGER (b. 1885); Carl LAEMMLE (1867-1939); Harold LLOYD (1893-1971); Victor McLAGLEN (1886-1959); *Louis B. MAYER (1885-1957); Tom MIX (1881-1949); Audie MURPHY (1924-71); Conrad NAGEL (b. 1897); Dick POWELL (1904-63); Roy ROGERS (b. 1912); Will ROGERS (1879-1935); Charles 'Chic' SALE (1885-1936), also known as the author of *The Specialist*; Richard 'Red' SKELTON (b. 1913); Sir C. Aubrey SMITH (1863-1948); Lewis STONE (1879-1953); *Irving THALBERG (1889-1936); Richard TODD (b. 1919); Henry B. WALTHALL (1878-1936); *Jack M. WARNER (b. 1916); *William WYLER (b. 1902), *Darryl F. ZANUCK (b. 1902); *Adolph ZUKOR (1873-?).

MEN OF LIGHT ENTERTAINMENT
(The Circus, Revue, Music Hall, Radio, Television)

Albert BURDON; William F. CODY ('Buffalo Bill') (1845-1917); Nat King COLE (1919-65); Cyril FLETCHER; GERALDO (Gerald Bright) (d. 1975); Robert HARBIN; Harry HOUDINI (1874-1926); Nat JACKLEY; Charlie KUNZ; Sir Harry LAUDER (1870-1954); Sidney

SOME FAMOUS FREEMASONS

LIPTON (b. 1906); Alfred MARKS (b. 1921); Bert MILLS; Bob MONKHOUSE; David NIXON; Ralph READER (b. 1903); The RINGLING Brothers (7) (b. 1852-68); Edmundo ROS; Fred RUSSELL; Cyril STAPLETON; Charles Sherwood STRATTON ('General Tom Thumb') (1838-83); Tommy TRINDER (b. 1909); Jimmy WHEELER; Paul WHITEMAN (b. 1891); Florenz ZIEGFELD (1869-1932).

SPORTSMEN

Sir Malcolm CAMPBELL (1885-1948), motorist; William 'Jack' DEMPSEY (b. 1895), boxer; John A. ('Jack') JOHNSON (1878-1946), boxer; Sir Thomas LIPTON (1850-1931), yachtsman; Daniel MENDOZA (1764-1832), pugilist.

OTHER NOTABLE BRETHREN

Elias ASHMOLE (1617-92), antiquary and astrologer; John Jacob ASTOR (1763-1848), financier; V. Rev. Sir Israel BRODIE (b. 1895), Past Grand Chaplain, Chief Rabbi 1948-65; Prince Chula CHAKRABONGSE of Siam (1908-63); Samuel COLT (1814-62), inventor and maker of pistols; Maharaja DHULEEP SINGH (1837-93); Jean Henri DUNANT (1828-1910), founder of the Red Cross; ERNST II, Duke of Saxe-Coburg-Gotha (1818-93), brother of Albert, Prince Consort; Francis Raymond, 1st Lord EVERSHED (1899-1966), Master of the Rolls 1949-62; Most Rev. Archbishop Lord FISHER of Lambeth (1887-1972), former Archbishop of Canterbury, Grand Chaplain 1937 and 1939; Henry FORD (1863-1947), car manufacturer; Dr. Joseph-Ignace GUILLOTIN (1738-1814), promoter of vaccination after whom the guillotine was named; Rt. Rev. Dr. Percy M. HERBERT (1885-1968), former Bishop of Norwich; J. Edgar HOOVER (b. 1895), of the American Federal Bureau of Investigation; ISMAIL Pasha (1830-95), Khedive of Egypt; Sir Jamsetjee JEEJEEBHOY (1783-1859), Indian merchant and philanthropist, the first Indian knight (1842) and baronet (1857); H. H. Jagatjit Singh Bahadur, Maharaja of KAPURTHALA (1872-1949); Most Rev. Archbishop George KINGSTON (1889-1950), Primate of Canada 1947-50; William, 1st Viscount LEVERHULME (1851-1925), founder of Port Sunlight; Jean Paul MARAT (1743-93), French revolutionary; Richard 'Beau' NASH (1674-1762), dandy; H. H. Bhupindra Singh, Maharaja Dhiraj of PATIALA (1891-38); H. H. Yadavindra Singh, Maharaja Dhiraj of PATIALA (1913-74) H. H. Syed Mohamed Raza Ali Khan, Nawab of RAMPUR (1906-66); Paul REVERE (1735-1818), American patriot; Edwin V. RICKENBACKER (b. 1890), aviator and aviation executive; James Meyer ROTHSCHILD (1792-1868), French financier; Nathan Meyer ROTHSCHILD (1777-1836), London financier; George SHILLIBEER (1797-1866), inventor of the hearse and promotor of the omnibus; John Passmore, Lord WIDGERY (b. 1911), Lord Chief Justice; John WILKES (1727-97), politician; Dr. Stephen S. WISE (1874-1949), American Zionist; Rt. Rev. Dr. Edward Sydney WOODS (1878-1953), Bishop of Lichfield.

INDEX

Compiled by G. Norman Knight and Frederick Smyth
(President and member respectively of the Society of Indexers)

Lodges, etc., are under the English Constitution (including the premier or Moderns' Grand Lodge, 1717-1813) unless otherwise indicated, e.g., (IC) Irish Constitution, (SC) Scottish, (A) Antients. Similar considerations apply to masonic ranks shown against the names of persons. G.L. stands for 'Grand Lodge'.
*against an English lodge number indicates that it was in use at a date prior to the final numbering of 1863 and, usually, that the lodge has been erased or is no longer on the English Register.
Page numbers in **bold type** denote the more important references; *bis* and *ter* after page numbers indicate two or three separate references on those pages; *passim* (e.g., 40-50 *passim*) denotes that the subject is referred to in scattered passages throughout the pages. q. stands for 'quoted'; q.v. for *quod vide* (which see).
The alphabetical arrangement is according to the word-by-word system.

A.Q.C., see *Ars Quatuor Coronatorum*
Abercorn, the Dukes of, G.M.s (IC) (1874-1913) **169**, 208
Aberdeen, Coopers, Wrights and Masons of 181
Aberdeen, Lodge of, No. 1³ (SC) 53, 75, 183, 184, 212
Aberdour, Lord (*later* 15th Earl of Morton), G.M.M. (SC) (1755-7) 190 and *n*.
Aboyne, 9th Earl of, G.M.M. (SC) (1796-8) 210 and *n*.
Abraham 33
Acception, the, of the Masons' Company **44**, 45-6
Adair, Maj.-Gen. Sir Allan, D.G.M. (1969-76) 135, 173
Adam 76
Adamson, Henry, *The Muses Threnodie* (1638) q. 182
'Additional' degrees, the **192**, 222-41
Adelphi, the 127
Adoptive Masonry 315-16
Africa, Freemasonry in **298-300**
Agar, James, D.G.M. (A) (1790-4) 121
Age of admission 93, 97, 154*n*.
Ahiman Rezon: the Antients' *B. of C.* (1756 et seq.) **91-2**, 104, 161-2, 205, 291; the Irish *B. of C.* (1804 et seq.) 161-2
Ailwyn Lodge No. 3535, Ramsey, Hunts. 248
Aisla, 4th Marquis of, G.Z. (SC) (1913-43) 287
Aitchison's Haven, Lodge of 22, 179, 180
Alabama, G.L. of 279
Alaska, Freemasonry in 283
Alban, St. 35, 46, 242
Albany, HRH Leopold, Duke of 70
Albert Edward, Prince of Wales Court, Porthcawl 117
Alberta, G.L. of 269

Alboyn, King 201
Aldworth, Hon. Mrs. Elizabeth **148-9**
Alexander, Lord (d. 1638) 183, 270
Alexander, Sir Anthony (d. 1637) 181, 183
Alexandra, HRH Princess 116, 118
Alexandria Washington Lodge No. 22 (Virginia) 275
Alfred the Great, King, 'Grand Master' 86
All England, G.L. of, *see* York, G.L. of
Allen, 3rd Viscount, G.M. (IC) (1744) 155
Alliance Fraternelle des Puissances Maçonniques 318
Allied Masonic Degrees of England 202, 222, **226-9**, 230, 237, 308; Grand Council (1884) 226, 227-9, 230, 287
Allied Masonic Degrees of U.S.A. 221, 227, 228, 230, 238, 287, 290, 315; Grand Council (1932) 227, **287**, 290; Sovereign College (1892) 228, 230, 287*n*.
Almoner, duties of the 143
Alnwick, old Lodge at 51-2, 54
Alost, Flanders, Lodge No. 341* (1765-1813) at 258
Alpha Lodge No. 116 (New Jersey), Newark 292
Alpina, G.L. of (Switzerland) 267
Amaranth, Order of the (U.S.A.) **289**
Ambulatory lodges, *see* Military lodges
American-Canadian Land Grand Lodge, Germany 250
American Civil War 229, 251
American Independence, War of 243, 251, **275-7**
American Lodge of Research, New York 11, 290, 321
American Rite, the 285
Amity, Lodge of, No. 137, Poole 254
Amity, Lodge of, No. 407* (1767-1813) Canton, China 309

333

INDEX

Amity Biscuit, the 253-4
Amphibal, St. 46
Ampthill, 2nd Lord, Pro G.M. (1908-35) 124, 247
Ancient, Free and Accepted Masonry, Order of 317-18
Ancient and Accepted (Scottish) Rite, the: America 231, 269, **286**, 292, 293-4; Australia 301; Co-masonic 316-17; Europe 258-64 *passim*, 266-7; United Kingdom and Ireland 110*n*., 226, 228 *bis*, **230-3**, 239-40, 248, 314
Ancient Order of Scots Knights Grand Architect 239
Ancient Union Lodge No.13(1C), Dublin 146
Anderson, Dr. James 27, 71, 72, **75-6**, 151, 185, 275; his *Constitutions* (1723) 42, 50, **76-7**, 152, 272, 273, (1738) **26**, 76, **86**, 110, 152; *Royal Genealogies* 75; see also *Book of Constitutions* (1723, 1738)
Anderson, James, senior 75
Anglesey, Earl of 155
Anglo-Dutch R.A. Chapter No. 5862, London 265
Annuity Fund (SC) 196
Anti-Masonry 46, **129-31**, **189-90**, **256-7**, **277-8**; see also Exposures
'Antient Manner of Constituting a Lodge, The' (Anderson) 76
Antient Masons of the Diluvian Order, Society of **219-20**
Antient Union Lodge No. 13 (IC), Limerick 146, 162
Antients, the 64, **88**, **90-4**, 105,6, 243; their Charities **102-3**, 119; their lodges 97, 102-3, 108, 109, 202; and the R.A. 202-6 *passim*; see also Antients and Moderns, Antients' G.L.
Antients and Moderns: dissension between 85, **88-94**, **202-3**; reconciliation of 94, 104, **105-7**, 108-9, **203-4**; see also Union (1813), the
Antients' Grand Lodge 64, 99, 105, 106, 160, 202; formation of 88, **90**; see also Union (1813), the
Antiquity, Lodge of, No. 1 (NSW) (*formerly* Australian Social Lodge No.260(IC)), Sydney 166, 301
Antiquity, Lodge of, No. 2, London **70**, 77, 89*n*., 97, 106, 113, 157, as a G.L. **96-7**; its number 108
Apollo University Lodge No. 357, Oxford 137
Appeal, Courts of **133**
'Apple-Tree'Tavern, Lodge at the 68
Apprentices 22, 76, 77, **179**; see also Entered Apprentices
Aprons 51-2, 176, 198, 205, 225, 228; Grand Stewards' 85; Scottish 198
Ara Lodge No. 1 (NZC), Auckland, N.Z. 306 *bis*
Ara Lodge No. 348 (IC), Auckland, N.Z. 166, 306
Architect, degree 287
Architects, the Travelling **15**, **49**
Ardent, HMS 246
Argentina, Freemasonry in 297
Arizona, G.L. of 279
Ark Mariners, G.L. (1772) of 219; Royal Ark and Mark Mariners 219

Arkansas, G.L. of 279
Arlington, 'Grand Master' 51
Ars Quatuor Coronatorum 7, 9, 146, 318, 321 (and in sundry footnotes)
Articles of Union (1813) **106-7**, 111, q. **203-4**, 223, 231
Ashley, H.V., G. Supt. Wks. (1937-45) 127
Ashmole, Elias 26, 39, **44-5**, 49, 54, 242
Assembly of Masons **25-6**, **35-6**, 39, 46, 52, 65
Asylum for Worthy and Decayed Freemasons **115**
Athelstan, King 25, 35, 39, 46
Athole Lodge No. 1004, Douglas, I.o.M. 191*n*.
Atholl, 3rd Duke of, G.M. (A) (1771-4), G.M.M. (SC) (1773) 92, 93
Atholl, 4th Duke of, G.M. (A) (1775-81), G.M.M. (SC) (1778-9) **93-4**, 103, 105, 106 *bis*
Atholl, 6th Duke of, G.M.M. (SC) (1843-64) 195
Atholl, 8th Duke of, see Tullibardine, Marquis of
'Atholl Masons' **93-4**, 117; see also Antients
Aubrey, John 15, 49, 55; *The Natural History of Wiltshire* (1686) q. **49-50**
'Ault Wharrie' (Scottish Masonic Home) 196
Australia, Freemasonry in 166, 218, 221, 225, 230, 235, 237 *bis*, **301-4**
Australia Felix, Lodge of, No. 697* (*now* No. 1 (Victoria)), Melbourne 303
Austria, Freemasonry in 250, **256-7**, 316
Avignon, Hermetic Schools at 223
Aynon 34
Ayr: old Lodge at 181; the Squaremen Incorporation of 181
Ayrshire, Prov. Grand Mastership 199

Baal's Bridge Square 146
Babel (Babylon), Tower of 32, 53, 64, 65, 200
Babylonish Pass, degree, see Red Cross of Babylon
Bacon's Hotel 221
Bagnall, Hon. Sir Arthur (Mr. Justice), P.S.G.W. (1974) 141, 142
Bagnall Report, The 117, 120, **141-3**
Baldwin, John, G. Sec. (IC) (1739-42) 153
Baldwin Rite, the 233, **239-40**
Ballincollig, Lodge No. 125 (IC) (1817-33) at 164
Bank of England foundation stone (1722) **74-5**
Barbados, Freemasonry in 166, 295
Barnard, J.D.E., Dep. G. Sec. (1971-) 9
Bath, Queen's Head Lodge (1724-36) at 84
Bathurst, Hon. W.R.S. 109, 110
Bauhütten (lodges) 16
Baxter, R.H. 40 *bis*, 91-2
Beale, Dr. John, D.G.M. (1721) 73
Beauceant, Social Order of the 289
Beaufort, 5th Duke of, G.M. (1767-71) 98-100
Begemann, Dr. W. 42
Belcher, Jonathan (USA) **270-1**, 272
Belfast, lodges in 153, 161
Belgium: Freemasonry in **258-9**; G.L.S. of **259**, 264
Belmore, Earl of 160
Benedict XIV, Pope (1740-58) 138
Benefit Societies (masonic) 104, **193-4**
Benevolence, Board of 83, 117
Benevolence, Fund of 97; Scottish 194, 196
Bengal, early lodge (1730) in 84, 308

334

INDEX

Benimeli, Father Ferrer, *La Masoneria depuis del Concilio* (1968) 139
Berlin, Grand National Lodge . . . in 262
Berlin Lodge No. 46 (Rhode Island), Berlin 250
Berosus (c.300 B.C.) 33
Besant, Mrs. Annie 316
Beswicke-Royds MS. q. **31-6**, q. **37-9**
'Beyond the Craft' 225
Bezaleel 63, 201
Bicentenaries: England **125-6**, R.A. **207-8**; Ireland 163, 186; Scotland **196**
Bills of Mortality 79, 83
Birkhead, 'Dr.' Matthew 151
Black Death, the 26, 35
Blanch, Nathan (init. 1721) 89n.
Blayney, 9th Lord, G.M. (1764-6), G.M. (IC) (1768) **98**, 203; his grandson 160
Blesington, 1st Earl of, G.M. (A) (1756-9) 92, 154, 155 bis
Blue Friars, the Society of (USA) **290-1**
Board of Benevolence 83, 117
Board of General Purposes 83, 109, 113-14, 132-3, 143, 245, 317; its members 109, 112-13, 122; its Presidents 124, 136, 217
Board of Installed Masters 106
Boardman, John, G. Treas. (IC) (1791-1813) 159. 167
Boaz 53, 182
'Bobbin, Tim' (John Collier), *Collected Poems* (1757), 'The Goose' q. **80**
Bolivar, Simon, liberator 296
Bolivia, Freemasonry in **296**
Bon Accord Mark Lodge (1851), London **216**, 217
Bon Accord R.A. Chapter No. 70 (SC), Aberdeen **216**
Bonneville, Chevalier de (Clermont Chapter) 230
Bonnie Doon Lodge No. 611 (SC), Colombo 310
Book of Constitutions (1723) 22, 42, 50, 72, **76-7**, 233, 242, 291; in America 272; in Ireland 149
Book of Constitutions (1738) 25-6, 50, 76, 78, 83, 85, **86**, 110; and the G.L. of York 82; as a record of G.L. of England (1717-23) **68-9**, 78
Book of Constitutions (1756) 73, 110
Book of Constitutions (1767) 110
Book of Constitutions (1784) 85, 95, 96, **102**
Book of Constitutions (1815) 110, **111-12**
Book of Constitutions ... of Ireland (1965) 176, q. **208**
Boston (USA), Freemasonry in **272-4**, 276; negroes initiated at 292; Royal Arch 283; Services lodge at 250; *see also* 'Boston Tea Party'
'Boston Tea Party', the 251, **276**
Boswell, James, D.G.M. (SC) (1776-8) 183 and n.
Boswell, John, of Auchinleck 183 and n.
Boyd, Lord, G.M.M. (SC) (1751-2) 190
Boys' Schools, *see* Masonic Schools (IC), Royal Masonic Institution for Boys
Bradford, initiations (1713) at 52
Brant, Joseph, Mohawk chief 251
Brazil, Freemasonry in **295-6**
Brian Boru Faislart, Order of Eri, London 238
Bridge, G.E.W., P.J.G.D. (1939) 236
Bristol: Freemasonry in 84, 92, 202, 222; unusual

degrees in 233-4, **239-40**
Bristol working 147
Britannia Lodge of Madeira No.3683, London **298**
British Broadcasting Corporation 131
British Columbia, G.L. of 269
British Freemasons (Germany), Association of 11, **249**
British Journal, The (1724) q. 80
British Land Grand Lodge, Germany 249
British Lodge No. 334, Cape Town **299**
Broadfoot, Philip, preceptor 113
Brooke, Raymond, G.M. (IC) (1948-64) **171-2**, 172n.
Brotherly Love, Order of 229
Brown, R.S. (Scotland) **225-6**
Bruce, Lord, G.M.M.M. (SC) (1961-5) **196-7**
Buchanan, Rt. Rev. Alan, Bishop of Clogher 168
Buchanan MS. (17th c.) q. **40**
Bucknill, Rt. Hon. Sir Thomas (Mr. Justice), Dep. G. Reg. (1915) **123-4**
Bulgaria, Freemasonry in 255
Burma, Freemasonry in 310
Burne, John (Dublin) 169
Burne, Dr. Joseph (Dublin) 169
Burnes, Dr. James (India) 309 bis
Burns, J.F., *Shop Window to the World* (1967) 168n.
Burns, Robert **191-2**
Burwood, William, S.G.W. (A) (1802) 102
Bushey, Boys' School at **119**
Butler, Hon. Humphrey, D.G.M. (IC) (1725) **150**
Byron, 5th Lord, G.M. (1747-51) 86

C.L.I.P.S.A.S. 318
Cadogan, 7th Earl, Pro G.M. (1969-) 117, 173
Calder, John, G. Sec. (IC) (1757-66) 153, 156
Caledonia, Lodge (SC) (1786-1838), Edinburgh **192-3**
Caledonian Lodge No. 134, London 97, 99, 191n.
California, G.L. of 279, 306
Cameroun, National Grand Orient of 298
Camp of Baldwyn **239-40**
Canceaux, HMS, Lodge (1762-92) in 246
Candidates, number of (SC) 194
Cane, Col. Claude, D.G.M. (IC) (1920-30) 171
Canonagate, (Craft) Incorporation of 181
Canongate and Leith . . . Lodge No. 5 (SC), Edinburgh 184 and n., 186, 187
Canongate Kilwinning Lodge No. 2 (SC), Edinburgh 184, **186**, 189, 191
Carbonari, the 138
Canal Zone, Freemasonry in the **294**
Canadian Grand Lodges **268-9**
Canada, Freemasonry in 165-6, 221, 233, 236, **268-70**, 283, 288 bis, 292
Canada: G.L. (1858) of 268-9; G.L. of (Ontario) 269
Caribbean, Freemasonry in the 166, 190, 231, 244, 273, **295**
Caribbean Lodge No. 4826, London 10
Carr, Harry, P.J.G.D. (1969) 9, 134, **139-40**, 182, 183n., 291; Foreword by **7-8**; references to his writings 98n., 136, 182, 185n., 291, 321-22
Castorius, mason and martyr 28
Caswell, Richard, G.M. (N. Carolina) 276

INDEX

Catechisms, the 52, **56-61**, 89, 182; R.A. 204
Catena (International Masonic Union) 318 *bis*
Catholics, *see* Roman Catholics
Central America, Freemasonry in **293-5**
Certificates of membership 154 and n., 176
Cerza, Alphonse (Illinois) 291
Ceylon (Sri Lanka), Freemasonry in 310
Changi Camp and Gaol, Singapore **248-9**
Charges, the (in *Beswicke-Royds MS.*) **37-9**; *see also* Old Charges
Charities, the masonic: American 271, 288, **289-90**; English **102-3, 114-21**, 121-2, **141-3**, **218-19**, 248; Irish **154-5**, **167-8**, **169-70**; Scottish **195-6**
Charity, the General 72, 73, **83**; American 271
Charity Steward, the office introduced (1975) 142, **143**
Charlemagne 34
Charles I, King 181
Charles II, King 66, 70
Charles XIII, King of Sweden, Order of 266
Charles Edward (Stuart), Prince 189
Charles Martel 17, 34-5
Charter of Compact (R.A., 1766), the 203 and n., 207
Charter of Incorporation (proposed, 1769) **99**
Chase, Jackson H. (New York) 225
Chester, Freemasonry in 47, 49, 54, 84 and n., 109, 110
Chesterfield, Earl of 100
Chetwode Crawley, W.J. 57, 68n., 147, 149, 163, 170
Chetwode Crawley MS. 56, **57**, 60
Chichester, old lodge in 83, 84
Chile: Freemasonry in **297**; G.L. of 296, 297
'Chin-Quaw Ky-Po' 79-80
China, Freemasonry in **311-12**
Chivalry, masonic Orders of 233-7, **239-41**, **284-5**
Church and Freemasonry **129-31**, **132-3**; *see also* Papal Bulls, Roman Catholics
Cibber, Gabriel, 'G. Warden' (1685) 51
Clare, Martin, D.G.M. (1741) 85
Claret, George, *The Ceremonies ...* (1838) 112n.
Clarke, J.R., on the 1st Charge 77
Clarke, Sir William, G.M. (Victoria) 302
Claudius, mason and martyr 28
Clement XII, Pope (1730-40) 138
Clermont Rite, the 230, 265
Co-Masonry **316-17**, **317-18**,
Coburn, A. Langdon 225
Coleraine, 3rd Lord, G.M. (1728) 82
Collectanea (USA) 290
Collegia, the **15**
Collier, John, *see* 'Bobbin, Tim'
Cologne Lodge of Instruction 249
Colombia, Freemasonry in 295
Colorado, G.L. of 279
Colquhoun of Luss, Sir Iain, G.M.M. (SC) (1935-6) 196
Columbia, District of, Freemasonry in the **279-81**
Columbine, Col. Francis, Pr.G.M., Cheshire (1725-7) 109
Columbus, Knights of (R.C., U.S.A.) 139
Comacine Masters, the **15-16**, 145

Combermere Lodge No. 752, Melbourne 303
Committee of Charity 79, **83**, 98, 105; Antients' 92; Irish 154
Committee of General Purposes, R.A. 207
Committee of Precedence 71
Compagnonnage, the **17-18**
Complete Free-mason, The (1763) 69
Conder, Edward 148n., 322
Conferences, masonic 171, 172n., 318
Confidant of St. Andrew, degree 266
Confidant of St. John, degree 266
Confidant of Solomon, degree 266
Connaught, HRH the Duke of, G.M. (1901-39) 121n., **124**, 125-8 *passim*, 171, 218, 234, 247
Connaught Army and Navy Lodge No. 4323, London 11
Connaught Court, Fulford, York 116
Connaught Rooms, the 122, 221
Connecticut, Freemasonry in 279, 284
Consecration ceremony, the 122
Constantinople, Knight of, degree 226, **227-8**, 287
Convent General, K.T. 234
Cooke, 'Major-General' George, impostor **121-2**
Cooke MS. (c.1410) 30, 37, 42, 43-4, q. 44n., 72
Cork, 1st Earl of 146-7
Cork: Lodge No. 1 (IC) of 151, 152, 153, 164; Lodge No. 3 (IC) of 164; Lodge No. 28 (IC) (1734-1818) of 164
Corker, Thomas, Dep. G. Sec. (IC) (1767-1800) 156, 159
Corks, Ye Antient Order of 287
Cormac's Chapel, Cashel 145
Cornwallis, Hon. Fiennes, D.G.M. (1976-) 144
Costa Rica, Freemasonry in 294
Coulton, Dr. G.G., *Art and the Reformation* (1928) 211-12
Council of the East and West 230
County Committees of Inspection (IC) 156, 166 and n.
Courts of Appeal 133
Coustos, John, and the Inquisition **255-6**
Cowans 25, 76, 178, 180
Cowper, William, Secretary to G.L. **78-9**
Coxe, Daniel (USA) **271**
Crawford, Lord 186
Crawley, W.J. Chetwode 57, 68n., 147, 149, 163, 170
Criminal Law Act 1967 105
Cromartie, 3rd Earl of, G.M.M. (SC) (1737-8) 187-8
Crossle, Philip, *see* Lepper and Crossle
'Crown' Ale-House, Lodge (1712-c.1736) at the, London 68, 70-1
Croydon, the R.M.B.I. Home at 115, 116
Crucefix, Dr. Robert, J.G.D. (1836) **114-16**, 121, 231
Cryptic Degrees, the, *see* Royal and Select Masters
Cuba, Freemasonry in 295
Culdees, the **14**
Cullen, Cardinal, of Dublin (c.1848) 162n.

336

INDEX

Cumberland, HRH Henry Frederick, Duke of, G.M. (1782-90) 101-2, 104
Cush, grandson to Noah 32, 64
Cyprus, Freemasonry in 313
Czechoslovakia, Freemasonry in 255

Daily Post, The (1724) q. **79-80**
Dalkeith, Earl of, G.M. (1723) 79, 82
Daniel, F. Columbine 119
Danske Store Landsloge, den (Denmark) 259
Dashwood, J.R. 203*n*.
Dassigny, Dr. Fifield, *A Serious and Impartial Enquiry* ... (1744) 148, **155-6**, **202**, 208, 291
Daughters of the Nile 289
David, King 34
David and Jonathan, Brotherhood of 229
Deacons 89, 106, 178, 197; as presiding officers (Scotland) 23, 178
Debtors' Prison, Dublin, Lodge No. 249 (IC) in the 153
Defence of Masonry, A (1730-1) 85
Degrees (Craft): how many? 55-6, **77-8**, 82, 274; interval between 112, **194**
Degrees (other), how many? **224**
De Grey and Ripon, Earl, *see* Ripon, Marquess of
Delaware, Freemasonry in 279, 285
de Molay, Order of 289
Denmark: Freemasonry in **259-60**; National G.L. of 259, 263
Denslow, Ray (USA) 293
Deraismes, Mlle. Maria 316
Dermott, Laurence, G.Sec. and D.G.M. (A) **90-1**, 92-4, 104, 175; see also *Ahiman Rezon*
Desaguliers, Dr. J.T., G.M. (1719) 72, **73-4**; as D.G.M. 75, 76, 79, 109; as P.G.M. 82, 85, **185**, 256, 275; his descendant 74, 128
Desaguliers, Lt.-Gen. Thomas 74
Devonshire, 10th Duke of, G.M. (1947-50) 128, 129, 138
Devonshire Court, Oadby, Leics. 116
Dewar, James, anti-mason 131
Dickey, William, G.Sec. and D.G.M. (A) 91, 93, 94
Dietrichstein, Count, G.M. (Austria) 257
Differences from English working: Irish practice **174-6**; Scottish practice **197-9**
Dillon, Hon. Charles, D.G.M. (1768-74) 99, 101
Diluvian Order, the 219
Diocletian, Roman Emperor (285-305) 28
District of Columbia, Freemasonry in the 279, 280, 281
District Grand Lodges: (EC) 269, 295-7, 305, **309**, 311, 312; (SC) 196, 269, **295** *bis*, 302; 304, 309, 311; title changed from 'Provincial' G.L. 110-11
Dodd, Rev. Dr. William, G. Chaplain (1775-7) 100, 123
Dominican Republic, Freemasonry in the 295
Donegall, The Marquess of G.M. (I.C.) (1981-) 173
Doneraile, 1st Viscount 148
Doneraile, 3rd Viscount, G.M. (IC) (1740) 155
Donoughmore, 1st Earl of, G.M. (IC) (1789-1813) **158-9**, 160, 162, 164, 173

Donoughmore, 2nd and 4th Earls of, S.G.W.s (IC) 173
Donoughmore, 6th Earl of, G.M. (IC) (1913-48) 135, 167, 170, 171
Donoughmore, 7th Earl of, G.M. (IC) (1964-81) 135, **172-3**, 174
Dorrington, John F., G.Comdr., Ark (1816-70) 220
Dougan, William, Master of Dublin Gild 145
Douglas, Rev. C.E., in Church Assembly, 1951 q. 130-1
Downes, Bro., printer 162
Draffen of Newington, George S., Dep.G.M. (SC) (1974-6) 9, 195 and *n*., 197, 291; *Pour la Foy* (1949) 235*n*.
Drake, Dr. Francis, J.G.W. (York G.L.) q. **82**
Drawing the lodge 87
Drei Kanonen, Lodge *zur den*, Vienna 256
Dress, masonic 51-2, 54
Druids, the **14**
Drummond, George, G.M.M. (SC) (1752-3) 190
Dublin: Lodge No. 2 (IC) of 150, 152, 158, 169; Lodge No. 6 (IC) of 150; Lodge No. 198 (IC) (1749-1821) of 162; Lodge No. 249 (IC) in the Debtors' Prison 153; Lodge No. 250 of 169
Dublin Evening Post, The (1734) 151
Dublin Masonic Hall Co. of Ireland, Ltd. 169
Dublin Weekly Journal, The (1725) 149, q. 151
Dugdale, Sir William 15, 49
Duke of Leinster's Lodge No. 283 (IC) (1821-54), Kingston, Canada 165, 166
Duke of Wellington's Regt. 243
Dumbarton Kilwinning Lodge No. 18 (SC), Dumbarton 185
Dumfries Kilwinning Lodge No. 53 (SC), Dumfries 61
Dumfries MS. No. 4 (c.1710) q. **41**, **61**, 62
Dunalley, 4th Lord, G.Sec. (IC) (1921-2) 170
Dunblane, Lodge of, No. 9 (SC), Dunblane 189
Dunckerley, Thomas **98-9**, 102, 110; and lodges in the Navy **245-6**; in the R.A. and other degrees 203, 205, **214**, 219-20, 233-4
Dundee, old Lodge at 181
Dunfermline, old Lodge at (*now* St. John No. 26 (SC)) 180, 181
Dunn, Thomas, operative/speculative mason 75
Durham, 1st Earl of, D.G.M. (1834-5) 115
Durham Cathedral 20
Dutch Guiana, Freemasonry in 295
Dyer, Colin F.W. 320; *Emulation – A Ritual to Remember* (1975) 113*n*., 320

Early Grand Encampment, K.T.: Ireland 234, 235, 236; Scotland 235
East, Knight of the 228, 241, 247
East, the Sword and Eagle, Knight of the 239
East and West, Knight of the 228, **241**
Eastern Star, Order of the 287, **288**, 316
Easton, Reginald, O.S.M. (1962) 129
Ecuador, Freemasonry in 296
Edgeworth (Edgware?), old Lodge in 84
Edinburgh, HRH Philip, Duke of 131-2

337

INDEX

Edinburgh (Mary's Chapel), Lodge of, No. 1 (SC) 22, 177, **180**, 181, 183, 184 *ter*; Dr. Desaguliers's visit to 73, **185**; first recorded *raising* in 190; initiations of Lord Alexander 270, and Sir Robert Moray 44, 188-9, 242; Grand Lodge and 186 *bis*; its Minutes 53, 179, 188, 192, 212; secession of **192-3**; speculatives appear in 183

Edinburgh Register House MS. (1696) 56, q. **57-60**, 182, 183

Edinburgh St. Andrew, Lodge of, No. 48 (SC) 193

Edward VII, King, P.G.M. **124**

Edward VIII, King, P.G.M. 128

Edwards, Miles, of Munster 164

Edwards, Morton A. (Ark Mariners) 220

Edwin, Prince 35-6, 39, 46, 52, 81-2

Effingham, 3rd Earl of, A/G.M. (1782-9) 102

Eglington, 17th Earl of, G.M.M. (SC) (1957-61) 179

Egypt: Freemasonry in 298; Mysteries of Ancient 14; National G.L. of 298, 311

89th Foot, Lodge No. 497 in the 245

Elizabeth, Queen, the Queen Mother 116, 126

Elizabeth I, Queen 26, 52

Elizabeth II, Queen 118, 124, 138

Elliot, Captain Joseph, S.G.W. (1717) 69

Emulation Lodge of Improvement 112 *bis*

England, Grand Lodge of 42, 75-6, **83-4**, 99, 100; its Bicentenary 125-6; its composition 85; its formation **68-9**; its jurisdiction 69, **83-4**; its Minutes 72, **78-9**; its 250th Anniversary **134-7**, 173; *see also* Moderns' G.L. *and* United G.L. of England

England, United Grand Lodge of **108-44**, 164, 165, 237, 255, 259, 264 *bis*, 267; its library **114**, 127; and the Mark degree **216-17**, 219; and the R.A. **204**

England South of the River Trent, Grand Lodge of 70, 94-5, **96-7**

Engraved List of Lodges (1725, 1729, 1732) 70, 84 *bis*

Enoch Lodge No. 11, London 92

Entered Apprentices 76, 77, 82, 107, 185 *bis*; in operative masonry 22, **182**, 183

Entered Apprentices' Song, the 54, 151, q. **152**

Entick, Rev. John 110

Eon, Chevalier d' **103-4**

Epworth (Methodist) lodges, the 130

Eri, Order (Red Branch) of 237-8, 287

Essenes, the **14**

Euclid 33, 76

Europäische Bruderkette 318

Euston, Earl of, Pro G.M., Mark (1893-1912) 228

Ewin, E.T. Floyd, on St. Paul's 50n.

'Excellent Masons' at Youghal (1743) 208 *and n*.

Excellent Master, degree 210, 215, 220, 222, 287, 301, 306

Exposures **64**, 84-5, 133, 277-8

Fairfax, Admiral Robert, his initiation (1713) 242

Falkirk, Lodge of (*now* St. John No. 16 (SC)) 187

Fallou, Frederick 16

F lkner's Dublin Journal (1740) 155

Favine, Andrew, *The Theater of Honour* ... (1623) q. **211**

Fellow 23, 76

Fellow Crafts 76, **77-8**, 185 *bis*; in Constitutions, etc. 107, 204, 208; in the Mark degree 214, 215, 217, 222; in operative masonry 23, 182 *bis*, 183, 212

Fellow of St. Andrew, degree 266

Ferrers, 5th Earl, G.M. (1762-3) 104

Fidelity, Lodge of, No. 3, London 109

Fiji, Freemasonry in 306

Fildes, Sir Luke, artist 124

Finland, Freemasonry in **260-1**, 316; A. & A.R. 233; R.A. 208

Fire of London, the Great (1666) 50, 66

First Foot (Royal Scots), Lodge No. 11 (IC) (1732-1847) in the 243

Fisher, David 92-3

Fisher of Lambeth, Most Rev. Lord, Archbishop of Canterbury (1945-61) 130, 131

Fitzgibbon, Lord Justice (Ireland) 170

Fleury, Cardinal (France) 223

Florence, Irish Lodge (1733) in 154 and *n*.

Florida, G.L. of 279

Flying Post, The (1723) q. 212-13

Fortitude, Lodge (1790-3) of, under G.L. of York 215n.

Fortitude and Old Cumberland Lodge No. 12, London 71

46th Foot, Lodge No. 227 (IC) (1782-1847) in the **251**, 277, 301

48th Foot, Lodge No. 218 (IC) (1750-1858) in the 166

Four Crowned Martyrs, the **28-9**

Four Old Lodges, the 68, **70-1**, 83, 153, 187; of Scotland 186-7

Fowler, John, D.G.M. (IC) (1818-24) 163 *bis*, 166

France, Freemasonry in **261-2**; early additional degrees **223-4**, 230, 240, 315-16; military lodges 246, 247; R.A. 208, 261; unrecognized Orders **316**, 318 *bis*

France, Grand Lodge of: (1743) 261; (1880) 261, 267, 295, 298

France, Grand Orient of 169, 247, **261**, 316; its influence – Africa 298, 299, America 295, 296, Asia 311, Europe 258, 263, 264, 266, 267

France, National Grand Lodge of 139, **261**, 312; an irregular imitation 262

Francis I, Emperor 73, **256-7**

Francis II, Emperor of Austria 257

Franklin, Benjamin **271-2**, 273 *ter*, 291

Frazer, Persifor (Pennsylvania) 270

Frederick II (the Great), King of Prussia 262

Fredericksburg Lodge No. 4 (Virginia), Fredericksburg 275, 282

Fredericksburg Minute, the 202, q. **282-3**

'Free', meanings of, in 'freemason' 24, 177

'Free-Masons, The' (1722-3), satirical poem q. **214**, q. 216

Free-thinkers, Lodge of (France) 316

'Freemason', origin of the term 23-4

Freemason's Journal, The (Dublin) 159

Freemason's Monthly Magazine, The 217

Freemason's Stone, Dublin 146

Freemasonry: attacks on 46, **129-31**, **189-90**,

338

INDEX

277-8; origin of **13-18**; pre-Grand Lodge **43-67**
Freemasons, famous 326-31
Freemasons' Hall, Dublin 150, **169**, 171
Freemasons' Hall, Edinburgh **195**
Freemasons' Hall, London: 1st (1776) **100**; 2nd (1866) **122-3**, 221; 3rd (1933) **127-8**, 135
Freemasons' Quarterly Review, The 112, 115 bis, 252, q. 253
Freemasons' Tavern, London 122
French, Thomas, G.Sec. (1768) 98, 101
French Guiana, Freemasonry in 295
French military lodges 246
French prisoners-of-war lodges 195-6, **246-7**
Frere, A.S., P.S.G.W. (1969) 136, 144
Friendship, Lodge of, No. 1 (S. Austr.), Adelaide 302
Friendship, Lodge of, No. 6, London 98 and *n*.
Friendship, Lodge of, No. 277, Oldham 215
Friendship, Lodges of, Mauritius 299
Friendship, R.A. Chapter of, No. 257, Portsmouth **214-15**, 213
Frimurerlauget af Gamle og Frie Antagne Murer (Denmark) 259
Fund of Benevolence, *see* Benevolence, Fund of
Fund of Scottish Masonic Benevolence, *see* Benevolence, Fund of

'G', the letter 87
Gambia, Freemasonry in the 298-9
Gamble, George S., D.G.M. (IC) (1959-62) 172
Garibaldi, Giuseppe, G.M. (Italy) 263
Gastvrijheid: Lodge No. 3970, London 247; Rose Croix Chapter 248
Gavel, The 315
General Assembly of Masons 25-6, 65; *see also* Assembly of Masons
General Grand Chapter, Royal Arch Masons International 283, 290; affiliated jurisdictions and chapters outside U.S.A. 262-3, 264, 269, 293, 294, 306, 312
General Grand Council of Royal and Select Masters 284
Geneva: Grand Orient of 266; Independent G.L. of 266
Gentlemen's Club, the, Spalding 223
Geometry, in the Old Charges 31-2, 34, 36
George II, King 98, 270
George III, King 99, 101, 102, 103, 106
George IV, King, P.G.M., *see* Wales, Prince of (George IV)
George V, King 119, 126
George VI, King, P.G.M., G.M.M. (SC) (1936) **128-9**, 132, 173, 196
Georgia, Freemasonry in 274, 279
Germany: Freemasonry in 248, **249-50**, 262-3, 283, 316 bis; *Steinmetzen* in **16-17**, 28
Gibraltar, Freemasonry in 84, 243, 267
Gilds, the, **20-1**, 37, **43-4**, 177; In Ireland 145-6; at Preston 49; in Scotland 178
Gilkes, Peter, preceptor 112-13
Girls' Schools, *see* Masonic Female Orphan School (IC), Royal Masonic Institution for Girls
Gist, Mordecai (USA) 276
Glammis, Lodge of, No. 99 (SC), Glamis 196

Glasgow: (Craft) Incorporation of 181; old Lodge at (*now* Glasgow St. John No. 3 bis (SC)) 181
Glittering Star, Lodge, No. 322 (IC), in the Worcestershire Regt. 167 and *n*.
Gloucestershire Regt., the 243
Gloves, presentation of 47 and *n*., 54
Gobhan Saor, mythical Celtic 'free smith' 145
Golden Chain, Order of the 289
Goldsworthy, J.H., preceptor 109, 113
'Goose, The', (Tim Bobbin) q. **80**
'Goose and Gridiron' Ale-House, the, London 68, 69
Gordon of Esselmont, Captain R.W., G.M.M. (SC) (1974-) 174
Gormogons, the **79-81**
Gould, R.F. 42, 80-1; *History of Freemasonry* (1882-7) 16, 322
Graeme, James (USA) 275
Graham (Chanceing), Thomas 63
Graham MS. (1726) q. **61-4**, 65, 183, 200, 201, q. **213**
Gran Loggia d'Italia 264
Gran Loggia Nazionale Italiana 264
Gran Logia (del) Archipelago Filipino 312
Gran Logia Cuscatlan de El Salvador 294
Gran Logia de la Republica de Guatemala 294
Gran Orient Filipino 312
Grand Architect, degree 287
Grand Charity, the 142, 143
Grand Collège des Rites, Le (France) 262
Grand College of Knight Templar Priests, *see* Knight Templar Priests
Grand College of Rites (USA) 290
Grand Commanderies of Knights Templar (USA) 285
Grand Committee (A) **90**
Grand Conclave, Knights Templar 234 bis
Grand Councils of R. & S.M., *see* Royal and Select Masters
Grand East of the Netherlands 247, 259, 265, 295 bis, 299 bis
Grand East of Ulster 159, **160-1**
Grand Encampment of Knights Templar (USA) **284-5**
Grand Festival, the 85-6
Grand High Priest, Order of the 226, **228-9**
Grand Lodge, 1717-1967 (1967) 109n., **135-6**, 321
Grand Lodge No. 1 MS. (1583) 30, q. 31, q. **41-2**, 201
Grand Lodge of Instruction (IC) 163, 173, 174
Grand Lodges (Craft), *see under* Alberta, Alpina (Switzerland), Antients'†, Austria, Belgium, Berlin†, Bolivia, British Columbia, Canada (1858)†, Costa Rica, Cuba, Dominican Republic, Ecuador, England, England South of the Trent, Finland, France§, Geneva (Independent)†, Greece, Guatemala, Honduras§, India, India (All Scottish Freemasonry in)†, Iran, Ireland, Israel, Japan‡, Liberia†, Luxembourg, Manitoba, Mexico, Moderns'†, Munster†, Netherlands†, New Brunswick, New South Wales (1877)†, New Zealand, Nicaragua§, Norway, Nova Scotia, Paraguay, Peru, Phillipines Prince Edward Island, Puerto Rico, Quebec,

† no longer in existence   ‡ not recognised by England   § irregular

339

INDEX

Queensland (1904, 1920)†, Royal York (Germany)†, Saskatchewan, Scotland, South Australia, Southern Africa, Tasmania, Three Globes (Germany)†, Turkey, Uruguay §, *Valle de Mexico*, Venezuela, Victoria (1883)†, West Australia, Wigan†, York† and the individual States of U.S.A., *see also* Grand Orients, National Grand Lodges, United Grand Lodges
Grand Lodges (Mark), *see* Mark Masonry
Grand Master's Lodge (IC), Dublin 156
Grand Master's Lodge No. 1, London 70, 93, 108
Grand Master's Order of Service to Masonry 129
Grand Master's Royal Ark Council 220
Grand National Lodge of German Freemasons in Berlin 262
Grand Orients, *see under* Austria§, Belgium§, Brazil, Cameroun§, France§, Geneva†, Greece†, Hungary†, Italy, Luxembourg§, Paraguay†, Peru†, Switzerland§
Grand Registrar, in charge of a Province 110
Grand Royal Arch Chapters: England **203-4**, 207-8, 216, 264; Ireland **208-9**; Scotland **209-10**, 216, 218, 220, 228-9; Africa 299; America 269, **282-4**, 293, 297; Asia **308**, 310; Australasia **301**, 302-3, 304 *bis*, **306**; Europe 260-7 *passim*
Grand Secretaries for Instruction (IC) 163
Grand Stewards 85-**6**, 275
Grand Stewards' Lodge, London 85, 108, 125
Grand Temple, London 123, 127
Grand Tiler of Solomon, degree 226, **228**, 287
Grand Wardens 89*n*., 98*n*.
Grande Loge Nationale Française 139, **261**, 311; an irregular imitation 262
Grande Loge Symbolique Ecossaise **316**
Grants, by Grand Lodge **137**, 138
Grasse-Tilly, Comte de 261
Grattan, Henry, Irish politician 160*n*.
Great Priories, K.T., *see* Temple, Order of the
Great Queen Street, London 100, 127
Greece: Freemasonry in 263. Mysteries of Ancient 14
Gretna R.A. Chapter No. 419 (SC), Gretna Green 189
Gridley, Jeremy (USA) 274
Griffith, Thomas, G.Sec. (IC) (1725-32) **150-1**, 152, 153
Grootloge der Nederlanden 265
Grootosten der Nederlanden 265
Grosse Landesloge von Deutschland 262
Grossloge von Österreich 258
'Grotto', the **288**
Guadeloupe, HMS, Lodge in 246
Guatemala, Freemasonry in 294
Gustav II Adolf, King of Sweden 83
Gustav V Adolf, King of Sweden 265
Guyana, Freemasonry in 108*n*., 295

Haddington, old Lodge at (*now* St. John Kilwinning No. 57 (SC)) 180
Haddon MS. (1723) q. 36
Hall, Edward, and the Charity (1732) 83
Hall Stone lodges 127-8
Halsey, Sir Frederick, D.G.M. (1903-26) 124
Halsey, Mrs. Marion 315

Halsey Memorial Pavilion (R.M.I.G.) 118
Hammerton, John (USA) 275
Hannah, Rev. Walton, anti-mason **130**, 131
Harewood, 6th Earl of, G.M. (1942-7) 128, 129 *bis*, 135
Harewood Court, Hove 116
Harleian MSS. q. 41, 48
Harper, Thomas, D.G.M. (A) (1801-13) 70, 105-7, 121
Harris, 5th Lord, G.M., Mark (1954-73) 116, 219
Harris MS. No. 1 (17th c.) q. **40-1**
Hart, John (init. 1721) 89*n*.
Harte, James O., G.Sec. (IC) (1954-), 168, 170
Hastings, 1st Marquess of, *see* Moira, Earl of
Haughfoot Lodge, its Minutes (1702) 55-**6**
Haunch, T.O., librarian to G.L. 9
Havers, John, J.G.W. (1862) 122
Hawaii, Freemasonry in 280*n*., 292, 306
Hawkins, E.L. 40
Hayes, Sir Henry Browne (Australia) **301**
Hazara Lodge No. 4159, London 11
Healey, Rev. K., in the Church Assembly (1951) 130
'Hedge Masons' 153
Heenan, Cardinal John, Archbishop of Westminster (1963-75) **139-40**
Helvetica Lodge No. 4894, London 267
Hely-Hutchinson, Hon. Abraham, D.G.M. (IC) (1807-18) 173
Hembroth (or Nembroth), King of Babylon 32
Hemming, Rev. Dr. S., S.G.W. (1813) 109
Henderson, John, G.Reg. (1857) 114, 217
Henry VI, King 27
Herbert, Rt. Rev. Bishop P.M., Pr.G.M., Norfolk (1943-46) 133-**4**, 207
Heredom of Kilwinning, degree and Order 240
Hermenes 32
Hermetic Schools at Avignon (*c.* 1740) 223
Hertfordshire, Province of 118
Heseltine, James, G.Sec. (1769-80) 96, 102
Hewers 24, 178
Hewitt, A.R., P.J.G.D. (1973) 135, 136, 203*n*., 207, 248*n*., *Guide for Masonic Librarians* (1965) 136
Higden, Ranulf, *Polychronicon* 32
High Priesthood, Anointed Order of 283; *see also* Grand High Priest
'Higher' degrees 224, 232
Hiram, King of Tyre 34
Hiramic legend, the 78, 183, 200
'History' in the Old Charges 31-6, **46-7**
Hogarth, William, artist 85
Holland, *see* Netherlands, the
Holme, Randle (1627-99) **47-9**, 54 *ter*, 55; *Academie of Armory* q. 48
Holmes-Dallimore, A., *The Three Constitutions* (1927) 174*n*.
Holy Royal Arch, *see* Royal Arch Masonry
Holy Royal Arch Knight Templar Priests, *see* Knight Templar Priests
Holy Sepulchre, Order of the 235
Holyrood House, Lodge of, No. 44 (SC), Edinburgh 185, 186, 189
Home, Earl of (*fl.* 1736) 186, 187
Honduras, Freemasonry in 293

† no longer in existence   § irregular

INDEX

Hong Kong, Freemasonry in **311**
Honor and Generosity, Lodge of, No. 165, London 249
Honorius I, Pope (625-38) 28
Honourable Fraternity of Ancient Freemasons 317
Honourable Fraternity of Antient Masonry 317
Hoppringle, John, of Haughfoot 56
Horn Tavern, (Old Horn) Lodge at the, London 71, 75, 246, 275
Hughan, W.J. 42, 57, 235, 237, **322**; *Origin of the English Rite* (3rd ed., 1925) 203, **322**
Hull, Richard (The Gambia, 1726) 298
Human Duty, Lodge of, No. 6 (Co-Masonic), London 316
Hund, Baron von (Strict Observance) **224**, 262, 267
Hungary, Freemasonry in 149, 255, 257-8
Hunt, Rev. C. Penney, anti-mason 129, 131

Iceland, Freemasonry in **263**
Idaho, G.L. of 279
Illinois; Grand Council of 225-6; G.L. of 279
Illustrations de l'Ordre, Lodge L', No. 376*, London 103
Inchiquin, 4th Earl of, G.M. (1727) 82, 151
Incorporation, proposed Charter (1769) of **99**
Incorporations of the Freemen-Masons and Wrights, Edinburgh 178, 179, 181
Incorporations of Masons and other Crafts **43-4**, 178, **181**
Independent G.L. of Geneva 266
India, Freemasonry in 84, 172, **244-5**, **308-10**
India, G.L. of All Scottish Freemasonry in 308
Indiana, G.L. of 279
Industry, Lodge of, No. 48, Gateshead 51
Initiation: age of 93, 97, 154 *n.*; fees for 112
Installed Masters' degree 89, 106, 201, **206**; Ireland 174; Scotland **194-5**
International Compact, the (1814) **111**, **164**, 165
Intrant (Scottish candidate) 194
Iowa, G.L. of 279
Ipswich, Ark Masonry (1790) at 219
Iran, Freemasonry in 312
Iraq, Freemasonry in 312-13
Ireland, Grand Lodge of 92, 149-76 *passim*, its Bicentenary 149, 171; its external relations 92, 105, 111, 165, 169, 172, 255, its formation **149-50**; and Freemasons' Hall 169. its G.L. of Instruction 163; meets in England 167, its Minutes 111, 164, and the penalties 170; and the R.A. 208; its 250th Anniversary **173-4**
Irish Freemasonry 53, **145-76**, differences from English **174-6**, in India **172**, 244-5, 309; military lodges 153, **167** and *n.*, 243-5; other than Craft – A. & A.R. **232**, 233, Knight Masons 228, **240-1**, K.T., etc. 232-3, **234-5**, 236, 241, Mark 218, R.A. 202, **205**, **208-9**, 301; *see also* Chapters XV to XVIII for other overseas references
'Irregular makings' 83, 86
Irvine, D'Arcy, G.Sec. (IC) (1796-1804) 159
Irvine, Col. W., G.M., Ulster (1808) 160
Israel, Freemasonry in 313

Italian 'travelling architects' 15, 49
Italy, Freemasonry in 153-4, **263-4**, 283

Jabal 32
Jachin 53, 182
Jachin & Boaz (1762), an exposure 278
Jackson, James (USA) 276
Jacobites, 80, 151, 223, 224; the '1745' **188-9**, 190, 243
Jacques, Maître 17
Jacquin 17
James VI, King of Scotland 179
Japan, Freemasonry in **310**
Jerusalem Lodge No. 44* (1731-80), London 101 and *n.*
Jerusalem Lodge No. 197, London 101 *n.*
Jesters, Royal Order of 288
Jewels: commemorative 128, 193; Craft/R.A. 176, 198; melted down in World War II 137 *n.*; of office-bearers (SC) **197-8**
Jewish freemasons, the earliest 77, 89 *n.*
Job's Daughters, Order of 289
John XXIII, Pope (1958-63) 139
John of Gloucester, master mason (*fl*. 1254-72) 23
Johnson, Dr. Samuel 100, 128 *n.*, 183
Jonathan and David and Jesus Christ, Order of 229
Jones, Bernard E. 73, 79, 291, **321**, **322**
Jones, John, of Trinity College 147
Jones, Paul (USA) **276**
Jordan, Freemasonry in 313
Joseph II, Emperor of Austria 257
Josephus, Flavius (37-c.100) 33
Journeyman Lodge of Dumfries (*now* Thistle No. 62 (SC)) 214-15
Journeymen Masons, Lodge of, No. 8 (SC), Edinburgh 185, 186
Jubal 32

Kansas, G.L. of 279
Kent, HRH Edward, Duke of, G.M. (A) (1813) 102, 106, 107, 134, 220, 235, 268
Kent, HRH Edward George, Duke of, G.M. (1967-) 70 *n.*, **134**, 141-3, 173
Kent, HRH George, Duke of, G.M. (1939-42) 128, 129, 132, 134, 135, 173, 218
Kent, HRH Katharine, Duchess of 116
Kent, HRH Prince Michael of 218
Kent, HRH Princess Alexandra of 116, 118
Kent, HRH Princess Marina, Duchess of 116, 118
Kent, Province of 120; divided 141
Kent Lodge No. 15, London 91, 219
Kentucky, G.L. of 279
Kevan MS. (*c*.1714) 56, 60
Kew Palace, occasional lodge at 74
Kilwinning, Lodge of, *see* Mother Kilwinning, Lodge
Kilwinning Scots Arms Lodge (SC) (1736-56), Edinburgh 186 *bis* and *n.*
King's Bench Prison, masons made in 101 *bis*
Kingsborough, 1st Lord, G.M. (IC) (1749-50) 156
Kingston, 4th Lord, G.M. (1728-9), G.M. (IC) (1731, 1735, 1745-6) 152 *bis*, 153, 155, 171
Kinnaird, Lord G.M.M. (SC) 111

341

INDEX

Kinsale: Lodge No. 31 (IC) (1787-1818) at 164, Mark certificate (1775) at 215
Kirk, Rev. Robert (*fl.*1691), of Aberfoyle q. 53, 182
Knight, G. Norman (other than as author) 146, 308
Knight Masons, Order of 228, **240-1**, 287
Knight Templar, *see* Temple, Order of the
Knight Templar Priests 226 *bis*, **237**, 286
Knighthoods, masonic, *see under* Constantinople; East, the; East, the Sword and Eagle; East and West; Malta, Order of; Nine Elected Masters, Pelican and Eagle; Rose Croix of Mt. Carmel; St. John of Jerusalem; St. Paul; Sword, the; Temple, Order of the
Knights Beneficent of the Holy City **267**, 286
Knights Commander of the Red Cross (Sweden) 266
Knoop, Professor Douglas 30, 42, 178, 181, 183, **321**, 322

'Lady freemason', the **148-9**
Lamball, Jacob, J.G.W. (1717) 69
Lamech 22, 76
Lanark, (Craft) Incorporation of 181
Lancashire, Provinces of: before division 113; Eastern 31, 119, 141; Western 141
Lancashire lodges, dissension (1821) in **113**
Landmarks 89
Layers (or setters) **24-5**, 178
Leather Apron Club (USA, 1728) 271
Lebanon, Freemasonry in the 313
le Bon, Captain Jacques, privateer 253-4
Leeson, Dr. H.B., and the A. & A.R. 231
Legh, Peter (USA) 275
Leicester, Lodge of Research No. 2429, Transactions of the 238
Leigh, 2nd Lord, G.M., Mark (1856) 217
Leinster, 2nd Duke of, G.M. (IC) (1770-71, 1777) 162
Leinster, 3rd Duke of, G.M. (IC) (1813-74), **162-3**, 165 *bis*, 169, 208; and the International Compact 111, 164; the length of his reign 121*n*., 169
Leith and Canongate, *see* Canongate and Leith
Leith Kilwinning Lodge (SC) (1736-56), Leith 186 *bis* and *n*.
Leo XII, Pope (1823-9) 139
Leo XIII, Pope (1878-1903) 139
Leopold I, King of the Belgians 258
Leopold II, Emperor of Austria 257
Lepper, J. Heron 90, 99, 149, 154*n*.
Lepper, J.H., and P. Crossle, *History of the G.L. of Ireland* (Vol. I, 1925) 145 and *n*., 154*n*., 167
Leslie, Robert, G.Sec (A) (1783-5, 1790-1813) 94
Leswarree Lodge No. 646 (IC), in the Royal Irish Hussars 167
Letter from the Grand Mistress, A (1724) **149**
Levander-York MS. (1560?) 52
Levi, Moses Isaac, S.G.W. (1785) 89*n*.
Lewis, Morgan (USA) 276
Liberal Catholic Church, the 316-17
Liberia, Freemasonry in 292, 298

Libres Penseurs, Loge Symbolique Ecossaise Mixte des 316
Light, August Order of **238**
Light Infantry Regiment, the 251, 277, 301
Limerick, Antient Union Lodge No. 13 (IC) at 146, 162
Literature, masonic **159**, 197, **290-1**, 318, **321-22**
Little, R. Wentworth 235, 237
Liverpool, erasure (1821) of lodge at **113**
Lodge Constitutions, sale of **98**
Lodges: early **21-2**; 18th c., practices in **87**; number of (EC) 108, 144; numbering of **108**, 191; precedence of 84, **187**, **192**
Lodges of Instruction **112-13**, **163**, 173, 174; none in Scotland 198
Lombard builders 16
London Grand Chapter Rank 125
London Grand Rank 125, **140-1**; L.G.R. Association 125, 142
London Lodge No. 108, London 245
London Mark Grand Rank 218
London masonic area, the **140-1**
London Masons' Company, the 19, **43-4**, **45-6**
Lord Harris Court, Sindlesham, Berks, 116, 219
Lorraine, Francis, Duke of 73, **256-7**, 264
Lottery scheme, Irish 154
Louis XV, King of France 103, 223
Louis XVI, King of France 103 *bis*, 104
Louisiana, Freemasonry in 279, 281
Lovel, 1st Lord (*later* Earl of Leicester), G.M. (1731) 256
Luxemburg, Freemasonry in **264**
Lyon, David, G. Tyler (A) (1760-5) 89*n*.
Lyon, D. Murray 195; *History of the L. of Edinburgh* (1900) 177, 187, 189, 321

McKisty, Captain, the saving of 251
Maçonnerie Internationale Mixte, Ordre de **316-17**
Madrid, old Lodge (1728) in 84, 242
Maine, G.L. of 279
Mainwaring, Col. Henry, and Ashmole 45, 242
Major General Henry Knox Lodge (Mass.), Boston 250
Malaya, Freemasonry in **311**
Mallow, Lodge No. 253 (IC) at 156
Malta, Freemasonry in 171, 244, 267
Malta, Order of 233, 234, 239; in Scotland 235; in U.S.A. 285
Manchester Association for Masonic Research 10, 57, 91, 321
Manitoba, G.L. of 269
Mansfield, Earl of, Chief Justice (1756-88) 103
Maria Theresia, Empress of Austria **256-7**
Marina, HRH Princess 116, 118
Mark Benevolent Fund 116, **218-19**
Mark Book, Aberdeen 53, 183, 212
Mark Centenary Hall (R.M.I.G.) 118
Mark Masonry 63, 116, 118, 202, **211-19**, 220, 226, 227; in America 269-70, 283, 297; in Asia 218, 308, 309; in Australasia 218, 221, 301-5 *passim*; Co-Masonic 317; in Europe 218, 226, 260, 261, 265; Irish 209, 215; Scottish 209, 210, 214-15
Mark Masons' Hall, London **221**

342

INDEX

Marks, masons' 40, 53, 147, **211-15**
Marquis of Granby Lodge No. 124, Durham 215
Martel, Charles 17, 34-5
Martiniste, l'Ordre 262
Mary, Queen 118, 126
Mary's Chapel, *see* Edinburgh, Lodge of
Maryland, G.L. of 279
Mason Word, the 43, 53 *bis*, 55, 177, **181-2**; form of giving **59-60**; the Kelso ruling 183-4; and the Lairds of Roslyn 53; in the Lodge of Aberdeen 183; in the Lodge of Journeymen Masons 185; in *MSS.* 57
'Mason's Confession, A' (1755-6) q. 213
'Mason's Examination, A' (1723) q. 213
Masonic Benefit Society, the (1799-1830) 104
Masonic Book Club, the (USA) 291
Masonic Female Orphan School (IC) **154-5**, 167
Masonic Foundation for the Aged and Sick 143
Masonic Literature **159**, **197**, **290-1**, 318, **321-22**
Masonic Order of Ancient Mysteries, the **315**
Masonic 'passports' 248
Masonic Peace Celebrations (1919) 126
Masonic Peace Memorial 122, **127-8**
Masonic Register for India, The (1869) 308
Masonic research 290-1, 305, **320-21**
Masonic Schools (IC) **154-5**, **167-8**
Masonic Trust for Girls and Boys 143
Masonic (or Royal Irish) Volunteers 159
Masonic Year Book, The (London, annual) 137, 319; *for* Scotland *see* Year Book
'Masonryes of the leige' (Aberdeen) 177
Masonry, definition of 'pure ancient' 107, 111, 204, 208
Masonry Dissected (Prichard, 1730) **84-5**
Masons' Company of London, the 19, **43-4**, **45-6**
Massachusetts: Freemasonry in 250, 272-5 *passim*, 283, 285, 292; Grand Lodges of 268, 272, 273, 279, 280, 312; lodges abroad 294, 297, 312
Master, the 23, **65-6**, 77, 78, 87
Master Masons 23, 78, 81, 178 *bis*, 185, 222; in Constitutions, Laws, etc. 107, 204, 208; and the Mark degree 214, 215; the substituted secrets of 89
Master of Tyre, degree 287, 315
Masters and Fellow Crafts 38, 78, 182, 183
Masters' lodges 206, 274
Mathew, Thomas, G.M. (A) (1766-70) **93**
Matier, C.F., G.Sec., Mark (1889-1914) 228
Mauritius, Freemasonry in 299
Mediterranean Pass, degree 233, 236
Melchiades, Pope (311-14) 37
Mellor, Alec, his initiation 139
Melrose No. 2 MS. q. 41
Memphis, Rite of 262, 314
Memphis et Misraïm, Rit de 262
Meredith, Sir James Creed, D.G.M. (IC) (1898-1911) 130n.
Meredith, Rev. R. Creed **130** and *n.*
Meridian Lodge No. 12 (IC), Dublin 172
Methodists and Freemasonry 129-30
Mexico, Freemasonry in 283, **293**
Michigan, G.L. of 279
Middlesex, Earl of (b. 1711) **153-4**
Milborne, A.J.B. 136

Military lodges 101, **243-8**, **250**, 310; French 246; Irish 153, **167** and *n.*, **243-5**, 303; stationed in America 243, 250-1, 268, 277, 292; stationed in Australia 301, 304
Military Lodges' Preceptory K.T. No. 300, London 245
Miller, David (the Morgan affair) 277-8
Minden Lodge No. 63 (IC) in the 20th Foot **243-4**
Minden Lodge No. 464 (IC), Calcutta 244-5
Minnesota, G.L. of 279
Miracle plays **21**
Mississippi, G.L. of 279
Missouri, Freemasonry in 279, 290, 321
Missouri Lodge of Research, Fulton, Mo. 290, 321
Mitchell, Dr. John, of Caledonian Lodge **192-3**
Mithraic cult, the 14
Mizraim, Rite of 262, 314
Moderns, the, *see* Antients and Moderns *and* Moderns' G.L.; for Strict Moderns, *see* Traditioners
Moderns' Grand Lodge 88, 95, 97, **98-102**, 250; and the Grand East of Ulster 160; and reconciliation 105; and the R.A. 203
'Modes of recognition' 89
Moira, 2nd Earl of (*later* Marquess of Hastings), A/G.M. (1790-1813) **104**, 105, 106, 160, 247; as A/G.M. of India 104, 308; as A/G.M. of Scotland 104, 105, **192**
Montagu, 2nd Duke of, G.M. (1721) 73, 74 *bis*, 82, 242
Montana, G.L. of 279
Moray, 9th Earl of, G.M.M. (SC) (1802-4) 210 and *n.*
Moray, Sir Robert, his initiation (1641) **44**, 49, 94, 183, 242
Morgan, William (USA) **277-8**
Morgan affair, the 252, **277-8**
Morin, Stephen (Rite of Perfection) 231, 261
Morison of Greenfield, Dr. Charles 195
Mornington, 1st Earl of, G.M. (IC) (1776) 158
Mornington, 2nd Earl of (*later* Marquess Wellesley), G.M. (IC) (1782) 158
Morrice, Thomas, J.G.W. (1718-19, 1721) 70
Most Excellent Master, degree 225, 283 *bis*
Mother Kilwinning Lodge No. 0 (SC): before G.L. 22, 25, 58, **179-80**, 184 *bis*, 185, G.L. and after 187, 188, 192, **199**; and Marks 212; its number 180, 192; its secession and re-conciliation **188**, **192**
Mount Sinai Lodge No.121, Penzance 108n.
Mountjoy, 3rd Viscount, G.M. (IC) (1738-40) (*later* Earl of Blesington, G.M. (A)) 92, 154, 155 *bis*
Mozart, Wolfgang Amadeus 258
Mozart Lodge (1956), Vienna 258
Muggeridge, Henry 112
Multa Paucis . . . (1763) 69
Munnich, Baron von (Denmark) 259
Munster, G.L. of **151-2**, 164
Munster, lodges in 151-2, **164**
Munster, Provincial G.L. of 164, 166
Murat, Prince Lucien, G.M., France 261
Muses Threnodie, The (Adamson, 1638) q. 182

343

INDEX

Music in lodge 132-3
Musical Society, the 81
Mysteries, the Ancient 14
Mystery of Free-Masonry, The (1730) 84

Napier-Clavering, Col. C.W., G.M., A.M.D. 230
Napoleon I, Emperor of France 244, 246, 253
National Grand Lodges, *see under* Austria†, Berlin†, Denmark, Egypt†, France, Iceland, Sweden
National Grand Orient of Cameroun 298
National Great Priory of England, K.T. (1872) 234
Naval Kilwinning Lodge (SC), not formed (1810) 246
Naval lodges 245-6
Navy Lodge No. 2612, London 129, 131-2
Naymus Graecus 34-5
Nebraska, G.L. of 279
Nebuchadnezzar, 'Grand Master' 86
Negro Freemasonry 291-2, 294, 298
Netherlands, The: Freemasonry in 229, 233, 247-8, 264-5, 318; Grand East of 247, 259, 265, 295 *bis*, 299 *bis*; the R.A. in 208
Netterville, 5th Viscount, D.G.M. (1731) and G.M. (IC) (1732) 153
Nevada, G.L. of 279
New Articles (in Old Charges) 40, 65-6
New Brunswick, G.L. of 269
New Guinea, Freemasonry in 307
New Hampshire, Freemasonry in 273, 279
New Jersey, Freemasonry in 271, 279, 292
New Mexico, G.L. of 279
New South Wales: Freemasonry in 225, 300-1; U.G.L. of 301, 304
New York: Freemasonry in 250, 271, 281 *bis*, 284, 288; G.L. of 260, 279, 312; research lodge in 290, 321
New Zealand, Freemasonry in 166, 171, 221, 237 *bis*, 305, 321
New Zealand Pacific Lodge No. 758* (*now* No. 2 (NZC)), Wellington 305
Newcastle upon Tyne Lodge No. 24 90
Newfoundland, Freemasonry in 269
Newman, F. Winton, G.Supt.Wks. (1946-53) 127
Nicaragua, Freemasonry in 294
Nicodemus, Roman Christian 28
Nicostratus, mason and martyr 28
Nimrod, son of Cush 64
Nine Elected Masters, Knight of the, degree (Baldwyn) 239
Nine Muses, Lodge of the, No. 235, London 102
Nine Sisters, Lodge of the, Paris 272
9th Foot, Lodge No. 183 (A) in the 247
Noah: in the *Graham MS.* 62, 183, 200; in the Old Charges 32, 200; and his sons 32, 62, 64
Noah's Ark 21, 65, 200, 219
Nobles of the Mystic Shrine, Ancient Arabic Order of 287, **288**
Noorthouck, John 85, **96**, 102
Nordiska Första, Lodge den (Sweden), Stockholm 265
Norfolk, 8th Duke of, G.M. (1729-30) 72, **82-3**, 150

† no longer in existence

Norske Store Landsloge, den 265
North Carolina, Freemasonry in 279, 281, 290
North Dakota, Freemasonry in 279, 281
Northamptonshire Regiment, the 166
Northern Freemason, The 11
Norway, Freemasonry in 265
Nova Scotia, G.L. of 269
Nurses' Training School (Royal Masonic Hospital) 127

Oath, the Mason's 37, 40-1, 66, 130, 162, 189
Obligation penalties, *see* Penalties
Obligations in the Old Charges 36, 39, **40-2**
O'Bryen, Hon. James, G.M., Munster (1726-30) 151, 152
O'Cahan, the 171
Occupation forces, Freemasonry among **249-50**
O'Connell, Daniel, Irish statesman **162**
Ohio, Freemaonry in 279, 290
Ohio R.A. Chapter of Research 290
Oklahoma, G.L. of 279
Old Bradfield Lodge No. 3549, London 10
Old Charges, the 16, 17, 21, 24, 25, **30-42**; at Alnwick 51; in America 270, 273; central organization hinted at 52; *MSS.* quoted 28-9, 61; new orders in 65; operatives' use of **39-42**; Payne, G.M., and 72; pillars and 200; in Scotland **178-9**, 183; speculatives' use of 54; at York 50
Old Exoinan Lodge No.9000, Exeter 143
Old Horn Lodge, *see* Horn Tavern, Royal Somerset House
Old King's Arms Lodge No. 28, London 72
Old Masonians' Lodges (5) 120-1
Operative masonry 18, 66; bridge from, to speculative 53, 73, 75, 181; and the Mark degree 211-12; medieval **19-29**; and other modern Orders 219, 227, 238; in Scotland **177-83**, 195, 212, 213
'Operatives, The' 238
Order of Service to Masonry, the **129**
Ordre des Francs Maçons Trahi, *L*' (1745) 201
Oregon, G.L. of 280
Orleans, Duc d', G.M., France 261
Orr-Ewing, Brig.-Gen. Sir Norman, G.M.M. (SC) (1937-9) 135
Orr-Ewing, Sir Ronald, G.M.M. (SC) (1965-9) 135
Osterreichischer Universaler Freimaurer-Orden 'Humanitas' 258
Overseas Grand Rank 125
Overseas Mark Grand Rank 218
Oxnard, Thomas (USA) **273-4**

Pacific Islands, Freemasonry in the **306-7**; *see also* Phillipines, the
Paisley, Lord (*later* 7th Earl of Abercorn), G.M. (1726) 82
Pakistan, Freemasonry in 308
Panama, Freemasonry in 294
Papal Bulls: anti-masonic 93, 100, **138-9**, 162 and *n*., 256; re travelling architects, etc. 15, 16, 49
Paper missive, the 216
Paraguay, Freemasonry in 296

INDEX

Parkinson, R.E., P.S.G.D.(IC) 9, 171, 172n., 174 and n.; *History of the G.L. of Ireland*, vol. 2 (1957) 145n., q. 163, 166n., 244, 321
Parthenon Lodge No. 112 (Greece), Athens 263
Passing the Veils 209, 210, 222, 239, 284
Passwords 89
Past Masters' Degree (virtual): 'Master of the Chair' 215; in Scotland (1845) 210; in U.S.A. 283 *bis*
Patoun, George (Edinburgh) 180
Paul VI, Pope (1967-) 139
Payne, George, G.M. (1718, 1720) **72-3**, 77, 81, 82, 275
Peace Memorial Committee 124
Pedro I, Emperor of Brazil 296
Pelican and Eagle, Knight of the, degree 231
Pemberton, Jeremy, Pres.B.G.P. (1972-) 144
Penalties, the Obligation **133-4**; Irish **170**; R.A. **207**; Scottish **197**
Penn, Springett, D.G.M., Munster (1726-7) 151-2
Pennell, John, G.Sec. (IC) (1732-9) 152, 161
Pennsylvania, Freemasonry in **271-2**, 273, 277, 280; Eastern Star forbidden 288; Mark, R.A., etc. 283, 284
Pennsylvania Gazette, The (1729) 271
Perdiguier, Agricol, *Livre du Compagnonnage* (1841) 17, 18
Perfection, Rite of 230
Peru, Freemasonry in 296
Peters, Rev. William, Grand Portrait Painter (1785) 100
Petre, 9th Lord, G.M. (1772-6) **100**, 138
Philalethes Society, The (USA) 290
Philippines, Freemasonry in and under the 283, 306, **312**
Philo-Musicae et Architecturae Societas 81
Phoenix Lodge No. 289 (A) (*now* No. 173), London 109
Pick, Fred L. 7, 9, **10**, 80, 114n., 270, 291
Pillars 48; antediluvian **32-3**, 61, 64, 200; J. & B. 53, 61, 64, 87, 200
Pilot, The (1837) 162
Pius VI, Pope (1775-99) 157
Pius VII, Pope (1800-23) 138
Pius IX, Pope (1846-78) 139
Plantagenet Lodge No. 1454, Albany, W. Australia 304
Plot, Dr. Robert, *Natural History of Staffordshire* (1686) q. **46-7**, 54
'Pocket Provincial Grand Lodges' 110
Points of Fellowship 59, 62, **63**, 183
Poland, Freemasonry in 253
Polychronicon (Higden) 32
Pomfret, George (India) 308
Poole, Rev. Herbert 42, 212, 322
Poole (Dorset) **253-4**
Poor Robin's Intelligencer (1676) 46
Pope, Alexander, *Moral Essays* (1731-5) q. 75n.
Portsmouth (Hants) 99, 214, 219
Portugal, Freemasonry in **255-6**
Prayer, in Old Charges **31**
Preceptors 97, 109, **112-13**
Premier Grand Lodge, *see* Moderns' G.L.
Preses, as presiding officers (Scotland) 23
Preston, William **70**, 88, 97, 100 *bis*, 102; *see also* England South of the River Trent, *Illustrations of Masonry*

Preston Gild, the 49
Prestonian Lectures, the 97, 113
Price, Henry (USA) **272-3**, 274 *bis*
Prichard, Samuel, *Masonry Dissected* (1730) **84-5**, 291
Primitive and Original Rite, the 315
Prince, HMS, Lodge in 99, 245
Prince Edward Island, G.L. of 269
Prince George Duke of Kent Court, Chislehurst 116
Prince Hall Freemasonry **291-2**, 298, 314
Prince Mason, degree 232
Prince of Wales's Lodge No. 259, London 121, 149
Princess Royal, HRH the, Dowager Countess of Harewood 196
Prisoners-of-War, Freemasonry among **246-9**
Pritchard, Dr. E.W., poisoner 123
Processions, masonic 72, 86, 96, 150
Professor of the Art ... of Speculative Freemasonry 106
Promulgation: Lodge (1809-11) of **106**; R.A. Chapter of 204
Provincial boundary changes **141**
Provincial Grand Lodges: (EC) **109-11**, overseas (*now* District G.Ls, q.v.) 268, 301, 305; (IC) 156, 157, 166, overseas 166, 301, 305; in North America 268 *bis*, 271-3, 277, 279-80; (SC) overseas (*now* District G.Ls, q.v.) 301, 305, 308
Provincial Grand Masters: (EC) 84 and n., 95, 99, **109-11**, overseas (*now* District G.M.s) 298; (IC) **156-7**, overseas 306; North America 268, 271-5 *passim*, 277; (SC) overseas (*now* District G.M.s) 308
Puerto Rico, G.L. of 295
'Punch Bowl', York, Lodge at the 95
Pythagoras 34, 76

Quarriers 178
Quatuor Coronati, the **28-9**, 242
Quatuor Coronati Lodge No. 670 (Italy), Rome 264
Quatuor Coronati Lodge No. 2076, London 7, 8, 29, 133n., 181, **320**; its Members 7, 9, 10, 11, 77; its publications **321**; its Secretaries 7, 9, 203; its Transactions: see *Ars Quatuor Coronatorum*
Quebec, G.L. of 269
Queen's Dragoon Guards, Lodge in the 167
'Queen's Head', Holles St., London, Lodge at the 81
Queen's Head Lodge (1724-36), Bath 84
Queensland: Freemasonry in **304**; United G.L. of 305, 307
Quiller-Couch, Sir Arthur, *The Westcotes* 246n.

Rabaul, Lodge, No. 4468, New Guinea 307
Rainbow, Order of 289
Rampur, Nawab of, 1st G.M., India 309
Ramsay, Chevalier Andrew 223, 240
Ramsay, Lord (*later* 1st Marquis of Dalhousie), G.M.M. (SC) (1836-8) 193
Rancliffe, 1st Lord, G.M., Ark and K.T. (1796) 220
'Randolph Hill' (Scottish Masonic Home) 196

345

INDEX

Ravenscourt Park, hospital at **126-7**
Raymond, 2nd Lord, G.M. (1739) 86
Reconciliation, Lodge of (1813-16) 107, **108-9**, 112, 113, 204
Rectified Scottish Rite, Grand Priory of the 267
Red Branch of Eri, Order of the **237-8**, 287
Red Cross of Babylon, degree 222, 226, 228, 236, 305; (IC, Knight Masons) 240-1; (SC, Babylonish Pass) 210, 220, 228; U.S.A. 285
Red Cross of Constantine, Order of the **235-7**, 269, 286; Grand Imperial Conclave (EC) 226, 235; Grand Imperial Council (SC) 236
Red Cross Knight, *see* Red Cross of Babylon
Red Cross of Daniel 236
Red Cross of Palestine 236 *bis*
Regensburg Rules (1459) of the *Steinmetzen* 16
Regius MS. (the 'Regius Poem', *c.*1390) q. **28-9**, 30, 37, 42, 291
Regulations, General 72, 77-8, 81, 112
Reid, William, Secretary to G.L. (1723-33) 42
Reilly, John, Pr.Dep.G.M., Munster (1754) 156
Religion and Freemasonry 77, 88, 111, **129-31**, **132-3**; in Ireland 176
'Re-makings', by the rival G.L.s **94**
Research, Lodge of, No. 200 (IC), Dublin 173, 174, 321
Research, Lodge of, No. 2429, Leicester 238, 321
Research, masonic **290-1**, 306, **320-21**
Revere, Paul, G.M., Massachusetts 284
Rhode Island, Freemasonry in 250, 280, 284, 285
Richardson, Samuel, *Clarissa Harlowe* (1747-8) 75
Richmond, 2nd Duke of, G.M. (1724) 71, 81, 82, 83
Rickmansworth, Girls' School at **118-19**, 142
Ripon, 1st Marquess of, G.M. (1870-4) 100, 119, 124, 140
Rising Star Lodge No. 342 (SC), Bombay 308 *bis*
Rit Ancien de Bouillon (1740) 201
Ritual: early **54-5**, **64-5**, 109; Irish 163, 174; Mark 216; R.A. 55, **204-5**; Scottish 183
Rivers, 'Grand Master' 50
Robbins, Sir Alfred, P.J.G.W. (1923) 124
Roberts family of Old Charges, the 65
Roberts MS. (1722) q. **65-6**
Robinson, Rev. H.I., and the *Graham MS*. 61
Roman Catholics and Freemasonry 80, **138-40**, 162; Catholic G.M.s 93, 100, 124; Catholic hostility (*see also* Papal Bulls) 130, 163, 165, 168
Rosae Crucis, degree 236
Rose Croix, degree **230-3** *passim*, 236, 239, 240, 247; unrecognized 315
Rose Croix of Mount Carmel, Knight of the, degree (Baldwyn) 239
Rosicrucians 14; *see also* Societas Rosicruciana
Roslin, Lairds of 53, **180-1**, 186
Rosse, 1st Earl of, G.M. (IC) (1725-30?) **150**, 151
Rosslyn, 4th Earl of, G.M.M. (SC) (1870-3) 195
Rosy Cross, degree 236, 240
Rosy and Triple Cross, degree 236
Royal Air Force Lodge No. 7335, London 250
Royal Albert Hall 124, 126-9 *passim*, 173

Royal Alpha Lodge No. 16, London 134
Royal and Select Masters (Cryptic degrees) 202, 219, **225-6**; overseas 221, 262, 269, 284, 285, 302, 306, 309
Royal Anglian Regt., the 243, 247
Royal Arch Lodge No. 190 (IC), Dublin 154-5
Royal Arch Mason, The 290
Royal Arch Masonry 89, 99, 107, **200-10**; early references 42, 155 and n., **202-3**; Installation ceremonies of **206-7**; Irish **205-6**, **208-9**, 222; legends in 205-6; qualifications for 206 and n.; its ritual **204-5**; and the Scandinavian Rite 266; Scottish 192, 205, 206, **209-10**, 217, 301, 304; Union (1817) in England **203-4**; in U.S.A. 205, 206, **282-4**, 285; unrecognized 315, 317 *bis*; *see also* Chapters XI and XII for connexion with other degrees and Orders, and Chapters XIV to XVIII for practice in other countries
Royal Arch Widows 289
Royal Ark Mariners **219-21**, 234; America 269, 287, 297, Australasia 301, 304, 306; Europe 249, 265; G.L. of 219; India 308; Royal Ark and Mark Mariners 219; Scottish 210, 220-1, 228
Royal Athelstan Lodge No. 19, London 91
Royal College of Surgeons, Research Fellowship Fund **136-7**
Royal Cumberland Free Masons' School 102
Royal Cumberland Lodge No. 41, Bath 94
Royal freemasons 73-4, **101-2**, 326; *see also* Kings Edward VII, George IV and VI, and William IV, *and* the Dukes of Connaught, Cumberland, Edinburgh, Kent (3), Sussex and Windsor, *also* Wales, Princes of
Royal Fusiliers, the 243
Royal Grand Conclave, K.T., Scotland 235, 236
Royal Highland Fusiliers, the 243
Royal Irish Fusiliers, the 243
Royal Irish Rangers, the 245
Royal Masonic Benevolent Annuity Fund 115, 122
Royal Masonic Benevolent Institution **114-17**, 121, 141, 219
Royal Masonic Hospital 117, **126-7**, 142
Royal Masonic Institution for Boys **102-3**, 117, **119-21**, 141-2, 248
Royal Masonic Institution for Girls **102-3**, **117-19**, 120, 121, 127, 141-2
Royal Master, degree 210, 225, 284
Royal Military Lodge No. 463* (1774-84) 101
Royal Naval Lodge No. 59, London 119
Royal Naval Volunteer Reserve Rose Croix Chapter No. 207, London 248
Royal Order of Heredom of Kilwinning 240
Royal Order of Scotland 223, **240**, 287
Royal Order of Scots Knights of Kilwinning (Baldwyn) 239
Royal Scots (1st Foot), lodges in the 243, 245, 251
Royal Society, the 223
Royal Somerset House and Inverness Lodge No. 4, London 71, 72-3, 99, 246
Royal Standard Lodge and Chapter No. 398, Halifax, N.S. 269
Royal Sussex Lodge No. 501, Hong Kong 311-12
Royal York, Grand Lodge, Germany 262

INDEX

Rudyard Kipling Lodge No. 8169, Uckfield 10
Rule of Three, the **201**, 213
Rumania, Freemasonry in 255
Rumbelow, Capt. A.G., G.M., A.M.D. (1964-9) 226*n*.
'Rummer and Grapes' Tavern, the, London 68, 71
Ruspini, Chevalier Bartholomew, G.Swd.B. (1791-1813) 102, 154
Russia, Freemasonry in 255, 260
Rylands, J.R., P.J.G.D. (1962) 133*n*.

Sackville, Lord Charles (Carolus) **153-4**, 154*n*., 263
Sackville, Sir Thomas, 'Grand Master' (1561) 26
Sadler, Henry, G. Tyler (1879-1909) 99, 114*n*.; *Masonic Facts and Fictions* (1887) 114*n*., 322; *Masonic Reprints and Revelations* (1898) 147
St. ..., *see under name of Saint*
St. Albans, Herts. 35
St. Andrew, Lodge of, Boston (Mass.) 276 *bis*
St. Andrew, Lodge of, No. 48 (SC) Edinburgh 193
St. Andrew's Day 187, 188
St. Andrew's Kilwinning, Lodge of, Inverness 189
St. Andrew's lodges 260 *bis*, 265-6
St. Andrews, old Lodge at, Scotland 180, 181
St. Bernard's Kilwinning, Lodge of, Kirkcudbright 276
St. Cecilia Lodge No. 250 (IC), Dublin 169
St. Clair Charters **180-1**
St. Clair of Roslin, William (1601 Charter) 180, 181
St. Clair of Roslin, William, G.M.M. (SC) (1736-7) **186-7**
St. Columba, Knights of (R.C.) 139
St. David's (Tarbolton) Lodge No. 133 (SC), Mauchline 191
St. George's Lodge No. 440, Montreal 269
St. Helena, Freemasonry in 299
St. John, Days of 69, 81, 88-9, 89*n*., 134, 174
St. John of Jerusalem, Knight of (Baldwyn) 239; *see also* Temple, Order of the
St. John the Evangelist, Order of 235
St. John's Kilwinning, Lodge of (*now* Old Kilwinning St. John No. 6 (SC)), Inverness 189
St. John's Lodge, Philadelphia 271-2
St. John's Lodge No. 1 (New Hampshire), Portsmouth 273
St. John's Lodge No. 126*, Boston (Mass.) 272-3
St. John's Lodge No. 134 (IC), Lurgan 154*n*.
St. John's Lodge of Colombo No. 454, Kandy 310
St. John's lodges 260, 266
St. Lawrence the martyr, degree 226, **227**, 287
St. Leger, Col. J. 149
St. Leger, Hon. Elizabeth **148-9**
St. Mary's Chapel, *see* Edinburgh, Lodge of
St. Paul, Knight of, degree 233
St. Paul, Lodge and Chapter of, No. 374, Montreal 269
St. Paul, Mark Lodge of, No. 131, Montreal 269-70

St. Paul's Cathedral 66, 97; its rebuilding 50-1, 70 *bis*
St. Thomas's Lodge No. 142, London 215
Salvador, Freemasonry in El **294**
Samber, Robert, *Long Livers* (1722) q. 213
Sandby, Thomas, Grand Architect (1776-98) 100
Sankey, Edward and Richard 39, 45 *bis*
Saskatchewan, G.L. of 269
Savannah, Lodge No. 139* at (Georgia) 274
Savile, Col. George, Lord 243
Sayer, Anthony, 1st G.M. (1717) 69, **71-2**, 82 *bis*
Scandinavia, Freemasonry in 144, **259-61**, 263, **265-6**, 316 *bis*
Scandinavian Rite, the 233, 235, 259, 260, 262, 263, **265-6**
Scarborough, J.R. (*fl.* 1847) 114
Scarborough, old Lodge at 52, 54
Scarborough MS. 40, 52
Scarborough, 11th Earl of, G.M. (1951-67), Pro G.M. (1967-9) 128-34 *passim*, **137-8**; and the R.A. 207 *bis*; and the 250th Anniversary of G.L. 134-5, 136-7
Scarbrough Court, Cramlington 116
Schaw, William 179, 180 *bis*
Schaw Statutes, the, 22, q. 25, **179**, 180 *bis*, 182, 212
Scotland, Grand Lodge of 177, 186-97 *passim*, 218, 246; 'Associated Lodges seceding from the (1807) 192; its Bicentenary **196**; its Centenary **193**; its *Constitution and Laws* 193; its external relations 92, 105, 111, 160, 180, 255, 303; its formation **186-7**; innovations, resisted by **190-1**; its Library **195**; and other degrees 192, **209-10**; and overseas Districts 196, **307**; its *Yearbook* **197**, 321
Scots degrees, the 223, 266
Scots Magazine, The (1755-6) q. 213
Scots Master, degree 247
Scots Philosophic Rite, the **223-4**
Scott, Sir Walter, ed. Swift's *Works* (1814) 147
Scottish Apprentice, degree 266
Scottish Freemasonry 43, **44**, **52-3**, **177-99***, 242; differences from English **197-9**; in India **308**; military lodges 243; other than Craft — A. & A.S.R. 231, **232**, K.T., etc. 235, Mark 212, **216**, 218, R.A. 202, **209-10**, 215, **301**, Royal Order of Scotland 223, **240**, 287, other degrees **225-6**, 228, **236-7**, 237
Scottish Masonic Benevolence 194, **195-6**
Scottish Master of St. Andrew, degree 266
'Scottish' rites **223**; *see also* Ancient and Accepted (Scottish) Rite
Seals of Cause (Scotland) **178**, 179, 181 *bis*
Sealy, John, G.Sec., G.L. of England S. of the Trent 96
Second degree 31; *see also* Fellow Crafts
Secret Monitor: degree 226, 229, 230, 287; Order of the **229-30**, 301, 302, 305, 310
Seddon, Frederick H., poisoner **123-4**
Selby Abbey, Yorks. 20
Select Mason of Twenty-Seven, degree 228
Select Master, degree 210, 225, 228, 284
Senior London Grand (Chapter) Rank 125
Sentimental and Masonic Magazine, The (1792) 159
Services lodges **250**

347

INDEX

Seton, Alexander, Dep.G.Sec. (IC) (1801-5) **159-61**, 162
Seton, Robert, Jacobite 189
Setters **24-5**, 58
Seven Liberal Arts and Sciences **31-2**
Seven Years' War, the (1756-63) 92, 103, 246
Shaftesley, John M. 89n.
Shanghai Tuscan Lodge No. 1027, London 311
Shekleton, Robert, D.G.M. (IC) (1870-97) 170
Sheldonian Theatre, Oxford 50
Shellard, Henry C., G.Sec. (IC) (1922-54) **170**
'Ship' (behind the Royal Exchange), Lodge (1723-45) at the 75
'Shrine', the (USA) 287, **288**
Shuttleworth, 4th Lord, J.G.W. (1951) 74, 128
Sibelius, Jean, composer 260
Sibly, Ebenezer (Noah) 219-20
Siddons, Mrs. Sarah, actress 154
'Side' degrees 224, 227, 229
Signs, the secret **20**, 53, 182
Simphorianus, mason and martyr 28
Simplicius, mason and martyr 28
Sincerity, Lodge, No. 3677, Wigan 113-14
Sinclair, Sir William 181
Singapore, Freemasonry in **311**
Slade, Alexander, *The Freemason Examined* (1754) **64**, 65
Sloane 3848 MS. (1646) 39, 45
Smith, Capt., George, Pr.G.M., Kent (1777-85) **101**; *The Use and Abuse of Freemasonry* 101
Smith, General John Corson (USA) 251
Smith, William, *Pocket Companion* (1735) 76, 161
Social Contract (Scots Philosophic Rite) 224
Social Friendship Lodge No. 497, London 245
Social Order of the Beauceant 289
Societas Rosicruciana: in Anglia **237**, 238 *bis*; in Civitatibus Foederatis 286, 290
Solomon, King 34, 53; *see also* Temple, King Solomon's
Somerset House Lodge, *see* Royal Somerset House
Sons of Solomon, of Maître Jacques and of Soubise 17
Soper, Rev. Lord 13:
Sorrell, Francis, S.G.W. (1723-5) 81
South Africa, Freemasonry in 225, **299-300**
South America, Freemasonry in 295-7
South Australia, Freemasonry in **302**
South Australian Lodge of Friendship No. 613* (*now* No. 1 (S.A.)), Adelaide 302
South Carolina, Freemasonry in 274-5, 280
South Dakota, Freemasonry in 280, 281
Southern Africa, G.L. of 299
Southwell, 2nd Lord, D.G.M. (IC) (1743) 150, 151
Sovereign Prince Rose Croix of Heredom, degree 231
Spain, Freemasonry in 84, 242, 255
Spalding, Gentlemen's Club at 223
Speculative Freemasonry 18, **147-8**, 187, 212; bridge from operative to 53, 73, 75, 181; earliest traces (England) **43-4**, 44n.; 'Professor' of 106; and Scotland 73, **183-4**
Spork, Count de (Prague) 256
Spratt, Edward, G.Sec. (IC) (1743-56) 91, 153, 155, 156, 161
Sri Lanka (Ceylon), Freemasonry in **310**

Stability Lodge of Instruction 112, 113, 252
Star in the East, Lodge, No. 67, Calcutta 308
Star of the East, Lodge, No. 880, Zante, Greece 263
Starck, Johann August von 224
Statutes affecting masons **26-8**, 66
Statutes of Labourers **26-7**
Steinmetzen, the **16-17**, 28
Stewards' Lodge (1735) 85
Stewards' 'Lodge' (Antients' Committee of Charity, 1754) 92
Stewart lodges 260, 266
Stirling, Associate Synod of (1745) 189
Stirling, old Lodge at 22, 181
Stirling Brass, the 219
Stirling Rock R.A. Chapter No. 2 (SC), Stirling 202
Stone, Nicolas, King's master mason 44
Storlogen af Danmark 259 *bis*
Storstora Frimurareglunnar a Islandi 263
Strachan, Sir Alexander 183
Stradbroke, 4th Earl of 218
Strasbourg, *Steinmetzen* chief lodge at 17
Strathmore, 7th Earl of, G.M. (1733) 150
Strathmore, 8th Earl of, G.M.M. (SC) (1740-1) **188**
Strathmore, 14th Earl of 196
Strict Observance, Rite of 224, 260, 262, 267 *bis*
'Strict Union', Antients' G.L. with Ireland and Scotland 92
Strong, Edward, 'G.Warden' (1685) 51
Stubbs, J.W., G.Sec. (1958-) 132 and n., 136
Studd, Sir Eric, Dist. G.M., Bengal (1930-7) 70n.
Stukeley, Dr. William, antiquary **74**
'Sublime degree', varying uses 78, 215
Sullivan, John (USA) 276
Sun Lodge, Chester 109, 110
Suomen Suur-Loosi (Finnish G.L.) 260
Super Excellent Master, degree 210, 215, 225, **284**
Superintendent, degree 287
Supreme Council MS. (1728) 42
Supreme Councils 33°, *see* Ancient and Accepted (Scottish) Rite *and under* names of countries in Chapters XIV to XVIII
Supreme Grand Council of Rites **314-15**
Supreme Grand R.A. Chapters, *see* Grand R.A. Chapters
Supreme Grand Royal Encampment, Bristol 233-4, 239
Surgical Research Fund **136-7**
Sussex, HRH the Duke of, G.M. (1813-43) 102, 106 *bis*, 111, 113, **121**, 165; his installation as G.M. 107; as member of Antiquity 70, 106; and 'other' degrees 215, 220, 231, 234; and the R.A. 204; and the R.M.B.I. 115 *bis*
Svenska Stora Landslogen (Sweden) **265-6**
Swalwell, Lodge at **51-2**
Swansea, 4th Lord, Pr.G.M., S.Wales (E.D.) 117
Sweden: Freemasonry in 260, **265-6**; 316; National G.L. of 83, 260, **265-6**
Swedenborgian Rite, the 313
Swedish Rite, *see* Scandinavian Rite
Swift, Dean Jonathan 147, 149
Switzerland: Freemasonry in **266-7**; R.A. in 208, 267
Sword, Knight of the, degree 228, 241

348

INDEX

Sword of State, the 83

Tall Cedars of Lebanon, the (USA) 288
Tarbolton Kilwinning St. James, Lodge of, No. 135 (SC) 191
Tasmania, Freemasonry in 303, **304**
Tasmanian Operative Lodge No. 1 (TC), Hobart 304
Tatler, The (1709) 46
Tegucigalpa, Templo Masonica de (Honduras) 293
Television, Freemasonry on **131**
Telfer, W.J. (Boston, U.S.A.) 254
Tempest, Sir George, Master (1705) of the York Lodge 52
Temple, King Solomon's 61, 182, 200, 205, 225; the building of 21, **33-4**, 53, 62-3, 65, 228
Temple, Order of the (Knights Templar) 202, 223, 224, 226, **233-5**; in America 269, **284-5**, 289; in Germany 262-3; in Ireland 232-3, **234-5**, 241; in New Zealand (irregular) 306; and other degrees and Orders 220, 232-3, 237, 239-40, 266, 267; in Scotland 192, 228-9, **235**
Templum Hierosolyma 204-5
Tennessee, Freemasonry in 280, 281
Texas, Freemasonry in 280, 283
Theology (1951) 130
Theosophical Society, the 316
Third degree **78**, 84, 109, **185**, 200, 202, 273-4; *see also* Master Masons
33rd Foot, Lodge No. 12 (IC) (1732-1817) in the 243
Thistle Lodge No. 62 (SC), Dumfries 214-15
Tho. Carmick MS. 270
Thompson, Andrew (Haughfoot) 56
Thompson, Lawrence, preceptor 113
Thompson, M. McBlain, purveyor of degrees 315n
Thomson, Peter, preceptor 113, 122
Three Globes, Grand National Mother Lodge of the, Berlin 230, 259, 262
Three Great Lights, the 89
Three Principles, Lodge of the, Vienna 256
Throne, Grand Master's 123, 135
'Time Immemorial' lodges **70-1**, 97, 151, 153, 220
Timson, Joshua, S.G.W. (1722) 83
To all Goodly People ... (anti-masonic leaflet, 1698) 46
Tomlinson, Robert (USA) 273, 274, 275
Torgau Statutes, the (1462) 16, 17, **212**
Torphichen Kilwinning, Lodge of No. 13 (SC), Bathgate 185
Townsend, John, operative/speculative mason 75
Traditioners **89-90**, 98, 99, 147
Travelling Architects **15**, **49**
Travelling Mark Lodge, Cheshire 193, **215-16**, 217
Trieste Masonic Association 250
Trim Lodge No. 494 (IC), Dublin (*formerly* at Trim) 158
Trinity College, Dublin 53, **147-8**
Trinity College MS. q. 54
Triple Tau, the **204-5**
Tripos MS. 147
Trowel, the 25, 143

Troy, Archbishop, of Dublin (18th c.) 162n.
True Blue Lodge No. 253 (1755-1892), Carrickfergus 156-7
True Kindred, Supreme Conclave (USA) 289
Tuam Cathedral, Ireland 145
Tubal Cain 32
Tucker, William, Pr.G.M., Dorset (1846-53) 110
Tullamore, 2nd Lord, G.M. (IC) (1741, 1760) 155
Tullibardine, Marquis of (*later* 8th Duke of Atholl), G.M.M. (SC) (1909-13) 195
Turkey, G.L. of 196, **311**
Turner, Robert, 1st G.M. (A) (1753) 90
12th Foot, Lodge (SC) (1747-1809) in the 243
20th Foot, Lodge No. 63 (IC) (1737-1869) in the **243-4**
21st Foot, Lodge No. 33 (IC) (1734?-1801) in the 243
27th Foot, Lodge No. 23 (IC) (1733-1801) in the 243
28th Foot, Lodge No. 35 (IC) (1734-1801) in the 243
Tyler, the 87, 175-6
Tyrconnel, Duchess of 150
Tytler, Lt.-Col., the sparing (1812) of 251

Ulster, Grand East of 159, **160-1**
Unanimity, Lodge of, No. 339, Penrith 108n.
Union (1813), the 85, 89, **105-9**, 157; additional degrees and 215, 220; Articles of **106-7**, 111, 203-4, 223, 231; ritual and 54
Union Lodge No. 310, Carlisle 191n.
Union Lodge No. 367 (IC), Downpatrick 157
United Grand Lodges, *see under* England, Germany, New South Wales, Queensland, Victoria
United Grand Lusitanian Orient 298
United Irishmen, Society of 159
United Mariners' Lodge No. 30, London 102-3
United Services Lodge No. 1118 (NY), New York 250
United States, Freemasonry in the 95, 221, 228 bis, 233, 236-7, **270-93**, 314, **315**
United States, Grand Lodges of the 277, **279-80**, 281; *see also* under names of individual States
Unity, Peace and Concord, Lodge of, No. 316, London 245, 251
Universal League of Freemasons **318-19**
Unlawful Oaths in Ireland Act (1823) 28, **165**
Unlawful Societies Act (1799) 28, 104, **105**, 165, 301
Uruguay, Freemasonry in **296-7**
Utah, G.L. of 280
Upper Canada, Provincial G.M. for 165

'Vails' (drink money, Scotland) 191
Vale Royal Abbey, building accounts of 22
Valle de Mexico, Grand Lodge 293
Vanguard, HMS, Lodge in 245
Variations in the established forms **85**, 89
Vatcher, Dr. Sidney 256
Vault, crypt, secret chamber 223, 225, 228
Veiled Prophets of the Enchanted Realm, Mystic Order of (USA) 288
Veils, passing the 209, 210, 222, 239, 284
Venezuela, Freemasonry in 295

349

INDEX

Vereinigte Grosslogen von Deutschland (Germany) 262
Vermont, G.L. of 280
Victoria, Freemasonry in 218, 225, **303**
Victoria Jubilee Masonic Annuity Fund (IC) **169-70**
Villenau, Josiah, S.G.W. (1721) 70
Virginia, Freemasonry in 275, 280, 281, 282-3, 283, 284
Voltaire, François Marie Arouet de 272
Volume of the Sacred Law 259, 297, 307
Von Tavel R.A. Chapter No. 1 (Switzerland) 267
Voorhis, Harold V.B. (USA) 9

Waite, A.E. 291
Wakefield Wing, Royal Masonic Hospital 126, 127
Wales, Prince of (Edward VII), G.M. (1874-1901) 119, **124**, 218
Wales, Prince of (Edward VIII), P.G.M. (1936) 128, 170
Wales, Prince of (Frederick) 73-4
Wales, Prince of (George IV), G.M. (1790-1813), G.M.M. (SC) (1805-20) 102 *bis*, 104, 106, 135, 192
Walpole, Horace q. 86-7
Waltham Abbey, Essex 20
Ward, Lt.-Col. Eric 77, 146
Wardens 23, 65, 66, 87, 89
Warrants, Irish 152-3, **164**, 167, 176
Warrington, Lodge (in 1646) at 39, 45, 242
Washington, George 251, **275-6**, 277
Washington, G.L. of 280
Washington (D.C.), see District of Columbia
Waterloo, Battle of 252
Waterloo Lodge No. 571 (IC), 1st Queen's Dragoon Guards 167; its R.A. Chapter 167
Weir, Thomas, Warden (Edinburgh) 180
Wellesley, 1st Marquess, see Mornington, Earl of
Wellington, 1st Duke of **157-8**
Wesley, Rev. John 157
Wesley, Samuel, G.Org. (1812-17) 157
West, Milbourne, Pr.G.M., Quebec (1764) 94
West India and American Lodge (Antiquity) 70
West Indies, Freemasonry in the 166, 190, 231, 244, 273, 293, **295**
West Virginia, Freemasonry in 280, 281, 283, 284
Western Australia, Freemasonry in **304**
Wharton, Duke of, G.M. (1722-3) 73, 75 and *n*., 79, 80, 82, 84, 242; as a Gormogon 80
White, Sir Sydney, G.Sec. (1937-57) 132
White, W.H., G.Sec. (1809-56) 122, 235
White Shrine of Jerusalem, Order of the 289
Whittington Lodge No. 862, London 129
Whitton, Charles, of Minden Lodge 244
Whole Institution of Free-Masons Opened, The (1725) 62
Wigan, Grand Lodge of **113-14**
Wilhelm of Hirschau, Abbot 16
Wilkes, John **101**
Willem van Oranje, Lodge, No. 3976, London 247

William IV, King, P.G.M. (1787) 102, 119, **121**
Williams, Lt.-Gen. Sir Harold, P.J.G.W. (1955), O.S.M. (1968) 172 and *n*.
Williams, Louis (USA) 291
Williams, William, Pr.G.M., Dorset (1812-39) 110, 111
Wilson, John, G.M., England S. of the Trent 96
Wilson, General Sir Robert (1777-1849) 252
Windsor, HRH the Duke of, P.G.M. (1936) 128, 170
Winning, St. 180
Wisconsin, G.L. of 280
Wolsey, Cardinal, 'Grand Master' 86
Women Freemasons, Order of 317
Women in Freemasonry 91, **148-9**, **288-9**, **317-19**
Woodford MS. (1728) 42
Worcestershire Regiment, Lodge in the 167
Working Tools 41, 54
World Wars: I 125-6, **247-8**, 262; II 97, 126, **248-9**
Worshipful Society of Free Masons ..., The 238
Wren, Sir Christopher **50-1**, 64, 66, 70 and *n*., 76, 86
Wren, Christopher, jun. 51
Wren, Stephen 51
Wren Maul, the 70 and *n*.
Wycherley, William, *The Country Wife* (1675) 151
Wyoming, Freemasonry in 280, 284

Yarker, John 237 *bis*, **314-16**
Year Book of the Grand Lodge of Scotland 197, 248*n*., 319
York, Archbishop of (C.F. Garbett) q. 131
York, HRH the Duke of, see George VI, King
York: Assembly at 26, 35-6, 39, 46, 52, 81; early Freemasonry in 52, 54, 81-2; Grand Lodge of 52, 70, **81-2**, 94-5, 96 *bis*, 203, 233
York Cross of Honour, Convent General of the 285
York Grand Lodge of Mexico 293
York Lodge No. 236, York 95
York MS. (1693) 52
'York Masonry' 95
York Minster, *Fabric Rolls* of 52
York Rite, the 95, **285**
York Rite Sovereign College of North America 285
Youghal (Ireland), Royal Arch in 155*n*., 208 and *n*.
Young, Col. John, Dep.G.M. (SC) (1736-52) 190 *bis*

Z, H and J **205-6**, 284
Zacharie, Dr. I., and the Secret Monitor 229
Zetland, 2nd Earl of, G.M. (1844-70) 118, 121, 122, 124
Zetland Fund, the 124
Zetland-in-the-East, Lodge, No. 508, Singapore 311
Zinnendorf, Nicolaus von (Berlin) 262